The Temple Church in London
History, Architecture, Art

The Temple Church, founded as the main church of the Knights Templar in England at the New Temple in London, is historically and architecturally one of the most important medieval buildings in London. Its round nave, modelled on the fourth-century Church of the Holy Sepulchre in Jerusalem, is an extraordinarily early and ambitious example of the Gothic style in England. It holds one of the most famous series of medieval effigies in the country. The luminous thirteenth-century choir, intended for the burial of Henry III, is of exceptional beauty. Major developments in the post-medieval period include the reordering of the church in the 1680s by Sir Christopher Wren, fascinating changes in the perception of the church's significance in the eighteenth century, and a substantial restoration programme in the early 1840s.

Despite its great importance, however, the Temple Church has until now attracted little scholarly or critical attention, a gap which is remedied by this volume. It considers the New Temple as a whole in the Middle Ages, and all aspects of the church itself from its foundation in the twelfth century to its war-time damage in the twentieth. Richly illustrated with numerous black and white and colour plates, it makes full use of the exceptional range and quality of the antiquarian material available for study, drawings, photographs, and plaster casts.

THE TEMPLE CHURCH
IN LONDON

HISTORY, ARCHITECTURE, ART

edited by
Robin Griffith-Jones *and* David Park

THE BOYDELL PRESS

First published 2010
The Boydell Press, Woodbridge

ISBN 978 1 84383 498 4

The Boydell Press is an imprint of Boydell & Brewer Ltd
PO Box 9, Woodbridge, Suffolk IP12 3DF, UK
and of Boydell & Brewer Inc.
668 Mount Hope Ave, Rochester, NY 14620, USA
website: www.boydellandbrewer.com

A CIP catalogue record for this book is available
from the British Library

The publisher has no responsibility for the continued existence or accuracy of URLs for
external or third-party internet websites referred to in this book, and does not guarantee that
any content on such websites is, or will remain, accurate or appropriate.

This publication is printed on acid-free paper

Designed and typeset in Columbus with Hadriano display by
The Stingray Office, Chorlton-cum-Hardy, Manchester

Printed in Great Britain by
CPI Antony Rowe, Chippenham and Eastbourne

Contents

List of Illustrations   vi
Editors' Preface   xv
List of Abbreviations   xvii
List of Contributors   xx

At the Heart of Medieval London: the New Temple in the Middle Ages   1
    Helen J. Nicholson

Gothic Architecture Transplanted: the Nave of the Temple Church in   19
    London
    Christopher Wilson

Light and Pure: the Templars' New Choir   45
    Virginia Jansen

Medieval Burials and Monuments   67
    David Park

The Thirteenth-Century Military Effigies in the Temple Church   93
    Philip J. Lankester

'An Enrichment of Cherubims': Christopher Wren's Refurbishment of   135
    the Temple Church
    Robin Griffith-Jones

'A neat structure with pillars': Changing Perceptions of the Temple   175
    Church in the Long Eighteenth Century
    Rosemary Sweet

Restoration and Recrimination: the Temple Church in the Nineteenth   195
    Century
    William Whyte

'The latter glory of this house': Some Details of Damage and Repair,   211
    1840–1941
    Robin Griffith-Jones

Black-and-White Plates   221
Index   279

List of Illustrations

FIGURES IN TEXT

1 New Temple and Environs, *c.*1250: Tentative Reconstruction   4
   Graphics: Reginald Piggott (Temple Church)

2 Temple Church choir, mouldings (not to same scale)   47
   Profiles after R. K. Morris, Warwick Mouldings Archive; graphics by Corri Jimenez

3 Mouldings compared to those of the Temple choir (not to same scale)   50
   From author's drawings unless otherwise noted; other profiles based on R. K. Morris,
   Warwick Mouldings Archive; Figs. 3s and 3t follow the Royal Commission on His-
   torical Monuments (England), *An Inventory of the Historical Monuments in London*, vol. 1:
   Westminster Abbey, London, 1924, 95; graphics by Corri Jimenez

4 Comparative plans of a few Templar churches and the Hospitaller church of St John's   55
   in Clerkenwell
   Re-worked by Virginia Jansen after B. Sloane and G. Malcolm, *Excavations at the Priory
   of the Order of the Hospital of St John of Jerusalem, Clerkenwell, London* (Museum of London Archaeology Service Monograph 20), London 2004, 7 and 45; Eugène Viollet-
   le-Duc, *Dictionnaire raisonné de l'architecture française du XIᵉ au XVIᵉ siècle*, 10 vols., Paris
   1858–68 [reprint 1967], IX, 15 and 19; P. Mayes, *Excavations at a Templar Preceptory,
   South Witham, Lincolnshire, 1965–67*, London 2002, 20; graphics by Corri Jimenez

5 Jerusalem in the Time of the Crusades   60
   Graphics: Reginald Piggott (Temple Church)

6 Map of stylistically related Purbeck marble effigies, centred on London   132

COLOUR PLATES *(between p. 44 and p. 45)*

I   Temple Church, interior elevation of main vessel of nave, looking north
    Photograph: Christopher Wilson

II Temple Church, west door, watercolour by Joseph Clarendon Smith, 1806 (Private Collec-
    tion). B, C. details of A
    Photograph: Christopher Wilson

III Temple Church choir, interior view to east
    Photograph: Christopher Wilson

IV   Temple Church, head of effigy in nave (William Marshal the Elder?)
     Photograph: Chris Christodoulou (Temple Church)

 V   Temple Church, effigy in south choir aisle (Silvester de Everdon, Bishop of Carlisle?)
     Photograph: Chris Christodoulou (Temple Church)

VI   Plan of the round nave, published by Edward Richardson in 1841, with added boxes show-
     ing: the present positions of the effigies from 1842 (red); the positions of the effigies until
     1841 (green); the nine coffins and one burial cavity found during the 1841–2 excavations
     (blue); and the vaults created to re-inter the coffins with their human remains (orange)
     From E. Richardson, *The Monumental Effigies of the Temple Church, with an Account of their Resto-
     ration in the Year 1842*, London 1843, pl. 1 (adapted)

VII Map of Temple, detail of 'A Large and Accurate Map of the City of London', 1676, by John
     Ogilby and William Morgan, showing western limits of Great Fire of 1666 (here in red);
     approximate extent of fire of winter 1678 (newly marked in green)
     Photograph: Middle Temple (adapted)

VIII Temple Church, interior of nave looking north-west, aquatint by Thomas Malton, 1796,
     from T. Malton, *A Picturesque Tour through the Cities of London and Westminster*, 2 vols., London
     1792–1801, II, pl. XLVI
     Photograph: Chris Christodoulou (Temple Church)

IX   Temple Church, interior of chancel looking east, drawing by George Shepherd (1811),
     engraved by J. Skelton (1812) and published in C. Clarke, *Architectura Ecclesiastica Londini*,
     London 1819, pl. 120
     Photograph: Guildhall Library, City of London

 X   Temple Church, chancel looking west with decoration designed by Thomas Willement,
     signed and with inscription on back of mount, 'Interior of the Temple Church, London.
     Viewed from the East End. In accordance with the present Restoration exclusive of the fit-
     tings. R. H. Essex. 1843.'
     Photograph: Chris Christodoulou (Temple Church)

XI   Temple Church, 'Elevation of Altar Piece', designed by Thomas Willement, published from
     drawing by William Richard Hamilton Essex in W. R. H. Essex and S. Smirke, *Illustrations
     of the Architectural Ornaments and Embellishments and Painted Glass of the Temple Church, London*,
     London 1845, pl. XXI
     Photograph: Middle Temple

XII Temple Church, chancel looking east with preacher in pulpit, engraving by Harden S. Mel-
     ville after George Cattermole for *London Interiors* [1841–4], May 1843 (pt 20), 153, pl. 40
     Photograph: Jeffrey J. Dean

Black-and-White Plates (*after p. 221*)

 1   Temple Church, plan
     From W. H. Godfrey, 'Recent Discoveries at the Temple, London, and Notes on the Topo-
     graphy of the Site', *Archaeologia*, 95, 1953, pl. XLVI; adapted by Jeffrey J. Dean

 2   Temple Church, west porch from north-west (west buttresses added in the 1860s and 1870s,
     upwards extension of aisle wall added in the 1950s)
     Photograph: Christopher Wilson

3   Saint-Denis, Benedictine abbey, chevet interior looking north-east
Photograph: James Austin

4   Temple Church, upper part of nave pier
Photograph: Christopher Wilson

5   Temple Church, plan and details of nave pier
From R.W. Billings, *Architectural Illustrations and Account of the Temple Church, London*, London 1838, pl. x, detail

6   Noyon Cathedral, north choir gallery, intermediate support
Photograph: Christopher Wilson

7   Temple Church, profiles of nave aisle vault ribs (above) and nave main arcade arches (below)
From R.W. Billings, *Architectural Illustrations and Account of the Temple Church, London*, London 1838, pl. viii, details

8   Temple Church, east–west section through nave
From R.W. Billings, *Architectural Illustrations and Account of the Temple Church, London*, pl. v, detail (the left-hand clearstorey window is shown opened out to its full original height)

9   Temple Church, triangular vault compartment in north part of nave aisle
Photograph: Christopher Wilson

10   Paris, St-Martin-des-Champs, Benedictine priory, detail of respond and vault on north side of axial chapel
Photograph: Courtauld, Conway Library (negative A99/87)

11   Dommartin, Premonstratensian abbey, plan of choir pier
From C. Enlart, *Manuel d'Archéologie Française*, 3rd edn, I, Paris 1927, 350 (broken lines showing projection of vault ribs added by C. Wilson)

12   Temple Church, south part of nave aisle looking south-west
Photograph: Christopher Wilson

13   Temple Church, quadripartite vault compartment in south part of nave aisle
Photograph: Christopher Wilson

14   Namps-au-Val, parish church, vault of chancel looking east, from C. Enlart, *Monuments religieux de l'architecture romane et de transition dans la région picarde*, Amiens and Paris 1895, pl. opp. p. 148, detail
Photograph: Christopher Wilson

15   Temple Church, capital of nave pier, detail
Photograph: Christopher Wilson

16   Tournai Cathedral, capital of main arcade of north transept apse
Photograph: Christopher Wilson

17   Temple Church, capital of nave pier, detail
Photograph: Christopher Wilson

18   Temple Church, capital on north side of westernmost transverse rib of vault of 12th-century chancel
Photograph: Christopher Wilson

19   Tournai Cathedral, north nave arcade, fifth freestanding pier from the east, capital on north-west face
Photograph: George Zarnecki, neg. 109/62 (Courtauld Institute, Conway Library)

20   Tournai Cathedral, spur on base of main arcade of north transept apse
Photograph: James F. King

21   Temple Church, west door, voussoirs
Photograph: Christopher Wilson

22   Dommartin, hemicycle capital, detail
Photograph: Christopher Wilson

23   Dommartin, hemicycle capital, detail
Photograph: Christopher Wilson

24   Saint-Denis, chevet, capital of columnar pier between two northernmost radiating chapels
Photograph: James Austin

25   Bertaucourt-les-Dames, Benedictine nunnery, detail of west door
Photograph: Christopher Wilson

26   Canterbury Cathedral, Benedictine priory, north-east corner pier of infirmary cloister (formerly with four shafts)
Photograph: Christopher Wilson

27   Paris, Temple Church, interior of nave looking west, detail of engraving by Jean Marot (1619?–1679),
From Yvan Christ, *Eglises parisiennes actuelles et disparues*, Paris 1947

28   York Minster, profile of choir main arcade
Photograph: Christopher Wilson

29   York Minster, choir crypt, base of pier at centre of north-east transept
Photograph: Christopher Wilson

30   Ripon Minster, north choir aisle, vault respond
Photograph: Christopher Wilson

31   Fontenay, Cistercian abbey, chapter house, pier
Photograph: Christopher Wilson

32   Bridlington, Augustinian priory, capital from cloister arcade
Photograph: Christopher Wilson

33   Temple Church, west porch, capital of east respond of north arch
Photograph: Christopher Wilson

34   Bridlington Priory, capital (original setting unknown)
Photograph: Christopher Wilson

35   Winchester, Hospital of St Cross, interior of choir looking south-east
Photograph: Christopher Wilson

36   Temple Church choir, exterior, south side
Photograph: Virginia Jansen

37   Salisbury Cathedral Trinity Chapel, view to north-east
Photograph: Virginia Jansen

38   Winchester Castle hall, interior view to north-west
Photograph: Virginia Jansen

39   Temple Church choir, piscina in south aisle
     Photograph: Chris Christodoulou (Temple Church)

40   Winchester Cathedral retrochoir, view to north-east
     Photograph: Virginia Jansen

41   Temple Church choir, head on north jamb of north lateral arch between nave and choir
     Photograph: Virginia Jansen

42   Temple Church, floor tiles found during the Victorian restoration of 1839–42
     From E. Richardson, *The Ancient Stone and Leaden Coffins, Encaustic Tiles, etc. recently discovered in the Temple Church*, London 1845, pl. VIII

43   Temple Church, St Anne's Chapel, 'copy by D. I. Smart of the original by J. C. Buckler [John Chessell Buckler, architect and author] 1823'
     Photograph: Chris Christodoulou (Temple Church)

44   Temple Church, grave cover in nave (for Richard of Hastings?)
     From E. Richardson, *The Monumental Effigies of the Temple Church, with an Account of their Restoration in the Year 1842*, London 1843, pl. 1

45   Temple Church, effigy in nave (William Marshal the Elder?)
     From E. Richardson, *The Monumental Effigies of the Temple Church, with an Account of their Restoration in the Year 1842*, London 1843, pl. 6

46   Temple Church, effigy in nave (Gilbert Marshal?)
     From E. Richardson, *The Monumental Effigies of the Temple Church, with an Account of their Restoration in the Year 1842*, London 1843, pl. 7

47   Temple Church, effigy in south choir aisle (Silvester de Everdon, Bishop of Carlisle?)
     From E. Richardson, *The Monumental Effigies of the Temple Church, with an Account of their Restoration in the Year 1842*, London 1843, pl. 11

48   Temple Church, head of bishop's effigy
     Photograph: Chris Christodoulou (Temple Church)

49   Temple Church, engraving showing original location of bishop's effigy in south choir aisle
     From J. T. Smith, *Antiquities of London and it's environs*, London 1791–1800

50   Temple Church, view of nave showing indent for brass in the foreground
     From C. Clarke, *Architectura Ecclesiastica Londini*, London 1819

51   Temple Church, detail of indent for brass
     From C. Clarke, *Architectura Ecclesiastica Londini*, London 1819, (detail)

52   Temple Church, effigy in nave south ambulatory of William de Ros?
     From E. Richardson, *The Monumental Effigies of the Temple Church, with an Account of their Restoration in the Year 1842*, London 1843, pl. 10

53   Temple Church, effigy of William de Ros? (detail)
     Photograph: Chris Christodoulou (Temple Church)

54   Bedale (North Yorkshire), effigy of Brian Fitzalan
     From T. and G. Hollis, *The Monumental Effigies of Great Britain, Drawn and Etched by Thomas Hollis and George Hollis*, London 1840–42

55   Bedale, tomb of Brian Fitzalan
     From E. Blore, *The Monumental Remains of Noble and Eminent Persons . . .* , London 1826.

56 Temple Church, layout of the thirteenth-century military effigies since 1842
Photographs: Bedford Lemere, about 1885

57 Temple Church, Purbeck marble effigy, RCHM no. 10. A. Etching of a drawing, published by
Thomas and George Hollis, 1840; B. After bomb damage in 1941
Photograph: (B) Temple Church

58 Temple Church, Purbeck marble effigies. Drawings and notes by Thomas Kerrich (d. 1828).
A. RCHM no. 5. B, C. RCHM no. 7
Photographs: British Library (MS Add. 6728, fols 67, 68)

59 A. Temple Church, Purbeck marble effigy, RCHM no. 6. Etching of a drawing by Charles
Stothard, January 1812. B. Merevale (Warwicks), Purbeck marble effigy.
Photograph: (B) Philip Lankester

60 A. Temple Church, Purbeck marble effigy, RCHM no. 3. Drawing by Thomas Kerrich (d.
1828). B. Temple Church, Reigate stone (?) effigy, RCHM no. 9. Etching of drawing by
Charles Stothard, 1811
Photograph: (A) British Library (MS Add. 6730, fol. 3)

61 Temple Church, Purbeck marble effigy, RCHM no. 4. Drawings and notes by Thomas Kerrich (d. 1828)
Photographs: British Library (MS Add. 6730, fol. 4; 6728, fol. 43)

62 Temple Church, RCHM no. 8. A, B. Drawings by Thomas Kerrich (d. 1828). C. Detail showing the straps visible through the armhole of the gown
Photographs: (A, B) British Library (MS Add. 6730, fol. 4, 6728, fol. 50); (C): Philip Lankester

63 Anthonis van den Wyngaerde, *Panorama of London* (detail), drawing, 1544
Photograph: Ashmolean Museum, Oxford

64 Temple Church, detail of engraving, 'A View of the Temple as it appeared in the Year 1671'
(from a reissue of 1770)
Photograph: Inner Temple

65 Temple, design for cloisters by Sir Christopher Wren, 1680
Photograph: Middle Temple

66 Temple Church, north face of nave Round, photograph 1861 following removal of neighbouring buildings
Photograph: Middle Temple

67 Temple Church, exterior of nave looking north, aquatint by Thomas Malton, 1796, from
T. Malton, *A Picturesque Tour through the Cities of London and Westminster*, 2 vols., London
1792–1801, II, pl. XLV
Photograph: Chris Christodoulou (Temple Church)

68 Temple Church, west porch, advertisement for stationers J. Penn and O. Lloyd, n.d. (a stationer Penn is mentioned in Inner Temple's accounts, 1677–99; Lloyd's shop, 1713/4 and
perhaps 1721), published without text in *Gentleman's Magazine*, 54 pt 2, Dec. 1784, opp. 911
('from an old shop-bill of Messrs O. Lloyd and S. Gibbons')
Photograph: Chris Christodoulou (Middle Temple)

69   Temple Church, chancel, engraving by L. Boydell after Thomas Boydell, 1750, published in 1750 and again in J. Boydell, *A Collection of One Hundred Views . . .* , 1770, pl. 42 (in 1790 edition, pl. 37)
Photograph: Chris Christodoulou (Temple Church)

70   'The South East Prospect of the Temple Church', engraving by Benjamin Cole, version of engraving by W. H. Toms, 1739, after Robert West, in R. West and W.H. Toms, *Perspective Views of All the Ancient Churches . . .* , 2nd series, London 1736–9, II, pl. 10
Photograph: Chris Christodoulou (Temple Church)

71   Temple Church and Lamb Building (built 1667, destroyed 10 May 1941), view from south-west, photograph *c.*1915–27
Photograph: National Monuments Record

72   Temple Church, interior of nave looking south-west, aquatint by J. Bluck after Thomas Rowlandson and Augustus Charles Pugin, from W. H. Pyne and W. Combe (for R. Ackermann), *The Microcosm of London*, 3 vols., London 1808–9, III, 174
Photograph: Chris Christodoulou (Temple Church)

73   Temple Church, interior of nave looking east, engraving by W. Woolnoth, 1805, after Frederick Nash, from J. Britton, The *Architectural Antiquities of Great Britain*, 4 vols., London 1807–14, I, 13, pl. 2
Photograph: Guildhall Library, City of London

74   Temple Church, Wrenian organ-case and screen looking west
Engraving reproduced from E. Macrory, *Notes on the Temple Organ*, ed. Muir Mackenzie, London 1911, opp. 34

75   Temple Church, Wrenian pulpit after its move to Christ Church, Newgate Street (pulpit destroyed, 29 December 1940), photograph
Photograph: Guildhall Library, City of London

76   Temple Church, 'View of the Interior from the Vestry Door', engraving by J. Le Keux after R. W. Billings, 1837, for G. Godwin, *The Churches of London: a History and Description of the Ecclesiastical Edifices of the Metropolis*, 2 vols., London 1839, I, 15, pl. 20
Photograph: Chris Christodoulou (Temple Church)

77   Temple Church, Wrenian reredos
Photograph: Chris Christodoulou

78   'The South Side of the Temple Church', engraving by William Emmett, 1702
Photograph: Guildhall Library, City of London

79   Church of Holy Sepulchre, Jerusalem, 17th-century model, probably made in Bethlehem, maple-wood, mother-of-pearl and ivory
Photograph: The Order of St John, Clerkenwell

80   Constantinople, 'The new Mosck or Achmet's Mosck', from G. Wheler, *A Journey into Greece by George Wheler Esq. . . .* , London 1682, opp. 187
Photograph: British Library

81   'A Prospect of the Ancient Church', from G. Wheler, *An Account of the Churches, or Places of Assembly, of the Primitive Christians . . .* , London 1689, pl. 5 opp. 63
Photograph: British Library

82   Temple Church, section of nave looking east, engraving by William Emmett, 1702
Photograph: Guildhall Library, City of London

83 'ICHNOGRAPHIA Templorum Veterum', engraving from W. Beveridge, *Synodicon, sive Pandectae Canonum SS. Apostolorum . . .* , 2 vols., Oxford 1672, II, opp. 71
Photograph: British Library

84 Temple Church, copy (dated 2 [or 3] August 1695 on reverse) of inscription over south-west door of nave
Photograph: Middle Temple

85 Temple Church, drawing of southern set of effigies (as laid out 1695–1841) made for Smart Lethieullier, 1736/7
Photograph: British Library (Add. MS 27348, fol. 90)

86 Temple Church, drawing of northern set of effigies (as laid out 1695–1841) made for Smart Lethieullier, 1736/7
Photograph: British Library (Add. MS 27348, fol.91)

87 Temple Church, engraving of southern set of effigies (as laid out 1695–1841), from R. Gough, *Sepulchral Monuments in Great Britain . . .* , 2 vols., London 1786–96, I, opp. 24
Photograph: Chris Christodoulou (Society of Antiquaries of London)

88 Temple Church, engraving of northern set of effigies (as laid out 1695–1841), from R. Gough, *Sepulchral Monuments in Great Britain . . .* , 2 vols., London 1786–96, I, opp. 50
Photograph: Chris Christodoulou (Society of Antiquaries of London)

89 Temple Church, busts on west doorway, drawings by Frederick Nash, *c.*1818
Photograph: Chris Christodoulou (Society of Antiquaries of London)

90 Temple Church, west doorway by Frederick Nash, engraved in 1818 and published in *Vetusta Monumenta*, 7 vols., London 1747–1906, V, 1828, pl. XXIII
Photograph: Chris Christodoulou (Society of Antiquaries of London)

91 Temple Church, arcading in nave, drawn (1809) and engraved (1813) by John Thomas Smith, published in J. T. Smith, *Antient Topography of London . . .* , London 1815, 7
Photograph: Middle Temple

92 'The Temple Church, as Restored', engraved by J. Carter, 1828, after Thomas Hosmer Shepherd for J. Elmes, *Metropolitan Improvements . . .* ('Shepherd's London'), 41 issues in 8 parts, London 1827–33, pt 6, no. 30, 1828, pl. 118
Photograph: Guildhall Library, City of London

93 Temple Church, exterior from south, showing Lamb Building and nave's roof as altered, 1860–62, photograph
Photograph: Middle Temple

94 Temple Church, monuments in triforium. From left to right: David Graham (d. 1770) and Edward Jennings (d. 1725); on buttress, William Petyt (d. 1707) and (above) John Wharry (d. 1812); William Freman (d. 1701) and (above) Roger Bishop (d. 1587) and William Moore (d. 1814); above openings John Denne (d. 1648). Photograph *c.*1915–27
Photograph: National Monuments Record

95 Temple Church, chancel from south-west, photograph by John Clerk, QC, Treasurer of Inner Temple, 1885
Photograph: Middle Temple

96 Temple Church, chancel from north-east, photograph by John Clerk, 1885
Photograph: Middle Temple

97   Temple Church, chancel from nave, photograph by John Clerk, 1885
Photograph: Middle Temple

98   Temple Church, design for east window of clearstorey made and presented by Thomas Willement, published from drawing by William Richard Hamilton Essex in W. R. H. Essex and S. Smirke, *Illustrations of the Architectural Ornaments and Embellishments and Painted Glass of the Temple Church, London*, London 1845, pl. x

99   Temple Church, design for painted decoration over chancel-arch looking west by Thomas Willement, published from drawing by William Richard Hamilton Essex in W. R. H. Essex and S. Smirke, *Illustrations of the Architectural Ornaments and Embellishments and Painted Glass of the Temple Church, London*, London 1845, pl. xviii
Photograph: Middle Temple

100   Temple Church, west porch and Round, lithograph by Thomas Shotter Boys for T. S. Boys, *London as it is*, 1842, title-page
Photograph: Guildhall Library, City of London

101   Temple Church, west doorway, photograph *c*.1915–27, from Royal Commission on Historical Monuments, *London,* iv (The City), London 1929, pl. 181
Photograph: National Monuments Record

102   Temple Church, two voussoirs of west doorway, one still in situ, the other in V&A, from drawing by Neil McFadyen published in N. McFadyen, 'Temple Church, London: The Great West Doorway', Association for Studies in the Conservation of Historic Buildings, *Transactions*, 9, 1984, 5
Photograph: Association for Studies in the Conservation of Historic Buildings

103   Temple Church, photograph 10 May 1941

104   Temple Church, nave looking east as damaged 10 May 1941, photograph
Photograph: Guildhall Library, City of London

105   The Temple, *c*.1945: View from Middle Temple Lane towards Temple Church
Photograph: Middle Temple

106   Temple Church, warriors of eight centuries gathered in nave, gouache, n.d. (after 10 May 1941)
Photograph: Guildhall Library, City of London

107   Temple, cloisters, photograph by Cecil Beaton published in *Vogue*, September 1941, 30
Photograph: Condé Nast

108   Temple Church, chancel from south-west, *c*.1954
Photograph: Arthur Bernard

109   Temple Church, effigies in nave with V&A's plaster-casts, photograph 2008
Photograph: Chris Christodoulou

Editors' Preface

THIS VOLUME RESULTS from a conference held at the Courtauld Institute of Art on Saturday 14 June 2008. Held in the Kenneth Clark Lecture Theatre, under the auspices of the Institute's Research Forum, the day was memorable not only for the quality of the papers presented but also for the lively and informative discussion engendered. The conference concluded with an evening reception in the atmospheric ambience of the Temple Church itself, an experience enhanced by an exhibition in the nave of antiquarian and other material relating to the history of the church. Particularly unforgettable was the juxtaposition of four nineteenth-century plaster casts brought from the Victoria and Albert Museum with the original thirteenth-century effigies so tragically damaged in the Second World War.[1]

Although the Courtauld and the Temple Church are only a stone's throw from one another, the conference represented our first collaboration in what we hope will become a series of academic initiatives. It was spurred by the lack of any comprehensive scholarly study of the church, despite its status as one of the most important surviving medieval monuments in London. Although the church has been the subject of much valuable antiquarian study in the past — as will be evident from many papers in this volume — the time is ripe for an up-to-date study of a monument so notable for its exceptionally important early Gothic architecture, magnificent series of medieval monuments, major post-Reformation furnishings by Sir Christopher Wren and others, and comprehensive refurbishment in the nineteenth century. Doubtless the past academic neglect can be attributed partly to the traumas the church has suffered, most famously the damage done by fire during the Blitz of 1941. No volume can claim to be entirely comprehensive, but most of the significant issues are addressed in detail in this book, which it is hoped will itself stimulate further research.

All of the papers presented at the conference are published here, though some have been substantially modified since. A further paper, on two major aspects of the nineteenth- and twentieth-century history of the church, has been added subsequently. A particular sadness was the death before the conference of Dr Thomas Cocke, who had been due to give the paper on the seventeenth-century refurbishment of the

---

[1] See Plate 109. A permanent record of the exhibition is provided in R. Griffith-Jones, *The Temple Church: a History in Pictures*, London 2008.

church. The affection and respect in which he was held was evident from the tributes paid to him at the conference.

The conference and resulting publication would have been impossible without the generous help of a number of individuals. We are particularly grateful to Sharon Cather and Professor Eric Fernie of the Courtauld Institute, Henrietta Amodio of the Temple Church, and Dr Paul Williamson of the Victoria and Albert Museum. Much invaluable photography was undertaken by Chris Christodoulou. Generous financial and logistical support for both the conference and publication have been provided by the Courtauld's Research Forum and the Temple Church. We are also greatly indebted to Caroline Palmer, to her team at Boydell & Brewer, and to Jeffrey Dean for all their skilful work in bringing the book to completion.

Robin Griffith-Jones
The Temple Church, London

David Park
The Courtauld Institute of Art, London   February 2010

List of Abbreviations

Addison, *Temple Church*	C. G. Addison, *The Temple Church*, London 1843
Baylis, *Temple Church*	T. H. Baylis, *The Temple Church and Chapel of St Ann, etc., an Historical Record and Guide*, London 1893
Billings, *Illustrations*	R. W. Billings, *Architectural Illustrations and Account of the Temple Church, London*, London 1838
BL	British Library
Bodl.	Bodleian Library, Oxford
CCR	*Calendar of the Close Rolls Preserved in the Public Record Office*, 47 vols. organised by reign, London 1892–1963
CPR	*Calendar of the Patent Rolls Preserved in the Public Record Office*, 73 vols. organised by reign, London 1891–1986
CR	*Close Rolls of the Reign of Henry III Preserved in the Public Record Office, 1227–72*, 14 vols., London 1902–38
Dugdale, *Origines*	W. Dugdale, *Origines Juridiciales*, London 1666
Dunstable Annals	Dunstable Annals in *Annales Monastici*, ed. H. R. Luard, Rolls Series 36, 5 vols., London 1864–9, III, 1866
Esdaile, *Temple Church Monuments*	K. A. Esdaile, *Temple Church Monuments*, London 1933
Essex and Smirke, *Illustrations*	W. R. H. Essex and S. Smirke, *Illustrations of the Architectural Ornaments and Embellishments, and the Painted Glass, of the Temple Church, London*, London 1845
Gardam, 'Restorations'	C. M. L. Gardam, 'Restorations of the Temple Church, London', in *Medieval Art, Architecture and Archaeology in London* (British Archaeological Association Conference Transactions for the Year 1984, x), ed. L. Grant, Leeds 1990, 101–17
Gough, *Sepulchral Monuments*	R. Gough, *Sepulchral Monuments in Great Britain, Applied to Illustrate the History of Families, Manners, Habits, and Arts, at the Different Periods from the Norman Conquest to the Seventeenth Century*, 2 vols., London 1786–96

Griffith-Jones, *Temple Church*	R. Griffith-Jones, *The Temple Church: A History in Pictures*, London 2008
ITA	Inner Temple Archives
ITR II	*A Calendar of the Inner Temple Records vol II, 1 James I (1603)– Restoration (1660)*, ed. F. A. Inderwick, London 1898
ITR III	*A Calendar of the Inner Temple Records vol. III, 12 Charles II (1660)–12 Anne (1714)*, ed. F. A. Inderwick , London 1901
ITR IV	*A Calendar of the Inner Temple Records vol. IV, 1 George I (1714)– 24 George II (1750)*, ed. R. A. Roberts, London 1933
ITR V	*A Calendar of the Inner Temple Records vol. V, 25 George II (1751)–41 George III (1800)*, ed. R. A. Roberts, London 1936
ITR VI	*A Calendar of the Inner Temple Records vol. VI, 41 George III (1801)–58 George III (1817)*, ed. B. Given, London 1992
JBAA	*Journal of the British Archaeological Association*
Lees, *Records*	*Records of the Templars in England in the Twelfth Century: the Inquest of 1185 with Illustrative Charters and Documents*, ed. B. A. Lees, London 1935
Lewer and Dark, *Temple Church*	D. Lewer and R. Dark, *The Temple Church in London*, London 1997
Life of William Marshal	*The Life of William Marshal*, ed. and tr. A. J. Holden, S. Gregory and D. Crouch, 3 vols., London, Anglo-Norman Text Society Occasional Publications, 4–6, 2002–6
Mordaunt Crook, 'Restoration'	J. Mordaunt Crook, 'The Restoration of the Temple Church: Ecclesiology and Recrimination', *Architectural History*, 8, 1965, 39–51
MTA	Middle Temple Archives
MTR	*Middle Temple Records: Minutes of Parliament of the Middle Temple*, tr. C. T. Martin, 3 vols., London 1904–5 (general editor C. H. Hopwood)
Nicholson, *Knights Templar*	H. J. Nicholson, *The Knights Templar: a New History*, Stroud 2001.
ODNB	*Oxford Dictionary of National Biography*, 60 vols., Oxford 2004
Paris, *Chronica*	Matthew Paris, *Chronica Majora*, ed. H. R. Luard, 7 vols., Rolls Series 57, London 1872–83
RCHM, *The City*	Royal Commission on Historical Monuments (England), *An Inventory on the Historical Monuments in London, IV, The City*, London 1929

Richardson, *Effigies of the Temple Church*	E. Richardson, *The Monumental Effigies of the Temple Church, with an Account of their Restoration in the Year 1842*, London 1843
Richardson, *Stone and Leaden Coffins*	E. Richardson, *The Ancient Stone and Leaden Coffins, Encaustic Tiles, etc. Recently Discovered in the Temple Church*, London 1845
RS	(Rolls Series) *Rerum Brittanicarum Medii Aevi Scriptores*, London 1858–96
Soo, *Wren*	L. M. Soo, *Wren's 'Tracts' on Architecture and other Writings*, Cambridge 1998
Stothard, *Monumental Effigies*	C. A. Stothard, *Monumental Effigies of Great Britain*, London 1817–32
Stow, *Survey*	J. Stow, *A Survey of the Cities of London and Westminster*, revised by J. Strype, London 1720
TNA:PRO	The National Archives: Public Record Office
Tummers, *Early Secular Effigies*	H. A. Tummers, *Early Secular Effigies in England: the Thirteenth Century*, Leiden 1980
Weever, *Monuments*	J. Weever, *Ancient Funerall Monuments within the United Monarchie of Great Britaine, Ireland, and the Islands adiacent . . .*, London 1631
Williamson, *Temple*	J. B. Williamson, *The History of the Temple, London*, London 1924

List of Contributors

Robin Griffith-Jones	Master of the Temple at the Temple Church
Virginia Jansen	Professor Emerita of History of Art and Visual Culture, University of California, Santa Cruz
Philip Lankester	Honorary Visiting Fellow, Department of History of Art, University of York
Helen Nicholson	Reader in History, Cardiff University
David Park	Professor, Courtauld Institute of Art
Rosemary Sweet	Director, Centre for Urban History, University of Leicester
William Whyte	Tutorial Fellow in Modern History, St John's College, Oxford
Christopher Wilson	Professor Emeritus of History of Art, University College London

Helen J. Nicholson

At the Heart of Medieval London:
the New Temple in the Middle Ages

T HE ORDER OF THE TEMPLE was a religious-military institution originally
founded by a group of warriors in Jerusalem in the decades following the First
Crusade.[1] The function of this order, institution or group was approved both
by the king of Jerusalem and by the patriarch (head of the Christian Church in the
kingdom) at a Church council at Nablus in 1120. The group was to protect Christian
pilgrims on the roads to the pilgrimage sites around Jerusalem, and the members also
helped to defend the territories that the participants in the First Crusade had con-
quered. In January 1129, at a Church council at Troyes in Champagne, in what is now
north-eastern France, the Templars were given papal approval and acknowledgement as
a formal religious Order, with an official uniform ('habit') and rule of life. As members
of a religious Order, the members called each other 'brother', and made three vows: to
obey their superior officer, to avoid sexual activity and to have no personal property.
They became known as 'Templars' after their headquarters in Jerusalem, which west-
erners believed had been King Solomon's Temple but in fact was the Aqsa mosque,
constructed from the seventh century AD onwards.[2]

The Templars first arrived in England in 1128 in the months before the Council
of Troyes, when the first grand master Hugh de Payns and his colleagues were in western Europe publicising their work in the East and recruiting. Possibly around 1135 and
certainly by 1144, they were given a site in Holborn just outside the city of London
and built a house with a circular-naved church.[3] A number of circular-naved churches

---

[1] The standard history of the Order of the Temple in English is M. Barber, *The New Knighthood: a History of the Order of the Temple*, Cambridge 1994. See also A. Demurger, *Les Templiers: une
chevalerie chrétienne au moyen âge*, Paris 2005; A. J. Forey, *The Military Orders: from the Twelfth to the Early
Fourteenth Centuries*, Basingstoke 1992; Nicholson, *Knights Templar*.

[2] On the Aqsa mosque in the Middle Ages, see D. Pringle, *The Churches of the Crusader Kingdom
of Jerusalem: a Corpus*, vol. III, *The City of Jerusalem*, Cambridge 2007, 417–34.

[3] M. Gervers, 'The Commandery as an Economic Unit in England', in *La Commanderie: institution des ordres militaires dans l'occident médiéval*, ed. A. Luttrell and L. Pressouyre, Paris 2002, 245–60
at 252 and n. 32. For discussion of the possible founder of Old Temple, see Park, pp. 68–74 below.

were being constructed in western Europe at this time, by returning crusaders or groups based in the Holy Land such as the Templars and their sister order the Hospitallers. They were modelled on the *Anastasis* of the church of the Holy Sepulchre in Jerusalem, the most holy site of Christendom which the crusaders had fought to recapture from the Muslims, which Christian pilgrims travelled to visit, and which the military religious orders were set up to protect. King Henry I, King Stephen and Queen Matilda were early patrons of the Templars, but it was from King Henry II (1154–89) that the order received most of its early holdings in London. At some time between 1159 and 1173, Henry II gave them a mill site on the River Fleet, a messuage or manor near Fleet Bridge, and the advowson of the church of St Clement Danes.[4]

In 1161 the Templars sold their original London site. They transferred their London base to a new site, which became known as the New Temple.[5] This was built on land between the main road from Ludgate to Westminster and the Thames, on the west bank of the river Fleet (Fig. 1, overleaf). The cemetery had been consecrated by 1163.[6] In spring 1185 Patriarch Heraclius of Jerusalem, who was in England trying to persuade Henry II to come to the aid of the kingdom of Jerusalem, consecrated the new Temple church, which had a circular nave like that at the Templars' previous house in Holborn.[7] He also consecrated the Hospitallers' new circular-naved church at Clerkenwell, to the north of the city.

THE TEMPLARS' WAY OF LIFE

In western Europe, away from the Muslim frontier, the Templars' purpose was to raise money and resources for their military work in the Holy Land, and to raise recruits. Their everyday life in the west was very like that of other religious orders. The Templars' rule was based on the Rule of St Benedict, which was the standard monastic rule in use in western Europe in the twelfth century. Their daily timetable was laid out in additions to their rule, and was as follows:[8]

[4] Gervers, 'The Commandery', 253; see also N. Hamonic, 'Londres', in *Prier et combattre: Dictionnaire européen des ordres militaires au moyen âge*, ed. N. Bérou and P. Josserand, Paris 2009, 558–60.

[5] Lees, *Records*, pp. lxxxvi–lxxxvii; D. Knowles and R. N. Hadcock, *Medieval Religious Houses: England and Wales*, 2nd edn, Harlow 1971, 294; E. Lord, *The Knights Templar in Britain*, London 2002, 26–30; Baylis, *Temple Church*.

[6] Lees, *Records*, p. lxxxvii, referring to the alleged burial of the earl of Essex in the cemetery of the New Temple in or about 1163. See also J. H. Round, *Geoffrey de Mandeville: a Study of the Anarchy*, London 1892, 225; Wilson, pp. 21–2 below; Park, pp. 71–4 below.

[7] 'Houses of Military Orders: the Temple', in *Victoria County History, History of the County of London*, I: *London within the Bars, Westminster and Southwark*, ed. W. Page, London 1909, 485, citing Stow, *Survey*, III, 270; *London and Middlesex Archaeological Society Transactions*, new series I, 257. See also Wilson, pp. 20–21 below.

[8] This table is taken from that in Nicholson, *Knights Templar*, 139, and is based on *Le Règle du Temple*, ed. H. de Curzon, Paris 1886, §§ 279–312, 340–65, translated as *The Rule of the Templars: the French Text of the Rule of the Order of the Knights Templar*, trans. J. M. Upton-Ward, Woodbridge 1992.

time	service in church	detail
At night	Matins in chapel (if house has one; otherwise in hall) Brothers then go and check horses and equipment and speak to squires. Sleep until dawn.	Brothers join in prayers.
'The Hours' follow, in chapel:		
c.6 am	Prime	
	Mass (or after sext)	
c.9 am	Terce	
c.midday	Sext	
	Mass (if not heard earlier)	Afterwards repair armour and equipment, make tent pegs, tent posts, or anything necessary.
	Dinner	Knights eat at first sitting; sergeants at second sitting. A clerk reads aloud while they eat.
	Brothers go to chapel and give thanks; then to their posts and work.	
c.3 pm	Nones	
	Vespers for the dead	
	Vigils for the dead	
Dusk	Vespers	
	Supper	
	Compline	Followed by a drink. Check horses and equipment, speak to squire if necessary.
Dark	Bed	

During periods of fasting there was only one meal a day, at 3 or 4 pm.

In Europe, away from the military frontiers, attention to horses and equipment would be replaced by whatever work was needed in the House, such as collecting rents, farming and conducting business. No time was set aside in the timetable for military practice. The Rule did allow jousting and military practice but only with the master's permission, and brothers had to be careful not to damage themselves or each other, or their equipment or horses.[9]

In houses with more than four brothers, every Sunday and at Christmas, Easter and Pentecost there would be a chapter meeting[10] — this was the traditional term used in monastic houses for a management meeting where house business was discussed by the members. Unlike monasteries, most Templar houses did not have a specially-built chapter house, in which case chapter meetings were held in the chapel. As there was

[9] *Règle*, §§ 95, 128, 315; *The Rule of the Templars*, trans. Upton–Ward, 43, 51, 89.
[10] *Règle*, § 385; *The Rule of the Templars*, trans. Upton-Ward, 105.

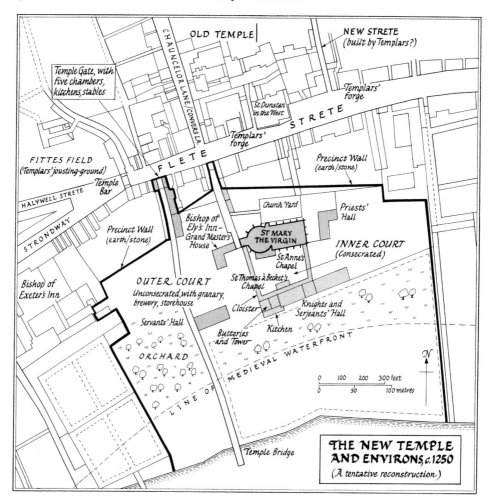

FIGURE I. New Temple and Environs, c.1250: Tentative Reconstruction

no chapter house at the New Temple, chapter meetings would have been held in the church, where the circular nave would form an excellent chapter house, with the brothers sitting in a circle against the walls, as in more traditional monastic houses.

The Templar province of England also held annual provincial chapter meetings, which the commanders of the English houses would attend; the commanders of Scotland and Ireland were also supposed to attend, although during the trial of the Templars some English brothers remarked that the Irish only attended every other year.[11] Initially, it seems, and up to at least 1244 the English provincial chapters were held

[11] Bodl., MS Bodley 454, fols. 66^r–81^v under charge 25; variant opinions on fols. 66^v, 67^r, 67^v, 68^r; MS Bodley 454, fols. 117^r–124^v, charge 6 (an abridged version of this manuscript was published by D. Wilkins, *Concilia Magnae Britanniae et Hiberniae*, London 1737, II, 329–93).

at the New Temple,[12] but by 1266 they were being held at Dinsley in Hertfordshire, which was more accessible for brothers from north of London, and possibly there was also more space there.[13] In addition, the church at New Temple may have been in constant use for other purposes, of which more below.

As a centre of Templar activity, the New Temple would have been a place for recruiting Templars, but in fact of the 108-odd Templars who gave evidence in the British Isles during the trial of the Templars, only eight had been received in London; one brother who was in France in 1307 had been received here.[14] Comparable numbers had been received at Temple Bruer in Lincolnshire[15] and at Balsall in Warwickshire[16] and far more at Dinsley.[17] So by 1307 London was not a major centre for admissions to the Order.

The central charge against the Templars in 1307 was that blasphemous proceedings occurred during reception ceremonies. Although the Templars denied these accusations, they were unable to establish their innocence because in many regions reception ceremonies took place without any non-Templars being present. The brothers in the British Isles all denied the charges, but their testimonies, and those of outsiders, suggest that Templar reception ceremonies in the British Isles may have taken place in two stages, the first in a public space, such as the commandery hall, in the presence of family and friends of the applicant; then the Templars and the applicant proceeded into the chapel, leaving all the others outside, for the second part of the ceremony, in which the applicant made his solemn vows to God — and the doors into the chapel could be left open or closed.[18] This could explain how (for instance) Brother William Raven could state at his first interrogation that he had 100 guests at his reception to the Order, yet state in his second interrogation that only Templars had been present.[19] Because the church had to be temporarily closed to outsiders during reception ceremonies, perhaps the London church was not convenient for receptions, if it was in continual use for other purposes.

[12] A royal donation of wine in April 1237 for the Templars' chapter was to the commander of the New Temple, where the chapter was to be held: *CR, 1234–7*, 440 (28 April 1237); in May 1244 and 1245 the master and congregation of the Knights Templar in London were given a donation of wine for their chapter at London: *CR, 1242–7*, 192, 307 (30 May 1244, 4 May 1245).

[13] The Templars' English provincial chapters were being held at Dinsley by 1266: *CPR, Henry III, 1258–66*, 586–7. Some of the witnesses in the trial noted that chapters were held here: MS Bodley 454, fols. 16^r, 36^r, 56^r, 60^r, 95^v, 96^r, 98$^{r–v}$; one witness recorded a chapter meeting there ten or eleven years before: ibid., fol. 94^v. One witness in MS Bodley 454, fol. 96^r, refers to a chapter house at Dinsley, as well as a chapel.

[14] MS Bodley 454, fols. 18^r, 33^v, 107$^{r–v}$, 109^v–110^r, 125^r, 127^v, 130^v, 148^r; J. Michelet, *Le Procès des Templiers*, 2 vols., Paris 1841–51, II, 398–401.

[15] MS Bodley 454, fols. 53^v, 112^v, 123^r, 130^r, 131^v, 139^v, 143^v, 155^r.

[16] MS Bodley 454, fols. 13^r, 27^r, 40^r, 45^v, 47^r, 49^r, 49^v, 54^r, 56^v, 104^v.

[17] MS Bodley 454, fols. 26^r, 30^v, 34^r, 36^r, 36^v, 38^v, 103^r, 103^v, 105^r, 105^v, 106^r, 108^r, etc.; see also A. Gilmour-Bryson, *The Trial of the Templars in Cyprus: a Complete English Edition*, Leiden 1998, 96, 99.

[18] This is discussed fully in H. J. Nicholson, *Knights Templar on Trial: the Trial of the Templars in the British Isles*, Stroud 2009, 171–3.

[19] MS Bodley 454, fols. 11^v, 22^v.

Apart from receiving people, the house could act as a centre to receive donations of money, property or rights.[20] This leads to the subject of the Templars' relations with their neighbours and society at large.

The Templars' financial and commercial services in London

Henry II was very favourably disposed towards the Templars, perhaps partly because his ancestors had played a leading role in the kingdom of Jerusalem, but also because he found that he could rely on the Templars as efficient and loyal officials. The New Temple early on played a role in the royal administration. In 1185, the same year that the church was consecrated, Henry II deposited some of his income at the New Temple for safe keeping: the Templars held the king's income from vacant churches, and the Temple was used as a depository for the exchequer's net receipts at Michaelmas, and also for mid-term receipts.[21]

Where, physically, was the money deposited? Was there a strong room where valuables were kept, or were they kept within the church itself, where no one would dare to touch them? The Dunstable Annals refer to 'The Templars' treasury' in 1263, and in the inventory of the New Temple taken by the sheriff of London in 1308 there is a reference to a 'dispensary', which could be the storeroom, though the situation is not at all clear.[22]

The New Temple's financial and administrative importance to the king of England was examined as long ago as 1925 by Agnes Sandys.[23] She pointed out that although the New Temple was 'never the sole or even the chief royal treasury', it acted throughout the thirteenth century as one of the 'ordinary and regular "treasuries" of the Crown'. The Exchequer officials used several places for depositing the king's revenue, but before there was a royal treasury at Westminster, the New Temple was much more convenient for the Exchequer officials in London than the royal treasury at Winchester.[24] The Exchequer continued to use the New Temple as a depository even after the royal treasury at Westminster was set up at the end of Henry II's reign. Monies due to the king were

[20] A story told by the Franciscan friar Nicholas Bozon, perhaps in the 1320s, relates how a corrodarian (pensioner) of the Templars who lived in the diocese of Lincoln used to bring all his income to London each year to donate to the Templars: *Les Contes moralisés de Nicole Bozon, frère mineur*, ed. L. Toulmin Smith and P. Meyer, Société des anciens textes françaises, Paris 1889, 181–2, no. 144.

[21] Lees, *Records*, p. lv; *The Receipt Roll of the Exchequer for Michaelmas Term XXXI Henry II, AD 1185*, ed. H. Hall, Studies in Economics and Political Science 7, London 1899, 30, 31.

[22] Dunstable Annals, III, 222; TNA:PRO E358/18 rot. 7(1–2); E358/20, rot. 3. The copy of the inventory at E358/20, rot. 3 is printed and translated by Baylis, *Temple Church*, 131–46; summarised by Lord, *Knights Templar in Britain*, 26–30.

[23] A. Sandys, 'The Financial and Administrative Importance of the London Temple in the Thirteenth Century', in *Essays in Medieval History presented to Thomas Frederick Tout*, ed. A. G. Little and F. M. Powicke, Manchester 1925, 147–62.

[24] Ibid., 151 and n. 8.

sometimes paid into the New Temple rather than to the Exchequer officials, and tax receipts were regularly stored there. Even in the 1280s, when the Italian banking families were taking over many of the responsibilities of tax collection and auditing, the money was still stored, audited and paid out at the New Temple.[25]

The New Temple not only acted as a depository for royal income, but also for royal valuables such as wine for important guests, important documents and the king's personal treasury, known as the Wardrobe.[26] The king's family and relations also kept valuables there.[27] In the 1230s the keeper of the king's Wardrobe was a Templar, Geoffrey, who was also royal almoner.[28] After 1266 the king's Wardrobe treasury at the New Temple was still in use, but was mentioned less often in the records, and in 1290 Edward I established two permanent treasuries, at the Chapter House at Westminster and at the Tower of London, so that he no longer needed to use the New Temple.

Sandys argued that the New Temple effectively acted as a bank. Through bills of exchange it could make payments for its clients at a distance: money was paid into the New Temple in London and paid out at any other Templar house in Christendom.[29] The Templars lent money to the king and his nobles; King John and his son Henry III made particular use of this service. Edward I preferred to borrow from Italian merchants, but sometimes he asked the Templars to repay a debt to the Italians on his behalf, promising to repay the Templars in the future.[30]

The Templars also loaned money to other leading nobles.[31] In addition, merchants

[25] Ibid., 152. *CPR, Edward I, 1281–92*, 184: Master Thomas of Brecdestret and the society of Lucca were to audit the accounts of the tax of a twentieth from the clergy; ibid., 244: the Riccardi of Lucca were to make a payment from the tax of a tenth in England to the papal nuncio.

[26] For example, in 1235 Henry III stored four tuns of his best wine in the Templars' cellar at the New Temple so that it would be in the best condition for the archbishop of Cologne when he arrived there. This procedure was repeated in 1243 for the visit of the archbishop of Embrun: *CR, 1234–7*, 55; *CR, 1242–7*, 42. Sandys noted that while the king's Wardrobe was kept at the New Temple, between 1225 and 1266, it was under the control of the treasurer of the Temple and the grand commander of the Temple in England rather than royal officials. The king's orders for money to be disbursed from his Wardrobe would be addressed to the grand commander or treasurer of the Temple, instructing him to give the keeper of the royal wardrobe money, or jewels or gold or silver to be spent as the king had instructed; Sandys, 'Financial and Administrative Importance', 149–51.

[27] Eleanor of Provence, queen of Henry III, owned a copy of the epic crusading poem *La Chanson d'Antioche*, described as a 'certain large book, in the French language, in which are contained the deeds of Antioch and of other kings, etc.', which was kept with the queen's valuables in the house of the Templars in London. On 17 May 1250, Henry III sent Henry of the Wardrobe to the Temple to fetch it 'for the queen's use'. Geoffrey of Lusignan, Henry III's half brother, left a chest at the New Temple for safe keeping when he was out of the country between 1260 and 1262: *CR, 1247–51*, 283; *Dunstable Annals*, 222; *CR, 1261–4*, 118; J. R. Maddicott, *Simon de Montfort*, Cambridge 1994, 234.

[28] Sandys, 'Financial and Administrative Importance', 150–51.

[29] Sandys, ibid., 155, cited Henry III's payments of 1,400 marks to the count of La Marche at Paris in 1224. The king allocated money from his revenues held at the New Temple in London; Brother W. Kadel, master of the Temple in France, paid the money to the count at Paris.

[30] Ibid., 157–8.

[31] For example, when Hubert de Burgh fell from power in 1232 he still owed the Templars

would arrange bills of exchange payable at the New Temple in London, and loans were specified as repayable at the New Temple in London.[32] Where exactly at the New Temple was not specified, but after the dissolution of the Templars such agreements would specify the church of the New Temple.

Bishops, nobles and merchants also kept their valuables at the New Temple.[33] In 1231 Henry III commanded the master or grand commander of the Temple in England not to allow the wool belonging to Geoffrey de la Lauzade and Isard his colleague to be removed without his permission from the New Temple, where it had been seized on the orders of the justiciars of the king's bench for a debt the two merchants owed to Stephen Raymond and Bartholomew of St Paul.[34] So, apparently, even merchants' goods could be kept in safe storage at the New Temple. Other private individuals kept money there, including the king's clerks.[35] In addition, people could take refuge there — the St Albans' chronicler Matthew Paris recounted that when in 1234 Henry III demanded a statement of accounts from Peter des Roches, bishop of Winchester, whom he had just removed from office, three royal clerks fled and that one of them, Robert Passelewe, 'concealed himself in the New Temple, pretending to be ill, in a certain secret cell, like a leper'.[36]

Extending its role as a safe deposit for anything valuable, the New Temple also housed legal and government records. In 1279 Roger of Seaton, who had been chief justice of the common bench until the previous year, had a chest at the New Temple which contained all the rolls recording his circuits around England and all the royal writs in his custody.[37] Under Edward I, the New Temple also began to act 'as a "record office" for the Chancery'. By 1289 there was a chest at the New Temple in which Chancery rolls were kept, and in 1291 the king's treasurer had to break into that chest in order to retrieve two documents which the king required — the treasurer could not get into the chest because the king and chancellor had the keys and they were in Scotland. When the king and chancellor returned to London, new keys were made for the broken lock.[38] The New Temple was also a place for the issue of legal documents. Many royal documents were dated there.[39]

So, generally the New Temple was regarded as a place of security, but in times

money, so the king had a manor in Surrey transferred to them to meet the debt; *CR, 1231–4*, 180, 187, 443: 9 January, 7 February 1233, 4 June 1234.

[32] Paris, *Chronica*, III, 329; T. W. Parker, *The Knights Templars in England*, Tucson 1963, 65–6, 157 n. 253.

[33] Sandys, 'Financial and Administrative Importance', 148–9.

[34] *CR, 1227–31*, 540, 4 August 1231.

[35] As did John Langtoft, clerk of the king's chancellor (d. 1261): *CR, 1261–4*, 1.

[36] Paris, *Chronica*, III, 293; R. Stacey, *Politics, Policy and Finance under Henry III, 1216–1245*, Oxford 1987, 39, 64, 142–3, 247, 251, 253.

[37] *Select Cases in the Court of King's Bench under Edward I*, ed. G. O. Sayles, Selden Society 55 (1936), p. cxxiii.

[38] Ibid., p. cxxiii; Sandys, 'Financial and Administrative Importance', 160, citing *CCR, Edward I, 1288–96*, 56, 245–6.

[39] *CPR, Edward III, 1327–30*, 427, *inspeximus* of deed dated 20 June 22 Edward I (1294). Many

of trouble it was not secure from the king. In 1232 Henry III had disgraced his former justiciar Hubert de Burgh and had confiscated all his property. According to Roger of Wendover, chronicler of St Albans abbey, Henry, having heard that Hubert had a great deal of money on deposit in the New Temple, summoned the Master of the Temple in England and demanded to know if this was so. The Master admitted that it was, but he had no idea how much. The king demanded that the money be handed over to him, on the grounds that Hubert had embezzled it from the king's treasury, but the Templars replied that they could not hand over any money deposited with them without the leave of the depositor. The king had to obtain permission from Hubert before the Templars would hand over the keys of his chests to the king.[40]

In 1263, Henry III was in severe financial straits and his government was under threat from opponents among the nobility. The annalist of Dunstable Priory explains what followed:

> The King came with the Queen [Eleanor of Provence] to the Tower of London on 26 May, while the Lord Edward [their eldest son, later Edward I] was staying at the Hospital [of St John] at Clerkenwell. All of them were short of money, and there was no one in London who would give them a penny on credit. So, since the Lord Edward did not like being in this embarrassing position, on the feast of Saints Peter and Paul he assembled Robert Walrampnum [Walerand] and many others and went to the New Temple when the doors were closed. On his request, he was admitted, and he said that he wanted to see the jewels of the Queen, his mother. The custodian of the treasury was fetched, and the Lord Edward fraudulently entered the Temple's treasury with his men; whereupon they broke open the chests of certain persons there with iron hammers which they had brought with them, took much money to the value of a thousand pounds, and carried it away. When they heard about this crime, the citizens of London rose up against them and other members of the King's council who were staying in the city.[41]

The Templars had often lent Henry III money, especially during the crisis years at the beginning of his reign; but clearly they had refused to do so on this occasion and a 'bank raid' was the result. Edward's initial request to see his mother's jewels was perfectly reasonable, in that the jewels were kept in the New Temple for safety; but the Templars, being unarmed, could not resist Edward and his men when they used force. It is also noteworthy that the citizens of London were particularly angry about the theft — presumably because they also kept their money at the New Temple.

On 20 September 1307 the possessions of Walter Langton, bishop of Coventry and Lichfield and royal treasurer, were taken into the hands of Edward II. The bishop

---

letters close were issued at the New Temple by government officials in 1272 and 1273, during Edward I's absence on crusade: *CCR, Edward I, 1272–9*, 1–2, 9, 44.

[40] Roger of Wendover, *Flores historiarum*, ed. Henry R. Hewlett, RS 84, 3 vols., London 1886–1889, III, 41; Paris, *Chronica*, III, 232–3.

[41] Dunstable Annals, 222; *CPR, Henry III, 1258–66*, 279.

himself had been arrested on charges of corruption and fraud. According to the continuation of Walter of Guisborough's chronicle, the king and Piers Gaveston also took the bishop's treasure stored in the New Temple in London, to the sum of 50 thousand pounds of silver, as well as a great quantity of gold, jewels and precious stones, which the king gave to Gaveston. The chronicler added: 'they were both present when the boxes were broken open', indicating that the bishop's possessions were taken by force rather than with the agreement of the bishop or the Templars.[42]

The Templars were not the only military order in England that undertook financial services. The Hospital of St John's house at Clerkenwell was also used by kings to deposit jewels, property and cash, and both orders made loans to the king.[43] But the New Temple remained the more important financial centre.

THE NEW TEMPLE AS A RELIGIOUS CENTRE

For a period in the 1220s and 1230s the Templars were the religious order most favoured by the king. The order maintained priests who celebrated mass regularly in New Temple church for the soul of King John.[44] In July 1231 Henry III granted the order of the Temple £8 a year to support three chaplains at the New Temple. They were to celebrate Masses daily: one for the king, one for the whole Christian people and one for the faithful departed.[45] At around the same time King Henry bequeathed his body to the order.[46] Queen Eleanor followed suit. As it was around this period that the Templars began to build a new chancel on to their round-naved church, it is likely that the chancel was intended to form a suitable shrine for the king and his wife. It was consecrated in 1240, in the king's presence.[47] In October 1246 Henry III annulled the bequest of his body to the Templars and left it instead to his own foundation, Westminster Abbey,

---

[42] *Chronicon domini Walteri de Hemingburgh*, ed. Hans Claude Hamilton, II, London 1849, 273–4 and 273 n. 2; *Chronica Walteri de Gyseburne: the Chronicle of Walter of Guisborough*, ed. H. Rothwell, Camden Society 3rd series 89 (1957), 383. I am indebted to Professor Ignacio de la Torre for bringing this incident to my attention. For Walter Langton's career, see R. M. Haines, 'Langton, Walter (d. 1321)', *ODNB*, vol. 32, 523–5.

[43] In time the Hospital's importance grew; by 1276 its headquarters at Clerkenwell was being designated the point of repayment for a debt, a role usually taken by the New Temple in London: *CCR, Edward I, 1272–9*, 428.

[44] *Register of Walter Gray, Lord Archbishop of York*, Surtees Society 56 (1872), 24, no. 115.

[45] *Calendar of the Charter Rolls Preserved in the Public Record Office*, 6 vols., London, 1903–27, *Henry III, 1226–57*, 135; *Calendar of the Liberate Rolls Preserved in the Public Record Office*, 6 vols., London 1916–1964, *Henry III, 1267–72*, 244 no. 2183 (1231), 254 no. 2267 (1235). There were still three priests there in 1278: *CCR, Edward I, 1272–9*, 490.

[46] *Calendar of the Charter Rolls, Henry III, 1226–57*, 135; *CR, 1237–42*, 6 (25 Nov. 1237); for Eleanor of Provence, see W. Dugdale, *Monasticon Anglicanum*, 6 vols. in 8, London 1846, VI, 818.

[47] Paris, *Chronica*, IV, 11. See also *CR, 1237–42*, 160, 179 (gifts from Henry to the Templars for the new church).

and on his death — while the Templars protested — the monks of Westminster had the honour of interring the royal corpse.[48]

A number of nobles, presumably patrons of the order, were buried in the church. The most famous of these was William Marshal, earl of Pembroke, who took the Templars' habit on his deathbed and was buried in the New Temple church in London in 1219.[49] His eldest son William the Marshal II died in 1231 and was buried in the New Temple Church as an associate of the order.[50] Such funerals would be public occasions. During the Templars' trial Brother Roger Norreys stated that he remembered seeing two deceased Templars being buried at Cressing in Essex, in the presence of a few Templars and up to 60 secular people, both from the families and others.[51]

Evidence given by outsiders during the trial of the Templars in Britain suggests that non-members of the Order entered Templar chapels on a regular basis, to pray and venerate relics.[52] The sheriffs of London, who recorded the contents of the New Temple when the Templars were arrested early in January 1308, did note that they had found many relics in the Templars' London house, but they did not identify them. Perhaps they did not know the saints' identities, but in any case their priority was to value the chattels for sale, not to identify them. Entries included: 'one silver-gilt case with various relics, price estimated at £10 . . . one piece of silver with a paten with the head of a certain saint, price of the silver 2s. A certain crystal vessel, with a silver foot and silver cover, with various relics, price of the silver, 1 mark. One little pix with various relics . . . One pix with various relics, enclosed with glass; two coffers made of pieces of ivory, closed with a lock, full of various relics, the price of which is unknown'.[53] If the New Temple had relics carefully stored in valuable containers, presumably there were also pilgrims coming to see those relics and to pray in New Temple church.

On 27 January 1310 Brother Michael of Baskerville, Templar commander of the New Temple, was interrogated by the papal inquisitors at London. When asked about the time of day that the order held chapter meetings, he replied:

---

[48] *Calendar of the Charter Rolls, Henry III, 1226–57*, 306; *Flores Historiarum*, ed. H. R. Luard, 3 vols., RS 95, London 1890, III, 28.

[49] *L'Histoire de Guillaume le Maréchal, comte de Striguil et de Pembroke, regent d'Angleterre de 1216 à 1219*, ed. P. Meyer, 3 vols., Paris 1891–1901, lines 18,351–442, 19,039–46.

[50] Paris, *Chronica*, III, 201. On the Marshal burials, see Park, 76–80, 82–3 below.

[51] Bodl., MS Bodley 454, fol. 82ᵛ.

[52] H. J. Nicholson, 'Relations between Houses of the Order of the Temple in Britain and their Local Communities, as Indicated during the Trial of the Templars, 1307–12', in *Knighthoods of Christ: Essays on the History of the Crusades and the Knights Templar, Presented to Malcolm Barber*, ed. N. Housley, Aldershot and Burlington, VT, 2007, 195–207.

[53] Baylis, *Temple Church*, 145; TNA:PRO E358/18 rot. 7(2): 'j capsa arg[e]nti de aur' cu[m] div[er]sis reliq[u]is p[re]c[ium] x lj' p[er] estimac[i]o[ne]m . . . j pecia arg' cu[m] patena capit' c[u]i[us]-d[am] S[anc]ti p[re]c[ium] arg' ij s[olidos]; q[u]od[am] vase c[ri]stall' cu[m] ped[e] arge[n]t' + coop[er]-tor' cu[m] div[er]sis r[e]liq[ui]s p[re]c[ium] arg' j mar. . . . J pixide p[ar]vo cu[m] div[er]sis Reliq[u]is . . . J pixid[e] cu[m] div[er]sis reliq[u]is in vit[r]o conclus[is]; ij cofr[e] de pec[iis] de eober[n'] f[ac]tis [?] s[u]b serur[a] claus[e], plene reliq[u]is div[er]sis q[u]or[um] p[re]c[ium] ignorat[ur]'.

quod circa horam prime, dicta missa ad quam potest venire quilibet de populo.[54]

about the first hour [that is, around 6.00 am, after dawn], after mass had been said; to which any of the people could come.

'People' could refer to servants of the brothers, or outsiders from the local community. Brother Michael did not specify which he meant, but his testimony indicates that access to New Temple church was not tightly restricted. As already mentioned, debt repayments and other legal procedures took place in New Temple church after the dissolution of the Templars; possibly this was also the case before the dissolution. When Pope Innocent II had in 1139 granted the Order the privilege of having its own chapels he specifically stated that this was to enable the brothers to worship separately from non-members of the Order.[55] But in practice, although Templar churches would have been closed during chapter meetings, they were apparently open to visitors at other times.

Further evidence that at least part of the Temple complex was not closed to non-Templars came from one Nicholas de Hynton, notary of London. He described to the inquisitors how he was invited into the New Temple for a drink by Brother Peter of Ottringham: 'idem Petrus duceret dictum Nicholaum ad quendam locum ut potaret cum eo'.[56] Nicholas reported that he had to drink up and leave the building quickly because he had allegedly spotted one of the Templars' secret idols; but his testimony implied that it was normal for outsiders to be allowed into other parts of the Temple complex, and not simply the church. Incidentally, of seventeen witnesses, lay and religious men, who came forward in London to give evidence against the Templars, only one had anything definite to say against the Templars, and he apparently had a grudge against the Order due to a land dispute.[57]

ACCOMMODATION IN THE NEW TEMPLE

To judge from the records of the trial and the inventory taken at the New Temple after the arrests, the Templars normally in residence at the New Temple at the beginning of 1308 were the commander Michael of Baskerville, the prior Ralph of Barton, the treasurer John of Stoke, and Adam the Mazun (who died 16 February 1308, just over a month after the arrests), William of Hereford or Hertford, Peter of Ottringham, Thomas of Standon and Richard of Herdwick — eight in all.[58] The Grand Commander,

[54] Bodl., MS Bodley 454, fol. 56ʳ.
[55] *Papsturkunden für Templer und Johanniter*, ed. R. Hiestand, Abhandlungen der Akademie der Wissenschaften in Göttingen, Phil.-hist. Klasse dritte Folge 77, Göttingen 1972, no. 3.
[56] Bodl., MS Bodley 454, fol. 94ʳ.
[57] Bodl., MS Bodley 454, fols. 60ʳ–62ᵛ; the hostile witness was Robert le Dorturer, MS Bodley 454, fols. 60ᵛ–61ʳ, on whom see TNA:PRO C 143/31/4; C 143/34/4; C 143/44/5 m. 2.
[58] Bodl., MS Bodley 454, fol. 58ʳ, with TNA:PRO E358/18 rot. 7(1); E. Gooder, *Temple Balsall*, Chichester 1995, 147. Lord, *Knights Templar in Britain*, 26, is incorrect to assume that Adam was an employee; he is clearly called 'frater', he received the Templars' standard pension of 4d per day, and

William de la More, was peripatetic and at the time of the arrests was at Ewell in Kent, although the fact that some of his possessions were at the New Temple indicates that it was his base.

There would also have been servants, but apparently these were not kept on at the Temple after the Templars were arrested as they were not recorded by the sheriffs. In addition, there were six priests saying mass for the king's ancestors, and clerks in their service, and some persons who were entitled to receive corrodies: food, drink, clothing and accommodation or financial support from the New Temple for their remaining lifetime.[59]

The sheriff's accounts from the arrests of the Templars in January 1308 to 14 November 1308 list various buildings and rooms in the New Temple.[60] There was a granary, and a garden with its produce. In the house itself, there was a cellar containing various miscellaneous items, an upstairs chamber over the dispensary (perhaps the storeroom where money and other valuables were kept), the kitchen, the stable, which contained not only horses but milling equipment, and the brewery. There were also the grand commander's wardrobe (that is, his private room), three entries labelled 'dormitory' — one containing the possessions of Michael of Baskerville, one the possessions of William of Hereford, and one those of Thomas of Standon — a room for the priest-brother, Thomas of Burton, whom the trial records indicate was otherwise based at Dinsley,[61] a room for the prior and a room for Brother Richard of Herdwick. Apparently Brother Peter of Ottringham did not have his own room. Finally, there was the 'great church', where the choir, the altar of St John, the altar of St Michael and the vestry were specifically mentioned. A second copy of the sheriffs' accounts also mentions the chamber of John of Stoke, the treasurer.[62]

These are only the Templars' private rooms. They must also have had a hall (*aula*) or refectory — one is mentioned in a document of 1336 — but none is mentioned in the

his pension ceased not on the Templars' arrest but on his death: TNA:PRO E358/18 rot. 7(1), under 'Exp.' Other Templars listed as at New Temple by Gooder, 147 (Hugh of Kirktoft, Robert of Sautre, Ralph of Malton, Thomas of Loudham), were in fact based at Stroud or Ewell in Kent, but were soon moved to London and so came under the responsibility of the sheriff of London.

[59] For Walter, 'lad' of the commander of the New Temple, see MS Bodley 454, fol. 98[r–v]. For other servants see TNA:PRO E358/18 rot. 7(1) under 'Exp.': a 'lad' looked after the horses, earning 1½d a day, and a *janitor* (porter) and gardener. The sheriff also employed a clerk to keep records and at first four, later two sergeants to guard the Templars; under E358/20, rot. 3, there are an additional 4 clerks serving the priests in the chapel (see also Lord, *Knights Templar in Britain*, 26). For the corrodiaries see, for example, *CCR, Edward II, 1313–18*, 18: in 1313 King Edward II confirmed the claim of William Lambert and his wife Caorsetta to 100s a year pension and 'a robe of the suit of the free servants of the house of the New Temple at London for him at Christmas and 50s yearly to her for life if she survives him'.

[60] TNA:PRO E358/18 rot. 7(1–2); E358/20 rot. 3. The copy of the inventory at E358/20 rot. 3 is printed and translated by Baylis, *Temple Church*, 131–46; summarised by Lord, *Knights Templar in Britain*, 26–30.

[61] Bodl., MS Bodley 454, fol. 58[v].

[62] TNA:PRO E358/20 rot. 3.

inventory.[63] In addition, although a 'dispensary' is mentioned, there is no information what was in it. If this was the strong room, where the deposits of kings, nobles and merchants were kept, then it must have been excluded from the inventory because there was nothing in it belonging to the Templars. In the same way, the hall may have been effectively a public room, in constant use by lawyers and depositors, who continued to use it for their business even when the Templars had been arrested, so there was nothing there belonging to the Order.

Finally, there is no mention of a guesthouse. The New Temple, like other religious houses, had always provided accommodation for the king and nobles when required.[64] A monastery would have a guest house outside the central monastic enclosure to house guests, but there is no mention of a guest house at Templar houses in England. Indeed, at the Templars' major Yorkshire house, Faxfleet, a friar commented that he and his colleague had been given a room next to the Templars' dormitory.[65] Perhaps, for important guests, the brothers had to vacate their own rooms.

As merchants, nobles and kings kept their property in the treasury of the house, they would need to be able to obtain access to it at reasonable hours. In 1329 Edward III noted that there was a public right of way through the middle of the court of the New Temple, from the main road to the bank of the Thames, from which secular persons could take boats up the Thames to Westminster, and that it had been the Templars' responsibility to maintain the bridge 'to the water of the Thames in the court of the Temple', so that secular persons could use this right of way. The king commanded the mayor of London to ensure that the gates of the New Temple were kept open from sunrise to sunset to allow the public to pass through to the wharf, implying that this had been the Templars' custom.[66] In 1374 the dispute arose again because the Hospitallers, who by then had obtained possession of the New Temple, had been closing the gate during the daytime and blocking the customary thoroughfare that had existed 'time out of mind' for carrying goods 'by wains, horses and otherwise'. In addition, any free man of London could request passage through the New Temple at night for the carriage of goods, but not by wain.[67] If these rights had indeed existed 'time out of mind', then the Templars of the New Temple had allowed a public thoroughfare through their main

[63] CPR, Edward III, 1334–8, 314: 'the chapel of St Thomas at the door of the hall of the Temple'.

[64] Apart from the archbishops mentioned above, other important guests lodged there included the messengers of King Alphonso of Castile in July 1255: CR, 1254–6, 114, 212; in April 1260 John Warenne was advised to lodge at Clerkenwell or the New Temple while attending Parliament: CR, 1259–61, 283.

[65] Bodl., MS Bodley 454, fol. 97ʳ. At Arles in the lower Rhône valley, the guest room was in the Templars' own residential wing of the house, between the commander's chamber and the room for sick knights: D. Carraz, L'Ordre du Temple dans la basse vallée du Rhône (1124–1312): ordres militaires, croisades et sociétés méridionales, Lyon 2005, 267.

[66] CCR, Edward III, 1327–30, 580; CCR, Edward III, 1330–33, 102; Foedera, conventiones, literae et cuiusque generis Acta Publica . . . , ed. T. Rymer, rev. R. Sanderson, A. Clarke and F. Holbrooke, vol. II.2: A.D. 1327–1344, London 1821, 774, 805.

[67] CCR, Edward III, 1374–7, 26–7.

English house by day and night. Such a thoroughfare would have been very valuable to local merchants who needed access to the Thames at all hours so that their merchandise could sail with the tide.

The expense of keeping 'Temple Bridge' in repair was substantial and ongoing. In 1354–5 it was again under repair, initiated by the king but to be paid for by the Hospitallers: six carpenters were required for the job.[68] In March 1398 Richard II noted that the bridge was again 'broken and ruinous' and ordered the Hospitaller Grand Prior in England, Walter de Grendon, to have it repaired before Whitsun.[69] It is clear that this was an important right of way for the people of London, especially its merchants.

THE NEW TEMPLE AFTER THE DISSOLUTION OF THE TEMPLARS

Both Aymer de Valence, earl of Pembroke, and Thomas, earl of Lancaster, claimed the New Temple; on 1 October 1314 Aymer surrendered it to Thomas of Lancaster, but the day after the earl's execution on 22 March 1322 Edward II granted it back to Aymer.[70] It was nominally handed over to the Hospitallers in 1324, but almost immediately afterwards Thomas Larcher, prior of the Hospital in England, granted it to the king's favourite Hugh le Despenser.[71] On Hugh's execution in November 1326 it reverted to royal control.

Edward II clearly decided to make use of the building, for in July 1326 the keeper of the king's 'cocket' seal was instructed to take the balance used for weighing wool for the Staple of London to the New Temple and store it there. But in September it was decided, on the request of the citizens of London, to move the balance back to its old place in the city. Although the New Temple was a good place for depositing money and goods, clearly it was less convenient for daily processing of wool.[72]

In 1332 Edward III repeated his father's instructions that all the former Templar properties should to be given to the Hospital,[73] but apparently this did not include the New Temple in London. The day-to-day maintenance of the New Temple remained the responsibility of the mayor of London, who was responsible for paying the daily wages of a man who looked after the houses, gate and gardens and was responsible for keeping the gates open during the day. In 1332 William de Langford was appointed custodian of the New Temple, and given responsibility for these tasks and for having the walls and buildings repaired.[74] In 1336 Philip de Thame, grand prior of the Hospital of St John of Jerusalem in England, claimed the New Temple, stating that Hugh Despenser had acquired it in 1324 by force. Edward III ordered an investigation, and the mayor and

[68] CCR, Edward III, 1354–60, 10; CPR, Edward III, 1354–8, 319.
[69] CCR, Richard II, 1396–9, 272–3.
[70] CPR, Edward II, 1313–17, 184; Foedera, II.I, 480.
[71] TNA:PRO E 40/1469.
[72] CCR, Edward II, 1323–7, 592, 615.
[73] CCR, Edward III, 1330–33, 496, 514.
[74] CCR, Edward III, 1330–33, 228, 241, 431, 434; CCR, Edward III, 1333–7, 246.

sheriffs of London, with four 'good men' of the city and William de Langford, went to look at the site. They established the area of the consecrated land around the church which should be annexed to the church, and noted that 'one Roger Blom, sometime messenger of the Temple, with the assent of the master and brothers, had caused some houses to be built on the plot of consecrated land in the front part near the highway to the north, to let these for the support of lights and ornaments of the said church, and that these had been unjustly taken by the said Hugh Despenser.' The mayor restored to the Hospitallers the houses and other properties which should belong to the Temple church.[75] William de Langford remained as 'custodian'.[76]

However, although they had been anxious to recover their legal property and the rents due to it, the Hospitallers did not need the New Temple as an administrative centre, because they already had their house at Clerkenwell. The six priests who had masses to say for the souls of the king's ancestors in the New Temple (according to the sheriff of London in 1308) needed only part of the Temple buildings.[77] By the mid fourteenth century the majority of the buildings at the New Temple were let out to lawyers, who had, as already mentioned, for some time been using the Temple as a place to store their documents. The lawyers were seldom mentioned in the government records, except occasionally when their servants were involved in criminal activities which came before the king's court.[78] The New Temple was still used as a location for legal processes.[79] From 1336 onwards a series of entries in the king's close rolls record that private individuals 'came to Chancery in the chapel of the New Temple, London, and acknowledged the preceding deed.'[80] The occasional grant was still dated at the New

[75] *CPR, Edward III, 1334–8*, 314. On 26 May 1337 the treasurers and barons of the Exchequer made a report of the inquest into the exact extent of the 'claustra et alia loca . . . sanctificata + deo dedicata' (cloister and other places consecrated and dedicated to God) at the New Temple and its ecclesiastical and secular revenues: TNA:PRO SC 1/55/101; see also *CCR, Edward III, 1337–9*, 72–73, 416–17.

[76] *CPR, Edward III, 1330–34*, 373; *CPR, Edward III, 1334–8*, 314, 352; *CPR, Edward III, 1338–40*, 99, 303–4. The Parliament of June 1338 formally agreed to hand over the spiritualities of the New Temple to the Hospital.

[77] TNA:PRO E358/18 rot. 7(1), under 'Exp.' In 1361 the New Temple was still employing a porter, but the job was granted not by the Hospital but by the king and was for life; the incumbent received wages and fees: *CPR, Edward III, 1361–4*, 4.

[78] In 1356 Hugh Lombard, servant of the manciple of New Temple, was murdered: *CPR, Edward III, 1354–8*, 377. In 1397 William Becke, servant in the Temple, was pardoned for the death of Richard Baron, servant of George Cressy of London, goldsmith, in Fleet Street on Palm Sunday: *CPR, Richard II, 1396–9*, 153.

[79] *CCR, Richard II, 1385–9*, 645–6.

[80] *CCR, Edward III, 1333–7*, 656, 657, 659, 669, 670, 673, 674; *CCR, Edward III, 1337–9*, 115, 117, 120, 121, 123–5, 142, 272, 273, 276, 288, 377, 378, 529, 610, 611, 613, 618, 625, 627; *CCR, Edward III, 1339–41*, 460; *CCR, Edward III, 1341–3*, 266, 271; *CCR, Edward III, 1343–6*, 577; *CCR, Edward III, 1369–74*, 345; *CCR, Richard II, 1377–81*, 87, 89.

Temple,[81] and debts were paid at the church.[82] In February 1381 a legal case was heard at the New Temple.[83]

Because the New Temple was a depository for legal records, during the 'Peasants' Revolt' in June 1381 it was sacked by the rebels. On Thursday 13 June 1381 Thomas Farndon led the rebels from Essex in an attack on the New Temple, London, which was burned; and on the Savoy Palace, the property of John of Gaunt, duke of Lancaster and uncle of Richard II, which was plundered and then deliberately blown up with gunpowder.[84] The rebels also destroyed the Templars' two forges on Fleet Street[85] and burned records at the Hospitallers' house at Clerkenwell. An important factor behind the rebellion was the desire to destroy unfavourable legal terms of tenure. The rebels destroyed the books, rolls and memoranda at the New Temple, as well as records of apprenticeship.[86] This must have caused considerable problems to the lawyers, and indeed in February 1384 it was noted in the king's patent rolls that a certain legal case could not be concluded because legal records kept in a chest in the church of the New Temple in London had been destroyed in the 'recent insurrection of the commons'.[87]

In the late fourteenth century, and throughout the following century, the New Temple continued to be used for legal transactions. Legal documents were sealed 'at the Temple in London', payments were made 'in the New Temple church London' and receipts issued at the same church.[88] There are fewer mentions of such transactions in the government's patent and close rolls than there were in earlier years, but presumably this is because such transactions only found their way into the royal records when some problem arose.

The lawyers continued in residence at the Temple. By the second half of the fifteenth century, individuals (invariably called 'gentilman') were using the term 'of the Middle Temple' or 'of the Inner Temple' as a suffix to their name.[89] Those lawyers based in the middle court would have been the 'Middle Temple' while those based in the Templars' former central building were the 'Inner Temple'. However, the New

[81] CCR, Edward III, 1339–41, 229.

[82] CCR, Edward III, 1349–54, 481; CCR, Edward III, 1354–60, 335; CCR, Edward III, 1364–8, 176; CCR, Richard II, 1381–5, 104, 603, 608; CCR, Richard II, 1385–9, 473.

[83] CCR, Richard II, 1377–81, 500.

[84] Anonimalle Chronicle, 1333 to 1381: From a MS written at St Mary's York, and now in the possession of Lieut.-Col. Sir William Ingilby, Bart., Ripley Castle, Yorkshire, ed. V. H. Galbraith, Manchester 1927, 135–51; CPR, Richard II, 1381–5, 394.

[85] CPR, Henry VI, 1441–6, 447; CCR, Henry IV, 1399–1402, 282, 476.

[86] Anonimalle Chronicle, 141; CPR, Richard II, 1381–5, 394.

[87] CPR, Richard II, 1381–5, 394: these were 'escheats and records of the justices, in the custody of Simon Lichfield, clerk of the common bench and clerk of the sessions'.

[88] CPR, Henry VI, 1446–52, 459 (1451); CCR, Henry IV, 1399–1402, 559 (1402); CCR, Henry VI, 1429–35, 247 (1433); CCR, Henry VI, 1441–7, 361 (1443); CCR, Henry VII, 1485–1500, 76, no. 282 (1487).

[89] CPR, Henry VII, 1494–1509, 214 (1500); CCR, Henry VI, 1447–54, 332 (1451); CCR, Henry VII, 1500–1509, 20, no. 63 (1501), 188 no. 480 (1505), 347–8, no. 937 (1508).

Temple was still owned by the Hospitallers. When Henry VIII suppressed the Hospitallers in England in 1540, ownership of the New Temple, which in 1535 had been valued at £162 11s, passed to the crown. The 'master of the Temple' (the chief cleric there) and the other chaplains were still given their stipends, and retained their posts. The master of the Temple, four priests and a clerk remained in post until at least the early seventeenth century. The lawyers continued to pay rent to the crown until 1608, when the Middle Temple and the Inner Temple were granted the freehold.[90]

From its beginnings, the New Temple played a spiritual role in London, its church being a place which recalled the Holy Land and Christ's Holy Sepulchre, a place where holy relics were kept and where the people of London could come to hear mass. It also quickly became a commercial and legal centre, where money and valuables were kept safe, debts were paid and legal transactions were recorded. A major public right of way ran through its outer courtyard, along which merchants and their wares, courtiers and other people travelled by day and night. Far from being a hidden, secretive place — as some modern writers might like us to believe — the New Temple in the Middle Ages was at the heart of the everyday life of the city of London.

[90] *Victoria County History, London*, 1, 489–90.

Christopher Wilson

Gothic Architecture Transplanted:
the Nave of the Temple Church in London

for Peter Fergusson

IN THE LITERATURE on English Gothic architecture the nave of the London church of the Knights Templar is conspicuous by its virtual absence.[1] Some responsibility for that state of affairs is mine, for although I delivered two conference papers on the subject as far back as 1983 and 1984 their content has remained unpublished apart from thumbnail sketches included in works which appeared in 1986 and 1990.[2] This paper is a belated substantiation of the two main propositions that

[1] The only attempts to integrate an account of the nave into a narrative of the history of English Gothic are: C. Wilson, *The Gothic Cathedral*, London 1990, 82, 84; G. Kowa, *Architektur der Englishen Gotik*, Cologne 1990, 74–5, the latter at my suggestion. Particularly puzzling is the absence of any references in the text of J. Bony, 'French Influences on the Origins of English Gothic Architecture', *Journal of the Warburg and Courtauld Institutes*, 12, 1949, 1–15, not least because a plan of the piers is illustrated at 10 (fig. 3). For the eastern parts of the twelfth-century church demolished to make way for the early thirteenth-century choir see W. H. Godfrey, 'Recent Discoveries at the Temple, London, and Notes on the Topography of the Site', *Archaeologia*, 95, 1953, 123–40 at 125–31, plates XLVI, XLVIII.

[2] Papers on English architecture of the decade 1155–65 given to the Association of Art Historians, 28 March 1983, and on the nave of the Temple Church read at the London conference of the British Archaeological Association, 11 April 1984; C. Wilson, 'The Cistercians as "Missionaries of Gothic" in Northern England', in *Cistercian Art and Architecture in the British Isles*, ed. C. Norton and D. Park, Cambridge 1986, 86–116 at 91 n. 14; idem, *Gothic Cathedral*, 82, 84. For partial adumbrations of my dating arguments, though not of their implications for the development of English Gothic architecture, see: W. Götz, *Zentralbau und Zentralbautendenz in der gotischen Architektur*, Berlin 1968, 292; C. N. L. Brooke and G. Keir, *London 800–1216: the Shaping of a City*, London 1975, caption to plate 44. My dating is adopted by M. Thurlby, review of P. Williamson, *Catalogue of Romanesque Sculpture [in the Victoria and Albert Museum, London]*, London 1983, in *Racar (Revue d'art canadienne/Canadian Art Review)*, 12,1985, 74–5; idem, 'Observations on the Twelfth-Century Sculpture from Bridlington Priory', in *Medieval Art and Architecture in the East Riding of Yorkshire* (British Archaeological Association Conference Transactions, IX), ed. C. Wilson, Leeds 1989, 33–43, at 40 n. 15; idem, 'The Place of St Albans in Regional Sculpture and Architecture in the Second Half of the Twelfth Century', in *Alban and St Albans: Roman and Medieval Architecture, Art and Archaeology* (British Archaeological

had to be made so laconically in those earlier publications: the dating of the Temple Church to shortly before 1160; and the attribution of the building to a French architect whose artistic formation had taken place to the north of the Gothic heartland of the Île-de-France, in the region represented today by the *départements* of Somme and Pas-de-Calais. An immediately obvious consequence of dating the church to the late 1150s is that the well-known record of its consecration in 1185 ceases to have any bearing on its building history other than to confirm that it existed by the early 1180s. I begin by presenting the case for discounting the 1185 consecration as evidence for the close dating of the church.

The only source for the consecration is the text of an inscription which, until its destruction in the late seventeenth century, occupied a tympanum over a small south-west door (itself now destroyed) which gave access to the nave from the enclosed court between the church and the Templars' domestic quarters to the south. The inscription recorded that on 10 February 1185 Heraclius, patriarch of the church of the Holy Re-surrection, consecrated the church in honour of St Mary and offered 60 days' indul-gence to those visiting it once a year.[3] Heraclius was in England as part of his mission to drum up desperately needed support among the rulers of Western Christendom for the Crusader kingdom of Jerusalem, a mission whose failure was to be a major factor in the disastrous defeat of the kingdom's forces at the Battle of Hattin in 1187.[4] Heraclius' English sojourn seems to have unfolded in a fairly leisurely way, for the crucial meeting with King Henry II took place five weeks after his consecration of the Temple Church, and he also had time to consecrate on 6 March the church of the Hospitallers at Clerk-enwell, to whose mid-twelfth-century circular nave a long aisled choir had recently been added.[5] This record of the other act of church dedication performed in London by Heraclius is surely the vital clue to the real nature of both consecrations, for it would

Association Conference Transactions, XXIV), ed. M. Henig and P. Lindley, Leeds 2001, 162–75 at 169–70. For sceptical responses to my dating, see P. Draper, 'Recherches récentes sur l'architecture dans les Iles Britanniques à la fin de l'époque romane et du début du gothique', *Bulletin monumental*, 144, 1986, 305–28 at 311; R. Stalley, 'L'Architecture gothique dans les Îles Britanniques: orientations et perspectives de la recherche', *Perspective (La revue de l'INHA, Institut national de l'histoire de l'art, Paris)*, 2, 2007, 261–80 at 266.

   [3] Esdaile, *Temple Church Monuments*, 6; Lewer and Dark, *Temple Church*, 32. See also Griffith-Jones, pp. 140, 170 below, and Plate 84.

   [4] For Heraclius' 1185 journey to Italy, France and England, see B. Z. Kedar, 'The Patriarch Eraclius', in *Outremer: Studies in the Crusading Kingdom of Jerusalem presented to Joshua Prawer*, ed. B. Z. Kedar, H. E. Mayer and R. C. Smail, Jerusalem 1982, 177–204 at 191–3; Klaus-Peter Kirstein, *Die lateinischen Patriarchen von Jerusalem: von der Eroberung der Heiligen Stadt durch die Kreuzfahrer 1099 bis zum Ende der Kreuzfahrerstaaten 1291*, Berlin 2002, 328–57 at 346–8. I am very grateful to Helen Ni-cholson for guidance on the bibliography of Heraclius and other Templar-related matters.

   [5] R. W. Eyton, *Court, Household and Itinerary of King Henry II*, London 1878, 261; British Li-brary, Cotton MS Nero E VI (early sixteenth-century cartulary of the Priory of St John of Jerusalem, Clerkenwell), fol. 3ʳ. For the London Hospitallers' Church, see most recently *Excavations at the Priory of the Order of the Hospital of St John of Jerusalem, Clerkenwell, London* (Museum of London Archaeology Service, monograph 20), ed. B. Sloane and G. Malcolm, London 2004, 191–3; *Survey of London, XLVI: South and East Clerkenwell*, ed. P. Temple, New Haven and London 2008, 124–8.

have been an astonishing coincidence if the city's churches of both military orders had just happened to be newly finished at precisely the same moment. It seems reasonable to suppose that in dedicating the Templars' and Hospitallers' churches in London the Patriarch was consciously imitating the honorific consecrations of French churches undertaken in 1095–6, 1147 and 1163 by Popes Urban II, Eugenius III and Alexander II respectively. Significantly, the first two of these pontiffs had journeyed out of Italy specifically to preach in support of the Crusade.[6]

The case for dating the completion of the Temple Church to c.1160 is partly based on analysis of the formal characteristics of the building (for which see below), but there exists strong documentary evidence that points in the same direction. The Templars' first London home lay on the south side of Holborn, just over half a kilometre north of the existing Temple Church, and there they built themselves a church at an unknown date before 1144. Its circular nave was nearly equal in diameter to that of the existing church, and it too had a central vessel bounded by an arcade, possibly also carried on six piers. It was demolished in 1595, but its vestiges have been observed several times in the course of the last few centuries, most recently in 2000.[7] In 1161 the whole of the Old Temple property was sold to the Bishop of Lincoln, and it remained the London house of his successors until 1547. The deed transferring the Old Temple, preserved in the *Registrum Antiquissimum* of Lincoln Cathedral, was given in a general chapter of the English province of the order and is dated May 1161 *apud Nouum templum*.[8] These details are probably in themselves sufficient evidence that the present Temple Church had been built and had become usable by 1161, for it would have made no sense to abandon a property which was equipped with a stone church constructed to the order's special requirements and virtually equal in size to the present church simply in order to be able to move to a vacant plot of ground or to temporary wooden buildings. The project of transferring to the present Thames-side site must have been conceived no later than the late 1150s, and in order to be ready by the spring of 1161 the Temple Church need not have been begun earlier than, say, 1158, if one makes the modest assumptions that the construction of this comparatively small building was well funded and was carried out by a highly organised and relatively large workshop.

The first historian to grasp that the transferral of the London Templars to their definitive site did not take place immediately before the 1185 consecration was Horace Round, who in 1898 wrote a monograph on the turbulent career of that would-be king-maker Geoffrey de Mandeville, earl of Essex. Geoffrey died excommunicate in 1144, and his body was taken to the Old Temple, where, according to one account, his coffin was suspended from a tree in an orchard instead of being buried in the cemetery. In 1163 Geoffrey's sentence of excommunication was annulled, and his body was given Christian burial in the churchyard of the New Temple. Round realised that this reference to

---

[6] R. Crozet, 'Le Voyage d'Urbain II en 1095–1096 et son importance au point de vue archéologique', *Annales du Midi*, 49, 1937, 42–69.

[7] On the Old Temple Church, see most recently A. Telfer, 'Locating the First Knights Templar Church', *London Archaeologist*, Summer 2002, 3–6. See also Lees, *Records*, 159 n. 4.

[8] Ibid., 158–60.

a churchyard implied the existence of a church, probably that whose nave exists today.[9] The late-twelfth-century chronicle written at Walden Priory, Geoffrey's Benedictine foundation in Essex, tells how the prior, on hearing of Geoffrey's impending burial, rushed to London in the hope of bringing back the corpse, only to find that the funeral had already taken place and that the earl now lay in the Templars' churchyard in a grave that the chronicler describes as 'somewhat ignoble'. Two other Walden Priory texts, those dubbed the 'roll of the founders' and the 'Walden Annals' by the modern editors of the chronicle, state that Geoffrey was buried in the porch before the west door of the Temple Church.[10] Unfortunately it is not possible to date the references to Geoffrey's tomb in these late-medieval texts, and therefore it cannot be known whether or not the earl's body had been moved to the porch after its initial burial at the New Temple. However, the chances that this happened are greatly reduced by the failure of the male line of the de Mandevilles in the early thirteenth century and by the improbability that Geoffrey would have seemed especially interesting in the eyes of the Templars or of the Hospitallers who succeeded them in the property in 1324. The Walden chronicler's locating of the grave in the churchyard and his characterising of its position as 'somewhat ignoble' seem perfectly consonant with a site under the north part of the west porch, for the churchyard was contiguous to the open arch on the north side of the porch (Plate 2). Burial before major church doors carried strong connotations of penitence and self-abasement and was expressive of the need of the deceased for the prayers of those entering and leaving church. All of this could well have been thought appropriate to the burial of one who had been excommunicated for his seizure of Ramsey Abbey during his rebellion against King Stephen.[11] The Walden chronicler's 'somewhat ignoble' epithet will have appeared entirely apt from his point of view, because if the prior had succeeded in bringing Geoffrey's body back to Walden it would undoubtedly have been given founder's honours by being buried prominently in the choir there. The probability is, therefore, that in 1163 Geoffrey de Mandeville's body was entombed below the then existing and still existing west porch of the Temple Church.

[9] J. H. Round, *Geoffrey de Mandeville: a Study of the Anarchy*, London 1892, 224 and n. 2, 225 and n. 3.

[10] *The Book of the Foundation of Walden Monastery*, ed. and trans. D. Greenway and L. Watkiss, Oxford 1999, pp. lviii–lix, 18, 19 and n. 34. BL, Cotton MS Titus D xx, fol. 74^{r-v}; BL, Arundel MS 51, fol. 17.

[11] I am very grateful to David Park for showing me the section of his paper in which he offers powerful arguments in favour of identifying Geoffrey de Mandeville as the founder of the London Templars' house on its original site and explaining his burial outdoors at the New Temple as an instance of the early Templars' Cistercian-inspired refusal to allow burial inside their churches. In deciding to leave my own text unaltered I was influenced by my only significant reservation, which is that by the early thirteenth century the considerable numbers of burials which had taken place inside the Temple Church would have made an outdoor site for the founder's burial seem disrespectfully modest. The clear implication of the texts referred to in n. 10, which evince great interest in the burial places of all of Walden Abbey's patrons, is that Geoffrey's body lay under the west porch in the fifteenth century. For David Park's discussion of the problem, including references to the penitential implications of burial near entrances, see pp. 71–4 below.

The uprooting of the Templars from their original site less than a generation after the completion there of a large custom-built church was a remarkable demonstration of the order's power, in particular its ability to attract important patronage and to command substantial resources. The motivation behind the move from Holborn to Fleet Street may well have been simple envy of the Hospitallers' spacious precinct at Clerkenwell,[12] but proximity to the Thames will have brought greatly improved access and also greatly enhanced prestige on account of the precinct's prominence in the London townscape as seen from the river, the pre-eminent viewpoint. Who were the patrons behind this extravagant enterprise? So far as I know, this is a question which has not been posed before. A possible clue is that the site was wholly or partly held of the Beaumonts, earls of Leicester and hereditary stewards of England.[13] Robert de Beaumont, the second earl, was Henry II's justiciar and effectively his vicegerent during his absence from England between 1158 and 1163. It is obviously significant that his name comes first among the laymen who were at the New Temple in May 1161 to witness the deed of sale of the Holborn site, but whether that placing was due to his status as vicegerent or to his role as major benefactor is not apparent. It is worth asking what the role of the king himself might have been. Most of the evidence for his practical support for the crusading project in general dates from 1166 onwards, and his only documented benefactions to the London Temple were his grant of the site for a mill on the River Fleet in 1159 and his gift, probably made in May 1157, of rents behind the garden of the Temple *tout court* but almost certainly meaning the New rather than the Old Temple.[14] We can be sure that Henry gave at least moral support to the creation of the New Temple, which served his interests to the not insignificant extent that the new church was, as will be shown below, a much more elegant and richly finished building than its counterpart in the capital city of his adversary Louis VII of France. A desire to please Henry II must lie behind the decision in 1155, the second year of Henry's reign, to replace the master of the English Province with Richard of Hastings. Richard came from a ministerial family and was entrusted by the king with some extremely important diplomatic missions, one of which had taken him abroad in May 1161 when the general chapter of his province was meeting on the new site and ratifying the sale of the old one.[15] His royal connections would have made him very well placed to solicit contributions from the

[12] Brooke and Keir, *London 800–1216*, 231.

[13] D. Crouch, *The Beaumont Twins. The Roots and Branches of Power in the Twelfth Century*, Cambridge 1986, 179; Lees, *Records*, p. lxxxix. There is, as Lees pointed out (ibid., p. xc n. 2) no documentary evidence to show how the site was acquired. Disappointingly, the 1185 survey of the Templars' English properties does not mention the New Temple; ibid., 13.

[14] Ibid., pp. lxxxvi, 156–7. In the confirmation charter of Richard I (ibid., 141) the property next to the Templars' garden is referred to as being 'retro gardinum suum apud Londoniam', the obvious implication of which must be that the property was next to the New Temple garden. There is no reason to suppose, as did Lees, that the grant refers to the Old Temple and that when the latter property was transferred to the Bishop of Lincoln in 1161 the Templars retained for their use a garden on this comparatively restricted site; ibid., 157 n. 2.

[15] I. Gatti, 'The Relationship between the Knights Templars and the Kings of England from the Order's Foundation to the Reign of Edward I', Ph.D. thesis, University of Reading, 2005, 27–9.

English baronage for the building of the new church if it was the case that there was no single patron funding this evidently very swiftly erected building. Another potentially influential figure is Osto de Saint-Omer, Richard of Hastings's predecessor as English provincial master. Osto's father was castellan of Saint-Omer in French Flanders and on that account a neighbour and vassal of the house of Boulogne, the family into which King Stephen had married.[16] Osto's roots were therefore in the very region of France whence, as will be argued below, the designer of the Temple Church was recruited. Despite ceasing to be English provincial master early in 1155, Osto continued to be involved in the order's affairs at a high level and he remained active at the royal court until the mid-1170s. A reference to him in a document issued by Louis VII in 1158 charts his presence in France close to the time when the new Temple Church in London is most likely to have been commissioned, and there will doubtless have been other earlier visits for which no documentation has survived.[17]

If one assumes, as most writers have done, that the Temple Church is a building designed around 1180, one is inevitably led to the highly problematic conclusion that an important and expensively finished building situated between England's capital city and its principal royal residence was entrusted to an architect who deliberately chose to ignore the remodelling of the eastern arm of Canterbury Cathedral from 1174, a building which, all the available evidence suggests, came as a revelation to architects and patrons alike. Unspoken awareness of this quandary could well lie behind the failure of architectural historians to offer any comments at all on the Temple Church's stylistic filiation. The main part of this paper will be devoted to the task of setting the Temple Church, or more precisely its surviving nave, into what I believe to be its contemporary artistic context, namely French Gothic of the period immediately after the building in the early 1140s of the earliest fully-fledged example of the style, the east end of the abbey church of Saint-Denis (Plate 3). The iconographic aspects of the design will not be discussed, for the simple reason that there is nothing in the London Temple Church's evocation of the rotunda of the Holy Sepulchre Church in Jerusalem which sets it apart from the relatively many other such exercises; indeed I shall treat the nave almost as if it were a building of conventional longitudinal format made up of a series of bays of rectangular plan. Only the west porch appears to embody a non-standard meaning and this is considered briefly in an appendix.

It is very striking how seldom in the meagre historiography of the London Tem-

---

[16] M.-L. Bulst-Thiele, 'Templer in königlichen und päpstlichen Diensten', in *Festschrift Percy Ernst Schramm*, ed. P. Classen and P. Sheibert, 2 vols., Wiesbaden 1964, I, 289–308 at 293–4.

[17] Ibid., 293, referring to a transcript by the Marquis d'Albon kept in the department of manuscripts in the Bibliothèque de France. Unfortunately, I have not been able to consult d'Albon's collections, and therefore the nature of the document, its exact date and its place of issue are unknown to me. After 1160 Osto was *persona non grata* to Louis VII and there are no further references to his being in France.

ple Church the word 'Gothic' occurs in relation to any feature of the interior other than the steeply pointed arches of the main arcade. But the aspect of the elevations to the central vessel which most clearly qualifies the Temple Church as post-Romanesque is not the form of these arches specifically but rather the extraordinary effect of openness created by the wide separation and slenderness of the supports of the main arcade (Colour Plate 1). The main arcade in the choir of Saint-Denis, especially when still borne on its original slim columnar supports, must have presented a similar invitation to look beyond the arcade into the peripheral spaces surrounding the main vessel (Plate 3), as its later imitations at Noyon and Senlis still do. Though not significantly bulkier than the columnar limestone piers which had become standard in the main arcades of French Gothic churches by the mid-twelfth century, the piers of the Temple Church are more complex in form and are made of Purbeck marble, a relatively costly material. At the Temple each pier consists of a cluster of four shafts, the two stouter ones receiving the arcade arches, the two smaller receiving the aisle vault ribs and the responds to the vault spanning the main vessel (Plates 4, 5). There is no centrally placed shaft forming a core. Some of the earliest of the very few French Gothic examples of coreless multi-shaft piers are the intermediate supports in the gallery-level arcade of the choir of Noyon Cathedral, which almost certainly dates from the early or mid-1150s (Plate 6).[18] Yet despite what I think is a very significant formal and conceptual likeness, the minor piers of the Noyon gallery differ from those of the Temple Church in being comparatively small, in possessing three shafts rather than four, in not supporting vaulting, and in being made of freestone similar to that used in the rest of the structure.

Alongside their widely spaced and slender supports, the most important component of the picture of structural slightness presented by the main arcades of the Temple Church and those of Saint-Denis and other French Early Gothic churches is the extreme shallowness of their arches in the horizontal plane (Colour Plate 1; Plates 3, 8). This feature probably owes its presence to the desire to conceal the true thickness of the upper walls that the arcades carry, walls which at the Temple were evidently sturdy enough to absorb the horizontal component of the thrusts exerted by the masonry vault that once covered the main vessel.[19] The way in which the upper walls oversail the

---

[18] The 1158 translation of the relics of St Eligius is seen as marking the likely end of work on the choir in D. Kimpel and R. Suckale, *Die gotische Architektur in Frankreich 1130–1270*, Munich 1985, 526. Although the architectural significance of this translation is discounted in M. Bidault and C. Lautier, *Île-de-France Gothique I*, Paris 1987, 249–59, a mid-century date for the choir's upper storeys seems to be favoured. Noyon also parallels the most distinctive trait of the wheel window over the west door of the Temple Church: sixteen arches at the rim but only eight spokes. The Noyon window is larger and slightly later than its Temple Church counterpart. The centripetal arrangement of the shafts in the Temple Church window is paralleled in a few other French Early Gothic wheel windows, but they are somewhat later in date.

[19] The earliest interior view of the Temple Church, that by the London carpenter William Emmett of 1702 (discussed by Griffith-Jones, p. 154 below; see Plate 82) shows the high vault of the nave replaced by a ceiling borne on a series of timber arches.. Since the spandrels over those arches are shown by Emmett with pierced rinceaux such as occur frequently in English architectural woodwork of the late seventeenth century, there must be a good chance that Emmett had installed the ceiling

normally invisible outer faces of the residual lower walls above the main arcades (Plate 9) is known as 'false bearing', a term indicative of the difference between the centres of the walls at the two levels. Admittedly, this technique had been introduced from Normandy into England in the late eleventh century, but its purpose then seems to have been to supplement the thickness of an already massive wall structure specifically to enable it to incorporate clearstorey passages.[20] Since false bearing seems to have virtually died out in England and Normandy by the mid-twelfth century, and since clearstorey wall passages are not present either in the Temple Church or in contemporary French Gothic churches, there can be no doubt that the former's false bearing was part and parcel of its indebtedness to the latter.

The complex profile applied to the undersides of the main arcade arches in the Temple Church (Plate 7) was in northern French Gothic terms a slightly old-fashioned feature by the late 1150s. In the choir of Saint-Denis, whose design was the best part of 20 years old when the Temple Church is likely to have been at the drawing-board stage, the analogous mouldings also consist of a row of small rolls (Plate 3).[21] The best comparison for the Temple's alternation of arrises with grooved rolls (the latter a rare motif) is to be found in the transverse ribs of the narthex to the Cluniac priory church of Saint-Leu-d'Esserent around 40 kilometres north of Paris, a building which probably dates from around 1140.[22] Proof of the very high importance of moulding profiles in

after the dismantling of the vault. Shortly before May 1838 the architect Robert Billings, who appears to have had direct access to the upper walls from scaffolding, stated that the wall ribs still bore traces of the masonry vault cells. His word for the latter, 'panelling', might suggest timber but it is clear from his description of the thirteenth-century choir vault that this term denotes the masonry vault cells between the ribs; Billings, *Illustrations*, 38–9, 43. Sydney Smirke, who restored the Temple Church in the early 1840s, believed that the clearstorey walls were too thin to have supported such a covering, a notion he put into practical effect with his installation of a timber fictive vault; Essex and Smirke, *Illustrations*, 3. However, the Paris Temple Church also combined thin clearstorey walls with a high stone vault, and no doubt both it and its London counterpart employed the very thin vault cells characteristic of French Gothic rather than the very massive webbing habitually used in English rib vaults. The horizontal component of the thrusts exerted by the high vault of the London Temple Church would have been greatly reduced further had tufa been employed (as in the minimally buttressed high vaults built over the east arm of Canterbury Cathedral some two decades later), but it seems more likely that clunch was used, as in the vaults of the aisle.

[20] The seminal building here is Saint-Étienne at Caen; J. Bony, 'La Technique normande du mur épais', *Bulletin monumental*, 98, 1939, 153–88 at 158–63. For false bearing in the eleventh and twelfth centuries, see E. Fernie, *The Architecture of Norman England*, Oxford 2000, 36, 101–2; Wilson, 'Missionaries', 90 n. 13, 91 n. 14; idem, *The Gothic Cathedral*, 41, 58, ills. 8a, 41a, c, d.

[21] The main arcade arches of the Saint-Denis hemicycle and easternmost rectangular-plan bay are recorded as belonging to the post-1231 remodelling of the church in C. A. Bruzelius, *The 13th-Century Church at St-Denis*, New Haven and London 1985, 77, 79. In my view the only thirteenth-century elements are recuttings of the twelfth-century profile, namely the small hollows between the rolls (replacements for arrises?) and the ogee profile facing the main vessel. The completely post-1231 main arcade arches in the two westernmost rectangular-plan bays of the east arm have the simple stepped profile with single angle rolls that is almost standard in French Gothic of the twelfth and thirteenth centuries.

[22] Wilson, 'Missionaries', 96, plate 23.

the mind of the Temple Church's architect is the use of different profiles for the diagonal ribs in each one of the six approximately square compartments in the ambulatory
vault (Plate 7). This is a unique feature, without parallel in France or England and, taken
together with the remarkable number and variety of the capital designs, it provides the
clearest possible indication that the Templars' London church was intended by its creators to be an exceptionally ambitious building.[23] The only element of the design which
is simpler than would be expected in a major English Romanesque building is the omission of any kind of profiling to the arched heads of the clearstorey and aisle windows.
This treatment, which had been widespread in French Romanesque, survived into the
Early Gothic period, probably because it conformed to the prevailing tendency to treat
residual walling around openings as a single plane.

Another unique feature is the three-dimensional form of the vaults covering the
triangular-plan compartments in the ambulatory vault, for they incorporate at their
centres horizontal triangular planes, in effect small ceilings (Plate 9). These ceilings,
which are inconspicuous under most lighting conditions, are a by-product of the decision to depart from orthodox Gothic design procedures by not including within the
triangular compartments any ribs analogous to the diagonal ribs in the approximately
rectangular compartments with which they alternate. An exactly parallel decision was
made, probably also in the late 1150s, by the designer of the ambulatory of Notre-
Dame in Paris, although there the three-dimensional geometry is different and more
improvised-looking than at the London Temple. In both cases it would appear that
there was a desire to keep to a minimum the number of ambulatory ribs springing from
each capital, but at the Temple the fact that there were two symmetrical pairs of ribs
and no central rib is acknowledged in the remarkable form of the capitals, whose abaci
have only two sides, arranged so as to form a sharp point. Capitals with these so-called
'beaked abaci' eventually became quite common in France, but the only earlier Gothic
examples that come to mind are those in the Lady Chapel at the east end of the choir
of Saint-Martin-des-Champs in Paris, to all appearances a building of the mid-1130s
(Plate 10).[24] The Saint-Martin examples are what might be described as a Siamese twin
version of the motif, particularly interesting in the present context in that it parallels the
Temple Church's use of two-sided beaked abaci as a way of expressing the inclusion of
only ribs that are set diagonally rather than orthogonally in relation to the main axis.
The vault over the Temple Church's main vessel is modern and, most inappropriately, of
unpainted wood, but it perpetuates the three-dimensional form of its medieval masonry
predecessor, whose still-surviving wall ribs and springers determine that the ridges are

---

[23] The only feature suggestive of economy is the use of rubble on the north side of the nave
aisle (Plates 2, 66). It is often said that the south side was also rubble-built until its encasing in ashlar
in the late seventeenth century, but this is disproved by the fact that ashlar facing was exposed in
1824 after the demolition of the chapel of St Anne built against the east part of the south side in the
early thirteenth century; Essex and Smirke, *Illustrations*, 4. The north side faced only the churchyard
whereas the south side faced the other principal buildings of the Temple precinct.

[24] P. Plagnieux, 'Le Chevet de Saint-Martin-des-Champs à Paris: incunable de l'architecture
gothique et temple de l'oraison clunisienne', *Bulletin monumental*, 167, 2009, 3–39 at 22–3.

not horizontal but slope down steeply from the centre (Colour Plate 1). High vaults with sloping lateral ridges are virtually unknown in English Romanesque but they occur frequently in French Early Gothic.

We turn now to the Temple Church's debts to recent architecture in the far north of France. The most obvious of these is the use of dark, polishable and marble-like limestone for the majority of its internal shafts. All of the Temple's Purbeck 'marble' shafts were 'edge-bedded' or *en délit*, which is to say that the stratification planes of the stone as it lay in the quarry changed from being horizontal to vertical once the dressed stone was set in place in the building. When edge-bedded monoliths are used as load-bearing members, as is the case with the two larger shafts in each of the Temple Church's piers, there is normally a high risk that the stones' constituent stratification planes will laminate and thereby render them incapable of carrying any significant load. In 1840 all the piers in the nave were replaced because of the damage done to the shafts when attaching post-medieval monuments to them, and the fact that none of the accounts written around that time mentions splitting is an indication that the stone from which the shafts were made had been chosen by someone who knew which were the better beds in the Purbeck quarries.[25] Discussion of the northernmost French origins of the idea of using dark polished shafts in buildings whose walls were of pale-coloured freestones is quite inevitably hampered by the fact that the French far north, like south-east England, is a veritable graveyard of major twelfth-century churches. However, it is clear that the latter region did not have what the former, together with the adjoining parts of what is now Belgium, undoubtedly did have, namely a well established tradition of employing ersatz marbles for load-bearing and non-load-bearing columnar elements as well as for capitals and bases.[26] The *locus classicus* of the use of the greyish- or bluish-black Carboniferous limestone usually referred to as Tournai marble is the cathedral of Tournai itself, which was probably begun in the second or third decade of the twelfth century. The main arcade and gallery piers there are coursed, and those in the nave have non-load-bearing monoliths attached, but on the exterior of the building the small shafts

---

[25] The shallowness of the beds at Purbeck means that there was no possibility of quarrying long horizontally bedded shafts. In the two most important accounts published around the time of the early Victorian restoration it is very strongly implied, though not explicitly stated, that all four shafts in each pier were edge-bedded monoliths; Billings, *Illustrations*, 37; Essex and Smirke, *Illustrations*, 5. When all the Purbeck work was renewed from 1840 coursed drums were used for the two load-bearing shafts in each pier, and in the further renewal in the 1950s all four shafts of each pier were made coursed. The use of edge-bedded and load-bearing Purbeck shafts remained rare in England, but a particularly audacious instance is the eastern chapel of Salisbury Cathedral.

[26] From the late eleventh century onwards considerable numbers of churches were built in the Low Countries (i.e. from northernmost France to the northern Netherlands) which have crypts with vaults borne on Tournai monoliths. For a useful short account of the traits of the various different beds of Tournai stone see L. Nys, *La Pierre de Tournai: son exploitation et son usage aux XIIIe, XIVe et XVe siècles*, Tournai and Leuven 1993, 39–43.

ranged along the front plane of the clearstorey passages are edge-bedded monoliths which carry a high proportion of the immense load imposed by the wall-heads and roofs of the central vessels.[27] A strong contender for the title of first church to incorporate a main arcade borne on Tournai monoliths is the lost cathedral of Thérouanne, whose choir, begun in or shortly after 1131, was completed by 1157.[28] Clearance of the site between 1898 and 1906 showed that the oldest parts, the outer walls, were built of cream-coloured limestone from Marquise north of Boulogne, whereas the piers of the main arcade, including their capitals and bases, were of Tournai. The absence of the latter material from the outer walls indicates that its use for the main arcade piers was an afterthought, albeit one made after only a short interval.[29] With a diameter of 69 cm, the twin shafts of Thérouanne's piers were much stouter than those of the likely model for their architectural form, Sens Cathedral's coursed coupled columns built out of limestone from c.1145, each of which has a diameter of 62 cm. It may be significant that in 1144 the patron of the Thérouanne choir, Bishop Milo I (1131–58) participated in the consecration of the choir of the abbey of Saint-Denis, where the original intention had been to incorporate reused Antique marble columns, almost certainly in emulation of the hemicycle arcade of the third church at Cluny.[30] Another of the region's great churches which might have pioneered the use of Tournai monoliths for main arcade piers was Amiens Cathedral as restored after a major fire in 1137. Its new roof is known to have been in progress in 1148 and its rededication was carried out in 1152, but nothing whatever can be known about the appearance of the work done at this time be-

[27] For a bibliography and summary of the extensive historiography of Tournai Cathedral see X. Barral i Altet, *Belgique Romane*, La-Pierre-qui-Vire 1989, 174–5, 211, 213–20, 225–8.

[28] As the cathedral was torn down in the 1550s, there are no visual records of its internal appearance.

[29] Camille Enlart, the first explorer of the site, never published his findings properly. In his popular work, *Villes mortes du moyen âge*, Paris 1920, 23–4 (and also in P. Héliot, 'Le Chevet de la cathédrale de Thérouanne', *Bulletin monumental*, 148, 1950, 103–16 at 103 n. 2, and in H. Bernard, 'Les Cathédrales de Thérouanne: les découvertes de 1980 et la cathédrale gothique', *Archéologie médiévale*, 13, 1983, 7–45 at 18–9, 21) the main arcade was dated to c.1200 or later. Bernard's excavations found no indication that the arcade's footings (whose shape was tailored to their two-shaft plan) had been preceded by footings for an earlier arcade, yet he failed to comment on the singularity of an approximately 70-year interval separating the arcade's supposed time of building from that of the outer wall, attributed to the early 1130s by all writers. Bernard also failed to draw the obvious inference from the record of the dedication in 1157 of an altar of the Holy Cross outside the choir, i.e. that this event concerned an altar associated with the rood screen at the west end of an already completed choir.The presence of early thirteenth-century fragments which Enlart regarded as deriving from the upper storeys of the choir (ibid., 43, fig. 13) would be explicable if the original superstructure had been replaced, as at Saint-Denis from 1231. So far as I am aware, no photographs or drawings of the piers of the choir's main arcade have ever reached print, but I have not succeeded in finding all of the published references to Enlart's activities at Thérouanne.Thérouanne's choir urgently needs some 'rescue archaeology' in the form of rigorous analysis of both the masonry fragments kept in the stores of the Saint-Omer Museum and Enlart's photographs held by the Boulogne municipal library.

[30] E. Panofsky, *Abbot Suger on the Abbey Church of Saint-Denis and its Art Treasures*, 2nd edn, Princeton 1987, 90, 112, 118, 136. For the Cluny hemicycle see K. J. Conant, *Cluny: les églises et la maison du chef d'ordre*, Mâcon 1968, 85, 142.

cause it was totally effaced in the course of the comprehensive rebuilding that followed a further fire in 1218.[31]

In the piers of the Temple Church the relationship between the different sizes of shaft in the piers and the arched elements they receive is unique, but a partial parallel is to be found in the Premonstratensian abbey church of Dommartin near Amiens, a building begun in 1153, dedicated in 1163 and mostly demolished after the French Revolution. The piers of the rectangular-plan bays at Dommartin were built from coursed limestone blocks and were therefore totally unrelated in their constructional technique to those of the Temple Church. Their visual effect was quite different too, for they comprised a tight cluster of eight shafts, an adaptation of a kind of pier which originated in Burgundian Cistercian chapter houses.[32] Dommartin's foreshadowing of the Temple Church piers was in fact confined to a single aspect: the clear hierarchical distinction made between the two large shafts allocated to the arches of the main arcade and the smaller shafts receiving the ribs in the vaults over the main vessel and aisles (Plates 4, 5, 11). Admittedly, that distinction had been made once before, at the Benedictine abbey of Saint-Germer-de-Fly near Beauvais, whose church was probably begun in the early 1130s, but it is the more recent example which is likely to have influenced the Temple Church, since all the piers at Saint-Germer include between their shafts rectangular-plan elements such as are totally eschewed at Dommartin and at the Temple.[33] Whereas Dommartin has groups of three small shafts facing inwards and outwards, the Temple Church has just single shafts, and in all probability that simplification was the germ of the very elegant design of the abaci and sub-bases at the Temple,[34] for their boldly projecting triangular parts can be readily understood as 'streamlined' versions of their Dommartin counterparts in which the frontal elements have been elided. Of course this explanation does not diminish the probability of influence from beaked abaci such as those at Saint-Martin-des-Champs in Paris.

The use of single vault shafts on the outer wall of the aisle (Plate 12) rather than

[31] G. Durand, *Monographie de l'église Notre-Dame Cathédrale d'Amiens*, 2 vols., Amiens and Paris 1901–3, I, 10–12. That Tournai 'marble' had been imported as far south as Amiens by the late eleventh century is clear from its use for the monolithic shafts supporting the crypt vault in the collegiate church at Nesle-en-Vermandois, some 45 kilometres east of Amiens; *La Picardie historique et monumentale, VI: Arrondissement de Péronne*, Amiens and Paris 1923–31, 267–70.

[32] For Cistercian influence on the Dommartin piers, including those in the hemicycle, see Wilson, 'Missionaries', 96, 100–111 passim, with references to earlier literature.

[33] The parts of the Saint-Germer hemicycle piers that face inwards, the only parts of the church's piers from which rectangular-plan elements have been eliminated (Kimpel and Suckale, *Gotische Architektur*, ill. 107), are likely to have been the immediate source of Dommartin's piers.

[34] The original form can be seen in the interior view of 1702 by William Emmett (discussed by Griffith-Jones, p. 154 below; see Plate 82). The octagonal sub-bases have found their way into several scholarly publications, despite the fact that they are an incorrect reconstruction of 1810 (replicated in the early 1840s and again after the Second World War) whose necessity arose from the obliteration of the originals when timber cladding was applied to the piers in the late seventeenth century.

the triple shafts that one would expect to find in this position may also be ascribed to the influence of Dommartin, where the diagonal ribs of the ambulatory vault sprang out of the ambulatory wall and only the transverse ribs were allocated shafts.[35] Despite being unique within French Early Gothic architecture, the Dommartin arrangement derives from Saint-Denis, where there is much emphasis on the high and virtually free-standing single shafts under the transverse ribs and where the shafts under the diagonal ribs are treated as part of the continuous window wall that encompasses all the apses of the radiating chapels (Plate 3). As an exercise in simplification the single vault shafts in the Dommartin ambulatory may fairly be regarded as instancing the Cistercianising spirit of Premonstratensian architecture, notwithstanding the Benedictine ancestry of the concept.[36] The aspect of the Temple Church which is not anticipated at Dommartin or Saint-Denis or anywhere else in northern France, so far as I am aware, is the way in which no fewer than four ribs spring from each shaft. In French Early Gothic the only shafts that normally receive multiple arches and ribs are the freestanding columnar piers of main arcades, but in each of the four-shaft groups which make up the main arcade piers at the Temple Church the shaft facing the aisle is made to resemble closely the shafts on the outer wall not only in supporting four ribs but in being of the same size and of the same material (Plates 4, 9). The near-perfect match in appearance and role between vault-bearing shafts on opposite sides of the aisle at the Temple Church leaves no room for doubt that the architect was consciously 'correcting' the marked imbalance between the supports used on opposite sides of the aisles of French churches. Perhaps it was because he was working abroad that he felt able to make such an important de-parture from what was rapidly becoming standard usage in his homeland. At all events the Temple Church's single shafts carrying multiple ribs would appear to have been the origin of a distinctive trait of English Gothic, one which was firmly established by the early thirteenth century and still current in the Early Tudor period.[37]

The quest for consistency and balance which is apparent in the design of the supports to the aisle vault found further expression in the unique equivalence achieved here between the internal elevation of the aisle and that of the central vessel above main arcade level, both of which have very similarly treated single round-headed windows set above horizontal bands of arcading (Colour Plate 1; Plate 8). It is pos-sible that once again Dommartin was the starting point, for it had tall round-headed windows lighting both the aisles and the main vessels. No interior views taken before the Revolution are known to exist and so there is no evidence for the treatment of the

[35] C. Enlart, *Monuments religieux de l'architecture romane et de transition dans la région picarde*, Ami-ens and Paris 1895, plate opp. 104, 107 (fig. 71).

[36] Some corroboration of this view is the influence exerted by Dommartin's ambulatory vault shafts on the Catalan Cistercian abbey of Poblet, begun in 1166.

[37] Twelfth-century examples include the high vaults of St Frideswide's Abbey, Oxford (Ox-ford Cathedral) and St Hugh's Choir, Lincoln Cathedral. Early-sixteenth-century examples include John Wastell's vaults in the crossing tower of Canterbury Cathedral and the eastern chapels of Peter-borough Abbey (Peterborough Cathedral).

main elevations between the clearstorey and the arcades.[38] The aisles certainly did not have wall arcading and it is very likely that the main vessel's elevations were a version of those at the major Cistercian abbey of Pontigny, where the wall between main arcade and clearstorey was flat and undecorated and where there was a fairly close equivalence between aisle and main elevations. Nevertheless, it needs to be stressed that whatever the architect of the Temple Church might have taken from Dommartin or its Cistercian antecedents, the equivalence he achieved between the internal elevations at upper and lower levels became a matter of far greater consequence than ever before because the slightness and openness of the main arcade made the aisle elevation exceptionally visible from the central vessel, the primary viewpoint.

An inconspicuous technical detail of the Temple Church's architecture which probably ought to be added to the tally of its debts to Early Gothic in the French far north is the construction of the cells of the quadripartite vaults over the ambulatory and the west porch. The courses of masonry making up the cells are laid so as to meet the ridges at an angle (Plate 13), whereas the normal French method was to make the courses range parallel to the ridges. This appears to be the only twelfth-century example of the technique to have survived in England, where, from the early thirteenth century onwards, it became the standard way of building vault cells. In northern France, by contrast, fewer than a handful of examples are known and all date from well before 1200. The nearest thing to a concentration occurs in the far north: the parish church chancels at Namps-au-Val (Plate 14), around 18 km south-west of Amiens, and Avesnes-le-Comte, some 48 km north-north-east of the same city.

The Temple Church's indebtedness to northernmost France is particularly evident in the domain of foliage carving, despite the fact that virtually all of the church's capitals are early-nineteenth-century replicas. It is immediately apparent that a clear division exists between the Caen stone capitals of the exterior and the aisle wall arcading, which exhibit a very high degree of variation, and the Purbeck marble capitals found throughout the rest of the building, which, though very far from being unvaried, make use of a repertory of forms that is both more restricted and more coherent.[39] By far the

---

[38] Enlart, *Monuments religieux*, 108, 119.

[39] Unfortunately, the renewal of the wall arcade capitals in 1826 under Robert Smirke was done with little concern to perpetuate the original forms; Gardam, 'Restorations', 111. In later restorations there seems to have been a conscientious effort to make replicas rather than new designs, and this is explicitly stated to have been the case with the capitals and bases of the triforium arcading; Essex and Smirke, *Illustrations*, 14–5. When the capitals of the nave piers were renewed at the beginning of the 1840s the carvers followed casts of the originals; Gardam, 'Restorations', 112, where an unduly negative assessment of the restorers' capacity to copy accurately is offered. For the restoration history of the Temple Church see also J. M. Crook, 'The Restoration of the Temple Church: Ecclesiology and Recrimination', *Architectural History*, 8, 1965, 39–51; G. Zarnecki, 'The West Doorway of the Temple Church in London', in *Beiträge zur Kunst des Mittelalters: Festschrift für Hans Wentzel zum 60. Geburtstag*, Berlin 1975, 245–53; Williamson, *Catalogue of Romanesque Sculpture*, 97–8; N. Macfadyen, 'Temple Church, London: the Great West Doorway', *Association for Studies in the Conservation of Historic Buildings, Transactions*, 9, 1984, 3–6; and pp. 195–216 below.

most frequently occurring motif in the decoration of the Purbeck capitals is waterleaf — the broad, fleshy leaf whose tip forms a distinctive upwards- and inwards-spiralling 'volute' at each corner. In the mid-twelfth century only northernmost France could show very large numbers of waterleaf capitals, which were eventually to achieve an even wider diffusion in England. At Dommartin variants of waterleaf seem to have been used throughout, except in the hemicycle and ambulatory, and the many examples that have survived from elsewhere in the region suggest that it was seen there almost as an 'everyday' type.[40] At the Temple one of the main arcade capitals and four in the triforium arcading combine waterleaf with a twin-leaved spray growing from a vertical stalk endowed with a rectangular collar, a motif which derives ultimately from the stems supporting the abacus flowers at the centre of the faces of Corinthian capitals (Plate 15). The incidence of this Antique form in earlier medieval capital sculpture is sparse but the one French church at which several versions of it can be seen is the mid-twelfth-century collegiate church of Lillers near Béthune, where waterleaf is also much in evidence.[41] It also occurs in at least one of the main arcade capitals in the north transept hemicycle of Tournai Cathedral which are likely to date from the 1140s or early 1150s.[42] A stock in trade of the mid-twelfth-century carvers of Tournai marble, both generally and in the cathedral transepts, is the simple volute capital whose tip ends in a prominent vertical disc resting on a plain, almost triangular leaf rising direct from the necking.[43] This type is quite well represented among the Purbeck capitals of the triforium arcading at the Temple Church, although it is almost invariably combined with other elements. In several capitals in the Tournai Cathedral transepts the edges of the broad leaves that end in volutes at the corners are linked to other volutes at the centres of the faces so as to set up a vigorously undulating rhythm (Plate 16). An echo of this type may be detected in part of a main arcade capital at the Temple Church (Plate 17), but the connectedness of the latter's capitals to the Tournai workshops is demonstrated most effectively by one of their simplest elements, the highly stylised leaves consisting of approximately triangular groups of radially arranged wedge-like forms ending in rounded tips and accompanied by a single rudimentary scroll (Plates 17, 18). These are found in the nave and transepts of the cathedral (Plates 19, 20) and they occur so often in Tournai-made fonts and tomb

[40] For waterleaf (as defined in the English rather than the French literature), see Wilson, 'Missionaries', 104–5, 106 n. 69, 111 n. 87.

[41] Early-eleventh-century examples are at St Lucius at Werden and St-Bénigne at Dijon and a late-eleventh-century example was until 1917 at Nesle-en-Vermandois. Illustrations of the Lillers examples are in H. Oursel, W. Sauerländer and J. Thiébaut, *Sculptures romanes et gothique du nord de la France* (exhibition catalogue, Musée des Beaux-Arts, Lille, 1978–9) Arras 1978, 88 (ills. 12, 14, 15).

[42] The variations in scholarly opinion regarding the dating of the twelfth-century parts of Tournai Cathedral are tabulated in E. Schwartzbaum, 'The Romanesque Sculpture of the Cathedral of Tournai', Ph.D. thesis, New York University, 1977, 235.

[43] Examples of the type are the capitals revealed during the Second World War in the ruins of the late medieval church of the Abbey of Saint-Bertin, perhaps part of repairs after a documented major fire in 1152; 'Abbaye de Saint-Bertin', *Société des Antiquaires de la Morinie, Bulletin historique*,16, 1938–46, 467–8.

slabs as to be almost a trademark.[44] There must be a good chance that the Purbeck capitals at the Temple were carved by sculptors recruited from Tournai and that after the building was complete some of these men sought further work in England. It is tempting to think that among them was the marbler with the quintessentially Low Countries name of Lambert who is documented working for the Bishop of Durham in 1183.[45]

The clearest evidence that sculptors from the far north of France were involved in the decoration of the Temple Church is the striking similarity between the small, tightly curled foliage scrolls on the archivolts of the west door, which are still mostly original, and the scrolls at the upper rims of some of the splendid capitals from the hemicycle at Dommartin, now in the museum at Amiens (Plates 21–3). Dommartin anticipates the design of the leaf forms, their rather metallic handling, their virtuosic undercutting, and even the rather curious conceit that the leaves have grown so as to form a very clearly defined front plane, almost as if they have been constrained by sheets of glass. One can be confident that the Dommartin hemicycle capitals were put in hand at the start of work in 1153, for their model was a capital carved in the early 1140s, that of the freestanding columnar pier between the two northernmost of the radiating chapels in the chevet of Saint-Denis (Plate 24). The likeness between Dommartin's hemicycle capitals and the archivolts of the Temple Church west door is so strong that in my view it would not be unreasonable to suppose both were made by the same sculptors. Some 30 km south-east of Dommartin is the Benedictine nunnery church of Berteaucourt-les-Dames, whose west portal shows that around the same time other sculptors in the region had anticipated the Temple Church's adaptation of Dommartin-type foliage scrolls to the archivolt format (Plate 25).[46]

If the Temple Church has the look of a building designed by a French architect 'parachuted' into the southern English milieu, much as William of Sens was to be nearly 20 years later at Canterbury Cathedral, it also resembles William's work in the way it takes account of a certain number of established English usages. A major example of the latter is the round-arched west portal, with its many recessed orders and its heavy reliance on abstract and foliate ornament rather than large-scale figure sculpture (Colour Plate II). The resemblances between the decoration applied to the door jambs and such recent south-east English exercises in decorative architecture as the St Albans Abbey chapter house and slype and the gate to the outer court of Canterbury Cathedral Priory indicate that the architect was going to considerable lengths to accommodate

[44] J. S. King, 'The Tournai Marble Tomb-Slabs at Trondheim (Norway) and Tortefontaine (France) and their Significance', *JBAA*, 161, 2008, 24–58 passim.

[45] J. H. Harvey, *English Mediaeval Architects: a Biographical Dictionary down to 1550*, rev. edn, Gloucester 1984, 170; R. Leach, *An Investigation into the Use of Purbeck Marble in Medieval England*, privately printed 1978, 86.

[46] Enlart, *Monuments religieux*, 72–87.

local preferences.[47] Other features classifiable as 'concessions' to English expectations are the elaborately treated wall arcade below the aisle windows and the intersecting arcading of the triforium. The latter might well have been based specifically on the middle storey of the Romanesque choir of Canterbury Cathedral, a building which would almost inevitably have been encountered by a north French architect using the most obvious approach to London, that from Dover.[48] The main cloister and infirmary cloister built next to the cathedral in the mid-twelfth century paralleled some other important aspects of the Temple Church, namely the employment of Purbeck for capitals and bases as well as for supports consisting of four separate and closely spaced shafts (Plate 26).[49] If he failed to penetrate either of the cathedral's cloisters a French architect en route for London was still likely to have been confronted by a major architectural use of Purbeck at Faversham Abbey, 16 kilometres west of Canterbury, in the choir of which King Stephen and Queen Matilda lay entombed.[50] Once he reached London our architect might have been told that the building works of Stephen's brother Henry of Blois had influentially switched from Tournai to Purbeck in the 1140s, but even if such a conversation did not take place his discussions with the patron or patrons of the new Temple Church will soon have clarified that in southern England Purbeck was on the way to becoming a *sine qua non* for high-status projects.[51] Just how far his willingness to embrace the prevailing English taste for elaborate ornament and rich materials was to take him away from the modest levels of architectural display generally favoured by the Knights Templar can be gauged by a comparison with the head church of the order's French province, the long-since-destroyed Temple Church in Paris. Probably built in the mid- or late 1140s, this building was slightly larger in area than its London counterpart, but its design was consistently plainer. As the only authentic view of its interior reveals, its elevations incorporated very large areas of undecorated ashlar and there was

[47] For bobbin ornament at St Albans which parallels that on the west door jambs see Thurlby, 'Place of St Albans', passim. For the Canterbury court gate's foliate ornaments comparable to those on the innermost order of the west door jambs, see *Courtauld Institute Illustration Archives, Archive 1: Cathedrals and Monastic Buildings in the British Isles, part 8, Canterbury, Romanesque Work*, ed. G. Zarnecki, London 1978, ill. 1/8/129.

[48] R. Willis, *The Architectural History of Canterbury Cathedral*, London 1845, fig. 15 opp. p. 73. Intersecting arcading was already known in northernmost France by the mid-twelfth century, as is evident from its use on the west front of the collegiate church of Lillers.

[49] T. Tatton-Brown, 'The Two Mid-12th-Century Cloister Arcades at Canterbury Cathedral Priory', *JBAA*, 159, 2006, 91–104.

[50] The one surviving capital from the site, whose size suggests it came from the abbey church, is carved from Purbeck marble; *English Romanesque Art 1066–1200* (exhibition catalogue, Hayward Gallery), London, 1984, 182 (no. 146). See also n. 55 below.

[51] Henry of Blois's works are likely to have pioneered the use of Purbeck marble in high-status buildings, not least because of the proximity of Purbeck to the religious houses of which he was the head, Glastonbury Abbey and Winchester Cathedral. For discussions of Henry of Blois's use of Tournai and Purbeck, see G. Zarnecki, 'Henry of Blois as a Patron of Sculpture', in *Art and Patronage in the English Romanesque*, ed. S. Macready and F. H. Thompson, London 1986, 159–72 at 168; Y. Kusaba, 'Henry of Blois, Winchester, and the 12th-century Renaissance', in *Winchester Cathedral: Nine Hundred Years*, ed. J. Crook, Chichester 1993, 69–79 at 71–4.

neither a wall arcade in the aisle nor a middle storey of any kind (Colour Plate 1; Plate 27). The capitals of its main arcade were decorated with foliage sculpture but the piers were fairly short single columns constructed from freestone drums in the usual way and the arches were devoid of moulded decoration. As in many northern French buildings of its period, the aisles were covered by groin vaults and rib vaults were reserved for the central vessel.[52]

The London Temple Church clearly represents an important moment in the reception of Gothic architecture in England during the third quarter of the twelfth century, but can we say that it was the country's first encounter with the new idiom? There are two immediately obvious obstacles to formulating a definite answer to that question: the very fragmentary physical evidence for other major English churches of the period, and the paucity of reliable evidence for dating most of the buildings that are potentially contemporary. The most important new church being built in south-east England during the decade preceding the start of work at the Temple was that of Faversham Abbey, where construction must have progressed with lightning speed from the mid-1140s in order to have brought all or most of the church to a state of readiness for the dedication in November 1148.[53] The ground plan revealed by excavation in the 1960s looks conventionally Anglo-Norman apart from the enormous elongation of the eastern arm to provide space for the royal burial chapel.[54] Obviously it is necessary to be cautious about interpreting the architecture of a site subjected to a ruthlessly thorough stripping by the agents of Henry VIII, but the very few moulded and carved details to have survived corroborate the evidence of the plan that the building was Romanesque in style.[55] The other most ambitious buildings erected in south-east England during the middle years of the twelfth century were improvements to monastic precincts, and the most

[52] Other Parisian examples are Saint-Pierre-de-Montmartre and Saint-Martin-des-Champs. There must be a possibility that the high vault of the Paris Temple Church was renewed in the early thirteenth century, when very large extensions were built to the east and west of the rotunda. What is probably the only extended discussion in print of this church is unfortunately mostly fantasy; E. Viollet-le-Duc, *Dictionnaire raisonné de l'architecture française du XIᵉ au XVIᵉ siècle*, 10 vols., Paris 1858–68, IX, 14–7.

[53] From an unknown date before 1148 Queen Matilda had taken up residence at St Augustine's Abbey, Canterbury, in order to be able to direct the Faversham works in person; D. Crouch, *The Reign of King Stephen, 1135–1154*, Harlow 2000, 261 n. 15. A near-contemporary annalist noted that the church was 'built' (*constructa*) in 1148; O. Lehmann-Brockhaus, *Lateinische Schriftquellen zur Kunst in England, Wales und Schottland vom Jahre 901 bis zum Jahre 1307*, 5 vols., Munich 1955–60, I, 464 (no. 1700). That at least the east arm was completed in 1148 is evident from the fact that the bodies of the founders and of their eldest son were interred there in 1152, 1153 and 1154. There are some interesting comments on the patronage of the abbey and its subversion by Henry II in M. Frohnsdorff, *The Foundation of Faversham Abbey*, Faversham 1998, passim.

[54] B. Philp, *Excavations at Faversham, 1965: the Royal Abbey, Roman Villa and Belgic Farmstead*, no place 1968, 14, 36, fig. 4 (folding plan).

[55] For the base see ibid., 43 (no. 12). Although very carefully finished, the profile of the base lacks the upper torus normally found in Early Gothic bases. The capital, already known before the 1965 excavation, is illustrated in *English Romanesque Art*, 182 (no. 146). It belonged to a respond of shaftless stepped plan without parallel in any major Early Gothic building.

extensive and sumptuous of these was the series of additions undertaken at Canterbury Cathedral Priory by Prior Wibert (1152/4–67). The handful of detached fragments attributable to the mid-twelfth-century renewal of Canterbury's main cloister includes two Purbeck marble voussoirs from arcades of pointed profile and small span.[56] These incorporate large roll mouldings sandwiched between parallel runs of chevron and one of them has at its centre two rolls flanking a broad hollow moulding decorated with boldly carved flowers, both of which are designs that first appeared in proto-Gothic buildings of the 1130s such as Saint-Germer-de-Fly. The other most important surviv- als from the main cloister are some roundels enclosing grotesque sculptured heads, and these probably extend the date bracket forwards by a few years, for one of them is very strongly reminiscent of a grimacing head in a roundel decorating one of the spandrels from the cloister built at Saint-Denis either towards the end of the abbacy of Abbot Suger or shortly after his death in 1151.[57] The possibility exists therefore that by the mid- or late 1150s Canterbury Cathedral Priory possessed a cloister or a part of a cloister with Gothic characteristics. Of course a structure consisting of nothing more than long runs of small-scale arcades carrying wooden roofs would have amounted to something rather less than a showcase for the new style of architecture, though its novel features might well have served to spark curiosity about their provenance in the minds of at least some viewers.

[56] If the marble shafts with complex fluted patterns are from the same phase of work on the main cloister, as shown in Tatton-Brown, 'Cloister Arcades', 100 (fig. 8), this might tend to indicate an earlier rather than a later date, as such shafts belong to a Late Romanesque formal repertory that was, to all appearances, eschewed in the Saint-Denis cloister. Caution is necessary here, however, for a decidedly non-purist approach was also evident in the main level of the choir begun c.1160 at York Minster, where French Gothic-derived structural elements were juxtaposed with very elaborate chevron and other geometric ornaments which seem to represent a revitalising of Anglo-Norman decorative traditions sparked by the realisation that chevron had also been part of the vocabulary of recent church architecture in the Île-de-France.

[57] This likeness was recognised independently by Jeffrey West and discussed by him in a lecture to the Society of Antiquaries on 4 December 1997. The Canterbury roundel in question is illustrated in *Courtauld Institute Illustration Archives*, ill. 1/8/145; D. Kahn, *Canterbury Cathedral and its Romanesque Sculpture*, London 1991, 168 (ill. 262); *English Romanesque Art*, 196 (no. 164i). During the preparation of this last publication I attempted, unsuccessfully, to persuade Professor George Zarnecki that this and the rest of the group of fragments previously associated by him with a screen of c.1180 in the cathedral church ought for three reasons to be attributed to the north walk of the cloister and the attached centrally planned lavatorium: firstly, the discovery of these pieces reused in the masonry of the north-west sector of the cloister built in 1397–1414 next to the site of the twelfth-century lavatorium; secondly, the stylistic evidence indicating a date well before c.1180; thirdly, the 135° angle incorporated into a length of decorated string course (ibid., 198, no. 164m, not illustrated; *Courtauld Institute Illustration Archives* (as above), ill. 1/8/160), an indication that its origin was on the outside of an octagonal structure identifiable as the lavatorium. For the Saint-Denis roundel see D. V. Johnson and M. Wyss, 'Saint-Denis II: Sculptures gothiques récemment découvertes', *Bulletin monumental*, 150, 1992, 355–81 at 371 (fig. 34). If Canterbury's head-enclosing roundels resembled their Saint-Denis counterparts in being set above cloister arcades, and if they are earlier than the Temple Church, they are potentially a source for the celebrated grotesque heads in the spandrels of the Temple's aisle wall arcade, a feature otherwise unique in the period.

Alongside the London Temple Church, the most important English building of the early years of Henry II's reign was the east arm added to York Minster by Archbishop Roger of Pont-l'Evêque (1154–81). How soon in Roger's episcopate the choir got under way is not known, but the designs must have been drawn up no later than 1160, for in 1162 work began on the new cathedral at St Andrews, a church which served the foremost Scottish see and whose very close stylistic kinship with the York choir was clearly intended as a rebuttal of Roger's aggressive assertion of York's claim to ecclesiastical suzerainty over Scotland.[58] The architectural vocabulary used in Roger's choir changed from predominantly Romanesque forms in its crypt to predominantly Early Gothic forms in its main upper level, but the knowledge of Durham Cathedral displayed in the geometric decoration of the crypt piers and the Durham-like proportioning of storeys in the upper level suggest very strongly that the architect was English by training. The most obvious explanation for the use of different formal repertories in the crypt and main level would be that the design was modernised in the course of execution, but that hypothesis is vitiated by its failure to account for the presence from the start of comparatively inconspicuous elements that betray the designer's awareness of mid-twelfth-century north French Gothic architecture. It is far more likely that the design was essentially an entity and that the contrast between the archaising crypt and the more modern upper choir was one deliberately contrived in order to express the lower and higher status attached to the two levels. A very similar contrast is to be seen in the choir of Saint-Denis, which could perfectly well have been the model for this aspect of York.[59] That a creative link of some sort existed between the York choir and the Temple Church cannot be doubted, for their complicated main arcade mouldings were almost identical (Plates 7, 28) and the bases of the piers that carried the vault in the east transept crypt at York provide for a rhomboid arrangement of four shafts which will have given them an unmistakable likeness to the piers at the Temple, despite their

[58] Wilson, 'Missionaries', 97.

[59] I no longer think that the crypt and main level were designed by different architects, the first one English-trained, the second one possibly French-trained, as argued ibid., 91–7. The chamfered corners of the sub-bases and abaci of the larger crypt piers, together with the design of the four-shaft piers in the parts of the crypt within the east transepts (Plate 29), indicate that the designer was aware of the Early Gothic great churches of northern France from the start. See also M. Thurlby, 'Roger of Pont-l'Évêque, Archbishop of York (1154–1181), and French Sources for the Beginnings of Gothic in Northern England', in *England and the Continent in the Middle Ages: Studies in Memory of Andrew Martindale* (Proceedings of the 1996 Harlaxton Symposium), ed. J. Mitchell, Stamford 2000, 35–47 at 37–8. A second aspect of my 1986 paper which I now realise is unsatisfactory is the suggestion that many of the Gothic elements in the York choir probably derived from Cistercian buildings in northern England; Wilson, 'Missionaries', 115 and passim. I think it is more likely that the blend of Gothic and Cistercian was taken over more or less ready-made from the French far north, as indeed I allowed for in ibid., 100–106. See also Thurlby, 'Roger of Pont-l'Évêque', 36 and passim. If one assumes that the architect was fully conscious of the origins of his source material he might have chosen to add to the blend further Cistercian (Romanesque) ingredients mostly derived from sources closer to home. For the pier plans that can readily be understood in this way see J. Bony, 'Origines des piles anglaises à fûts en délit', in *Gedenkschrift Ernst Gall*, ed. M. Kühn and L. Grodecki, Munich 1965, 95–122 at 109–13.

considerably larger scale and their lack of either beaked sub-bases or differentiated shaft sizes (Plates 4, 29).[60] If one uses as a surrogate for the dismantled upper choir at York the still-existing choir of Ripon Minster, which was also patronised by Archbishop Roger, one can identify as further northernmost French borrowings common to York and the Temple Church the predominance of waterleaf in the decoration of capitals, the false bearing technique, and high vaults with sloping lateral ridges.[61] A further point of comparison between the Temple Church and York/Ripon is that the chancel of the former and the aisles of the latter both possess clustered vault responds with half-octagonal abaci in the manner of the Fontenay chapter house, the building whose fully octagonal freestanding supports were the model for the clustered piers at Dommartin (Plates 18, 30, 31).

How is it possible to account for the overlapping formal repertories and shared sources of these two buildings, the one apparently designed by a French architect, the other by an Englishman? There appear to me to be two main options. The first, which does not entail deciding whether York or the Temple Church is the earlier, would be to ascribe their similarities to the fact that most English travellers going to Paris and beyond would have become quite familiar with the far north of France because the Boulonnais was where they usually disembarked. The large number of major churches recently completed or in progress in the 1150s would, on this argument, have made the far north seem as worthy, or almost as worthy, of attention as the Île-de-France, which modern scholarship privileges on the strength of its having been the birthplace of Gothic; and the presence of very similar far northern French features at York and the Temple would merely be parallel instances of borrowing ideas which were in evidence at many of the region's mid-twelfth-century churches before these were so brutally culled in later ages. The second option, which places more emphasis on the probability

---

[60] The likeness of these two designs was tacitly acknowledged by their near-juxtaposition in Bony, 'French Influences', 10 fig. 3, even though the text does not comment on their relationship. The very rare horn-like element in the profile of the transverse arches of the aisles of the main choir at York and in the radiating chapel ribs at Dommartin (Wilson, 'Missionaries', 96 n. 35) is to be seen in the diagonal ribs of two compartments of the Temple Church aisle vault (Plate 7). The only original base surviving at the Temple Church, that in the south-west corner of the probable sacristy south of the original aisleless chancel (Griffith-Jones, *Temple Church*, 20), anticipates the rare cylindrical treatment of the outermost part of the lower torus in the bases from the main level of the York choir, although the closest parallels are with a base in Suger's work at the west end of Saint-Denis; J. Browne, *The History of the Metropolitan Church of St Peter, York*, 2 vols., London and York 1847, II, plates XIIIE, XXXI; Crosby, *Royal Abbey*, 443 (L.2.). The profile shown in Godfrey, 'Recent Discoveries', plate XLVIII, is extremely inaccurate.

[61] The over-early dating of the Ripon choir in Wilson, 'Missionaries', 88, is corrected in P. Barker and S. Harrison, 'Ripon Minster: an Archaeological Analysis and Reconstruction of the 12th-century Church', *Journal of the British Archaeological Association*, 112, 1999, 49–78 at 51. For a discussion of the evidence that the high vault at Ripon was at first meant to have had an acutely pointed transverse profile with steeply sloping lateral ridges (much as in the so-called chapter house at Trondheim Cathedral, Norway, and presumably also as in the lost high vault of the York choir) see the entry on Ripon Cathedral by C. Wilson, in P. Leach and N. Pevsner, *Yorkshire West Riding: Leeds, Bradford and the North* (The Buildings of England), New Haven and London 2009, 637–64 at 648–9.

that York differed from the Temple Church in being designed by an English architect, is to assume that the Temple was earlier by a small margin and to postulate that the architect of York made contact with his French colleague, who showed him sketches and drawings he had brought over from France and perhaps offered suggestions about which buildings were most worth crossing the Channel to study 'in the flesh'. The main advantage of this second option is that it eliminates the necessity of postulating the former existence of rather large numbers of far northern French churches which were stylistically closely akin to the York choir and the Temple Church, but the evidence that in my view decisively tips the scales in favour of the second option is the presence at the Augustinian Priory of Bridlington, some 60 kilometres east of York, of several capitals whose carved decoration is so closely paralleled at the Temple that the most obvious way of accounting for the likenesses would be to postulate a northwards trans- fer of craftsmen around 1160 after the completion of the Temple Church. Four of these capitals derive from the cloister arcades and incorporate variations on a very sophisti- cated design, a simulation of elaborate pleating in thin cloth or parchment whose upper edges paraphrase one of the stock elements of English Romanesque, the multi-scallop capital (Plate 32). So far as I am aware, the only example of this kind of capital still in situ is that on the east side of the north arch of the Temple Church porch (Plate 33).[62] Another capital at Bridlington, whose original context within the priory's buildings is unknown, has the only mid-twelfth-century English example of a beaked abacus other than those on the main arcade at the Temple Church and, no less remarkably, foliage carving which is in the style of the Dommartin choir capitals (Plates 22, 23, 34).[63] The long-term consequences of the indebtedness of Archbishop Roger's choir to the Temple Church were extremely important in the north of England, because York inaugurated a new style of architecture which was to dominate the region's output, and that of Scotland also, until the end of the twelfth century.

    What impact, if any, did the Temple Church have in the south-east of England in the years following its completion? It has been recognised for some time that the orna- ments of the west door were imitated in the western entrances at Dunstable Priory and Hemel Hempstead church,[64] but in the realm of architecture strictly defined no influ- ence has been detected so far. I suggest that there is a case for seeing the lateral eleva- tions of the choir of the hospital church of St Cross in Winchester as a highly eccentric and not altogether intelligent response to the nave elevation at the Temple. I concur

    [62] For illustrations see Thurlby, 'Sculpture from Bridlington Priory', 33–43, plate iva, c; S. Harrison, 'Benedictine and Augustinian Cloister Arcades of the Twelfth and Thirteenth Centuries in England, Wales and Scotland', *JBAA*, 159, 2006, 105–30 at 111–9. For the related Temple Church capital before restoration in the 1860s, see the watercolour dated 1861 by J. W. Archer in the Prints and Drawings Department of the British Museum; Gardam, 'Restorations', plate xxivc; Lewer and Dark, *Temple Church*, ill. 89. An ex-situ capital of this kind, formerly at St Albans Abbey but now lost, is illustrated in Kahn, *Romanesque Sculpture*, 108 (ill. 165).

    [63] J. Bilson, 'The Fragments of the Cloister Arcade [of Bridlington Priory]', *Yorkshire Archaeo- logical Journal*, 21, 1911, 174–5.

    [64] R. C. Marks, 'The Sculpture of Dunstable Priory c.1130–1222', MA report, Courtauld Insti- tute of Art, University London, 1970, 18–35; Thurlby, 'Place of St Albans', passim.

with the majority of recent students of the topic in thinking that St Cross should be dated late in the career of its founder Henry of Blois, that is to say to the early 1160s.[65] The St Cross designer was clearly determined to keep faith with the well-established English Romanesque preference for thick walls and clearstorey passages, both features decisively rejected at the Temple.[66] However, the proportions of the three storeys are very similar to those of the Temple Church, the vault springs from a similarly high level, and the intersecting arcading of the triforium is comparable in its overall design (Colour Plate 1; Plate 35). Moreover, if one reinstates in one's mind's eye the original form of the piers carrying the two-bay main arcades at St Cross, the likeness becomes considerably enhanced. The piers currently in this position are mid-nineteenth-century replacements for late fourteenth-century replacements, but enough of the originals remains to show that they consisted of five Purbeck marble shafts, one in the middle and one at each corner.[67] They must have resembled nothing so much as elongated versions of the supports under the bowls of mid-twelfth-century Tournai marble fonts, and given that one of the most important of these stands in Winchester Cathedral, it seems quite likely that the St Cross architect was indeed using this somewhat improbable local exemplar in order to 'correct' what may well have seemed to him, as an unreconstructed aficionado of the traditional English thick wall, the rather risky design of the coreless piers of the Temple Church nave. In the end it was he who miscalculated the risks inherent in his design, for his piers eventually proved unequal to the enormous load placed upon them by the very thick walls of the choir. The similarities of St Cross to the Temple Church could perfectly well have been due entirely to the architect's response to an obvious exemplar, but if I am justified in my suspicion, tentatively voiced at the start of this paper, that the relocation and rebuilding of the Templars' English headquarters was an initiative due ultimately to Henry II, it is perhaps worth considering the possibility that Henry of Blois' decision to build a hospital church far grander than any other was a gesture intended to demonstrate that, morally at least, the ancien régime headed by the bishop's brother and the bishop himself was not entirely a spent force. A possible pointer towards a context of rivalry is the fact that St Cross was in the hands of the Hospitallers, the only other military order active in England besides the Templars.

It is tempting to connect the London Temple Church's relative lack of influence on the subsequent course of architectural development in south-east England with the fact that this, like all Templars' churches, was a very private place, open to the populace on only one day in each year.[68] But we should not suppose that that restriction was

[65] Y. L. Kusaba, 'The Architectural History of the Church of the Hospital of St Cross in Winchester and its Place in the Development of English Gothic Architecture', Ph.D. thesis, Indiana University, 1983, 25–38.

[66] The upper walls of the Temple Church nave are approximately half as thick as those of the St Cross choir, c.92 as against c.183 cm.

[67] Kusaba, 'St Cross in Winchester', 163–85, figs. 36–8.

[68] A papal bull of 1139 had specified two days a year, but another of 1179 reduced this to one; Gatti, 'Relationship between the Knights Templars and the Kings of England', 216. For a discussion

applied to members of the elites who commissioned major church buildings. The real reason for the lack of influence in the south-east must surely be that the Temple Church was put up at the wrong time in the cycle of building and renewing the great churches which were the natural leaders of architectural fashion. It was only with the reconstruction of the eastern arm of Canterbury Cathedral that there emerged a building capable of initiating a long-term regional trend not only in architectural style but in the very purposes served by grand church architecture, namely the reinforcement of episcopal authority and the glorification of English saints. Yet Canterbury's lavish use of Purbeck marble could very well have been influenced by the Temple Church, which appears to have been England's first demonstration of the possibilities of the material for church architecture. Moreover, the phase of English Gothic inaugurated by Canterbury, the so-called 'Early English' style, probably owed to the Temple Church two of its more idiosyncratic traits, the tendency to spring many ribs from single shafts, and the infilling of vaults with masonry courses set at an angle to the ridges. But if the nave of the Temple Church is viewed in the context of English medieval art as a whole it appears significant on two main counts: it testifies to the permeability of mid-twelfth-century England by the artistic innovations emanating from the newly resurgent kingdom of France, an attitude of openness which was to enable the English to develop their own versions of Gothic architecture much earlier than any other part of Europe outside northern France; and it exemplifies what was to be a persistent and widespread tendency of elite English patrons, their predilection for the highly wrought and the refined even in contexts where simplicity and restraint might be expected.[69] Its rich and varied decoration and its bays formatted like those of a great church leave no room for doubt that the creators of this building intended it to be something wholly exceptional. Acknowledgement of their success in that respect is long overdue, for London's Temple Church far exceeds in ambition and accomplishment all the other churches erected for the Knights Templar during the twelfth century.

APPENDIX: THE ARCHITECTURAL ICONOGRAPHY OF THE WEST PORCH

The only feature of the London Temple Church which seems to evoke a prototype other than the Church of the Holy Sepulchre is the west porch (Plate 2). Its form would have appeared

of access to the church by the faithful at large in the early and mid-fourteenth century, see Nicholson, pp. 11–12 above.

[69] Wilson, 'Missionaries', 112–16; Fernie, *Architecture of Norman England*, 192.

exotic to many contemporary viewers, for its placing before the west door, its square plan and its openness on three sides were all unprecedented in England.[1] Of several such porches surviving in France, the west porch to the mid-twelfth-century Templars' chapel at Laon provides the most suggestive parallel. Elie Lambert showed in 1954 that the Laon church was associated with the Templars' acquisition of the right to have a cemetery and that in its octagonal nave and apsidal chancel it followed the funerary chapel built by a recent abbot of the Benedictine abbey of Saint-Vincent, hitherto the only religious house in Laon permitted to have its own cemetery.[2] Lambert's assertions that the centralised plan of the aisleless nave of the Laon Templars' chapel was due entirely to its belonging to the genre of funerary chapel, and that it had nothing to do with evoking the Holy Sepulchre, are surely wrong. The immediate prototype of the chapel, that at Saint-Vincent, was dedicated to St Mary Magdalen, first-mentioned of the three women to visit Christ's empty tomb and the follower to whom the resurrected Christ first appeared; and there can be little doubt that the Saint-Vincent and Templar chapels in Laon, in common with all the other cemetery chapels of centralised plan, were conceived as evocations not of the Holy Sepulchre Church itself but of the structure which stood at its centre, namely the Aedicule over Christ's tomb, the main chamber of which was treated externally like a miniature rotunda. Within a very short time of its completion the Laon Templars' chapel acquired a west porch, an addition that will have served to reinforce the chapel's likeness to the Aedicule, which possessed such a feature both before and after its partial destruction in 1009.[3] Although it is aisled, the London Temple Church shares the basic rotunda concept with the Aedicule, and at least some viewers would have been able to recognise that its west porch enhanced the capacity of the church as a whole to recall the shrine which lay at the heart of the Templars' mission. It may be suspected that in its combination of references to the Holy Sepulchre Church and to the Aedicule the Temple Church was simply following its now-destroyed Parisian counterpart of c.1145–50, for the two-bay, open-sided west porch which the latter acquired around 1240[4] was an uncommon feature in its time and could well have owed its overall form to its being a replacement for a single-bay porch belonging to the primary building campaign. The existence of such a porch at such a prestigious church would help account for the diffusion of the type within France.[5]

[1] In 1862 what were interpreted as foundations for two nave buttresses flanking the west door were found and interpreted either as evidence that the west porch was secondary or as an indication that it was an addition made during the course of building the nave; Gardam, 'Restorations', 103. In the absence of any precise record of what was found in 1862 it seems right to stress that the still partly original vault of the porch appears to belong to the primary work because it is formally and technically of a piece with the nave aisle vaulting.

[2] E. Lambert, 'L'Architecture des Templiers', *Bulletin monumental*, 112, 1954, 7–60, 129–65 at 54–60.

[3] M. Biddle, *The Tomb of Christ*, Stroud 1999, 20–40, 82 (fig. 66) and passim.

[4] R. Branner, *Saint Louis and the Court Style in Gothic Architecture*, London 1965, 72 (plate 81).

[5] It is almost certainly apropos that before 1149 a similar square-plan porch, admittedly with only two open sides, had been built out from the east part of the south transept front of the Church of the Holy Sepulchre in Jerusalem. The porch sheltered the entrance to the Calvary Chapel at gallery level in the south transept; D. Pringle, *The Churches of the Crusader Kingdom of Jerusalem: a Corpus, Vol. III: The City of Jerusalem*, Cambridge 2007, 54–6.

PLATE I. Temple Church, interior elevation of main vessel of nave, looking north

A

B   C

PLATE II. Temple Church, west door, watercolour by Joseph Clarendon Smith, 1806 (B and C: details of A)

PLATE III. Temple Church choir, interior view to east

PLATE IV. Temple Church, head of Purbeck marble effigy in nave (William Marshal the Elder?)

PLATE V. Temple Church, Purbeck marble effigy in south choir aisle (Silvester de Everdon, Bishop of Carlisle?)

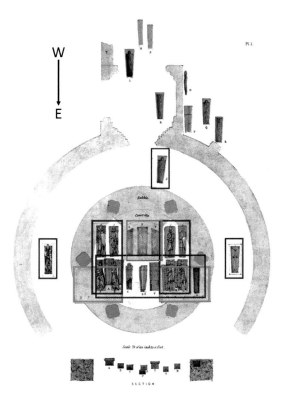

PLATE VI. Plan of the round nave, published by Edward Richardson in 1841, with added boxes showing: the present positions of the effigies from 1842 (red); the positions of the effigies until 1841 (green); the nine coffins and one burial cavity found during the 1841–2 excavations (blue); and the vaults created to re-inter the coffins with their human remains (orange)

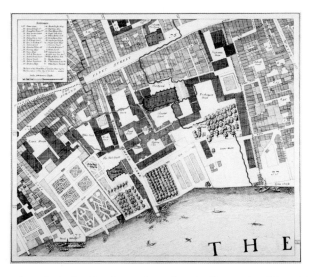

PLATE VII. The Temple, 1676, detail of map by John Ogilby and Willam Morgan, showing western limits of Great Fire of 1666 (here in red); approximate extent of fire of winter 1678 (newly marked in green)

PLATE IX. Temple Church, interior of chancel looking east, drawing by George Shepherd, 1811

PLATE X. Temple Church, chancel looking west, 1843, decoration designed by Thomas Willement

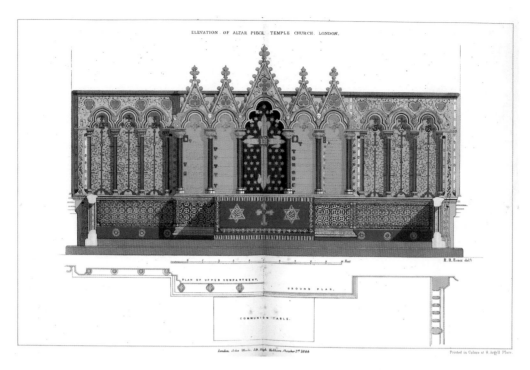

PLATE XI. Temple Church, altar piece, 1845, design by Thomas Willement

PLATE XII. Temple Church, chancel looking east, engraved by Harden S. Melville, 1843, after George Cattermole

Virginia Jansen

Light and Pure:
the Templars' New Choir

INTRODUCTION

O N ASCENSION DAY in 1240, the new choir of the Temple Church was consecrated before a prestigious congregation, including King Henry III and many magnates of the realm.[1] It replaced an earlier choir, presumably built by the time the Templars moved to this new site in *c.*1161. Although popular interest in the Temple Church focuses on the tombs in the round nave, architectural designers and historians admire the superlative beauty of the choir. It prompted the nineteenth-century architect Lewis Nockalls Cottingham to assert that 'the choir or square part of the church is decidedly the most exquisite specimen of pointed architecture existing' (Colour Plate III and Plate 36).[2] It is not only the beauty of the choir that warrants attention, however, but also the multi-faceted aspects of historical interpretation that this addition raises.

ARCHITECTURAL FORM

The Temple choir

Especially striking are the qualities of openness and spaciousness, today bringing an overall effect of bright lightness to the choir. These traits follow from the choir's structure, defined as a hall church; that is, a form with three or more aisles of generally equal height, so that the walls of the centre aisle lack the clearstorey that characterises the

My grateful thanks go to the conference speakers and audience, in particular to Helen Nicholson and the organizers Robin Griffith-Jones and David Park for providing congenial discussions on several issues and for responding to persistent questions.

[1] Paris, *Chronica*, IV, 11.

[2] As quoted in W. Burge, *The Temple Church: an Account of its Restoration and Repairs*, London 1843, 16.

basilican form.[3] This construction means that the relationship between central vessel and side aisles is more regular and that lighting comes from windows placed only on the periphery. It usually allows a more even tonality to permeate the building, whatever glazing originally filled the windows. In the case of the choir of the Temple Church, to quote Nikolaus Pevsner, 'It is in fact one of the most perfectly and classically proportioned buildings of the C13 in England, airy, yet sturdy, generous in all its spacing, but disciplined and sharply pulled together.'[4]

The regular and even proportions of the choir are indeed notable (Colour Plate III). The internal width of the choir of 59′ 6″ (as measured from the internal face of the walls, a length correlated with the diameter of the nave of 60′ 2″) and its length of 86′ 6″ provide the ratio of nearly 2:3 (.69).[5] The height of 37′ 7/8″ in relation to the width produces the ratio of .623, close to the golden mean of .618. The bay length is 17′, the same as the width of the aisle; the central aisle as measured on pier centre (25′ 6″) is half again as wide, yielding the ratio between the widths of the aisle and centre vessel as 2:3. The number of bays across the width of the choir — three — related to their number along its length — five — again yields approximately the golden ratio.

The repetitive forms of the architecture also contribute to a sense of calm balance. With the same profile as the ribs, not even the transverse arches between the bays interrupt the flow of space. In contrast to the architecture of most greater churches of Gothic England, the choir is reticent and simple. For example, there is no decorative wall arcade as there is in the nave; only a thin stringcourse in Purbeck marble outlines the sill. All the windows are graduated triplets of lancets, echoing purely the rise of the rib vaulting. Blank walling (undoubtedly originally painted) rather than blind niches flanks the windows; only the eastern spandrels bear any sculptural decoration. The vaults are minimally quadripartite with a small foliage boss knitting the ribs together at the crown. The five-bay choir has uniform, slender quatrefoil piers of Purbeck marble, moulded bases and capitals rather than luxuriant foliage capitals, as well as very regular moulded arches (Fig. 2). With a fillet only on the larger axial roll, the mouldings consist primarily of evenly designed rolls and hollows. A uniformity seems to rule everywhere.

Despite much restoration and severe war damage from 1941, the details are essentially reliable even if renewed.[6] For too long it has been believed that restoration has obliterated historical forms, but often surviving physical evidence and illustrations

---

[3] For an extensive set of drawings including sections and mouldings, see Billings, *Illustrations*.

[4] N. Pevsner, *London: the Cities of London and Westminster* (The Buildings of England), 3rd edn, rev. B. Cherry, Harmondsworth 1973, 315.

[5] Without a modern, large-scale measured plan and elevation, only fairly accurate numbers can be calculated. Measurements are taken from Godfrey's plan illustrated here as Plate 1, and his elevation as reproduced in J. Butler, *Saxons, Templars and Lawyers in the Inner Temple: Archaeological Excavations in Church Court & Hare Court* (Pre-Construct Archaeology Limited Monograph no. 4), London 2005, 52, fig. 69. I appreciate Robert Bork's help in formulating this paragraph, although any mistakes are mine.

[6] In addition to William Whyte's contribution to this volume, see Gardam, 'Restorations'. Medieval fragments found in the 1999–2000 excavations discussed by Butler in *Saxons, Templars and Lawyers*, 47, corroborate the general accuracy of the restored details even if some of the stones

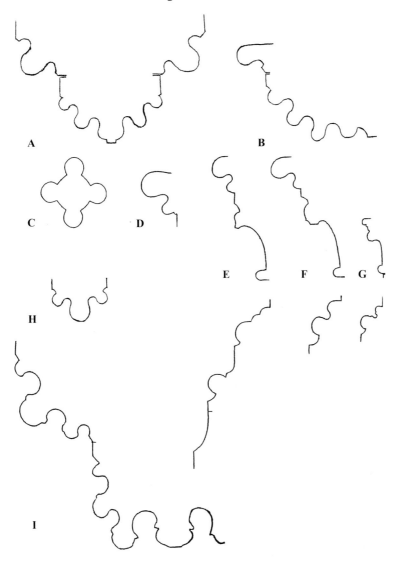

FIGURE 2. Temple Church choir, mouldings (not to same scale)

Profiles after R. K. Morris, Warwick Mouldings Archive [WMA]; graphics by Corri Jimenez

    A. arch of main arcade (WMA.0110)

    B. rere-arch of lancet window (WMA.0120)

    C. pier section (WMA.0111)

    D. stringcourse of window sill (WMA.0127)

    E. capital of main arcade (WMA.0136) and base (WMA.0113)

    F. capital of window rere-arch (WMA.0122) and base (WMA.0123)

    G. capital of piscina (WMA.0152) and base (WMA.0155)

    H. rib and transverse arch (WMA.0128)

    I. lateral north arch between choir and nave (WMA.0130)

have allowed restorers to reconstruct the original form and architectural historians to determine it even if the pieces are modern rather than historic.

Although the date when the choir was begun is unknown, the architectural forms are similar to many buildings of the 1220s and 1230s in southern England. These are mostly connected with the patronage of advisers of young King Henry during his minority, which was ending in 1227. Possibly the rebuilding of the choir began in 1231 when the king decided to be buried at the Temple. David Carpenter believes this decision can be associated with the death of Henry's beloved brother-in-law William Marshal the Younger, the distraught king desiring interment in the Temple, where both William and his father had been buried. It is recorded that in 1231 Henry granted the Temple £8 for supporting three chaplains, each to celebrate a daily mass.[7] These decisions might well have stimulated a rebuilding of an aisled choir, which would provide space for three altars and presumably for the king's tomb

The new choir originally had at least three altars: the high altar and two others dedicated to St John and to St Nicholas, presumably in the side aisles. Not only are these altars documented in the 1307–8 Inventory taken at the Suppression of the Order, but the thirteenth-century aumbries still exist: one each at the east end of the north and south aisles, and a series of arches in the central bay of the eastern wall, now hidden behind the Wren reredos.[8] Near these last aumbries the main altar would have been located somewhat west of where it is now, even if its precise location is unknown. It was placed on a raised platform as was usual. During the nineteenth-century restorations, some of the original paving was found *in situ*, indicating that the medieval level of the thirteenth-century church was 9″ lower than the early-modern level on the altar dais and 15″ lower in the choir. The change in pavement level occurred between the two eastern freestanding piers. Perhaps, like the late twelfth-century chancel at St John's, Clerkenwell, the altars may have been raised two steps.[9]

restored in the 1950s differed slightly in size. These excavations also turned up evidence of the thirteenth-century cloister; ibid., 23–6 and fig. 30.

    [7] Paris, *Chronica*, III, 201. See D. A. Carpenter, *The Reign of Henry III*, London 1996, 433–44, and idem, 'King Henry III and Saint Edward the Confessor: The Origins of the Cult', *English Historical Review*, 122, 2007, 865–91, esp. 871–2. Gifts to support the three daily masses, one for the king, one for all Christians living, and one for those departed, are found in the *Calendar of the Charter Rolls of Henry III, 1226–57*, I, London 1895, 135. In 1235, Henry restated his intent, but in 1246 Henry ordered his burial for Westminster Abbey; ibid., 210 and 306.

    [8] The full Inventory is given in Baylis, *Temple Church*, 131–46, and excerpted in Lewer and Dark, *Temple Church*, 178–9. The central aumbries are illustrated in Griffith-Jones, *Temple Church*, 25; presumably there were four arched niches originally, the two central ones having been remade into one large niche.

    [9] A difference of nine inches for the altar pavement was cited by Richardson, *Stone and Leaden Coffins*, 19–20, and Burge, *The Temple Church*, 25 and 45. The variation of fifteen inches was mentioned in Essex and Smirke, *Illustrations*, 6, and following them in Lewer and Dark, *Temple Church*, 97. (D. Lewer in 'Restorations in the Temple Church with Notes on Middle Temple Hall', *Transactions of the Ancient Monuments Society*, ns 16, 1968–9, 24, wrote 10″.) Butler, *Saxons, Templars and Lawyers*, 8, referred to the original paving as being buried under two feet of soil in the seventeenth century. B. Sloane and G. Malcolm, *Excavations at the Priory of the Order of the Hospital of St John of*

Comparative buildings

The architecture of the Templars' new choir most closely resembles that of the Lady Chapel, or more accurately the Trinity Chapel, of Salisbury Cathedral, begun by 1220 and consecrated in 1225 (Plate 37).[10] It, too, was built as a hall structure, and its architecture shows similar Purbeck marble piers, moulded capitals, triple roll bases, plain dado walling, simple quadripartite vaulting (without bosses in the Trinity Chapel), and a triplet group of lancets in the east window. Some of the moulding profiles are the same as or very similar to those in the Temple (Fig. 3, overleaf).

The work at Salisbury Cathedral provides a close, but only one precedent. Another related building is Henry III's castle hall in Winchester of 1222–1236 (Fig. 3 and Plate 38). The moulded capitals have a profile like the Temple's and tall, thin Purbeck piers, although their section differs from the Temple's. While the domestic arch mouldings of the hall are simpler than those in the church, the hall also contains even rolls between the chamfered orders.

Close by the Temple, the Archbishop's Chapel at Lambeth Palace, undated but probably completed after the Interdict was lifted (that is, after 1213), exemplifies an early instance of these formulae.[11] Although a simple rectangular chapel rather than a hall church, it has similar lancet triplets, Purbeck shafting, and regular roll mouldings and capital profiles; its vaults are modern (Fig. 3). Not surprisingly other work at Canterbury itself of this period after the Interdict — such as the hall of the archbishop's palace and the cloister doorway to the refectory, of which only fragments survive — reveals a similar use of Purbeck marble and repetitively even roll mouldings (Fig. 3).

Two further features of the Temple underscore the comparisons already drawn: first, in the southeastern corner the beautiful but damaged double piscina, which has a composition of a quatrefoil surmounting two rounded trefoil arches and flanked by roundels (Plate 39); and, second, the elongated quatrefoils of the eastern spandrels of the central aisle. Although such figures as quatrefoils and trefoils are common Gothic

---

Jerusalem, Clerkenwell, London (Museum of London Archaeology Service Monograph, 20), London 2004, 46 and fig. 31, show Clerkenwell with a rise of about .35m, or 13 ¾″. Billings, *Illustrations*, pl. v, showed the altar dais two steps higher in the eastern bay only, but since he published before the restoration, the figure must have been hypothetical. The north and south aumbries are approximately 5′ above the present floor-level, suggesting that the dais extended across the side aisles.

[10] For detailed discussion of the dating of Salisbury Cathedral, see P. Z. Blum, 'The Sequence of the Building Campaigns at Salisbury', *Art Bulletin*, 73, 1991, 6–38, esp. 9–10, and most recently, T. Tatton-Brown and J. Crook, *Salisbury Cathedral: the Making of a Medieval Masterpiece*, London 2009.

[11] V. Jansen, 'Lambeth Palace Chapel, the Temple Choir, and Southern English Gothic Architecture of *c.*1215–1240', in *England in the Thirteenth Century* (Proceedings of the 1984 Harlaxton Symposium), ed. W. M. Ormrod, Grantham 1985, 95–9 and fig. 1; see also pl. XIIA in V. Jansen, 'Salisbury Cathedral and the Episcopal Style in the Early Thirteenth Century', in *Medieval Art and Architecture at Salisbury* (British Archaeological Association Conference Transactions, XVII), ed. L. Keen and T. Cocke, Leeds 1996, 32–9. T. Tatton-Brown, *Lambeth Palace: a History of the Archbishops of Canterbury and their Houses*, London 2000, 31–2, has found evidence of three phases; he assigns the upper chapel to the period *c.*1218–28.

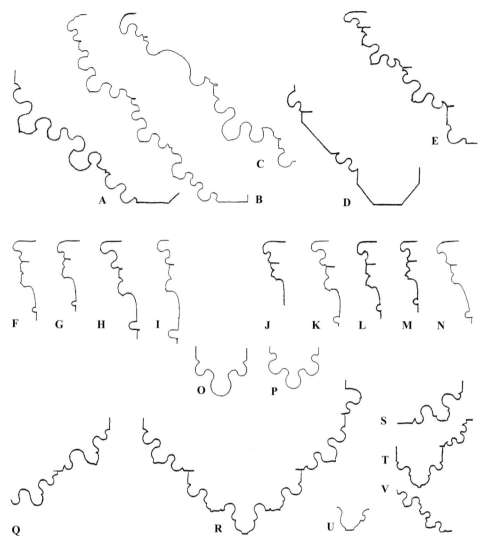

FIGURE 3. Mouldings compared to those of the Temple choir (not to same scale)
    From author's drawings unless otherwise noted; other profiles based on R. K. Morris, Warwick Mouldings Archive [WMA], and additional sources; graphics by Corri Jimenez
    (legend on opposite page)

currency, they can be found in several buildings in the context we have been discussing: in the archbishop's palace at Canterbury; the eastern wall and piscina of the related church at Hythe on the coast; the entry door to Lambeth Palace Chapel (where there are pointed trefoil arches, but rounded ones in the restored crypt windows); the windows at Winchester Castle Hall (Plate 38); the windows in Bishop Jocelyn's palace at Wells; the parapet around Salisbury Cathedral; and the piscinae of the Salisbury

A. Salisbury Cathedral, arch of triforium of eastern transept (WMA.0241)

B. Lambeth Palace Chapel, London, arch of west doorway (WMA.0900)

C. Canterbury, arch of doorway from cloisters to former refectory (WMA.0836)

D. Winchester Castle hall, arch of arcade

E. Winchester Castle hall, exterior arch of south doorway (after Harold S. Sawyer, 1903)

F. Winchester Cathedral retrochoir, capital of dado arcade

G. Beaulieu Abbey, capital of refectory

H. Salisbury Cathedral, capital of window jamb of presbytery aisle (WMA.0133)

I. Wells Bishop's Palace, capital of undercroft central pier (WMA.0905)

J. Chichester Cathedral, capital from north arm of transept

K. Salisbury Cathedral, capital of triforium of east transept (WMA.0247) and of piscina of south aisle of presbytery

L. Winchester Castle hall, capital of arcade

M. Beaulieu Abbey, capital of refectory pulpit

N. Portsmouth Garrison church, chancel capital (WMA.0112)

O. Winchester Cathedral retrochoir, diagonal and transverse rib of aisle (WMA.0124)

P. Salisbury Cathedral, diagonal rib of main vault, type 2 (WMA.0271)

Q. Windsor Castle Lower Ward, arch of cloister arcade

R. Westminster Abbey, arch of doorway of St Faith's Chapel

S. Westminster Abbey, transverse arch of vault of transept (RCHM[E])

T. Westminster Abbey, arch of presbytery arcade (RCHM[E])

U. Clarendon Palace, fragment in Salisbury and South Wiltshire Museum

V. Beaulieu Abbey, arch of lavatory

churches of St Nicholas Hospital, St Martin's and St George's.[12] A telling comparison is found in the earlier retrochoir of Winchester Cathedral, of c.1200 – the 1230s, where the wall arcading and upper walls of the eastern chapels show such foiled shapes (Plate 40).[13] But more than the similarity of the Temple and Winchester motifs, their function is particularly revealing. The use in the richly decorated Winchester retrochoir contributes to the context of funereal and shrine architecture, whereas in the Temple choir the forms serve to enrich the choir's most sacred part in contrast to the reticence presented elsewhere. Overall, the simpler architecture of the choir accords well with the monastic values of the Templars, who from their beginnings had ties to the Augustinian and Cistercian Orders.[14]

[12] For Canterbury see J. Rady, T. Tatton-Brown and J. A. Bowen, 'The Archbishop's Palace, Canterbury', *JBAA*, 144, 1991, 1–60, and Tatton-Brown, *Lambeth Palace*, 37; for the Lambeth portal and windows, ibid., 31–2 and 111; for Wells, Jansen, 'Salisbury Cathedral', pls XA and XIB; and for the Salisbury churches, Royal Commission on Historical Monuments (England), *Ancient and Historical Monuments in the City of Salisbury*, 1, London 1980, pl. 40.

[13] The dates reflect protracted construction with several breaks; see J. Crook, 'St Swithun of Winchester', in *Winchester Cathedral: Nine Hundred Years 1093–1993*, ed. J. Crook, Chichester 1993, 61 and 67 n. 18, as well as P. Draper, 'The Retrochoir of Winchester Cathedral', *Architectural History*, 21, 1978, 1–17.

[14] Nicholson, *Knights Templar*, 28 and *passim*.

The forms of the Temple choir thus fit unproblematically into a stylistic frame-work of buildings constructed throughout southern England and connected with royal, clerical, and noble patrons who were associated with the government during the king's minority. Such sites as Beaulieu Abbey, Clarendon Palace, other work at Salisbury Cathedral, the north arm of the transept at Chichester Cathedral, and still further examples both earlier and later provide comparison, even if the precise architectural relationships are less telling than those that have been cited already.[15] Given Henry III's intention to be buried in the New Temple, the correspondences are unsurprising, even if we cannot specify other locations where the masons who worked on the Temple Church had been active.

Somewhat later in style than the choir itself, the two arches joining the side-aisles of the new choir and the older nave remain stylistically within the same milieu. Completing the connection of the two sections, they may date from near the time of the consecration in 1240, a second phase in the architecture of the choir. In contrast, the moulding of the centre arch indicates that it belonged to the twelfth-century chancel arch between the first choir and the round nave. The lateral entrances with their luxuriant decoration make a fitting entrance to the choir. The moulded rolls now include lateral fillets, a sharper linearity such as that seen in the Windsor cloister of 1240, Westminster Abbey, and Salisbury in the door between the south arm of the main transept and the cloister (Figs. 2 and 3). The beautiful heads with classically square, softly modelled faces, wide-opened eyes, parted lips, and full wavy hair (Plate 41) seem stylistically situated somewhere between the dainty features of the sculpture of c.1230–50 on the west façade of Wells Cathedral and the early heads at Westminster Abbey with their square stereometry and similar treatment of the eyelids from c.1250.[16] The finished Temple heads were painted and their pupils filled with blue glass beads.[17]

These heads remind us that the medieval choir was colourful. On the evidence of finds made during the restoration of the 1840s, it had been embellished with painted walls, vaults and mouldings; tile floors (Plate 42); and glazing with geometric shapes and shields.[18] Given the knightly status of the Templars, shield imagery is not sur-

[15] Jansen, 'Southern English Gothic', 95–9.

[16] For Wells, see P. Williamson, 'Sculpture', in *Age of Chivalry: Art in Plantagenet England 1200–1400*, ed. J. Alexander and P. Binski, London 1987, 100, and ibid., cat. 243, for a quatrefoil angel, similar to some of the queens from the middle tier of the facade. For Westminster Abbey see the head of a king over the door of the north arm of the transept and corbel heads in the eastern triforium and St Faith's Chapel in L. E. Tanner, *Unknown Westminster Abbey*, Harmondsworth 1948, pls. 15, 16, 33, and 36. P. Tudor-Craig in *Age of Chivalry*, 320, remarks that the Gabriel Master of the Westminster chapter house Annunciation might be the carver of the St Faith heads. The Temple heads are also generally like the painted head of a king in the cloister at Windsor.

[17] Richardson, *Stone and Leaden Coffins*, 23; on p. 24 he describes the colouring as follows: 'the cheeks and lips were red, the eyes grey, the brows and long flowing hair gilt, and the fillet or band across the head blue'. Also quoted in Lewer and Dark, *Temple Church*, 105; they reproduce a head on p. 119, ill. 91.

[18] As recorded by Richardson, *Stone and Leaden Coffins*, 23, 'the ceiling had been decorated with colours and metallic plating in straight-sided oblongs, with semi-circular heads'. Stones from

prising; however, since the original location of these pieces is no longer known, it is unclear whether they were made in *c*.1240 or later. As glazing may follow the building by some years, possibly the original painted glass did include shields, since they were beginning to appear by mid-century.[19] As the architecture is related to that of Salisbury Cathedral, so might the glass be. In this case the prevalence of coloured panels in geometric armatures set in grisaille glass (perhaps including the shields) would coordinate admirably with the restrained architecture yet show off the costly marble piers, which strongly coloured glass would have obscured. One remnant at Salisbury that may be relevant displays repeating quarries surrounding an inscribed quatrefoil; others employ lozenge patterns.[20] Discussion of the Temple glazing is, however, problematic given the state of the evidence.

THE HALL-CHURCH CHOIR AND ITS TYPE

More problematic than this assessment of the architectural context of the Temple choir are the complex questions concerning the decision to employ the hall-church type. Because convincing evidence is lacking, working toward conclusions requires evaluation of several issues. These include Templar traditions, the site and topography of the London Temple, the hall-church type, rituals and practices, iconographic links with Jerusalem, and practical considerations of structure. As ever, all of these are interwoven within the contexts of the politics of the period. Finally, consideration of the role of the

the choir that had earlier been used to seal up the triforium of the Round were painted with 'not only rich bands of colour and metallic plating, but some gilding'. These were painted with yellow, dark grey, red, blue, and a 'metallic plating, like silver'; no figural images were uncovered, an absence which would have been in accordance with the Templars' Cistercian-influenced sensitivity.

Richardson illustrated the tiles known to him in pls. VIII and IX; examples 1, 3, 4, 6 and probably 2, 5, 8, and 9 were thirteenth-century. One tile is in the British Museum and two are at the Museum of London; one of the latter is illustrated in Griffith-Jones, *Temple Church*, 26. Butler, *Saxons, Templars and Lawyers*, 80–83, reproduces the finds of 1999–2000 and Richardson's two plates showing tiles. The tiles were either glazed plain green or yellow with the decorated tiles brownish red and yellow or yellow-orange. I. M. Betts, *Medieval 'Westminster' Floor Tiles* (Museum of London Archaeology Service Monograph, 11), London 2002, 25, dates 'Westminster' tiles to the 1250s at the earliest.

Essex and Smirke, *Illustrations*, 6, mentioned that only 'a few shields remained' of the medieval glass.

[19] R. Marks, *Stained Glass in England during the Middle Ages*, Toronto 1993, 10, states that the earliest known example is dated 1247, which would suggest that such glazing at the Temple had been added after the dedication. But see Park, p. 84 below, for further discussion of the Temple glazing.

[20] R. Marks, 'The Thirteenth-Century Glazing of Salisbury Cathedral', in *Medieval Art and Architecture at Salisbury*, 106–20, Figs 3D and 3A–C respectively. Marks, *Stained Glass*, 113–40, emphasizes the prevalence of grisaille for several churches of this era, including Lincoln, York and Westminster as well as Salisbury. The Cistercians were also known for employing grisaille glass. P. Mayes, *Excavations at a Templar Preceptory, South Witham, Lincolnshire, 1965–67*, London 2002, 131, refers to a few fragments of quarry glass from that mid-thirteenth-century church, but the glass itself is undated.

Temple Church itself and of comparable structures in the life and reign of Henry III as he passed beyond his minority expands any understanding of the new Templar choir.

Templar traditions

Since most Templar commanderies in the West were actually small rural manor-like establishments, many chapels were simply single-cell buildings, or had a small aisleless chancel attached to a nave.[21] Several churches were round or polygonal structures, as were some Hospitaller churches; these made reference to the origins of both Orders in the vicinity of the Holy Sepulchre (Fig. 4).[22] Likewise, chapels in the eastern provinces of the Order, often existing within the defensive framework of a castle, were of simple type. Similarly, the first church at the New Temple was comprised of a round nave with an aisleless chancel. Excavation has revealed the latter's plan, except for its termination, which could have been either apsidal or square-ended (Plate 1).[23] In time, however, the important headquarter complexes of the provinces, such as those of London and Paris which were also nationally significant as banking institutions and depositories for kings and magnates, grew much larger.[24] Yet it is difficult to envisage how the financial services of the Templars would have affected the form of the choir. Even the huge thirteenth-century enlargement of about one hundred feet long in the vast Paris complex retained a single-aisled choir (Fig. 4).

Topography and site

In London there seems to have been no compelling reason why the choir could not have been extended as it was in Paris. Clerical housing seems to have stood to the east, which the Church's expansion in width rather than length allowed to remain, even

[21] Nicholson, *Knights Templar*, *passim*; E. Lambert, 'L'Architecture des Templiers', *Bulletin monumental*, 112, 1954, 7–60 and 129–65; P. Ritoók 'The Architecture of the Knights Templars in England', in *The Military Orders: Fighting for the Faith and Caring for the Sick*, ed. M. Barber, Aldershot 1994, 167–78; J. Folda, *The Art of the Crusaders in the Holy Land 1098–1187*, Cambridge 1995, *passim*.

[22] M. Gervers, 'Rotundae Anglicanae', in *Évolution générale et développements régionaux en histoire de l'art* (Acts of the 22nd International Congress of the History of Art, Budapest 1969), 3 vols., Budapest 1972, I, 359–76 and III, figs. 91–6.

[23] W. H. Godfrey, 'Recent Discoveries at the Temple, London, and Notes on the Topography of the Site', *Archaeologia*, 95, 1953, 125–7.

[24] E. Ferris, 'The Financial Relations of the Knights Templars to the English Crown', *American Historical Review*, 8, 1902, 1–17; C. Perkins, 'The Wealth of the Knights Templars in England and the Disposition of it after their Dissolution', *American Historical Review*, 15, 1910, 252–63; and A. Sandys, 'The Financial and Administrative Importance of the London Temple in the Thirteenth Century', in *Essays in Medieval History Presented to Thomas Frederick Tout*, ed. A. G. Little and F. M. Powicke, Manchester 1925, 147–62. See also Helen Nicholson's paper, pp. 1–18 above. The Fine Rolls make it clear how much royal financial business involved the Temple, including providing a place of deposit for many national taxes and subsidies: *Calendar of the Fine Rolls of the Reign of Henry III*, http://www.finerollshenry3.org.uk/cocoon/frh3/content/indexes/place/lo-lz.html (accessed 18 October 2008). In Paris the Templars held the treasury of the kingdom of France.

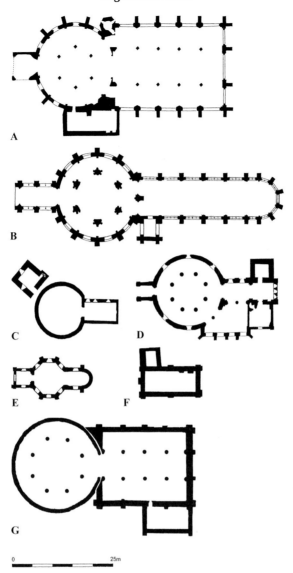

FIGURE 4. Comparative plans of a few Templar churches and the Hospitaller church of
St John's in Clerkenwell, London
    Reworked by Virginia Jansen after Sloane and Malcolm, Viollet-le-Duc, and Mayes;
graphics by Corri Jimenez
    A. London
    B. Paris
    C. Garway (Heref.)
    D. Temple Bruer (Lincs.)
    E. Laon
    F. South Witham (Lincs.)
    G. St John's, Clerkenwell, London

though such housing could surely had been moved, had a longer chancel been desirable. Thus, the London hall church remains unusual, probably unique, within Templar architecture.

Typology

Many aisled parish churches started out as hall churches in the Middle Ages before acquiring clearstoreys, but these are essentially halls by default. Like domestic halls derived from timber structures, the walls of these churches are there essentially to enclose space and to support a pitched roof.[25] They generally eschew expensive architectural embellishments such as clearstoreys and vaulting. Given the strictly even heights of all three aisles in the Temple Church and its canopied vaulting (expressed on the exterior by three long parallel roofs), a distinction between the types covered by the category 'hall church' may be drawn. The vaulted type may be more closely related to developments evolved from hall crypts than from domestic timber hall structures.[26] Moreover, hall churches of the Temple type are infrequent in England, but they are found regularly in western and southern France, where the English controlled territory in the Middle Ages; in Flanders; and in regions of Germany and Italy. Because no compelling reason links the New Temple's choir to any of these areas, other matters, such as ritual and service practices, might be more constructively pursued.

Function: rites and practices

Akin to the chancel with a single aisle, the hall-church format is practical for a collegiate community. The members can sit facing one another, as in the seating arrangement of the Temple choir today or in the placement of canons' stalls. The *Rule* of the Templars indicates that the Templars sat for part of the service; standing too much was said to be 'immoderate'.[27] Moreover, since weekly chapter meetings were normally held in the church, lending authority to the investigations undertaken and the corrections

[25] Richard Morris reminded me about parish hall churches. For the interrelationships between domestic halls and hall churches, see W. Horn, 'On the Origins of the Mediaeval Bay System', *Journal of the Society of Architectural Historians*, 1958, 17, 2–23; and W. Horn and E. Born, *The Plan of St Gall: a Study of the Architecture and Economy of, and Life in a Paradigmatic Carolingian Monastery*, 3 vols., Berkeley 1979; and P. Crossley, 'The Nave of Stone Church in Kent', *Architectural History*, 44, 2001, 195–211.

[26] Although unvaulted, the Galilee at Durham of the 1170s shows that a hall structure with aisles of even height was built in England before the thirteenth century. Another hall form is found in the large aisled, vaulted chapter houses, as at Fountains and Furness, but these examples — simple enlargements from a unified space — seem unconnected with the hall church as such. Jean Bony portrayed the categories of hall churches somewhat differently in *The English Decorated Style: Gothic Architecture Transformed 1250–1350*, Oxford 1979, 34–6.

[27] *The Rule of the Templars: the French Text of the Rule of the Order of the Knights Templar*, trans. and intro. J. M. Upton-Ward, Woodbridge 1992, 23, § 15. C. Dondi, *The Liturgy of the Canons Regular of the Holy Sepulchre of Jerusalem: a Study and a Catalogue of the Manuscript Sources* (Bibliotheca Victorina,

imposed there, such a design would have served well, although the centripetal form of the nave would serve even better.[28] It is possible, then, and perhaps more likely, that the knights attended chapel in the nave, even if the evidence remains far from clear. The *Rule* instructed, 'While the office is being said, no brother should remain in that part of the chapel in which the priest and the clerk stay when they perform the office of Our Lord . . . because he may perhaps hinder them in performing their office.'[29] Similarly, Sloane and Malcolm assert that at the Hospitallers' church of St John's in Clerkenwell 'the chancel was the province of the chaplains only'.[30] And the Inventory of Templar possessions in 1307–8 lists an altar with mass book, seven tropers, and chalice in the 'Church of the Blessed Mary', which has been interpreted as referring to the nave.[31] The cross in the church, before which the Marshals were said to have been buried, most likely referred to a cross at the chancel arch.[32] There would, if these readings are correct, have been a setting for mass — whether for the knights, sergeants, servitors or visitors — in the nave.

None of these remarks, however, provides unquestionable evidence for the location of the brothers during chapter, the offices or mass. The church cross, especially prior to the late thirteenth century, could be located on or near the altar, but this placement was uncommon.[33] Whereas the *Rule* strongly suggests that the brothers should not occupy the east end of the chancel, it says nothing about their presence — at an appropriate distance from the chaplains — at its west end. Assuming a small number of brothers, we can envisage their attendance at services at the western end even of the first, smaller chancel. We have no real evidence for the number of brothers, just imprecise indications from a later date, but nothing indicates that they were ever too numerous to fit into the western part of such a chancel. There is also no information on the number of sergeants who were present at services.[34] It is hard, then, to believe that

16), Turnhout 2004, 41, points out that Templar houses in the West followed the liturgy of the local diocese.

[28] I appreciate Helen Nicholson's comments on these matters.

[29] Upton-Ward, *The Rule*, 100, § 363.

[30] Sloane and Malcolm, *Excavations*, 71, without including further evidence. R. Gilchrist, *Contemplation and Action: the Other Monasticism*, London 1995, 71, notes that at Garway (Herefs.), only the western side of the chancel arch was decorated, suggesting that the Templars viewed the arch from seats in the nave, at least in the early period.

[31] Baylis, *Temple Church*, 144; Lewer and Dark, *Temple Church*, 49–50 and 179, who suggested that the Church of the Blessed Mary was meant to identify the nave, since the Inventory also mentioned 'The Great Church' and 'The Choir' separately. As the text referred to a church 'beyond the door of the hall', Godfrey, 'Discoveries', 130, supposed that it was a misnomer for the Chapel of St Thomas Becket. Despite the dedication of the entire church to the Virgin, the designation may have been meant specifically to identify the first church on the site, of which only the rotunda survives; see, for example, Lees, *Records*, 163, charter 8.

[32] See n. 64 below, and Park, pp. 77–9 below.

[33] C. D. Cragoe, 'Belief and Patronage in the English Parish before 1300: Some Evidence from Roods', *Architectural History*, 48, 2005, esp. 26–33.

[34] The Inventory of 1307–8 (Baylis, *Temple Church*, 131–46, and extracts in Lewer and Dark, *Temple Church*, 178–9) listed twelve brethren and three officers in addition to six chaplains, four

the number of brothers and sergeants, wherever they participated in the services, would by itself have prompted the building of a new and enlarged choir.

Might the enlargement have been made necessary by the grant of ever more indulgences to those visiting the Church and by the consequent growth in the number of visitors?[35] Especially in the period 1228–79, nearly twenty indulgences were added to those first granted in the second half of the twelfth century.[36] Although there must have been some increase in the traffic of visitors in the first decades of the thirteenth century, it is difficult to know how significant it was and what effects it might have had on the spaces of the church.

It is clear, however, that Templars' churches were less closed than has been previously thought. In London the faithful attended morning mass and regularly visited the important relics, which included wood from the cross, Christ's blood, and the sword that was used to kill Becket.[37] The hall type, related to hall crypts under choirs for the visitation of relics, has a long history, with a large early example found at Santa Maria in Cosmedin, Rome, from the time of Pope Hadrian I (772–95).[38] Other types of structures, however, could accommodate the devotion of relics as well; it has been notoriously difficult for architectural historians to connect a certain type with specific religious practices and liturgies.

Thus, it seems that the old single-aisle, three-bay chancel (assuming that its structural condition remained satisfactory), was not too small, except perhaps on special occasions that included visits of illustrious guests. Indeed, the single-aisled form, so frequently used because of its simplicity, modesty and practicality, would seem to have

clerks serving the chaplains and some choristers (the Inventory recorded four little copes for them); see also Lewer and Dark, *Temple Church*, 49. Perhaps only coincidently there were twenty-two silver spoons in the cellar, twenty-two banners in the vestry, and twenty-two pieces of Birmingham in the wardrobe of the Grand Master, but whether these connoted twenty-two brothers at some time is unclear. Sloane and Malcolm, *Excavations*, 42, tentatively estimated fourteen brethren at Clerkenwell in c.1200, with an unknown number of sergeants and servants.

[35] The British Library's MS Cotton Nero E vi, fols. 24ʳ–25ᵛ, records these indulgences. Most specify a visit at the time of the Church's dedication or on the day constituted for the veneration of the Church's relics. I am grateful to Robin Griffith-Jones for contributing this information. For further evidence from the trials of 1307–12, see Helen Nicholson's paper, pp. 11–12 above.

[36] Lees, *Records*, 162–3.

[37] See Helen Nicholson's paper, p. 11 above, and eadem, 'Relations between Houses of the Order of the Temple in Britain and their Local Communities, as Indicated during the Trial of the Templars, 1307–12', in *Knighthoods of Christ: Essays on the History of the Crusades and the Knights Templar, Presented to Malcolm Barber*, ed. N. Housley, Aldershot 2007, 195–207. Important visitors are mentioned in Williamson, *Temple*, 26–8. The relics are recorded in the Inventory in Baylis, *Temple Church*, 145, and Lewer and Dark, *Temple Church*, 179. The Templars were strongly connected with the sites of the source of the cross, as discussed by Folda, *Art*, 173, and in *Jerusalem Pilgrimage, 1099–1185* (Hakluyt Society, 2nd ser. no. 167), ed. and trans. J. Wilkinson, London 1988, 74–7, for the Templars' finding the wood of the cross.

[38] R. Krautheimer, 'The Carolingian Revival of Early Christian Architecture', in *Studies in Early Christian, Medieval, and Renaissance Art*, New York 1969, 215, esp. n. 109 (reprinted from *Art Bulletin*, 24, 1942, 1–38).

remained the best form for a Templar church, even for the head church of a province, as existed in Paris. After Henry III granted support for three chaplains saying daily mass, the Templars may have needed to enlarge the choir in some manner; but the context for that grant must still be clarified after considering iconographic models.

Architectural iconography

As is well known, the Temple's round church is modelled on the Holy Sepulchre, the supreme monument which the Military Orders protected and adjacent to which the Templars first resided under the aegis of the Augustinian canons (Fig. 5). London's Templars, perhaps motivated by their possession of relics of Christ, might have wished to underscore the link between the Jerusalem Sepulchre and their own church. In the fourth century, an aisled basilica in Jerusalem was added to the tomb structure, which was rebuilt on a grand scale, so that there was an aisled structure adjoining a round. More recently, in about the 1140s, the crusaders had added a new choir, again with a clearstorey elevation.[39] Might this choir and its relation to the rotunda have inspired and shaped the extension of the London chancel? Such a conclusion would be plausible only if those responsible for the work in London thought in terms of a ground plan regardless of elevation or exterior volumes. Despite Richard Krautheimer's famous essay on medieval copies, not much about this kind of thought process is really known.[40]

There is in Jerusalem a second possible iconographic model for the London chancel.[41] Soon after their establishment, the Templars were given residence in King Baldwin's palace, located in the aisled Aqsa Mosque on the Temple Mount (Fig. 5). Under the crusaders the mosque was referred to as the Temple of Solomon, and the Templars became known as the Knights of the Temple of Solomon of Jerusalem. The Augustinian canons, who had control of the nearby Dome of the Rock (then known as the Temple of the Lord), allocated space to the Templars for their services.[42] Might the multi-aisled 'Temple of Solomon' and the octagonal 'Temple of the Lord', built almost on a single axis on the same platform, have been regarded in Templar minds as associated buildings?[43] At this distance it is hard to know how closely coupled the two structures may have been in medieval minds. They were some distance apart, in different precincts, and under different control, but both were visible and present every day up on the Mount. Taken together they might, to some degree, have informed the enlargement of the

[39] For plans of the several stages of building at the Holy Sepulchre, see R. Ousterhout, 'Architecture as Relic and the Construction of Sanctity: the Stones of the Holy Sepulchre', *Journal of the Society of Architectural Historians*, 62, 2003, 4–23; Folda, *Art*, 177–245.

[40] R. Krautheimer, 'Introduction to an "Iconography of Mediaeval Architecture"', in *Studies*, 115–50 (reprinted from *Journal of the Warburg and Courtauld Institutes*, 5, 1942, 1–33).

[41] I appreciate Carol Krinsky's help in discussing the Jerusalem material.

[42] Folda, *Art*, 78.

[43] Krautheimer, 'Iconography', 118–19, explained how medieval minds equated a polygon with a circle.

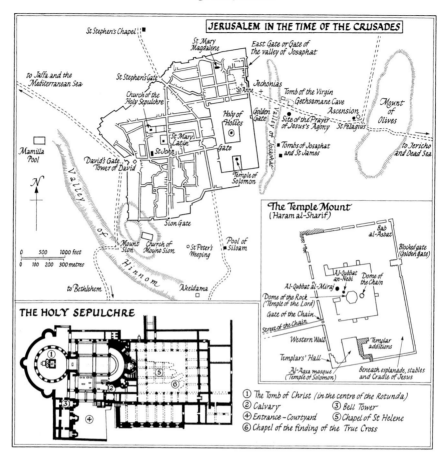

FIGURE 5. Jerusalem in the Time of the Crusades

London Temple.[44] If the Mount's buildings had formed a potent symbol, however, it would surely have been deployed more than just once, in London.[45] Moreover, when Jerusalem was back in crusader hands in 1229–44, the Temple Mount itself remained under Muslim control.[46]

[44] Rather than regarding such a conflation of models as confused, one might conceive of it as mixed, or 'co-associated', in this way extending John Wilkinson's idea that the reused capitals in the crusader choir attached to the Holy Sepulchre 'came from the Haram, perhaps from the Al-Aqsa Mosque', as relayed in Ousterhout, 'Architecture', 18–19, where Ousterhout notes that the columns could have been consciously and symbolically linked with the Temple of Jerusalem as well. Similarly 'co-associated' was the building shape between the Holy Sepulchre and the *Templum Domini* on the Mount.

[45] The assumption that London is the only example is based, of course, on present knowledge.

[46] Dondi, *Liturgy*, 87 and n. 67. In the forefront entering Jerusalem in 1229 was the bishop of Winchester, Peter des Roches, who played key roles in King Henry's minority government, as noted below; N. Vincent, *Peter Des Roches: an Alien in English Politics, 1205–1238*, Cambridge 1996, 25, and J. Crook, *Winchester Cathedral*, Andover 2001, 22.

The practicalities of structure

Whatever meanings lie behind the form of the choir, the practical consequences of joining two dissimilar sections engender further thoughts. One reason for attaching a simple, single-aisled chancel to a round is to avoid overshadowing the more meaningful
form with the greater height that a basilica would present;[47] the hall type provides additional space in an aisled structure but keeps to a low silhouette. With nearly the same
width as the nave, the current choir of the Temple harmonizes so well with the nave
that this match might supply the entire explanation of the choir's hall form, particularly
for those who emphasise the structure of buildings.

Once more, the hall type

Nonetheless, there are instances of hall churches near the Temple Church that need to
be considered. After a fire in 1212, the Augustinian priory of Southwark was rebuilt
with a two-bay, four-aisled retrochoir in hall form at the east end. The priory was situated within the diocese of Winchester and enjoyed the patronage of the bishops of
Winchester, whose palace is situated immediately to the west.[48]

Despite triplet lancets, moulded capitals, simple quadripartite vaulting and four-
shafted thin piers, the precedent of a hall at Southwark does not cast significant light
on the Temple's choir. The small, low space at Southwark essentially serves to provide
access to the chapels at the east end; it is not itself a choir. This type is developed from
outer crypts, a different tradition from the larger, independent space of the Temple
choir.[49]

Surely more relevant is the work of the Hospitallers of St John's of Jerusalem
at Clerkenwell. They were rebuilding their choir attached to a round nave at about
the same time as the Templars were building the nave and first chancel of their New
Temple Church.[50] As the Templars would rebuild their choir a few decades later, the

---

[47] Stuart Harrison, pers. comm., proposed thinking about the relationship of the sections.
Despite the Holy Sepulchre, few examples of basilican attachments to rounds exist, according to
G. Schwering-Illert, *Die ehemalige französische Abteikirche Saint-Sauveur in Charroux (Vienne) im 11. und
12. Jh.: ein Vorschlag zur Rekonstruktion und Deutung der romanischen Bauteile*, Düsseldorf 1963, 78 and
n. 100, and figs. 36–7, where the rectangular arms of Benedictine Charroux were reconstructed with
a one-storey elevation, but the eleventh-century church of St Michael's in Fulda included a clearstorey (fig. 52).

[48] S. C. Kaines-Smith, 'Southwark Cathedral', in *Victoria History of the Counties of England, Surrey*, IV, London 1912, 153–8, who mentioned that the vaults were restored and the detached shafts
were originally of Purbeck; see also Draper, 'The Retrochoir of Winchester', 9. Similarly, the Cistercian line of retrochoirs are additive spaces, e.g. at Abbey Dore.

[49] For these developments, see M. F. Hearn, 'The Rectangular Ambulatory in English Mediaeval Architecture', *Journal of the Society of Architectural Historians*, 30, 1971, 187–208, esp. 196–200,
and on Southwark, the Temple, and Winchester, 206; Hearn relates crypt developments to choir
plans in general, 202 and 205.

[50] Sloane and Malcolm, *Excavations*, 43–57. The dedication at Clerkenwell in 1185, like that of

Hospitallers transformed their choir from a single-aisled chancel to a three-aisled church (Fig. 4). It is unclear what elevation its clustered piers supported, but the small four-bay choir might not have been a basilican structure.[51] Could it have been a hall church? The excavation report left the issue open, simply commenting, 'There may originally have been a clerestory above the central aisle.'[52] Possibly; but when the choir was remodelled in the late fifteenth or early sixteenth century, its exterior profile looked like an aisled hall, its dimensions similar to those of the Temple choir.[53] The evidence suggests the possibility of a hall structure even if such a conclusion remains speculative. If St John's had been a hall church, it would have provided an immediate architectural and monastic typological model for the Temple choir.

At this point, it is time to reconsider the eastern addition, traditionally referred to as a retrochoir, to the apse of Winchester Cathedral (Plate 40). Usually, a retrochoir is a minor affair, as the Southwark or Cistercian examples show, but the Winchester supplement is unusual, more like a separate church and even slightly larger than the Temple choir itself.[54] Although the retrochoir is not so long as the Temple choir, it is as

---

the Temple Church, by the patriarch of Jerusalem Heraclius was a ceremonial act that cannot be used for precise dating, ibid., 42; Godfrey, 'Discoveries', 125; and see Wilson, pp. 20–21 above.

[51] Sloane and Malcolm, *Excavations*, 47, listed .81m (nearly 32″) for the pier diameter.

[52] Ibid., 51. I am grateful to Stuart Harrison for discussing this issue with me.

[53] Ibid., 43 and 46, described the late-twelfth-century choir as 21.7m long × 15.8m wide (71.176′ × 51.824′), with a general bay length of 5.12m (16.794′, nearly the same as the Temple's of 17′). The late medieval height I estimated at roughly 12.5m (41.01′), as measured from fig. 110 in Sloane and Malcolm, *Excavations*, 156–7, i.e., only slightly taller than the internal height of the Temple choir of approximately 37′; cf. ibid., 132, 154, and 156–9: figs. 110–11. The late medieval exterior is shown in the Utrecht Panorama of the later sixteenth century and in Hollar's engraving of 1661, illustrated ibid., figs. 145–6.

At the conference it was queried whether the first New Temple chancel might have had an aisle on the north side to correspond in plan to the rectangular chamber on the south (which is partly below ground-level and thus not an aisle) and to what at Clerkenwell appear in plan as aisles. Godfrey, 'Discoveries', 128, states that nothing to the north was found; moreover, at Clerkenwell it is only at the crypt level that flanking chambers (rather than an aisle) existed on the north; there is a south aisle there and at the choir level aisles, where Sloane and Malcolm, *Excavations*, 46, found pier bases *in situ*. They suggest (56) that the middle northern room of the crypt served as a treasury; Godfrey, 'Discoveries', 130, had suggested that the southern crypt-like chamber at the Temple had been a treasury. He believed that this function was taken over by the undercroft of St Anne's Chapel. St Anne's was built after the nave, sometime in the decades around *c.*1200, to judge by the architecture painted by J. C. Buckler. Specifically, a crocket capital with square abacus looks similar to some of the small capitals in the Trinity Chapel and Corona at Canterbury Cathedral, and circular moulded capitals are reminiscent of those on the tomb of Archbishop Hubert Walter (died 1205) in Canterbury. For the copy of Buckler's watercolour showing the chapel just before its demolition, see Plate 43.

[54] The use of 'retrochoir' to refer to a separate space behind (east of) the high altar, is modern; the medieval usage referred to a reserved area *west* of the choir. See J. H. Parker, *A Glossary of Terms used in Grecian, Roman, Italian, and Gothic Architecture*, 5th edn, Oxford 1850, 386; Parker's work was based on Du Cange's *Glossarium*.

spacious and as high.[55] It was under construction in c.1200–1235, just before the Temple choir was begun and in a period when Henry III was frequently staying in Winchester.[56] Its purpose may have been to offer not only generous access to both St Swithun's tomb located behind the high altar and other relics in the eastern chapels but also to provide an impressive burial site for the patron, Bishop Geoffrey de Lucy, originally entombed in the eastern bay of the centre aisle.[57]

The model of the Winchester retrochoir was surely meaningful for the king. Not only was 'Henry of Winchester' born in the royal castle there in 1207 and baptized in the cathedral, but also Bishop Peter des Roches, under whose episcopate most of the Winchester eastern end was built, had been variously Henry's tutor, guardian, and mentor as well as a leader in Henry's minority government from 1212 to 1221, and then the King's close government advisor from 1231 to 1234.[58] If the Templars' choir lacks the episcopal richness of the Winchester retrochoir, the architecture followed its majesty of space and adopted details such as piers of Purbeck marble, foiled forms, and quadripartite vaulting with central bosses. In accordance with Templar principles, however, the cathedral opulence was transformed into an edifice light and pure.

CONCLUSIONS

How might the various possibilities here presented be disentangled and evaluated? Given the destruction of Templar records in 1381, there is little or no evidence for most suppositions.[59] It is unknown who the designers of the choir were and whether they were working principally for the king or the Templars, or both. One might assume, however, that the Templars paid the masons since royal records show no indication of the king's financial role in this instance. The rebuilding may have occurred owing to a straightforward sense that the mid-twelfth-century chancel was too small and perhaps too old for the major role that the Temple was playing in thirteenth-century London. If the decision were taken to retain the priests' quarters to the east and to widen the Church and not (as in Paris) to lengthen it, then the Templars would have been led to the practical solution of an aisled building such as the Hospitallers had just built close by.

[55] P. Draper and R. K. Morris, 'The Development of the East End of Winchester Cathedral from the 13th to the 16th Century', in *Winchester Cathedral: Nine Hundred Years*, 178, explain that the Winchester retrochoir was meant to be four bays long, not the present three. It is actually slightly taller than the Temple choir: the central aisle rises to almost 43' whereas the aisle vaults are about 37' 2" high. Originally, the space may have been designed as a basilica. I thank John Crook for providing me with the heights and for showing me the complicated evidence for a basilica.

[56] See n. 13 above.

[57] Draper, 'The Retrochoir of Winchester', 12, and Crook, *Winchester Cathedral*, 21.

[58] D. A. Carpenter, *The Minority of Henry III*, London 1990, *passim*, esp. 17, 53, 106, 131, 238; Vincent, esp. 10, 71, and chap. 5.

[59] Williamson, *Temple*, 89–90; Lewer and Dark, *Temple Church*, 55.

The architectural forms of the Temple choir, however, tie in closely with what seems to be a kind of governmental or 'court' style in the early part of Henry III's reign, in the 1220s and 1230s, even if the word 'court' must be very loosely understood for this period. This milieu accords with Henry's desire to be buried in the Temple Church, underscored after his marriage in 1236, when it was decided that Queen Eleanor of Provence would also be buried here.[60]

Might then the Temple choir be understood not only as the appropriate height and width for a chancel attached to the round nave, but also, and more specifically, as a spacious setting for the tomb of the king just beginning his reign in his own right? It seems that in 1231 it was Henry's particular desire to live throughout eternity close to his beloved friend and brother-in-law, William Marshal the Younger, who was himself entombed next to his renowned father, the Marshal.[61] After a tumultuous minority, the king undoubtedly would have appreciated the security within the Temple, a place where he had often stayed during his youth;[62] and in a variety of capacities the Templars had long been trusted servants of the Crown.[63]

Even though the Marshal tombs were most probably placed in the nave, either Henry or the Templars might have found it more appropriate for a king to be buried in a specially marked space in the choir.[64] There may have been simple considerations of

[60] Williamson, *Temple*, 21, citing William Dugdale, *Monasticon*, VI, 818. Also see Nicholson, *Knights Templar*, 175, who thinks that the choir enlargement was meant to serve as 'a royal mausoleum'.

[61] Paris, *Chronica*, III, 201, recorded the king's emotional response at seeing William's corpse and the information that William was interred next to his father.

[62] T. Craib, 'The Itinerary of King Henry III, 1216–1272', ed. S. Brindle and S. Priestley, unpublished, English Heritage 1999; after 1227, no further stays were noted in the 'Itinerary', nor in the *Calendar of the Fine Rolls*, as marked by the issuance of charters and orders; the activity of government was now being run from royal residences. Furthermore, in 1219, for example, the king's revenues were sent to the Temple; Carpenter, *Minority*, 130. Carpenter also stresses Henry's feelings of insecurity (62).

[63] H. Nicholson, 'The Military Orders and the Kings of England in the Twelfth and Thirteenth Centuries', in *From Clermont to Jerusalem: the Crusades and Crusader Societies 1095–1500* (Selected Proceedings of the International Medieval Congress, University of Leeds 1995), ed. A. V. Murray, Turnhout 1998, 203–18; and eadem, *Knights Templar*, 161–70, esp. 162 (Henry's almoner from 1229–40, the Templar Geoffrey, served also as his keeper of the wardrobe).

[64] For discussion of the original location of the Marshal family burials, see Park, pp. 77–9, 82 below. The Marshal was said to have been buried in the 'middle of the church' ('in medio ecclesiae honorifice tumulatus') according to Matthew Paris, *Historia Anglorum*, ed. F. Madden, Rolls Series 44, 3 vols., London 1866–9, II, 232, and 'in front of the cross in the church' ('Dedevant la croiz del moster, Leiz le liu al buen chevalier, Cel qui frere Willeme a non') in the *History of William Marshal* (Anglo-Norman Text Society Occasional Publications Series 4–6), ed. A. J. Holden, trans. S. Gregory, notes by D. Crouch, 3 vols., London 2002–6, II, lines 18415–17. Since the Templars were most probably restricted to the nave, it is highly likely that the Marshal men were buried there among the brothers. Burial in the nave would also follow the model of Christ buried in the Holy Sepulchre. Further, when the elder Marshal's tomb was opened in 1240 (Paris, *Chronica*, IV, 493–5), there was no mention that the tomb had been moved; this weak argument *ex silentio* also nods slightly toward an original placement in the nave.

size. The Templars would have faced the prospect of a royal tomb (and after Henry's marriage in 1236, two tombs) in a space 25′ wide that was already required for the offices, mass and pilgrims. A larger traffic in visitors could be expected. Thus, the Templars had good reason to widen and lengthen the choir.

Yet the choir's form as a hall church enlarges the discussion by pointing to other traditions: to the development of east ends to mark tombs and shrines of special note and to create spacious areas to accommodate visitors. Templar commanderies officially opened their chapels to patrons once a year. But in London the church was also and more frequently open to accommodate pilgrims viewing the relics of Christ and the saints, Christians seeking indulgences, many eminent and governmental visitors dealing with a variety of business, and those attending mass.[65] More specifically, an aisled hall was a type associated with the burial of saints and patrons in the Winchester retrochoir and probably in the Trinity Chapel of Salisbury. Such a form might well have appealed to an emotional and religious king such as Henry III, who eventually was first entombed in the very coffin of St Edward the Confessor near the high altar at Westminster Abbey.[66] It may also be decisive that the body of the king's father was moved in 1232 to a location before the high altar at Worcester Cathedral between Saints Oswald and Wulfstan.[67]

As so often, it remains unclear how many of these factors were operative in the creation and design of the Templars' new choir. If the Hospitallers' choir of St John, Clerkenwell, was a hall church, it would have provided an essential model from the architecture of a companion Military Order. Whether there were also distant allusions to typologies in Jerusalem can only be surmised. I have doubts about any such model despite the crusaders' recent recapture of Jerusalem. Unlike the clear resonance of the Holy Sepulchre in the nave, the hall-church choir bears no readily comprehensible relationship to structures in Jerusalem. More likely a combination of motives lay behind the building of a hall church. These include such aspects as making space for three altars, for visits to the king's tomb near relics like his father's tomb, which was situated between saints, and for retention of the priests' quarters east of the church. These may have been fused with resonances of distinctive burial spaces for special figures, such as those for a bishop of Winchester and one of Salisbury. Selecting only one solution seems reductionist when many issues were circulating that the hall-church type resolves

[65] Lees, *Records*, p. lvi; Nicholson, 'Relations between Houses', and pers. comm.

[66] A slight hint toward this line of thinking might be seen in Henry's wail at viewing the corpse of William Marshal the Younger and connecting it with his comment that St Thomas of Canterbury had been vindicated, as reported by Paris, *Chronica*, III, 201; in this regard, recall that the Temple possessed the sword that had killed Becket. Although not documented, it is likely that the Trinity Chapel at Salisbury was meant for the saintly remains of Osmund, finally canonised in 1457. Tim Tatton-Brown asserts that Osmund was meant for the centre of the chapel in 'The Burial Places of St Osmund', *Spire*, 69th Annual Report of the Friends of Salisbury Cathedral, 1999, 21, and in *Salisbury Cathedral: the Making of a Medieval Masterpiece*, 48. For Henry III's burial at Westminster, see Carpenter, *Reign*, 428, and n. 7 above.

[67] U. Engel, *Worcester Cathedral: an Architectural History*, Chichester 2007, 207–8. I am very grateful to Dr Engel for providing me with a copy of her book.

better than other forms. Because this structure was specific to the needs of the London situation, it is unsurprising that it has not been found in Templar churches elsewhere. Whereas much has been recovered about the history of the Templars and their church in London, much remains obscure. Yet obscurity, in addition to beauty, significance and history, enhances the fascination with the Temple Church.

David Park

Medieval Burials and Monuments

EW CHURCHES IN ENGLAND are more famous for their medieval monuments than the Temple Church. While Philip Lankester's paper in this volume provides a detailed discussion of the thirteenth-century military effigies, this chapter will focus on the evidence that burials and monuments at the church provide not only for medieval attitudes to death and commemoration in general, but also for specifically Templar attitudes. It will also show how they throw light on other aspects of the church and the London Temple as a whole, including its foundation. With the exception of some of the thirteenth-century effigies discussed in Lankester's paper, it will consider all the most important medieval monuments in the church, concluding with a particularly fine example which — uniquely — was never associated with a burial there.

ST HUGH OF LINCOLN (D. 1200)

It is necessary, however, to start with the burial of the bowels of St Hugh of Lincoln at the Old Temple in Holborn in 1200. Hugh's main place of burial was of course Lincoln Cathedral, which as a result developed into a major pilgrimage site, and where his funeral procession is shown in the thirteenth-century stained glass.[1] Although only his bowels were buried at the Old Temple, and almost forty years after the Templars' move to the New Temple in 1161, the episode is interesting for several reasons, not least for the rare evidence it provides for the Old Temple itself.

In 1161 the Old Temple site was bought by the bishop of Lincoln, and thereafter used as the bishops' town house.[2] St Hugh died there in 1200, and a lengthy account

For help in the preparation of this paper, I am much indebted to Sharon Cather, Robin Griffith-Jones, Virginia Jansen, Philip Lankester, Helen Nicholson and Christopher Wilson. Valuable advice on particular points has also kindly been provided by Janet Burton, Anna Eavis, John Goodall, Catherine Walden, and Paul Williamson.

[1] J. Lafond, 'The Stained Glass Decoration of Lincoln Cathedral in the Thirteenth Century', *Archaeological Journal*, 103, 1946, 137–8.

[2] Nicholson, p. 2 above; Wilson, p. 21 above.

of his death and funeral appears in the *Life* written by Adam of Eynsham, an eyewitness to these events.[3] It was decided to remove Hugh's bowels before the body was taken to Lincoln — a normal hygienic precaution at this time if a corpse had to be transported a considerable distance[4] — but most unusually Adam's account provides a picture of the argument which occurred over whether it was proper to do so: 'by the advice of his doctors and in spite of strong opposition from others who felt that it was wrong, his bowels were removed from his body because it had to be taken a long distance for burial'.[5] The *Life* tells us that Hugh's bowels 'shone like glass', a common topos at this period in referring to saints' bodies.[6]

More importantly, in our context, the account of Hugh's death provides valuable but strangely neglected evidence for the Old Temple itself. Its record that Hugh's bowels were 'placed in a leaden casket and honourably interred under a marble slab near the altar steps in the church of the Old Temple which is dedicated to the blessed Mary' is the only evidence for such steps.[7] In his account of a strange vision he experienced on the night of Hugh's death, Adam also provides a detailed description of the surroundings of the chamber where Hugh died, including a garden, an orchard, a cemetery, a ditch blocked with undergrowth, and 'a remarkably tall and beautiful pear tree', which throws interesting light on the setting of an earlier 'burial' at the Old Temple, which must now be examined.

GEOFFREY DE MANDEVILLE (D. 1144)

The only 'burial' known to have occurred at the Old Temple while it was still in Templar hands was in fact not a burial at all, and has always been regarded as a particularly bizarre episode. Analysis of this episode, however, not only indicates the probable founder of the Old Temple, but also its likely foundation date, while also throwing

---

[3] Adam of Eynsham, *Magna Vita Sancti Hugonis: the Life of St Hugh of Lincoln*, ed. and trans. D. Douie and D. H. Farmer, ii, Oxford 1985, 184–232.

[4] See D. Westerhof, 'Celebrating Fragmentation: the Presence of Aristocratic Body Parts in Monastic Houses in Twelfth- and Thirteenth-Century England', in *Sepulturae Cistercienses: Burial, Memorial and Patronage in Medieval Cistercian Monasteries* (Cîteaux: Textes et documents; 56, fasc. 1–4), J. Hall and C. Kratzke, eds., Cîteaux 2005, 39.

[5] Douie and Farmer, *Magna Vita Sancti Hugonis*, 217–18. For a general discussion of anxiety in the twelfth and thirteenth centuries concerning bodily partition, see C. W. Bynum, *The Resurrection of the Body in Western Christianity, 200–1336*, New York 1995, 205–6.

[6] Bynum, *Resurrection of the Body*, 209–10; for Ailred of Rievaulx's flesh described as 'clearer than glass', see *The Life of Ailred of Rievaulx by Walter Daniel*, ed. and trans. F. M. Powicke, London 1950, 62.

[7] Douie and Farmer, *Magna Vita Sancti Hugonis*, 218, where however the editors fail to translate 'Vetus' in 'eadem ecclesia Beate Marie ad Vetus Templum'; hence the mistaken implication in R. Bartlett, *England under the Norman and Angevin Kings, 1075–1225*, Oxford 2000, 597, that the burial occurred at the present Temple Church.

entirely new light on the most notorious baron of the Anarchy of King Stephen's reign — Geoffrey de Mandeville, earl of Essex — who, it transpires, died a Templar.

Excommunicated following his sack of Ramsey Abbey in 1143, Geoffrey died the following year at Mildenhall in Suffolk after receiving a fatal wound at the siege of Burwell Castle. Details of his 'burial' at the Old Temple are provided both by the twelfth-century chronicle of Ramsey Abbey itself and by the chronicle composed after 1163 at the Benedictine priory founded by Geoffrey at Walden in Essex. Predictably, both are biased: the former against Geoffrey, and the latter against the Templars who deprived Walden of their founder's body. According to the Ramsey Chronicle, the body of the excommunicate Geoffrey was sealed in a box and thrown in a pit or ditch outside the cemetery of the Old Temple.[8] A different and more detailed account is provided by the Walden chronicler:

> . . . when he was on the point of death and drawing his last breath, some Templars arrived on the scene who laid upon him the habit of their order marked with the red cross; then when he was dead, they took his body away with them, encased it in a lead waterpipe and hung it from a tree growing wild in their orchard at the Old Temple.[9]

Geoffrey's body remained at the Old Temple for almost twenty years, until, as we shall see, it was transferred to the New Temple and buried there. Whether it was swinging from a tree for all that time is uncertain, but the Walden account is so graphic that it is perhaps more reliable than the Ramsey version, and it is even possible that the tree was the very fruit tree described in Adam of Eynsham's vision at the Old Temple on the night of St Hugh's death.[10] The use of lead to encase the body, and the care taken to avoid actually burying it, would also accord with the canon of the Legatine Council of London (probably 1143) prohibiting the burial of excommunicates 'within churchyards either in stone or wood'.[11]

Yet the story still seems very strange. Does the Walden account that while Geoffrey was dying 'some Templars arrived on the scene' tell the whole story, and if so why did they take him all the way to London? The same chronicler goes on to record that the Templars 'laid upon him the habit of their order marked with the red cross', which would signify that the dying Geoffrey was received into the Templar Order, just as in 1219 William Marshal was to be received into the Order by receiving the mantle on his

[8] *Chronicon Abbatiae Rameseiensis*, ed. W. D. Macray, RS 83, London 1886, 332: 'Corpus vero defuncti comitis in trunco quodam signatum, et propter anathema quo fuerat innodatus Londiniis apud Vetus Templum extra cimiterium in antro quodam projectum est.'

[9] *The Book of the Foundation of Walden Monastery*, ed. and trans. D. Greenway and L. Watkiss, Oxford 1999, 18–19: 'Illo autem in discrimine mortis ultimum trahente spiritum, quidam superuenere Templarii, qui religionis sue habitum cruce rubea signatum ei imposuerunt, ac deinde iam mortuum secum tollentes et in pomerio suo Veteris scilicet Templi apud London canali inclusum plumbeo in arbore torua suspenderant.'

[10] See p. 68 above.

[11] *Councils and Synods with Other Documents Relating to the English Church*, I (871–1204), ed. D. Whitelock, M. Brett and C. N. L Brooke, Oxford 1981, I, pt. ii, 801.

deathbed.[12] And just as William's deathbed was attended by the Master of the Temple in England, so it appears that Geoffrey's deathbed was attended by the leading Templar in England of his time. The evidence for the latter is provided by a charter of Geoffrey's, confirming land to Holy Trinity, Aldgate, in London.[13] Two of the witnesses are doctors, suggesting — as first noted by Round — that the grant to Holy Trinity is likely to be a restitution made on Geoffrey's deathbed.[14] Prominent among the witnesses is 'Payn of the Temple', identifiable as Payen de Montdidier, one of the leading Templars of the day. Described in 1130 as master of the Templars in France 'north of the Loire', Payen subsequently came to England, and appears as witness to grants to Templar preceptories.[15] He also witnessed Geoffrey's foundation charter of c.1140 for Walden Priory.[16] The likelihood is, therefore, that it was Payen who arranged for Geoffrey's body to be taken to the Old Temple. But why transport it all the way to London, when it could more easily have been taken to the Templar preceptory at Cressing in Essex? If the foundation dates of Templar preceptories throughout Europe are considered, virtually all are of the mid 1130s or later; even Paris is as late as 1146.[17] Although the foundation of the Old Temple in London is often assigned to 1128 or shortly thereafter,[18] such a date would be uniquely early. But there is no evidence for such an early foundation date, a year before the Order was formally established at the Council of Troyes. It is merely an inference from the visit of the founder of the Order, Hugh de Payns, to England in 1128. But all the *Anglo-Saxon Chronicle* says of this visit is that Henry I 'sent him to England and there he was received by all good men and they all gave him treasure'.[19] Even if some rudimentary establishment was created then at Holborn, it would not have had a church or cemetery, which were only permitted to the Templars by the papal bull *Omne datum optimum* of 1139.[20] All the other early Templar preceptories in England were founded in Stephen's reign, during which Payen de Montdidier was active, and

[12] See p. 77 below. If taken literally, the description of the habit in Geoffrey's case as 'marked with the red cross' would be of particular interest as the earliest known reference to the Templars' distinctive mantle. William of Tyre (writing in the 1180s) attributed their adoption of the cross to the time of Pope Eugenius III (1145–53): 'in the time of Pope Eugenius, it is said, they started to sew on their mantles crosses of red cloth to make them more distinctive'; M. Barber and K. Bate, *The Templars: Selected Sources Translated and Annotated*, Manchester and New York 2002, 26.

[13] *English Historical Documents, II, 1042–1189*, ed. D. C. Douglas and G. W. Greenaway, London 1968, 952–3.

[14] J. H. Round, *The Commune of London and Other Studies*, London 1899, 100.

[15] R. Barber, *The New Knighthood: a History of the Order of the Temple*, Cambridge 1994, 20–21; Lees, *Records*, 180, 231–2.

[16] Greenway and Watkiss, *Book of the Foundation*, appendix 2, 169–72.

[17] For a convenient map, see R. Barber, *New Knighthood*, fig. 2.

[18] See, for example, A. Grakiis, 'Anglo-Norman England and the Holy Land', in *Anglo-Norman Studies*, VII (Proceedings of the Battle Conference, 1984), ed. R. A. Brown, Woodbridge 1985, 141; C. W. Hollister, *Henry I*, New Haven and London 2001, 412.

[19] See also Henry of Huntingdon, *The History of the English People 1000–1154*, trans. and ed. D. Greenway, Oxford 1996, 61: 'Hugh of Payns, master of the knights of the Temple at Jerusalem, came to England and took with him many to Jerusalem.'

[20] *Papsturkunden für Templer und Johanniter*, ed. R. Hiestand, Vorarbeiten zum Oriens Pontif-

it is much more likely that this was also true of the Old Temple.[21] This would make its church approximately contemporary with the Hospitallers' church in London, with its similar circular nave.[22] If the Old Temple was founded in or around the early 1140s, who is more likely to have been the founder than Geoffrey de Mandeville, especially in his role of constable of the Tower of London, which 'virtually gave him the control of the capital' before he was forced to surrender the office in 1143?[23] If Geoffrey was the founder of the Old Temple, this would not only explain why his body was taken there, but also — if the Walden chronicler is to be trusted — the temporary expedient of hanging his body from a tree (since he was excommunicate), and the subsequent trouble taken by the Templars to transfer his body to the New Temple.

In 1163 Geoffrey's absolution from excommunication was finally obtained by his son from Pope Alexander III, and his body was transferred to the New Temple for Christian burial, despite the efforts of the prior of Walden to transfer it there.[24] As has been emphasised by Christopher Wilson, this is the earliest evidence for the existence of a church at the New Temple.[25] The Walden chronicle says that the body was consigned to 'a somewhat ignoble grave in the cemetery',[26] whereas later medieval Walden accounts which partly derive from the chronicle say that it was buried in the west porch,[27] which still exists. As Wilson argues, even the chronicle's reference to the cemetery could in fact mean the porch, and as emphasised by him this porch is exceptionally elaborate. Geoffrey's burial here, combined with all the other evidence, yet again seems to underline his status as founder or at least major patron of the London Temple.

But would the founder of the Temple have been buried in the cemetery or the porch, a location described by the Walden chronicler as 'somewhat ignoble'? From the late eleventh century onward, the normal burial location for a founder and his kin was either the choir or, more normally, the chapter house.[28] Thus, Geoffrey's own eldest

icius, vol. 1, Abhandlungen der Akademie der Wissenschaften zu Göttingen, 77, Göttingen 1972, no. 3, 204–10. For interpretation of the relevant wording of *Omne datum optimum*, see n. 37 below.

[21] The foundation of the preceptory at Shipley (Sussex) is dated to 1134–9, so it might be marginally earlier. For the foundation of monastic houses generally in Stephen's reign, at 'a rate unequalled in any other period', see R. H. C. Davis, *King Stephen 1135–1154*, London 1967, 88; see also D. Knowles, *The Monastic Order in England . . . 940–1216*, 2nd ed., Cambridge 1963, 297–8.

[22] For the Hospitallers' church, see Wilson, p. 20 and n. 5 above.

[23] A. L. Poole, *Domesday Book to Magna Carta 1087–1216*, 2nd ed., Oxford 1954, 146–7.

[24] Greenway and Watkiss, *Book of the Foundation*, 18–19. Characteristically, the Walden chronicler attributes the grant of absolution to the efforts of the prior of Walden, though it was achieved by Geoffrey's son making restitution to Ramsey Abbey; Macray, *Chronicon Abbatiae Rameseiensis*, 332–3.

[25] Wilson, pp. 21–2 above. See also the indulgence by Thomas Becket referring to 'Domum Templi que Londoniis super Tamesem fluuium sita est', which may date from the beginning of his archbishopric in 1162; Lees, *Records*, 162–3.

[26] Greenway and Watkiss, *Book of the Foundation*, 18–19.

[27] BL, Arundel MS 51, fol. 17; BL, Cotton MS Titus D xx, fol. 74[r–v]: 'cuius corpus iacet London humatum apud Templebar in porticu ante hostium ecclesie occidentalis'.

[28] The chapter house seems, from the surviving evidence, to have been more usual. See also a thirteenth-century Tewkesbury chronicler's remark that it was the normal place for nobles to be buried; B. Golding, 'Anglo-Norman Knightly Burials', in *The Ideals and Practice of Medieval Knighthood*

son, Geoffrey de Mandeville III, was buried 'between the high altar and the choir' of Walden Priory in 1166.[29] Even by the time of the Council of Mainz in 813, the Church's traditional hostility to burial inside churches was weakening, permitting the internal burial of not only bishops and abbots, but also 'fideles laici' (that is, kings, princes, patrons and founders).[30] Liminal burial, in the porch or under the eaves of a church, would often have had a penitential purpose, as captured in a letter by Baudri of Bourgeuil, archbishop of Dol (1107–30): 'so that the soaking of the dripping drops running off the holy roof should wash the bones' of sin.[31] Burial specifically at an entrance would have been designed to attract the prayers of the religious entering and exiting, as made explicit in the case of the burial of Henry I's concubine Ansfrid at Abingdon Abbey, 'in claustro ante ostium ecclesiae, ubi fratres intrant in ecclesia, et exeunt'.[32] We can well imagine that such prayers were felt to be needed for the notorious and only recently absolved Geoffrey de Mandeville, about whom even the Walden Chronicler felt a certain queasiness, ending his account of his later career and death: 'the more monstrous a man may appear in human estimation because of his more serious sins, the more earnest should be everybody's prayer on his behalf'.[33] Such a motive may also explain the external burial of the similarly notorious Hugh d'Avranches, earl of Chester — nicknamed 'the Wolf' for his violence to the Welsh — who was buried in the cemetery of the Benedictine abbey he founded at Chester.[34] But explicit evidence that a founder could himself wish to be buried at an entrance for penitential reasons is provided by the case of Duke Richard I of Normandy at Fécamp Abbey in 996, who donned a penitent's hair shirt shortly before his death, and when asked where he wished to be buried, responded 'So wicked a corpse ought not to rest within the entrance of this temple, but at that doorway, under the eaves of the monastery.'[35] Duke Richard II (d. 1026) was

(Papers from the first and second Strawberry Hill Conferences), ed. C. Harper-Bill and R. Harvey, Woodbridge 1986, 42. The Temple, of course, had no chapter house.

[29] Greenway and Watkiss, *Book of the Foundation*, 40–41.

[30] For this, and earlier opposition to internal burial, see C. Wilson, 'The Medieval Monuments', in *A History of Canterbury Cathedral*, ed. P. Collinson, N. Ramsay and M. Sparks, Oxford 1995, 453 n. 8.

[31] *Dudo of St Quentin: History of the Normans*, ed. and trans. E. Christiansen, Woodbridge 1998, 227 n. 490.

[32] *Chronicon Monasterii de Abingdon*, ed, J. Stevenson, 2 vols., RS 2, London 1858, vol. 2, 124; 122–3; D. Postles, 'Monastic Burials of Non-Patronal Lay Benefactors', *Journal of Ecclesiastical History*, 47, 1996, 629.

[33] Greenway and Watkiss, *Book of the Foundation*, 18–19.

[34] Hugh was subsequently reinterred in the chapter house by his nephew. It is unclear whether there was any penitential aspect to two other cases which might be mentioned: the burial in 1102 of Walter Giffard, earl of Buckingham, at the entrance of the church ('In introitu uero basilicae') of his Cluniac foundation of Longueville in Normandy (*The Ecclesiastical History of Orderic Vitalis*, VI, ed. and trans. M. Chibnall, Oxford 1978, 36–7); and the burial of Cecily (wife of William d'Aubigné who died in or after 1148) 'under the wall' ('sub pariete') at Belvoir. For both these examples, and for a general discussion of the burial of founders and their kin, see Golding, 'Anglo-Norman Knightly Burials', 35–48, esp. 43, 46.

[35] Christiansen, *Dudo of St Quentin*, 171.

subsequently buried in the same location, but in 1162 Henry II expressed grief at the lowly burial of his ancestors — echoing the 'ignoble' epithet of the Walden chronicler — and had their remains removed to the choir, to the richly carved sarcophagus that survives there today.[36]

Although Geoffrey de Mandeville's external burial most likely had penitential connotations, this was not the principal reason for its location. While Henry II was able to move his ancestors into the choir at Fécamp, and the prior of Walden would likewise have been able to bury Geoffrey in the choir of his Essex priory, this was because both were Benedictine foundations, in which such burials were commonplace. In Templar churches, by contrast, it appears that no one was buried internally before the end of the twelfth century, not even brothers.[37] Consequently, Geoffrey simply could *not* have been buried inside. Although the detailed French text of the Templar *Rule* does not specifically forbid internal burials, it assumes that all burials would be in the cemetery; for example, article 541 referring to prayers for benefactors, says that 'he should pray . . . especially for those who lie in our cemeteries'.[38] All other early Templar documents referring to burial likewise appear to refer only to cemeteries, and in terms of surviving physical evidence it may be that the late twelfth-century carved grave cover at the New Temple, discussed below, constitutes the earliest evidence of internal burial in a Templar church. In their early opposition to internal burial, the Templars were doubt- less influenced, as was so often the case, by the Cistercians, who maintained a stricter attitude to internal lay burial than any other monastic order, first permitting it in their legislation in a statute of 1180.[39] Consequently, Cistercian founders were often buried

[36] For the thirteenth-century poem describing the transference of the remains, and for the twelfth-century sarcophagus to which they were moved, see S. E. Jones, 'The Twelfth-Century Re- liefs from Fécamp: New Evidence for their Dating and Original Purpose', *JBAA*, 138, 1985, 79–88. The original burial place of Richard I was under the eaves on the south side of the church, where Richard II built a mortuary chapel and was himself buried; see Christiansen, *Dudo of St Quentin*, 227 n. 494.

[37] *Omne datum optimum* (1139) states 'We equally grant permission to build oratories in places adjacent to the Holy Temple where your company lives in which it may hear the divine offices and where any of you of that household may be buried after death', and a subsequent bull, *Milites Dei* (1145), uses similar wording, 'we grant them permission to build oratories in places adjacent to it [the Temple], where indeed the household lives, in which to hear the divine services and for the burial of any brother or sergeant who dies'. However, *Milites Dei* goes on to say 'we recommend and instruct your brotherhood that when requested by these brothers you consecrate these oratories without any ill will and bless the cemeteries in the aforesaid places for the burial of this household' (translations from Barber and Bate, *The Templars: Selected Sources*, 63, 66). It therefore seems clear that both bulls are referring to cemeteries *around* the churches, as interpreted by Barber, *New Knighthood*, 57–8.

[38] *The Rule of the Templars: the French Text of the Rule of the Order of the Knights Templar*, ed. and trans. J. Upton-Ward, Woodbridge 1992, 141.

[39] 'No-one except for a king or queen, or archbishops and bishops, is to be buried in our churches. In the chapter house abbots only, or any of the aforesaid persons'; for variant wordings of this statute, see J. Hall, S. Sneddon and N. Sohr, 'Table of Legislation concerning the Burial of Laity and Other Patrons in Cistercian Abbeys', in *Sepulturae Cistercienses*, 378. This legislation may have followed the burial of Louis VII (d. 1180) at Barbeau; A. Gajewski, 'Burial, Cult, and Construction at the Abbey Church of Clairvaux (Clairvaux III)', in *Sepulturae Cistercienses*, 57. The earliest Cistercian

in the porch, like the dukes of Burgundy at Cîteaux itself.[40] Geoffrey's burial in the cemetery or porch at the New Temple would have been entirely consistent with this quasi-Cistercian tradition, and if it was indeed in the porch — as Christoper Wilson has persuasively argued[41] — there was in fact no more prominent location in which he could have been interred. This is underlined by the unprecedented (in England) and superbly exotic nature of the porch itself, emphasised by Wilson, who argues that it imitates the similar feature of the Aedicule over Christ's own tomb in the Holy Sepulchre Church. Indeed, one motive for the exceptionally elaborate nature of the porch may well have been provided by the founder's burial there.

In summary, therefore, there can be little doubt that the turbulent Geoffrey de Mandeville was the founder of the Temple in London. All the evidence fits: the much greater likelihood that the Old Temple was founded not at the uniquely early date of 1128, but c.1140 when Payen de Montdidier was in England; the presence of Payen himself at Geoffrey's deathbed, when Geoffrey became a Templar; the transference of his body from East Anglia to the Old Temple in London, the city where Geoffrey had been pre-eminent; its careful preservation there for almost twenty years; Geoffrey's absolution and transference to the New Temple at precisely the right moment; and his probable interment in the porch there, the most privileged location in which he could have been buried. *Contra* J. H. Round's ironical comment that 'around the nameless resting-place of the great champion of anarchy, there was destined to rise, in later days, the home of English law',[42] there was every reason for Geoffrey to be buried at the New Temple.

RICHARD OF HASTINGS? (D. C.1185)

The earliest monument inside the church is the carved Purbeck marble grave cover on the north side of the nave (Plate 44). It may well have always been inside, since it is much more elaborate than any of the grave covers still surviving outside the church. Its *dos d'âne* ('ass's-back') form is comparable to the Purbeck marble tomb at Winchester now attributed to Bishop Henry of Blois (d. 1171),[43] but its decoration is considerably

---

reference to the burial of founders is in a statute probably of c.1179 — 'For burial, none may be received except founders' — but this does not refer explicitly to internal burial. In 1198 the abbot of Vauluisant was condemned to light penance for burying his founder in the chapter house, but no condemnation of founders' burials occurs after this date.

[40] M-F. Damongeot and M. Plouvier, 'Cîteaux-nécropole: la "Saint-Denis bourguignonne"', in *Pour une histoire monumentale de l'abbaye de Cîteaux*, ed. M. Plouvier and A. Saint-Denis, Dijon 1998, 281–307. For the geography of burial in northern English Cistercian houses, including burial in the church porch, see M. Cassidy-Welch, *Monastic Spaces and their Meanings: Thirteenth-Century Cistercian Monasteries*, Turnhout 2001, 232–6.

[41] Wilson, p. 22 above.

[42] J. H. Round, *Geoffrey de Mandeville: a Study of the Anarchy*, London 1892, 226.

[43] J. Crook, 'The "Rufus Tomb" in Winchester Cathedral', *Antiquaries Journal*, 79, 1999, 187–212, especially 192. For a similar twelfth-century coped marble slab decorated with foliate or-

richer, with a ridge-swallowing lion's head at one end and a 'ram's' head at the other, and stylised foliage dateable to c.1180.[44]

The 'ram's' head indicates the type of person who must have been commemorated by the tomb, since — despite its ferocious appearance, with tongue lolling out — its identity can be established through comparison with Templar seals. The Agnus Dei was the symbol of the Masters of the Temple in England, and invariably employed on their seals, where its horns give it an even more ferocious appearance than on the tomb — a fitting symbol for the monks of war. It appears, for example, on the seal of Richard of Hastings, Master in England from the 1150s to the 1180s, and it therefore seems very likely that it is Richard whom this Purbeck marble tomb commemorates.[45]

As Wilson has shown, it was probably Richard who was responsible for the building of the New Temple church in c.1160, characterised by its lavish use of Purbeck marble.[46] The iconography of its richly carved west doorway can be interpreted partly in the light of the tomb, since the innermost order appears originally to have featured alternating rams' heads and lions' heads.[47] The former are likely to have referred to the Templars, with the alternation perhaps suggesting a contrast between good and evil.[48] If so, this would add further weight to Zarnecki's interpretation of the curious half-length figures at the top of the columns as representing Christians contrasted with Muslims; as he observed, it appears from Nash's pre-restoration drawings of c.1818 (Plate 89) that the figures on the north side were shown with turbans, and also with buttons — a detail associated in the West before the fourteenth century with pagan figures.[49]

nament, see N. Saul, 'The Medieval Monuments of Rochester Cathedral' in *Medieval Art, Architecture and Archaeology at Rochester* (British Archaeological Association Conference Transactions, xxviii), ed. T. Ayers and T. Tatton-Brown, Leeds 2006, 166, fig. 1.

[44] Crook, 'The "Rufus Tomb"', 192, suggests that the ridge on the cover of the Winchester tomb may originally have terminated in foliate bosses or animal heads.

[45] For illustrations of relevant seals, see Nicholson, *Knights Templar*, pls. 6c, 6d (Richard of Hastings), and pl. 8a. The date of Richard's death is uncertain; although Lees, *Records*, p. lvii, suggests that he went on pilgrimage to the Holy Land in the 1180s, the evidence is not compelling.

[46] Wilson, pp. 23–4, 28 above.

[47] Although the doorway was heavily restored in the nineteenth century, two of the original voussoirs survive in the Victoria and Albert Museum; P. Williamson, *Catalogue of Romanesque Sculpture [in the Victoria and Albert Museum, London]*, London 1983, nos. 45–46, pp. 96–8. The restoration is discussed by Griffith-Jones, pp. 211–16 below, and see also Plate 102.

[48] I am indebted to Paul Williamson for suggesting the Templar significance of the voussoirs to me.

[49] G. Zarnecki, 'The West Doorway of the Temple Church in London', in *Beiträge zur Kunst des Mittelalters: Festschrift für Hans Wentzel zum 60. Geburtstag*, Berlin 1975, 252–3. Excellent reproductions of Nash's drawings are provided by Griffith-Jones, *Temple Church*, 18–19.

AIMERY OF ST MAUR (D. 1219) AND WILLIAM MARSHAL I (D. 1219)

In considering the thirteenth-century monuments at the Temple, there has been much debate about which effigies commemorate whom, and also concerning their original location — in particular, were they in the nave, as they are now? Crucial evidence that they were indeed in the nave is provided by the earliest documented burials in the church: those of Aimery de Saint-Maur, one of Richard's successors as Master of the Temple in England, and William Marshal, earl of Pembroke and the greatest knight of his age, both of whom died in 1219. The same evidence is also invaluable for what was once another major feature of the church: the rood.

The main evidence for William's burial, and the only evidence for Aimery's, is provided by the work known as *L'Histoire de Guillaume le Maréchal*. The *Life* is an astonishing work — an unparalleled biography of a non-royal layman of the period, comprising 19,214 lines in rhyming couplets in Middle French. It was completed no later than 1229, under the patronage of William's eldest son.[50] The *Life* devotes more than a thousand lines to the death of William at his manor of Caversham near Reading, and his funeral procession to London and burial at the Temple. It tells us that William had already assigned his body to the Templars many years earlier: 'when I was away in the Holy Land, I gave my body to be buried by the Templars at the time of my death, in whatever place I happened to die ... with the Templars is where I shall lie, for so I have vowed and arranged it'.[51] We further learn that he had brought back from the Holy Land precious silks 'to be draped over my body when I am laid in the earth'.[52] The *Life* also tells us that William composed his will on his deathbed, and supplies many touching details of how he was surrounded by his family and knights, of how his daughters sang for him, and of how he was shown the cross before he died.[53] Of particular sig-

---

[50] *Life of William Marshal*, III, 3–5; see also D. Crouch, *William Marshal: Knighthood, War and Chivalry, 1147–1219*, 2nd edn, Harlow 2002, 1–11.

[51] *Life of William Marshal*, II, 414–15, lines 18233–43. This must have been during his two-year sojourn in the Holy Land in the 1180s, of which little else is known.

[52] *Life of William Marshal*, II, 410–13, lines 18183–224; 414–15, lines 18251–56. This was no doubt a common practice; for the silks found in the tomb of Archbishop Hubert Walter (d. 1205) at Canterbury, and the suggestion that these may have been among the gifts to Hubert by Saladin during the Third Crusade, see N. Stratford, P. Tudor-Craig and A. M. Muthesius, 'Archbishop Hubert Walter's tomb and its furnishings', in *Medieval Art and Architecture at Canterbury before 1220* (British Archaeological Association Conference Transactions, v), London 1982, 74, 79 n. 18, 80–87, pls. XVIII–XXIII; M. Henig, 'Archbishop Hubert Walter's Gems', *JBAA*, 136, 1983, 60. William Marshal himself provided silk(s) for the tomb of King John; see J. Martindale, 'The Sword on the Stone: Some Resonances of a Medieval Symbol of Power (The Tomb of King John in Worcester Cathedral)', in *Anglo-Norman Studies*, xv (Proceedings of the Battle Conference 1992), ed. M. Chibnall, Woodbridge 1993, 205 and n. 16.

[53] The best English pictorial parallel for this deathbed scene, with the dying figure similarly surrounded by family members and being shown the cross, was a mid-thirteenth-century tomb painting formerly at Starston (Norfolk); E. W. Tristram, *English Wall Painting of the Fourteenth Century*, London 1955, 251–2, pl. 56a (where however it is wrongly dated to the fourteenth century).

nificance for our purposes is the account of Aimery de Saint-Maur's visit to the dying man, at which William formally became a Templar, to the distress of his wife and family. William informed the assembled company that 'It is some time since I pledged myself to the Temple, and now I wish to become a monk in it', and to this end instructed his almoner, Geoffrey (a Templar) to bring him the cloak that he had 'made for him a year before, keeping it in his possession without anyone else knowing of its existence'.[54] Following William's death, his body was brought to the Temple after resting at Reading Abbey, Staines, and a further night at Westminster Abbey, where there was a vigil and mass.[55] His funeral at the Temple, probably on 20 May 1219,[56] was presided over by the archbishop of Canterbury, Stephen Langton, and 'As the Marshal had willed it with his own voice, the grave was in front of the cross alongside that of brother Aimery de Saint-Maur, his friend.'[57] As for Aimery, we are told that on returning to London after visiting William on his deathbed, he had contracted an illness and died himself, which the *Life* oddly describes as 'no laughing matter'.[58]

The *Life* also records that, before Aimery died, 'he said that, in the love of God, he wished to be buried in front of the cross in the church, "next to the resting place of that worthy knight brother William the Marshal"'.[59] This oft-repeated phrase — 'in front of the cross' — is crucial. It does not mean in front of a cross on an altar, but is the standard phrase for burial in the nave before the rood. This was always one of the most desirable locations for burials, and there are many examples of episcopal burials in this position — for example, Lanfranc (d. 1089) and Anselm (d. 1109) at Canterbury.[60] An amusing case from the fourteenth century is that of William Courtenay, archbishop of Canterbury (d. 1396), whose eagerness to be buried in this position at Exeter Cathedral led him to state in his will the wish that the three deans already buried there should be disinterred and buried elsewhere at his expense.[61] But burial in this location was by no means confined to ecclesiastics: notable lay examples include Queen Margaret of Scotland (d. 1093), who was buried 'over against (*contra*) the altar and the venerable sign

---

[54] *Life of William Marshal*, II, 420–21, lines 18351–87. For the similar use of the Templar mantle at Geoffrey de Mandeville's deathbed, see p. 69 above.

[55] *Life of William Marshal*, II, 452–55, lines 18997–19038; III, 193–4. For the location of the vigil and mass at Westminster Abbey, see *Chronicles of the Reigns of Stephen, Henry II and Richard I*, ed. R. Howlett, 4 vols., RS 82, London 1884–9, II, 526.

[56] *Life of William Marshal*, III, 194.

[57] *Life of William Marshal*, II, 454–5, lines 19043–6.

[58] *Life of William Marshal*, II, 420–25, lines 18409–29. The view that Aimery died abroad (*The Victoria History of the Counties of England: London*, I, London 1909, 490) is clearly mistaken.

[59] *Life of William Marshal*, II, 422–3, lines 18413–18.

[60] K. Blockley, M. Sparks and T. Tatton-Brown, *Canterbury Cathedral Nave: Archaeology, History and Architecture*, Canterbury 1997, 121, fig. 53. Other early examples of bishops buried 'ante crucifixum' include Sampson (d. 1112) and Theulf (d. 1123) at Worcester; U. Engel, *Worcester Cathedral: an Architectural History*, Chichester 2007, 57. Richard, abbot of Saint-Évroul, was buried 'ante crucifixum' at Thorney Abbey in 1140; Chibnall, *Orderic*, VI, 536–9.

[61] C. Daniells, *Death and Burial in England 1066–1550*, London and New York 1997, 95–6. In the event, Courtenay was buried in the even more prestigious location of the choir at Canterbury, beside Becket's shrine; Wilson, 'Medieval Monuments', 472–5, pl. 112.

of the Holy Cross' at Dunfermline Abbey in accordance with her wishes;[62] and Count Geoffrey of Anjou, who was buried before the rood in Le Mans Cathedral in 1151, and commemorated by a celebrated enamel tomb plaque which still survives.[63] Even for the Temple Church, there is a will as late as 1524 expressing the wish to be buried 'afore the Roode'.[64]

It is clear, therefore, that there was a rood at the Temple by 1219, which must have been placed between the nave and the choir, and that Aimery and William were buried in the nave in front of it. No roods of such an early date survive in England, though there is ample evidence for their former existence; for example, the 'great cross' erected at Canterbury Cathedral in the late eleventh century, flanked by 'two cherubim, and the images of St Mary, and St John the Apostle'.[65] However, continental examples such as that at Halberstadt (c.1215–20), with its resurrecting figure of Adam at the base, provide the explanation for why such a burial location was so desirable: the intercessory nature of Christ's sacrifice on the cross, and the hope that the deceased lying at its foot would arise like Adam to be saved.[66] In many cases, as at Canterbury, there was an altar of the Holy Cross before the rood, facing the nave, though whether this was so at the Temple is uncertain.[67] In medieval sources, this position was often described as 'in medio ec-

[62] E. Fernie, 'The Romanesque Churches of Dunfermline Abbey', in *Medieval Art and Architecture in the Diocese of St Andrews* (British Archaeological Conference Transactions, XIV), ed. J. Higgitt, London 1994, 28–30.

[63] For Robert of Torigni's reference to Geoffrey's burial 'before the crucifix', see *Church Historians of England, vol. 4, pt 2: The History of William of Newburgh; The Chronicles of Robert de Monte*, trans. J. Stevenson, London 1856, 727. Other twelfth-century lay examples include William d'Aubigné (d. in or after 1148), buried 'before the cross' at Belvoir (Golding, 'Anglo-Norman Knightly Burials', 42–3), and 'the lesser members of the lineage [of the counts of Eu] in the twelfth century, about a dozen of them, . . . customarily laid before the roods of the abbey churches of Foucarmont and Eu'; D. Crouch, *The Birth of Nobility: Constructing Aristocracy in England and France 900–1300*, Harlow 2005, 164. For many other examples from throughout the medieval period, see A. Vallance, *Greater English Church Screens*, London 1947, esp. 3–4; also 28, 47, 61, 79, 94, 101, 105, 133, 156.

[64] R. Newcourt, *Repertorium Ecclesiasticum Parochiale Londinense*, London 1708–10; for Philip Tredeneck's will of 1524, see the annotations by Challoner Smith opposite p. 545 in the interleaved copy at the Society of Antiquaries. I am indebted to Robin Griffith-Jones for this reference.

[65] For a general discussion, see C. Davidson Cragoe, 'Belief and Patronage in the English Parish before 1300: Some Evidence from Roods', *Architectural History*, 48, 2005, 21–48. Fragments of a twelfth-century figure of Christ from South Cerney (Gloucestershire) may derive from a rood.

[66] For the Halberstadt rood, see P. Williamson, *Gothic Sculpture 1140–1300*, New Haven and London, 83, 288 n. 69, pl. 125. A similar iconography appears in England in the Crucifixion miniature of the mid-thirteenth-century Amesbury Psalter (Oxford, All Souls College MS 6, fol. 5), which Morgan suggests may have been derived from a rood sculpture; N. Morgan, *Early Gothic Manuscripts [II] 1250–1285* (A Survey of Manuscripts Illuminated in the British Isles, 5), London 1988, 60, ill. 29.

[67] For altars of the Holy Cross, and the redemptive function of burial before the rood, see K. Imesch, 'The Altar of the Holy Cross and the Ideal of Adam's Progeny: "*ut paradysiace loca possideat regionis*"', in *Death and Dying in the Middle Ages*, ed. E. E. DuBruck and B. I Gusick, New York 1999, 73–106.

clesiae' — that is, between the nave and the chancel.[68] This phrase was employed by Matthew Paris in describing the location of William Marshal's burial at the Temple,[69] providing further confirmation that William and Aimery were buried before the rood.

The present paper will not in general consider which effigies might commemorate whom — a thorny problem discussed by Philip Lankester — but there does appear to be a strong case for interpreting one of them as William Marshal. This is the celebrated effigy which has normally been interpreted as his since 1843 (Plates 45, 57).[70] Several factors appear to support this interpretation. The effigy is undoubtedly one of the earliest at the Temple, and is distinguished from the others in various ways: its more formal, frontal pose; the depiction of the figure as holding an unsheathed sword at his side, with which he pierces the head of a lion at his feet; his polygonal rather than merely square cushion; and the lush foliage flanking the cushion. The only other Purbeck effigy similarly shown holding a sword downwards and piercing a lion at his feet is that of King John at Worcester, dating from about the time of his translation to the choir in 1232.[71] As often observed, John's effigy is stylistically similar to the figures on the west front of Wells Cathedral, dating from c.1220–30.[72] Many of the crowned figures at Wells are shown wearing a large pennanular brooch,[73] and exactly the same type of brooch is a distinctive feature of the Temple effigy. But its occurrence here on the surcoat of a knight appears to be unparalleled, and is again suggestive of the special status of this figure. There is, however, another feature which points particularly strongly to the identification of this figure as William Marshal: the face is shown as *old*. Richardson remarked on its 'aged' features,[74] and these are unmistakeable: the wrinkled brow, and deep lines etched from either side of the nose (Colour Plate IV). Such a representation of old age is most unusual, since effigies at this period normally show the deceased at the ideal age at which it was believed the resurrection of the body would occur.[75] But

---

[68] Imesch, 'Altar of the Holy Cross', 75; F. Oswald, '*In medio Ecclesiae*: die Deutung der literarischen Zeugnisse im Lichte archäologischer Funde', *Frühmittelalterliche Studien*, 3, 1969, 313–26.

[69] Matthew Paris, *Historia Anglorum*, ed. F. D. Madden, 3 vols., RS 44, London 1866–69, II, 232.

[70] Richardson, *Effigies of the Temple Church*, 22–3, pl. 6. In the sixteenth century, Stow identified one of the 'crosse legged' effigies as William Marshal (*A Survey of London by John Stow reprinted from the text of 1603*, ed. C. L. Kingsford, Oxford 1908, 51), but his account, ending 'these are all that I can remember to haue read of', seems highly unreliable. See also Lankester, pp. 112–13, 117–18 below.

[71] Martindale, 'Sword on the Stone', 237, and for a discussion of the rarity of early monuments with the deceased shown holding a drawn sword, ibid., 223–37. Further examples appeared in the spectacular series of twelfth-century patronal monuments to the Beaumont family at Préaux in Normandy, now lost but illustrated in an eighteenth-century woodcut. Two held a sword in front of their bodies to pierce the dragon at their feet; see Crouch, *Birth of Nobility*, 165 n. 19, pl. 4.

[72] For King John's tomb, see Williamson, *Gothic Sculpture*, 111, pl. 170; for the similarity of the effigy to William Marshal's, Martindale, 'Sword on the Stone', 237.

[73] See, for example, P. Tudor-Craig, *One Half of our Noblest Art: a Study of the Sculptures of Wells West Front*, Wells 1976, pl. 10.

[74] Richardson, *Effigies of the Temple Church*, 22.

[75] For the concept of resurrection at the perfect age, see Bynum, *Resurrection of the Body*, 77, 98 ff., 122 n. 15; S. Oosterwijk, '"A Swithe Feire Graue": the Appearance of Children on Medieval

since William Marshal was famous for living to an advanced age — actually seventy-two, though he claimed to be over eighty when attempting to refuse the regency in 1216 — it would be an appropriate way of distinguishing his effigy. It appears that only one other Purbeck effigy of the period deliberately characterises the deceased as old: that of Bishop Giles de Bridport (d. 1262) at Salisbury. Marion Roberts has drawn attention to the wrinkles around the bishop's eyes and mouth, and his sagging jowls, but the depiction of age is still much less explicit than in the Temple effigy.[76] Although, stylistically, it is conceivable that the latter could be as early as William's death in 1219, the parallels cited at Worcester and Wells suggest a slightly later date of c.1225–30. But this need not worry us. As with King John, a significant amount of time frequently elapsed between the date of death and the erection of a funerary monument. This is a theme that will recur at the end of this paper, but it is also worth bearing in mind in relation to William's own sons, in relation to whom the strange subsequent history of their father's tomb will also be considered.

ROBERT DE ROS (D. 1226/7)
AND ROBERT DE VIEUXPONT (D. 1227/8)

Before considering William Marshal's sons, however, we need to address the cases of Robert de Ros and Robert de Vieuxpont, two of the leading barons of the reign of King John and the minority of Henry III. Both were prominent 'Northerners', the former married to an illegitimate daughter of William the Lion of Scotland and generally loyal to King John before 1215, though subsequently a leading opponent and one of the twenty-five barons elected to ensure the observance of the provisions of Magna Carta.[77] Robert de Vieuxpont, a grandson of one of Becket's assassins, was a protégé of King John's and by 1207 'probably the greatest pluralist in the country'; in the civil war at the end of the reign, he was a leading member of the royal government.[78]

Robert de Ros has been said to have been buried in the Temple Church since at least the sixteenth century, when Stow recorded that '*Robert Rose*, otherwise called *Fursan*, being made a Templar in the yeare 1245. dyed and was buried there'.[79] Although

Tomb Monuments', in *Family and Dynasty in Late Medieval England* (Harlaxton Medieval Studies, IX), ed. R. Eales and S. Tyas, Donington 2003, 180–87.

[76] Caroline Walden kindly drew my attention to the Salisbury example; see M. E. Roberts, 'The Tomb of Giles de Bridport in Salisbury Cathedral', *Art Bulletin*, 65, 1983, 567. Exceptionally early instances of old age depicted in effigies occurred in the twelfth-century series at Préaux, where the eleventh-century ancestors of the Beaumont earls were distinguished by staffs and, in one case, a long beard; Crouch, *Birth of Nobility*, 165, pl. 4.

[77] B. English, *The Lords of Holderness, 1086–1260*, Oxford 1979, 37–9, 151–2; J. C. Holt, *The Northerners: a Study in the Reign of King John*, corrected edn, Oxford 1992, esp. 24–6; *ODNB*, vol. 47, 725–6.

[78] Holt, *The Northerners*, 220–21, 226–8; *ODNB*, vol. 56, 464–5.

[79] *A Survey of London by John Stow*, 51.

Robert de Ros was indeed nicknamed Fursan (or Furfan), he died in 1226 or 1227, and no other evidence connects him directly with the Temple Church. Moreover, Robert established the Templar preceptory at Ribston (Yorkshire) at the end of his life; the charter of 1226 survives whereby he gave the Templars various gifts including the manor and advowson of the church at Ribston, and his body for burial, for the maintenance of the Holy Land: 'Hoc autem donum feci Deo et sancte Marie et predictis fratribus militie templi. cum corpore meo. Et ad sustentationem sancte terre orientalis.'[80] At first sight, this would seem to indicate that he gave his body to Ribston, but from the phrasing it is evident that Robert was bequeathing his body not to a particular preceptory but to the *Order*, just as William Marshal had done earlier.[81] Indeed, it is clear that at the end of his life, like William Marshal and Geoffrey de Mandeville, Robert actually became a Templar, since he is referred to as 'brother'.[82] From the combined evidence therefore — the phrasing of Robert's charter, the fact that the Ribston preceptory was only barely established by the time of his death, and the antiquarian evidence dating back to Stow — we must suppose that the tradition of his burial in the Temple Church is correct.

One of the witnesses of Robert de Ros's charter of 1226 was Robert de Vieuxpont, himself dead by February 1228. In 1227 he too bequeathed his body to the Templars, together with his estate at Wycombe (Buckinghamshire); as in the case of Geoffrey de Mandeville's grant to Holy Trinity, Aldgate, a doctor was a witness to this bequest, suggesting that Robert was already close to death.[83] Since his widow, Idonea, made a bequest to support a chaplain at the Temple Church to pray for her own soul and that of her husband,[84] it seems very likely that Robert de Vieuxpont was buried there.

Whether any of the existing military effigies commemorate de Ros or de Vieuxpont is impossible to say, though none shows the distinctive de Ros heraldry displayed by the fourteenth-century effigy in the nave, which commemorates an altogether different member of the family.[85]

[80] *Early Yorkshire Charters, X: The Trussebut Fee with Some Charters of the Ros Fee*, ed. C. T. Clay, 1955, 40–41; for Robert de Ros and Ribston, see also J. E. Burton, 'The Knights Templar in Yorkshire in the Twelfth Century: a Reassessment', *Northern History*, 27, 1991, 38–9.

[81] I am indebted to Janet Burton for discussing Robert's intentions with me. For William Marshal, see p. 76 above.

[82] Thus, a confirmation of his gifts by his aunt includes the phrase 'pro anima fratris Roberti de Ros nepotis mei'; *Early Yorkshire Charters*, 42; Burton, 'Knights Templar in Yorkshire', 39.

[83] *ODNB*, vol. 56, 465.

[84] BL, Cotton MS Nero E. vi, fol. 30ᵛ (fifteenth-century Cartulary of the Hospitallers in England; W. Dugdale, *Monasticon Anglicanum*, ed. J. Caley and H. Ellis, 6 vols. in 8, London 1817–30, vi, pt. ii, 818.

[85] See pp. 88–91 below.

William Marshal II (d. 1231), Gilbert Marshal (d. 1241), and the Temple as a 'Marshal mausoleum'

Two of William Marshal's five sons were buried at the Temple. The first was his eldest son, also named William, who was the patron of his father's biography and who died in London in 1231. The other was William's fourth son, Gilbert, who died at an illicit tournament in Hertford in 1241; a celebrated drawing by Matthew Paris shows Gilbert being dragged to his death after his harness had broken.[86] As in St Hugh's case, Gilbert's bowels were buried locally — in the Benedictine priory at Hertford — before his corpse was taken to its resting place at the Temple.

Matthew Paris records that William was buried next to his father ('juxta patrem suum'), and Gilbert next to his father and brother ('juxta patrem suum et fratrem').[87] In all probability, therefore, this means the nave, and it may well be that they are commemorated by two of the existing effigies. One plausible candidate is the effigy with the lion carved on his shield (Plates 46, 60B), since the Marshal arms were a red lion rampant on a gold and green field. This is the only thirteenth-century effigy at the Temple still displaying authentic heraldry, and remains of red were recorded on the surface of the shield by Richardson, which — as Philip Lankester observes — is precisely what would be expected as a ground for gold.[88] Although Lankester observes that the drapery style of the effigy suggests that it is unlikely to date from before the late 1250s,[89] it could have been erected somewhat later than the date of death. If so, Gilbert would seem the most likely candidate.

The Temple was clearly becoming something of a Marshal mausoleum, with the sons being buried there — 'near' their father — if possible. But this was not always possible. William's second son, Richard, was killed in Ireland in 1234 while in rebellion against Henry III, and was buried at Kilkenny.[90] The two youngest sons — Walter and Anselm — died in 1251 at Goodrich and Chepstow respectively, and were buried at nearby Tintern, a Cistercian monastery of which the family were patrons.[91] Remarkably, therefore, despite William's having had five sons, the male line of the Marshal family ran out in the early 1250s. This was attributed by contemporaries to a curse connected with a dispute over their lands in Ireland. For, even more remarkably, William Marshal himself — generally regarded as the paradigm of the perfect knight — had died excommunicate, like Geoffrey de Mandeville before him. This was the result of a dispute with

---

[86] Cambridge, Corpus Christi College MS 16, fol. 147ᵛ; S. Lewis, *The Art of Matthew Paris in the* Chronica Majora, Berkeley, Los Angeles and London 1987, 236–8, fig. 152.

[87] Paris, *Chronica*, III, 201; IV, 136.

[88] Lankester, p. 116 below.

[89] Ibid., pp. 128–9 below.

[90] A. Gwynn and R. N. Hadcock, *Medieval Religious Houses: Ireland*, London 1970, 226, 252.

[91] For effigies at Tintern which might well commemorate them, see D. M. Robinson, *The Cistercians in Wales: Architecture and Archaeology 1130–1540*, London 2006, 278 and n. 18, fig. 183.

the Bishop of Ferns over property, which continued to fester under William's sons.[92] Matthew Paris provides a vivid account of the extraordinary episode when the bishop and Henry III visited the Temple Church after William's death, with the bishop still refusing to absolve him.[93]

In 1245, according to Matthew Paris, William Marshal the Elder's tomb was opened and his body found corrupt.[94] This has sometimes been taken as evidence that William's tomb was affected by the recent rebuilding of the choir, but as we have seen William was buried in the nave, so his tomb must have been opened for other reasons. We now need to consider the new choir as the proposed burial place of Henry III, and the relevance of Henry's relationship with the Marshal family.

HENRY III (D. 1272) AND ELEANOR OF PROVENCE (D. 1291): TWO NON-BURIALS AT THE TEMPLE

In 1231 Henry made a grant to 'St. Mary and the master and brethren of the Temple, to whom the king has entrusted his body for burial after his mortal end', and in 1236 confirmed that he 'has given his body after his death to St. Mary and the house of the knights Templars of London there to be buried; and if hereafter the king shall found any religious house, the said house shall not oppose the burial as aforesaid'.[95] David Carpenter has suggested that Henry's decision to be buried at the Temple was influenced by his close friendship with William Marshal the Younger, whose death in 1231 he mourned deeply.[96] Royal commitment to the Temple was underscored after Henry's marriage to Eleanor of Provence in 1236, when she also affirmed her wish to be buried there.[97] In the event, of course, neither were buried at the Temple: Henry changed his mind in favour of Westminster Abbey, while Eleanor was buried in 1291 at the nunnery of Amesbury in Wiltshire.[98]

Whatever Henry's original motive, it seems very likely that the new choir at the Temple — consecrated in his presence in 1240 — was intended from the outset to form his burial place. It is not known when the choir was begun, but as Virginia Jansen has shown, this may well have been at about the time Henry first affirmed his wish to be

[92] For the dispute with Ailbe (Albinus), bishop of Ferns from 1186 to 1223, see Gwynn and Hadcock, *Medieval Religious Houses: Ireland*, 79; Crouch, *William Marshal*, 114.

[93] Paris, *Chronica*, IV, 493–4.

[94] Paris, *Chronica*, IV, 495.

[95] *Calendar of the Charter Rolls Preserved in the Public Record Office, I: Henry III, A.D. 1226–1257*, London 1903, 135, 210–11.

[96] D. A. Carpenter, *The Reign of Henry III*, London and Rio Grande 1996, 433–4.

[97] BL Cotton MS Nero E. VI, fol. 25 (Cartulary of the Hospitallers in England), transcribed by Dugdale, *Monasticon Anglicanum*, VI, 818: 'Alianora Dei gratia regina Angliae . . . postquam diem clauserimus extremum, corpus nostrum in praedicta domo militiae Templi, debitae, sicut praedictum est, tradatur sepulturae.'

[98] M. Howell, *Eleanor of Provence: Queenship in Thirteenth-Century England*, Oxford 1998, 309–12.

buried there.[99] There can be no doubt that Henry would have intended to be buried in the choir rather than the nave, just as his father was buried in the choir at Worcester, and his Angevin ancestors in the nuns' choir at Fontevraud. It appears that the new choir was appropriately decorated to house a royal tomb, since John Aubrey (writing in c.1670) recorded that 'the Scutcheons in the Temple-church are as those in our Ladies ch at Sal. Viz. G. 3 Lyons O./ The Scutcheon long and sharp pointed, as in the first order'.[100] The shields would thus have been the appropriate shape for this period, and can probably be linked with the 'few shields' mentioned as surviving in the medieval glass at the Temple in the mid nineteenth century.[101] Although Aubrey refers specifically to the Lady Chapel at Salisbury — a building whose similarity to the Temple choir is emphasised by Jansen[102] — it is possible that he instead meant the heraldic glazing of c.1260 still surviving in the chapter house there. If so, and the Temple choir windows did indeed have such a scheme, this would be the earliest evidence for heraldic glazing in England.[103]

In 1246, however, Henry affirmed his wish to be buried in Westminster Abbey.[104] Carpenter has plausibly associated Henry's change of mind with his increasing devotion to Edward the Confessor,[105] and it is obvious that Westminster Abbey was becoming an obsession with him. An additional factor, however, may well have been Henry's changed relationship with the Marshal family. While William Marshal the Elder had been regent at the beginning of the reign, and the younger William Marshal such a loved friend that his death in 1231 led to an outpouring of grief, Henry's relationship with the other Marshals was distinctly more fraught. As already mentioned, Richard died in 1234 in rebellion against him, and Henry was even accused of his murder. Gilbert died in a tournament held against the king's wishes, and Henry harassed his successors over their inheritance. It must have seemed increasingly unattractive to Henry to be buried in a church so closely associated with the Marshal family, especially since that family seemed so ill-fated. His change of mind, however, must have been deeply disappointing to the Templars, who at his death in 1272 still claimed that his body rightfully belonged to them.[106]

[99] Jansen, p. 48 above.

[100] J. Aubrey, *Chronologia Architectonica* (Bodl., MS Top. gen. c. 25), fol. 155ᵛ (renumbered 6). I am indebted to Robin Griffith-Jones for this reference.

[101] Essex and Smirke, *Illustrations*, 6.

[102] Jansen, p. 49 above.

[103] Otherwise, the earliest recorded evidence for heraldic glazing in England is that ordered by Henry III for Rochester Castle in 1247, while the earliest surviving shields are those of c.1254–9 at Westminster Abbey; R. Marks, *Stained Glass in England during the Middle Ages*, London 1993, 10, 134–5, fig. 5. See also Jansen, pp. 52–3 above.

[104] *Calendar of Charter Rolls, 1226–1257*, 306.

[105] D. A. Carpenter, 'King Henry III and Saint Edward the Confessor: the Origins of the Cult', *English Historical Review*, 122, 2007, 871–2.

[106] *Flores Historiarum*, ed. H. R. Luard, 3 vols., RS 95, London 1890, III, 28; W. C. Jordan, *A Tale of Two Monasteries: Westminster and Saint-Denis in the Thirteenth Century*, Princeton and Oxford 2009, 154–5.

SILVESTER DE EVERDON, BISHOP OF CARLISLE? (D. 1254),
AND WILLIAM, FIFTH SON OF HENRY III? (D. 1256? OR 1259?)

Only one medieval monument now occupies the choir at the Temple: the superb mid thirteenth-century effigy of a bishop (Colour Plate v, Plates 47–8) in the south aisle. Originally situated at the east end of the aisle (Plate 49), it was placed in a recess in the south wall in the nineteenth century, and consequently escaped damage in the War. The bishop is shown blessing and holding a crosier, while the snake-like creature at his feet is actually a winged dragon. Two angels appear in the canopy, one censing and one praying. The effigy is generally similar to other mid-thirteenth-century Purbeck effigies of bishops, such as that of Archbishop Walter de Gray (d. 1255) at York. The latter is comparable in its drapery style, and in the vexillium suspended from the crosier, though the Temple figure has a much less elaborate canopy around the body, and of course no elaborate shrine-like canopy above.[107]

Whom does this effigy commemorate? It was apparently Browne Willis who first ascribed it to Bishop Silvester de Everdon of Carlisle, who died in 1254.[108] It is a strange name to pluck out of the air, and while there is no firm evidence for the identification, the date would fit. Although a mid-thirteenth-century Purbeck marble effigy of a bishop does survive at Carlisle,[109] it may commemorate Silvester's successor, Robert Vipont, who died in 1256. Circumstantial evidence might also support the identification. Although once mocked by Henry III as 'my little clerk', Silvester was an important figure at court, and keeper of the great seal for a period. He died in 1254 at Northampton while on his way to London, as a result of being thrown from his horse.[110] It is easy to envisage his entourage continuing their journey to London, bearing his corpse to the town house of the bishops of Carlisle located in the Strand, close to the Temple.[111] A curious find made when the tomb was opened in 1810 was the skeleton of an infant lying at the bishop's feet. This burial has been associated with that of William, fifth son of Henry III, who according to Sandford's *Genealogical History* was buried at the New Temple in c.1256, and thus only about two years after Silvester's death.[112] However, a recent study has cast doubt on William's existence, though shown that if he did exist

[107] The style of de Gray's effigy, and of related mid-thirteenth-century Purbeck episcopal effigies, is discussed by M. Roberts, 'The Effigy of Bishop Hugh de Northwold in Ely Cathedral', *Burlington Magazine*, 130, 1988, 77–84; see also M. Sillence, 'The Two Effigies of Archbishop Walter de Gray (d. 1255) at York Minster', *Church Monuments*, 20, 2005, 5–29.

[108] See Richardson, *Effigies of the Temple Church*, 31.

[109] For the Carlisle effigy, see J. W. Hurtig, *The Armored Gisant before 1400*, New York and London 1979, 149, pl. 254.

[110] For Silvester's career, see H. Summerson, 'The King's *Clericulus*: the Life and Career of Silvester de Everdon, Bishop of Carlisle, 1247–1254', *Northern History*, 28, 1992, 70–91.

[111] For Carlisle Inn on the Strand, see J. Wilson, *Rose Castle: the Residential Seat of the Bishop of Carlisle*, Carlisle 1912, 16–21.

[112] Richardson, *Effigies of the Temple Church*, 31. F. Sandford, *A Genealogical History of the Kings and Queens of England and Monarchs of Great Britain*, 2nd edn, London 1707, 92.

he may have died in 1259.[113] This would still, of course, be close in date to Silvester's death.

Constant de Hoverio?

Similar uncertainty concerns the existence of another individual supposedly buried at the Temple. Burton's *Description of Leicester Shire* (1622) records 'in the body of the church a large blue marble inlaid with brass, with this inscription: Hic requiescit Constantius de Hoverio quondam visitator generalis ordinis Militiae Templi in Anglia, Francia, et in . . . . . .'.[114] In Nichols's *History and Antiquities of the County of Leicester* (1804), the same inscription is recorded as ending 'et in Italia'.[115] This monument, which no longer exists, has recently been discussed by Lack and Whittemore.[116] While rightly interpreting the phrase 'the body of the church' as referring to the choir,[117] they identify the monument with the indent of a large figural brass in the nave — now lost but shown in an engraving of 1819 (Plates 50–51) — and therefore conclude that the slab must have been moved during a restoration of the church.[118]

The engraving shows a full-length figure wearing a long gown and set beneath a canopy, with six flanking shields and a surrounding marginal fillet (Plate 51). Even from the engraving, it is evident that this was a very early example of a figural brass, and since they interpret it as the memorial of 'Constance de Hover' wearing his Templar robes, Lack and Whittemore are obliged to date it before the suppression of the Order; the date they give is '*c.*1308'.[119] But there are difficulties with this interpretation. The addition of 'Italia' to the inscription first recorded by Burton is unlikely to be correct, since there was no Templar Visitor for 'England, France and Italy'; Italy was a separate province.[120] Moreover, there was no Visitor of the Order named Constant de Hoverio

---

[113] M. Howell, 'The Children of King Henry III and Eleanor of Provence', in *Thirteenth Century England IV* (Proceedings of the Newcastle upon Tyne Conference 1991), ed. P. R. Coss and S. D. Lloyd, Woodbridge 1992, 57–72, esp. 57–8, 60–61, 65–6, 70–72.

[114] W. Burton, *The Description of Leicester Shire*, London 1622, 235.

[115] J. Nichols, *The History and Antiquities of the County of Leicester*, London 1804, III, pt. 2, 945.

[116] *A Series of Monumental Brasses, Indents and Incised Slabs from the 13th to the 20th Century*, ed. W. Lack and P. Whittemore, vol. 2, pt. 3 (April 2002), 15–16.

[117] For seventeenth-century examples of the use of the phrase to refer to the choir, see *Death Records in the Register of Burials in the Temple Church, London England* (http://ancestorsatrest.com/cemetery_records/temple_church_cemetery.shtml; accessed 30 August 2009).

[118] The head of the indent is also shown in a view of the nave by Thomas Malton, of 1796 (Colour Plate VIII).

[119] Lack and Whittemore, *Series of Monumental Brasses*, 15.

[120] Barber, *New Knighthood*, 245, 380n. 80. It is possible that the record of the inscription at the Temple may have become confused with a similar inscription recorded by Weever, *Monuments* (1631) as carved on one of the effigies in the nave: 'Hic requiescit . . . R . . . Ep . . . Quondam visitator generalis ordinis Militiae Templi in Anglia et in Francia et in Italia . . .'. Weever's reference itself seems unreliable, partly since it was made not from personal observation but from a work read in Sir Robert Cotton's Library.

in the period around 1300, and indeed it is far from clear that such a figure ever existed; examination of the main Templar sources has failed to produce any such evidence.

Nevertheless, it is hard to believe that Burton invented the inscription, particularly since a few references to a Templar of the same name do exist. Foxe's Book of Martyrs refers to a Constans de Hoverio as one of two prominent Templars — the other being Richard of Hastings — who confronted Thomas Becket at the council in 1164 at which the Constitutions of Clarendon were drawn up.[121] Although this is incorrect, since Richard's companion was Osto de Saint-Omer,[122] it nevertheless suggests a memory of a Templar by this name when Foxe was writing in the sixteenth century. More to the point, perhaps, are recent references in Alias's Prosography of the Templars and on web sites to a Visitor by this name, the latter assigning him a date in the mid thirteenth century.[123] Although none of these references supply any supporting evidence, and must be treated with extreme caution, it seems unlikely that they derive from the record of the inscription at the Temple.

Burton's description does not explicitly state that the tomb showed a figure, and it is possible therefore that there was only an inscription in brass, as in the mosaic grave slabs of Margaret and John de Valence (d. 1276 and 1277) at Westminster Abbey.[124] On the other hand, the figural brass illustrated in the 1819 engraving (Plate 50) certainly appears to show a Templar in his robes, and it is likely to have had a surrounding inscription, like such other early brasses as that of Margaret de Camoys (c.1310) at Trotton, which also shows a similar arrangement of flanking shields.[125] More research is needed before such matters can be clarified, but at present the balance of evidence suggests that there was a Templar Visitor named Constant de Hoverio who was buried at the Temple. Whether the brass depicted in the engraving was his memorial or not, it was clearly one of the earliest figural brasses in England, and the only known example commemorating a Templar.

[121] J. Foxe, *Acts and Monuments: The Variorum Edition* (hriOnline, Sheffield 2004), available at http://www.hrionline.ac.uk/johnfoxe/main/4_1570_0266.jsp; 1570 edn, book 4, 266.

[122] Lees, *Records*, pp. liii–liv; F. Barlow, *Thomas Becket*, London 1986, 98–9.

[123] J.-L. Alias, *Acta Templarorium*, Fontenay-le-Comte 2002, 220, no. 2316, describing Constant de Hoverio as 'Précepteur d'outremerc [*sic*]', without any further information; http://www.templiers.net/maitres/index.php (accessed 25 May 2008) includes 'Constant de Hoverio', against the date 1242, in its list of 'Les Grands Visiteurs de France'; http://templis.free.fr/dignitai.htm (accessed 25 May 2008) cites him as a 'Visiteur Cismarin', between Hugues de Jouy (1251) and Gui de Basenville (1257–62). I am grateful to Helen Nicholson for drawing my attention to the Alias reference.

[124] P. Binski, *Westminster Abbey and the Plantagenets: Kingship and the Representation of Power, 1200–1400*, New Haven and London 1995, 113, fig. 137.

[125] For the Camoys brass, see P. Binski, 'The Stylistic Sequence of London Figure Brasses', in *The Earliest English Brasses: Patronage, Style and Workshops 1270–1350*, ed. J. Coales, London 1987, 80, fig. 62.

William de Ros? (d. 1316): an Effigy from Elsewhere

Finally, we come to an effigy without a burial. This is the splendid early fourteenth-century figure, so different in style as well as date from the others at the Temple, in the ambulatory on the south side of the nave (Plates 52–3). With its lavishly curled hair, graceful pose and gloriously detailed armour, this effigy fortunately escaped wartime damage. Although only transferred to the Temple in the seventeenth century, it merits discussion here not only as a superb work in its own right, but also because of the confusion it has engendered at its new home, and since it highlights dating issues of a type similar to those already encountered with other effigies at the Temple. Indeed, its study helps to redate many of the most important fourteenth-century effigies in northern England.

The *New View of London* (1708) records that the effigy was 'brought from York, by Mr. Serjeant Belwood, Recorder of that city, about the year 1682, and is said to be the Figure of one *Rooce*, of an honourable family'.[126] The water bougets carved on the shield confirm that the effigy does indeed commemorate a member of the Yorkshire family of de Ros. As already discussed, an earlier member of this family — Robert de Ros (d. 1226/7) — was buried at the Temple, and the present effigy is still sometimes identified as his.[127] In fact, it dates from about a century later, and was plausibly identified as William de Ros (d. 1316) by I'Anson in his systematic study of fourteenth-century Yorkshire effigies published in the 1920s.[128] Although another de Ros effigy of similar date survives in York, and may have come from the Greyfriars there,[129] the Temple effigy seems more likely to derive from the mausoleum of the main branch of the family at Kirkham Priory, to the north-east of York. The only burial there of appropriate date was that of William de Ros, one-time claimant to the Scottish throne, whose tomb was on the north side of the presbytery.[130]

---

[126] E. Hatton, *A New View of London*, ii, London 1708, 574. For a discussion of the possible circumstances of its removal to the Temple, see Griffith-Jones, pp. 171–3 below.

[127] B. English, *Lords of Holderness*, 152; *ODNB*, vol. 47, 726.

[128] W. M. I'Anson, 'Some Yorkshire Effigies', *Yorkshire Archaeological Journal*, 27, 1923–24, 137–8, pl. opp. p. 133; idem, 'The Mediaeval Military Effigies of Yorkshire (Part ii)', *Yorkshire Archaeological Journal*, 29, 1927–29, 9–10.

[129] I'Anson, 'Some Yorkshire Effigies', 136–7; this very battered effigy has been set up on Hob Moor, York, since the eighteenth century.

[130] Evidence for William's tomb is provided by a genealogy of the de Ros family, where he is described as being 'in tumba marmorea ex parte boreali' (*Cartularium Abbathiae de Rievalle*, Surtees Society, 83, 1889, ed. J. C. Atkinson, Appendix 1, 361). The word 'marble' should not be taken literally; for the limestone or sandstone used for Yorkshire effigies at this period, see B. Gittos and M. Gittos, 'Yorkshire Effigies c.1300 and their Place in English Sculpture', Pre-printed Papers of a Conference on Medieval Archaeology in Europe, University of York, vol. 7, *Art and Symbolism*, York 1992, paper G8d. It does, however, raise the possibility that the effigy rested on an elaborate tomb chest like those of the similar effigies at Bedale (see below, and Plate 55), Howden and elsewhere. For the de Ros mausoleum at Kirkham, see G. Coppack, S. Harrison and C. Hayfield, 'Kirkham Priory: the Architecture and Archaeology of an Augustinian House', *JBAA*, 148, 1995, 73, and for a plan showing

Recently, however, the effigy in the Temple has been dated to 'c.1300–03' by Brian and Moira Gittos, as part of their radical redating of Yorkshire effigies of this period. Whereas I'Anson had already recognised that the Temple effigy belonged to a group of stylistically similar monuments, which he dated partly on the grounds of their style and armour to c.1318–1330,[131] the new chronology is determined by the date of death of those known (or thought) to be commemorated by particular effigies, around which the other effigies are arranged in a supposed stylistic sequence.[132] In this new chronology, the Temple effigy belongs to the group of effigies dubbed 'Series B', a revised version of I'Anson's grouping, but now dated to c.1300–c.1317.[133] Although the individual commemorated by the Temple effigy is not identified in the Gittos studies, they regard the effigy as falling early in the stylistic sequence.[134]

The revised dating of the Temple and other Yorshire effigies has not been universally accepted.[135] In particular, Claude Blair has argued that since a detail characteristic of all the military effigies — the metal rings shown attaching the sword-scabbard to its belt — is otherwise first seen in a fully developed form in an English context on the effigy of Aymer de Valence (d. 1324) in Westminster Abbey, it is unlikely to have been represented significantly earlier in Yorkshire.[136] But the revised dating is also unconvincing on other grounds. Although the type of bare-headed praying figure seen at the Temple and in several of the related Yorkshire monuments is of French derivation, its closest parallel in England is the Setvans brass at Chartham (Kent), formerly assigned to c.1306 but now dated to c.1323;[137] indeed, at a casual glance, the de Ros effigy resembles a three-dimensional version of this famous brass. One difference is the effigy's long-sleeved surcoat, also a feature of its closest Yorkshire counterparts at Howden and East Harlsey,[138] as also the slightly more elaborate bare-headed effigies at

the position of the tombs, S. Harrison, *Kirkham Priory, North Yorkshire* (English Heritage guidebook), London 2000, 28.

[131] I'Anson, 'Some Yorkshire Effigies', 136.

[132] Although refined in numerous articles, the most comprehensive account of the new chronology is Gittos and Gittos, 'Yorkshire Effigies'; see especially its 'Summary Table' of Yorkshire effigies.

[133] Gittos and Gittos, 'Yorkshire Effigies'; see also S. Badham, B. Gittos and M. Gittos, 'The Fourteenth-century Monuments in the Saltmarshe Chapel at Howden, Yorkshire: their History and Context', *Yorkshire Archaeological Journal*, 68, 1996, 119.

[134] The figure is assigned to 'c.1300–03' in Badham, Gittos and Gittos, 'Howden', 119; see also Gittos and Gittos, 'Yorkshire Effigies', 'Summary Table'.

[135] See, e.g., R. Knowles, 'A Civilian Effigy in Birkin Church, North Yorkshire', *Yorkshire Archaeological Journal*, 57, 1985, 87–92.

[136] C. Blair, 'Yorkshire Effigies and Ring Scabbard-attachments', *Church Monuments Society Newsletter*, vol. 11, no. 1 (summer 1995), 4–5; see also the subsequent debate on this matter between Blair and Gittos and Gittos, ibid., 6; vol. 11, no. 2 (winter 1995–6), 38–40; vol. 12 (1996), 16–19.

[137] For the style and dating of the Setvans brass, see Binski, 'Stylistic Sequence', 86–90. For earlier French effigies of this type, see Hurtig, *Armored Gisant*, esp. 22, 26, pls. 9, 13, 19, 21–7.

[138] For useful drawings of these effigies, see I'Anson, 'Some Yorkshire Effigies', 122 (Howden), and idem, 'The Mediaeval Military Effigies', fig. 75 (East Harlsey).

Bedale (Yorkshire) and Norton (Durham).[139] None of these effigies is securely dated; for instance, identification of the Norton figure as Sir John de Lythegranes (d. 1303), and its consequent dating to the beginning of the fourteenth century, has recently been described as 'far from certain'.[140] Indeed, the dimunitive carved figures accompanying the Norton effigy and that at Bedale would suggest a significantly later date, anticipating the profusion of such figures on the tomb of Sir John Harrington (d. c.1347) at Cartmel Priory (Cumbria).[141] Similarly, the richly decorated swordbelts so characteristic of the group, often — as on the Temple effigy — carved with elaborate lions' masks, are closely paralleled in French effigies of the second quarter of the fourteenth century, and in an English context anticipate such later effigies as the mid fourteenth-century example at Warkworth (Northants).[142]

For our purposes, however, it is sufficient to consider the most famous of these Yorkshire effigies: that of Brian Fitzalan at Bedale (Plate 54), rightly regarded by Brian and Moira Gittos as providing 'key' evidence for dating the various effigies.[143] Although they date it to about the time of Fitzalan's death in 1306, all the stylistic evidence indicates that it is unlikely to date from before the 1320s. The nodding ogee form of the gable at the head of this effigy (and of some others of the group) is most obviously paralleled in northern England by the nodding ogees at York Minster, in the nave and on the tomb of St William, dating from c.1330–40.[144] The ballflower ornament on the gable is a type of decoration rarely found in the North; it appears to occur there first on a window of the King's Tower of Knaresborough Castle, built by London masons for Edward II in 1307–12, but is again most conspicuous in the nave of York Minster, in work most likely dating from the 1320s.[145] The elaborate tomb chest on which the effigy originally rested, carved with various figures including Fitzalan on his deathbed, and a knight wearing a short surcoat reaching only to his knees (Plate 55), again suggests a date not earlier than the 1320s.[146] The combined evidence indicates

[139] Bedale is discussed below; for Norton, see P. R. Coss, 'Heraldry and Monumental Effigies in the North East', in *Northumbrian Panorama: Studies in the History and Culture of North East England*, ed. T. E. Faulkner, London 1996, 22–6, figs. 12–13.

[140] Coss, 'Heraldry and Monumental Effigies', 26.

[141] M. Markus, '"An Attempt to Discriminate the Styles": the Sculptors of the Harrington Tomb, Cartmel', *Church Monuments*, 11, 1996, 5–24.

[142] For French examples of c.1318–20 and later, see Hurtig, *Armored Gisant*, pls. 38, 41, 49, and for Warkworth, ibid., 164, pl. 282.

[143] Gittos and Gittos, 'Yorkshire Effigies', 211.

[144] S. Brown, *'Our Magnificent Fabrick': York Minster: an Architectural History c.1220–1500*, Swindon 2003, 112–13, fig. 3.38.

[145] Brown, *'Our Magnificent Fabrick'*, 112, 117, 129, fig. 3.36; see also J. Goodall, 'A Royal Gift' [Knaresborough Castle], *Country Life*, 202, 2008, 72–4.

[146] The engraving reproduced here from E. Blore, *The Monumental Remains of Noble and Eminent Persons . . .*, London 1826, shows the tomb as re-erected in the post-medieval period with a later fourteenth-century effigy behind Fitzalan. The carvings on the tomb chest, of which only a fragment now survives, included a priest attending Fitzalan's deathbed, and the Coronation of the Virgin (both shown in Blore's engraving), and knights and ladies holding shields (illustrated in R. Gale, *Registrum Honoris de Richmond . . .*, London 1722, 242).

that this tomb was commemorative, erected substantially later than Fitzalan's death, and expressing the same sort of filial devotion as the family heraldry once displayed throughout the church in stained glass and wall painting. Although Fitzalan died in 1306 without male issue, his arms still appeared in the chancel east window, which is dateable to as late as c.1370.[147]

It is ironic that while recent scholarship has assigned the military brasses of this period to some twenty years later than previously thought, the finest series of contemporary effigies — which are so similar to the brasses in many respects — have been redated in the reverse direction.[148] At Bedale, the lapse of time between death and commemoration need not surprise us. The most famous monument of the Decorated period — the Percy Tomb at Beverley — can be confidently regarded as commemorating Eleanor Percy (d. 1328), but cannot be dated before 1340 on heraldic grounds.[149] The combined evidence suggests that the most likely dating of the de Ros effigy in the Temple, and of the similar effigies still in northern England, is c.1325–30. This would mean that the Temple effigy dates from some ten or fifteen years after the death of William de Ros in 1316, but such a gap is consistent with evidence elsewhere. As argued in this paper, it is likely to apply to the monument of the great William Marshal, and perhaps to one or more of his sons, in whose mausoleum William de Ros would doubtless be surprised to find himself.

[147] Fitzalan's arms were recorded in the east window in a visitation of 1665; for two repainted fourteenth-century shields surviving on either side of the window, see H. B. McCall, 'Finds at Bedale Church', *Yorkshire Archaeological Journal*, 28, 1924–6, 450 and pl. opp. 450.

[148] Coales, ed., *Earliest English Brasses*.

[149] P. Lindley, *Tomb Destruction and Scholarship: Medieval Monuments in Early Modern England*, Donington 2007, 167–98.

Philip J. Lankester

The Thirteenth-Century Military Effigies in the Temple Church

INTRODUCTION

O N THE NIGHT OF 10 May 1941 the Temple Church was hit by an incendiary bomb (Plates 103–4). In the resulting fire the roof of the round nave collapsed, causing severe damage to the most important collection of thirteenth-century military effigies in the country. Sadly, the precautions which had been taken to enclose the effigies in protective boxes against damage from bomb blasts were of little use against fire and falling roof timbers (Plate 57B).[1]

Consequently, despite the careful post-bomb restoration of the effigies by Harold Haysom,[2] the study of the thirteenth-century effigies today relies heavily on drawings, casts and photographs taken before 1941. Moreover, there is another phase of very significant, though less drastic, interference with the effigies which must also be taken into account — the repairs and restorations carried out by the sculptor Edward Richardson in 1842, to which I shall return later. During his work Richardson radically reorganised the physical arrangement of the effigies, and this too has to be taken into account, especially when reading earlier descriptions. Further confusion is potentially caused by the different numbering systems used by various authors who have written on the

I am most grateful to Robin Griffith-Jones, Henrietta Amodio, Claire Ryder, Celia Charlton and their colleagues at the Temple for their considerable help; also to Sally Badham and the late Claude Blair, who, at short notice, helpfully corrected and commented on my text. Thanks for help are also due to Stephen Church, Mark Downing, Rod Joyce, Richard Knowles, Helen Nicholson, Christopher Norton, David Park, Rosemary Sweet, Pamela Tudor-Craig (Lady Wedgwood), and Roger Weick.

    [1] It is said that the protective cases were of wood, which caught fire and 'baked' the effigies. Photographs taken soon after the bomb damage show the effigies surrounded by low brick walls (Plate 57B). Dr Claude Blair informed me that the late Sir James Mann (who was consulted about the effigies after the damage: Royal Armouries, Leeds, archives, Mann correspondence, Box C) told him that they were covered with railway sleepers.

    [2] For a photograph of Mr Haysom kneeling over one of the effigies, see Lewer and Dark, *Temple Church*, ill. 120. See also n. 196 at the end of this chapter.

effigies. The present account will therefore begin with an explanation of the current arrangement of the effigies and how they are to be numbered for reference, together with
a summary of what is known about their earlier disposition in the building.

NUMBERING AND ARRANGEMENT

This study concerns the eight thirteenth-century military effigies which have, since
Richardson's restoration, been arranged in two groups of four, on the north and south
sides of the central space of the circular 'nave' of the church, known as the Round.
Various authors have adopted different numbering systems over the years (see Table,
pp. 96–7 below), and it was decided to use the Royal Commission on Historical Monuments' numbering (of 'monuments and floor slabs') for all the effigies discussed in this
volume.[3] This means that the eight effigies to be discussed here are numbered 3–10 (in
the centre of the Round) (Plate 56). The two remaining medieval effigies are discussed
in David Park's paper: the bishop's effigy, no. 1 (in the choir) and the early fourteenth-
century military effigy, no. 12 (on the south side of the ambulatory of the Round). No.
2 in the RCHM's numbering was allocated to the inscription from the post-medieval
monument to John Selden (d. 1654),[4] and RCHM no. 11 is the Purbeck marble coped
grave-marker on the north side of the ambulatory of the Round: neither monument will
be discussed here.[5]

[3] RCHM, *The City*, 140–41.

[4] For an account of the original monument to which it belonged, see Esdaile, *Temple Church
Monuments*, 161–3 and pl. xvii. Large parts of the frame to Selden's monument and the lower part of
the inscription (all broken) survive, currently stored in the Church's crypt.

[5] For the coped grave marker (illus. in RCHM, *The City*, pl. 184 [bottom]), see Park, pp. 74–5
above, and Plate 44; also an article by James King in preparation. There are now six tapered 'coffin
lids' outside the church, to the north and north-west of the nave (listed by RCHM, *The City*, 140),
on several orientations and all apparently in a shelly limestone. Some are slightly coped and all have
a central, longitudinal ridge or fillet. Most have low plinths, some of which at least are probably
coffins which are now mostly below pavement level. More of the sides of these six coffins are shown
(in their present positions) in an old photograph taken when the ground level was lower (Griffith-
Jones, *Temple Church*, 16). Richardson's plan (present Colour Plate vi) shows three coffins north of
the west porch (P, Q and R), all aligned west–east, and one has a lid with a central ridge, similar to
the six just described (Richardson, *Stone and Leaden Coffins*, 16 and pl. 1). A Purbeck marble incised
cross-slab was found by Richardson on one of the three Purbeck stone coffins found during excavations inside the Round (see p. 95 below) along with other plain Purbeck slabs, some of which may
have originally been coffin lids. John Stow describes, in addition to the effigies (and presumably also
inside the church), three 'coaped stones al in gray Marble' (J. Stow, *A Survay of London*, London 1598,
327; see also see the modern edition, *Stow's Survey of London reprinted from the edition of 1603*, ed. C. L.
Kingsford, 2 vols., amended reprint, Oxford 1971, ii, 50–51) agreeing with William Dugdale who
describes, 'three . . . Gravestones lying about five inches above the level ground' (Dugdale, *Origines*,
173). One of these three was almost certainly the coped grave-marker now there (RCHM no. 11). The
other two may be among those discovered by Richardson inside or among the six now outside the
church. Dugdale's statement that one of the three 'gravestones' bore 'a large Escocheon with a Lion
rampant graven thereon' is almost certainly a confused reference to the same arms which actually

Before Richardson's intervention the nine military effigies (RCHM nos. 3–10 and 12) and the coped grave-marker (RCHM no. 2), making ten monuments in all, were arranged in a line across the Round, centrally divided into two groups of five (Plates 50, 82, 85–8). The restoration and rearrangement were prompted by excavations of 1841 in the centre of the Round to stabilise the building. The arrangement of the effigies, both before and after Richardson's restoration, is shown in the plan published in Richardson's account of the discoveries during the excavations, which concentrated on the coffins found at that time.[6]

As observed by Robin Griffith-Jones,[7] Richardson's plan (Colour Plate VI) superimposes several layers of information. Shown most prominently is the arrangement of the effigies as carried out by Richardson, which is how they remain today[8] (see also Plate 56). Also shown is the arrangement of the nine effigies and the coped grave-marker (RCHM nos. 3–12) as found by Richardson.[9] Richardson also showed nine coffins and a burial cavity which had been encountered inside the Round during the excavations to stabilise the structure.[10] Eight of the coffins — two of Purbeck marble and six of lead — and the burial cavity were arranged in an untidy line just east of the north–south axis, and a further Purbeck marble coffin was found in the ambulatory, just north of the west entrance. Lastly, Richardson showed a line of three brick vaults which were newly constructed at the western end of the space between the two groups of four effigies, for the reinterment of the nine coffins and their human remains.[11] At the top of the central vault (about 1 foot below the pavement) he placed the Purbeck marble coffin lid or grave-marker decorated with an incised cross, which was found on one of the coffins,[12] and this appears in his plan.

While it is tempting to see some relationship between the eight original effigies and the single coped coffin lid (together making nine monuments) and the line of nine burials discovered very slightly further west, it is not safe to do so, since we do not know the positions of the effigies in the Middle Ages, nor whether the eight coffins

occur on the shield of one of the effigies (RCHM no. 9; discussed here on p. 116). If Dugdale had just sketched the arms in his notes he could easily later have mistakenly associated them with the grave-markers rather than with the effigies.

[6] Richardson, *Stone and Leaden Coffins*, pl. 1; reproduced in Lewer and Dark, *Temple Church*, ill. 28, and in Griffith-Jones, *Temple Church*, 28; present Colour Plate VI.

[7] Ibid., 29.

[8] Numbered 1–10. It is important to note that, in Richardson's plan, 'the effigies [in their new positions] are drawn to a scale one eighth part greater than that of the Coffins and the rest of the Plan'. (Richardson, *Stone and Leaden Coffins*, 13 n.).

[9] Again numbered 1–10.

[10] Lettered A–J. At least one of the coffins had already been encountered during earlier works in 1827 (Richardson, *Stone and Leaden Coffins*, 10 n.). The dating of these coffins is beyond the scope of this paper, but there seems no reason why any should date from after the suppression of the Templars in the early fourteenth century.

[11] All lettered S.

[12] Richardson, *Stone and Leaden Coffins*, 15 and pl. 1. Richardson later regretted the reburial of this cross-slab (see n. 55 below).

TABLE: Concordance of Numbering of and References to the Medieval Effigies

RCHM (material)	Stothard	Kerrich	Saunders	Tummers	Plates in this volume	Kerrich Drawings (BL Add. MSS)
1 (Pm)					v, 47–9	
3 (Pm)	4	4	H	VIII	56, 60A	6728, fol. 40 (whole)
						6728, fol. 41 (whole)
						6730, fol. 3 (whole)
						6730, fol. 3 (whole)
4 (Pm)	8	7	G	VII	56, 61	6728, fol. 42 (whole)
						6728, fol. 43 (dets., incl. head)
						6730, fol. 4 (whole)
5 (Pm)	7	6	F	IV	56, 58A	6728, fol. 67 (whole)
6 (Pm)	1	1	E	III	56, 59A	6728, fol. 38 (whole)
						6728, fol. 39 (whole)
						6728, fol. 39 (dets., head)
7 (Pm)	10	9	D	VI	56, 58B–C	6728, fol. 67 (dets., incl. head)
						6728, fol. 68 (det., head)
8 (Rs)	9	8	C	V	56, 62	6728, fol. 50 (dets., incl. head)
						6730, fol. 4 (whole)
9 (Rs?)	2	2	B	II	46, 56, 60B	6728, fol. 48 (whole)
						6728, fol. 49 (dets., incl. head)
10 (Pm)	6	5	A	I	IV, 45, 56, 57	6728, fol. 65 (whole)
						6728, fol. 66 (dets., incl. head)
12 (Ml)	3	[3]	—	—	52, 53	6728, fol. 80 (whole)

Abbreviations etc.

det./dets.	detail(s)
incl.	including
Pm	Purbeck marble
Rs	Reigate stone
Ml	Magnesian limestone
whole	view of whole effigy

References

The numbering by Kerrich and Stothard relates to the pre-1841 arrangement; the numbering by Richardson, the RCHM, Saunders and Tummers is based on Richardson's post-1842 arrangement.

Hollis	T. and G. Hollis, *The Monumental Effigies of Great Britain, Drawn and Etched by Thomas Hollis and George Hollis*, London 1840–42 (unpaginated).
Kerrich	Unpublished drawings by the Rev. Thomas Kerrich, British Library, Additional Manuscripts 6728 and 6730. 6730, fols. 3 and 4, are high quality finished pen-

RCHM Plates	Saunders	Stothard Plates	Hollis Plates	Richardson Plates	Richardson Casts (V&A)
184 (whole)		28		11	
182 (whole) 187 (head)		15		4	
182 (whole) 187 (head)			unpag.	5	
182 (whole) 187 (head)	Fig. 75B			2	
182 (whole) 185 (shield) 187 (head)	Fig. 75A	10		3	
183 (whole) 186 (head)				9	A1938-10
183 (whole) 186 (head)				8	A1938-8
183 (whole) 185 (shield) (mis-captioned no. 8) 186 (head)		26 27		7	A1938-9
183 (whole) 186 (head)			unpag.	6	A1938-7
184 (whole) 185 (shield)		38		10	A1938-6

cil drawings; 6728, fols. 38–43, 48–50, 65–8 and 80, contain drawings and sketches of differing quality (most very good), both in ink and pencil. Kerrich's numbering, based on the pre-Richardson arrangement, ran from left to right across the two groups of five monuments but *excluded* the coped grave marker (RCHM no. 11).

RCHM — Royal Commission of Historical Monuments (England), *An Inventory of the Historical Monuments in London*, IV, *The City*, London 1929. The numbering based on the present layout — see Plate 56. No. 2 referred to a post-medieval monument, no. 11 to the coped grave-marker.

Richardson — E. Richardson, *The Monumental Effigies of the Temple Church, with an Account of their Restoration in the Year 1842*, London 1843. No. 1 is the coped grave-marker, nos. 2–10 the military effigies, and no. 11 the bishop's effigy in the choir. The numbering begins at the north-west, with all four effigies in the northern group being numbered before moving to the south-west corner of the southern group.

Richardson Casts — Taken in 1853 (see p. 102 below) and now in the Victoria and Albert Museum. The V&A Accession numbers are given.

(references to table cont. on next page)

(references to table, cont.)

Saunders	O. E. Saunders, *A History of English Art in the Middle Ages*, Oxford 1932, 203–206. The numbering begins at the south-west, all four effigies in the southern group being numbered before moving to the south-west corner of the northern group.
Stothard	C. A. Stothard, *Monumental Effigies of Great Britain*, London 1817–32 (plate numbers unchanged in 2nd edn of 1876). The general plate on p. 1 (2nd edn, p. 23) shows the effigies in their pre-Richardson arrangement. The numbering, referred to in the text, p. 2 (2nd edn, p. 24), ran from left to right across the two groups of five monuments but *included* the coped grave-marker as no. 5 (RCHM no. 11, not included in the present table).
Tummers	H. A. Tummers, *Early Secular Effigies in England: The Thirteenth Century*, Leiden 1980, 'List' at 139. The numbering is from the south-west to the north-east, passing along each row of four from north to south.

in this line were in their original positions or whether some or all of them had been moved there from elsewhere.[13] One cannot rule out the possibility that some of the stone coffins may have borne effigies, and Richardson thought this was probably the case with all three of the Purbeck marble coffins and another of Reigate stone which was found in the west porch;[14] but this cannot be verified and, even if he was correct, this is still no guarantee that the Purbeck marble coffins were in their original positions, while the porch would be an improbable location for any effigy. In the case of the Purbeck marble coffins, Richardson noted that the sides were smooth and highly finished, which makes it possible that at least part of the sides were intended to be seen above ground.[15]

The effigies, in their pre-Richardson arrangement of two linear groups of five, were illustrated in sufficient detail by both Gough (Plates 87–8)[16] and Stothard[17] for the individual effigies to be distinguished. The earliest reliable visual evidence we have of the location of the effigies in these positions is a sectioned view of the nave, looking from west to east, drawn by William Emmett (Plate 82[18]). It was dated between

[13] Cf. Esdaile, *Temple Church Monuments*, 67: the effigies' 'original arrangement can safely be determined by Richardson's plate showing the position of the coffins over which they would naturally be placed'.

[14] Richardson, *Stone and Leaden Coffins*, 10, 12–15. Richardson specifically compared the large size of one of the coffins (F on his plan) and the exceptionally large size of the plinth of one of the effigies (RCHM no. 6), and noted that the size of the Reigate stone coffin was close to that of the plinths of the two Reigate stone effigies (RCHM nos. 8 and 9).

[15] Ibid. See also pp. 110–11 below.

[16] Gough, *Sepulchral Monuments*, 1/1, pl. v (southern row), pl. xix (northern row). The original drawings for these plates are in Bodl. MS Gough Maps 225, fols. 151, 152. There are also some notes on the effigies in MS Gough Maps 221 (an interleaved copy of Gough, *Sepulchral Monuments*, vol. 1), between p. 24 and pl. v of the printed text.

[17] Stothard, *Monumental Effigies*, 23. Some of the drawings were issued in parts by Stothard with a title page dated 1817. After Stothard's death further plates were etched, and all the plates were published with additional text by Alfred Kempe in 1832. A second edition, with further additional text by C. A. Hewitt, appeared in 1876.

[18] Reproduced in Esdaile, *Temple Church Monuments*, pl. 1a, and Griffith-Jones, *Temple Church*,

1682 and 1685 by Esdaile,[19] but documentary evidence recently discovered by Robin Griffith-Jones appears conclusively to indicate that this arrangement of the effigies was carried out in 1695 and that Emmett's view was made in 1702.[20]

The relevant work, detailed in the 1695 accounts, involved dividing the effigies into two groups (presumably to create a central processional way from the west door that would formerly have been blocked by them), repairing and painting the effigies, and adapting and extending the surrounding railings. This would agree with the evidence of William Dugdale, who, publishing in 1666, describes the effigies as being in 'Within a spacious grate of iron in the midst of the round walk'.[21] This clearly implies that the effigies were all in a single, railed enclosure, though without the evidence of the 1695 accounts we might not be warranted in reading that degree of precision into Dugdale's comment.

ANTIQUARIAN DESCRIPTIONS
AND LATER WRITINGS, DRAWINGS AND CASTS

The earliest mention of the effigies appears to be in a book on heraldry, Gerard Legh's *Accedens of Armorie*, published in 1576:

> And passing forward, [I] entered into a Church of auncient building, wherein were many monuments of noble personages armed in knightly habit, with their cotes depainted in auncient shields, whereat I tooke pleasure to behold.[22]

47. The coped grave-marker (RCHM no. 11) can be distinguished, and with effort some at least of the other effigies could probably also be identified.

[19] Esdaile, *Temple Church Monuments*, 66.

[20] See Griffith-Jones, pp. 153–6 below. This agrees with the statement by Addison, *Temple Church*, 93 (quoting the *Flying Post*, 2 January 1696), that it was Treasurer Roger Gillingham who marshalled 'the Knight's Templars in uniform order'. Gillingham was elected Treasurer in 1694, to serve in 1695 (pers. comm. Robin Griffith-Jones). His involvement with the effigies recorded by the *Flying Post* may have been in an obituary notice, but I have been unable to locate a copy of that issue. There remains the problem of an engraving of the west porch — an advertisement for a stationer's shop located there — which also shows, below and detached from the main picture, the effigies and grave-marker in their two groups of five (Plate 68). This engraving has been recently published and captioned with the improbably early date of c.1678 (Lewer and Dark, *Temple Church*, ill. 54). For the probable explanation, see Griffith-Jones, p. 137 n. 11 below. The reference to the *Gentleman's Magazine* included in Lewer and Dark's caption (vol. 54, p. 911) turns out to be to an issue published in December 1784, which included an illustration taken from the original engraving (pl. facing p. 911).

[21] Dugdale, *Origines*, 173. The iron railings are also mentioned by the Dutchman, William Schellinks, who visited in August 1661 (*The Journal of William Schellinks' Travels in England 1661–1663*, transl. and ed. M. Exwood and H. L. Lehmann, Royal Historical Society Camden Series, 5th ser., 1, 1993, 58). Shellinks's description of eleven monuments, eight of which were effigies (five of them cross-legged) agrees completely with the accounts of Dugdale and Stow, *Survay of London*.

[22] G. Legh, *The Accedens of Armory*, London 1576, fol. 120ʳ, quoted by Esdaile, *Temple Church Monuments*, 63, but without comment.

However, this passage occurs in the context of an account of an imaginary journey by the narrator, during which he visits the Inner Temple in London, and while it was clearly inspired by a knowledge of the actual London Temple, its details — like those of the subsequent account of a visit to the office of an imaginary King of Arms (called Palaphilos[23]) — cannot be relied upon. Nevertheless it is possible that Legh saw remains of colour on some of the shields.[24]

Subsequently there are many further references by early antiquaries such as Stow, Camden, Weever and Dugdale, and by other writers during the eighteenth century, though some sources appear to copy the accounts in earlier publications, suggesting their authors were not writing from first-hand observation. These earlier accounts are referenced (and some quoted in more detail) by Richardson, Esdaile and Baylis;[25] consequently, they will not be listed here and will be cited only when they contribute significant additional information about the effigies. The effigies have been discussed and illustrated in several nineteenth-century works on sculpture and monumental effigies, most importantly by Richardson, and in various twentieth-century studies including those by Prior and Gardner, Saunders, Andersson, Bauch, Hurtig, and Tummers.[26] They have also been mentioned in writings on armour by such authors as Meyrick, Hartshorne, Laking, and Blair.[27]

---

[23] Named after the fictitious 'Constable Marshall of the Inner Temple' of the same name (Legh, *Accedens of Armory*, fols. 118^v, 119^v).

[24] For a recent discussion of and further references for Legh's *Accedens of Armorie* (originally published in 1562, with the first word of the title spelt *Accedence*), see J. Wilson and E. J. Kenny, 'The Monument to Gerard Legh (d. 1563) in St Dunstan-in-the-West, Fleet Street, London', *Church Monuments*, 22, 2008, 88–99. Richardson notes that Camden is silent on the matter of colour (Richardson, *Effigies of the Temple Church*, 11); Richardson cites the 1586 edition of Camden's *Britannia*, but the earliest edition to mention the effigies is that of 1594 (W. Camden, *Britannia . . .*, London 1594, 321; see n. 85 below). However, Camden's relevant text is quite short and he would probably not have mentioned colour on the shields unless he could identify the arms.

[25] Richardson, *Effigies of the Temple Church*, 10–12; Baylis, *Temple Church*, 94–115 ('The Writers upon the Effigies' — though not all the sources cited discuss the Temple Church effigies); Esdaile, *Temple Church Monuments*, esp. chap. v.

[26] E. S. Prior and A. Gardner, *An Account of Medieval Figure-sculpture in England*, Cambridge 1912, esp. 552 (table), 588–90 (incl. figs. 663–6); O. E. Saunders, *A History of English Art in the Middle Ages*, Oxford 1932, 203–6, fig. 75; A. Andersson, *English Influence on Norwegian and Swedish Figure Sculpture in Wood 1220–1270*, Stockholm 1950, 30, 46, 54–5; K. Bauch, *Das mittelalterliche Grabbild*, Berlin and New York 1976, 126–8, 130–33, Abb. 200, 207, 210; J. Hurtig, *The Armored Gisant before 1400*, New York and London 1979, esp. 112–14, 117–18, 126, and pls. 180–81, 193–5, 206–8; Tummers, *Early Secular Effigies*, *passim*, list at 139 and pls. 27–30, 98. Apart from Tummers, authors writing since 1945 have tended to mention them only briefly, probably being deterred by the 1941 damage and the earlier restoration: see Andersson, op. cit., 55 n. 2; also L. Stone, *Sculpture in Britain: the Middle Ages*, 2nd edn, Harmondsworth 1972, 117, 150, 251 n. 27. Bauch, op. cit., confined his detailed discussion to one of the least damaged of the thirteenth-century effigies (RCHM no. 8) and to the similarly well preserved early-fourteenth-century effigy (RHCM no. 12).

[27] S. R. Meyrick, *A Critical Inquiry into Antient Armour . . .*, 3 vols., London 1824, 1, pl. 21 (based on RCHM, no. 12); A. Hartshorne, 'The Sword Belts of the Middle Ages', *Archaeological Journal*, 48, 1891, 320–40, illus. nos. 1, 2, 5, 6, 8, 10, 11, 13; G. F. Laking, *A Record of European Armour and Arms*

The earliest record of drawings being made of the effigies is in February 1718/19, when the Society of Antiquaries resolved to employ a Signor Grisoni for that purpose.[28] The whereabouts of these drawings (assuming they were executed and still survive) is unknown. In 1736/7 Smart Lethieullier informed the Society that he owned drawings of the effigies, which he had commissioned himself.[29] These are presumably those included in a collection of drawings that formerly belonged to Lethieullier and are now in the British Library.[30] There are two drawings, each showing one of the two lines of five monuments (Plates 85–6). While they contain some interesting details which can be compared with later pre-Richardson drawings, they are generally not accurate enough for detailed study.

The earliest published illustrations to show the effigies in detail are those by Richard Gough (Plates 87–8),[31] but the drawings are again insufficiently accurate for detailed study and are slightly less accurate than those made for Lethieullier in the 1730s. The same goes for the watercolours executed by the Rev. John Skinner during a visit in 1826, when he also took some brief notes, and which are also now in the British Library.[32]

The earliest drawings so far found which are useful for detailed study were made by the Rev. Thomas Kerrich (1748–1828), Principal Librarian of the University of Cambridge, and are also now in the British Library.[33] They include some important annotations. Kerrich's more finished drawings resemble those of Charles Alfred Stothard, who was inspired by the drawings of Kerrich and corresponded with him.[34] Stothard's own drawings (executed before 1821) were published between 1817 and 1832 and included three of the thirteenth-century Temple Church military effigies (RCHM nos. 3, 6 and 9) together with the bishop's effigy and the early fourteenth-century effigy (RCHM nos. 1 and 12);[35] the original drawings are in the British Museum.[36] Stothard's published

through Seven Centuries, 5 vols., London 1920–22, I, 109–10, fig. 132; C. Blair, *European Armour* circa *1066 to circa 1700*, London 1958, 27 (fig. 8), 39.

[28] Esdaile, *Temple Church Monuments*, 72, citing Society of Antiquaries of London, Minute Book, I, 20, 25 February.

[29] Esdaile, *Temple Church Monuments*, 72, citing Society of Antiquaries of London, Minute Book, II, 269, 10 February.

[30] BL, Add. MSS 27348–50. The drawings of the Temple effigies are in Add. MS 27348, fols. 90–91. The three volumes, which formerly belonged to Horace Walpole, were compiled by Lethieullier in conjunction with Charles Frederick, who executed many of the drawings. For further information on these volumes, see P. Whittemore, 'The Slab to Dame Eve Goldsburgh', *Monumental Brass Society Bulletin*, 107, January 2008, 133.

[31] See n. 16 above.

[32] BL, MS Sloane 33695, fols. 181–93.

[33] BL, Add. MS 6728, fols. 38–43, 48–50, 65–8 and 80; Add. MS 6730, fols. 3 and 4. See the Table, pp. 96–7 above, for details. Only a few of Kerrich's drawings (and none of the Temple Church effigies) were ever published: see R. Knowles, 'French Excursions: Charles Alfred Stothard and the Monumental Effigies of France', *Church Monuments*, 13, 1998, 46 and nn. 11–13.

[34] Ibid., 46–7

[35] Stothard, *Monumental Effigies*, respectively pls. 15, 10, 26–7, 28 and 38. See n. 17 above.

[36] British Museum, Dept of Prints and Drawings, reg. nos. 1883.0704.481–750; nos. 492, 497,

corpus of drawings of effigies was extended by the father and son George and Thomas Hollis, whose drawings were published between 1840 and 1842 and included two further Temple Church effigies (RCHM nos. 4 and 10).[37] The Hollises' original effigy drawings are also in the British Museum.[38] These sets of drawings by Kerrich, Stothard and the Hollis brothers together form the main visual evidence for the condition and appearance of the effigies before Richardson's restoration. The coverage for each effigy is uneven. To avoid frequent referencing, the illustrations relating to each effigy are set out in the Table, pp. 96–7 above.

Richardson published drawings of all the effigies to accompany his account of their restoration in 1842,[39] but all these drawings were done after his restoration. In the summer of 1853, Richardson returned to take casts of four of the thirteenth-century effigies (RCHM nos. 7–10) and of the early fourteenth-century effigy (RCHM no. 12)[40] for the huge display of casts then being set up at the Crystal Palace, which opened in June 1854.[41] The Temple effigy casts were placed, with casts of three other military effigies, outside the Romanesque and Byzantine Court.[42] The Crystal Palace was largely destroyed by fire in November 1936, and the Temple effigy casts, together with others which had survived the fire, were moved out and are now in the cast courts at the Victoria and Albert Museum.[43] There are also references to casts of four of the effigies being made in or shortly before March 1841 for L. N. Cottingham (then architect to the Temple Church).[44] It seems doubtful that these casts survive but, as they were taken

514, 516, 525 (resp. RCHM nos. 6, 3, 9, 1 and 12). See P. J. Lankester, 'Charles Stothard's Drawings for *The Monumental Effigies of Great Britain*', *Church Monuments Society Newsletter*, 20/1, Summer 2004, 6–9. The drawings of the Temple Church effigies do not differ from the published etchings to any significant degree.

[37] T. and G. Hollis, *The Monumental Effigies of Great Britain, Drawn and Etched by Thomas Hollis and George Hollis*, London 1840–42 (the plates, originally issued in parts, are unnumbered). Their drawings of the two Temple effigies were done in or shortly before 1840, narrowly escaping Richardson's restoration. The drawings of the Temple Church effigies do not differ from the published etchings to any significant degree.

[38] British Museum, Dept of Prints and Drawings, reg. nos. 1903.1002.53 (RCHM no. 4), 54 (RCHM no. 10).

[39] Richardson, *Effigies of the Temple Church*. For the plate numbers for each effigy, see the Table, pp. 96–7 above. If they still survive, the location of Richardson's original drawings has not yet been discovered.

[40] Richardson was granted permission to take the casts during the long vacation in 1853: ITA, BEN/1/20, 19 April 1853. I owe this reference to Celia Charlton.

[41] J. Kenworthy-Browne, 'Plaster Casts from the Crystal Palace, Sydenham', *Sculpture Journal*, 15, 2006, 184. I owe this reference to Dr Stephen Church.

[42] Ibid., 187.

[43] For the Victoria and Albert Museum accession numbers, see the Table, pp. 96–7 above. The casts were each displayed alongside the relevant effigies in the exhibition in the Temple Church in 2008 (see p. xv above and Plate 109). For the damage to the Crystal Palace and the survival of some of the casts housed towards the northern end, see *The Times*, 2 Dec. 1936 (issue 47547), 14, col. D. I am indebted to Stephen Church for this reference.

[44] The 1841 casts were taken by Messrs Williams, Landuchi and Bishop and two others unnamed: (memorandum of 16 March by Mr. Burnell for Mr. Wyatt, ITA, TEM/2/7 B). The casts are

before Richardson's restoration, if ever found they would be of great importance. However, even with casts, we have to be aware of restorations, and one of those taken by Richardson now differs from the original in details of the belt, presumably as a result of damage and inaccurate repair.[45]

The pre-bomb damage evidence of Richardson's casts is supplemented by a number of photographs covering all the effigies. These include an important series of 'bird's eye' views taken by Bedford Lemere in about 1885, which are reproduced in small scale in Plate 56.[46] Other photographs, now in the collection of the National Monuments Record at Swindon, were taken for the Royal Commission on Historical Monuments, and a number were published in its 1929 London 'City' volume.[47]

THE EFFIGIES: DESCRIPTION AND RESTORATION

Of the eight thirteenth-century effigies, six are in the stone called Purbeck marble — a hard, dark, fossiliferous, polishable limestone, quarried on the Isle of Purbeck in Dorset, which was also used extensively in the building.[48] It is chiefly composed of fossils of the small mollusc *Viviparus cariniferus*.[49] It is not clear why Richardson identified the stone of two of these six (RCHM nos. 6 and 10) as of Sussex marble (which is similar in appearance to Purbeck but with much larger fossils).[50] There is now no visible basis

referred to in a letter of 19 March 1841 from Cottingham (ibid., TEM/2/7 Id), and this letter is referred to in the Bench Table order book, under 23 April 1841 (ibid., BEN/1/16). I owe all these references to Celia Charlton.

[45] RCHM no. 7. The parts of the sword belt below the buckle on the cast (A1938–10) are quite different and lack the sets of three lateral studs. These studs were inaccurately restored by Richardson: they were originally bars with a central knop, as may be seen by careful examination of the effigy in its present state. The loss of Richardson's restoration overlay from the sword belt reveals, on the first of these bars below the figure's right forearm, that its original form was closer to those on some of the other stylistically related Purbeck marble effigies (see p. 131 ff. and n. 189 below) and also seen on RCHM no. 8.

[46] Another set of bird's-eye views was apparently taken some time before the war damage by R. B. Fleming. The present author has seen a partial set of prints, and those of two of the effigies are reproduced in Saunders, *English Art*, fig. 75. Fleming's negatives have not yet been located.

[47] RCHM, *The City*, pls. 182–7; for details, see the Table, pp. 96–7 above.

[48] For Purbeck marble generally see J. Blair, 'Purbeck Marble', in *English Medieval Industries: Craftsmen, Techniques, Products*, ed. J. Blair and N. Ramsay, London 1991, 41–56; G. Dru Drury, 'The Use of Purbeck Marble in Mediaeval Times', *Proceedings of the Dorset Natural History and Archaeological Society*, 70, 1948, 74–98; R. Leach, *An Investigation into the Use of Purbeck Marble in Medieval England*, 2nd edn, Crediton 1978.

[49] W. J. Arkell et al., *The Geology of the Country around Weymouth, Swanage, Corfe and Lulworth* (Memoirs of the Geological Survey of Great Britain: England and Wales), reprint with additional references, London 1968 (1st edn 1947), chap. VII, esp. 104 ff.

[50] For Sussex marble, sometimes known by local names such as Petworth or Bethersden marble from the places of extraction, see W. Topley, *The Geology of the Weald* (Memoirs of the Geological Survey of Great Britain: England and Wales), London 1875, chap. VIII, esp. 104 ff. Topley described three beds: two had large fossils (here described as 'Large *Paludina*' — *Paludina* being the old generic

for this distinction, and both effigies appear to be in Purbeck marble. The remaining two effigies (RCHM nos. 8 and 9) are in a calcareous sandstone, one certainly and the other very probably of the variety called Reigate stone.[51]

All the recent mainstream authors[52] date these effigies to the thirteenth century, which there is no reason to dispute. Dating them more precisely is fraught with difficulties. Armour appears to have changed very little during the century, compared with the first half of the fourteenth century, when developments were comparatively rapid. Our study is further hampered because hardly any original armour survives from the period and it is not always clear how we should interpret the visual and documentary evidence. The armour and other approaches to dating are discussed below.

Apart from the war damage, the major problem in studying these effigies is to determine the extent of Richardson's restoration work undertaken between March and October 1842. Our starting point is his discussion of this work in his publication of 1843.[53] While the amount of text for each effigy dealing specifically with condition and restoration averages only about 100 words, it is much more than we have for most restoration work of this period. To what extent Richardson's account is a reliable guide to his work is difficult to assess. In general, his account gives the impression of a careful and methodical approach by the standards of the time and he clearly wished to leave a more detailed published record than either his patrons or publisher would allow:

> In the following description of the Plates it has in many cases been found impossible to describe, with the minuteness and precision the Author desired, the extent of decay and restoration. It will however, it is trusted, suffice for those interested in these figures to be assured that no part of the originals was removed, and that, on carefully examining the Effigies, the extent of every restoration may be traced.[54]

The accounts of the individual effigies appear to be reasonably accurate in describing major losses and replacements, but there is insufficient detail on less significant losses and practically no information on the reworking or 'crisping up' of existing

name for *Viviparus*; this large variety is now called *Viviparus fluviorum*) and the third bed had small *Paludina* (i.e. *Viviparus*) fossils. This latter bed might be visually confused with Purbeck marble, but the normal thickness was given as 3–4 in. (7.5–10 cm) and the greatest recorded thickness was 6–8 in. (15–20 cm) so it is extremely unlikely it could have been used for effigies. See also J. Potter, '*Viviparus* Limestone ("Purbeck Marble"): a Key to Financially Well-Endowed Churches in the London Basin', *Church Archaeology*, 5–6, 2004, 79–89; 7–9, 2005, 192 (bibliography), esp. 82–4; S. Badham, 'The Use of Sedimentary "Marbles" for Church Monuments in Pre-Reformation England', *Church Archaeology*, 11, 2007, 1–18, esp. 3–5.

[51] I am grateful to Martyn Owen of the Geological Survey for his opinions on the stones of the effigies during a visit in 1977 or 1978. The slight doubt he expressed about the stone of RCHM no. 9 was due to the unclean surface.

[52] See nn. 26, 27 above.

[53] Richardson, *Effigies of the Temple Church*. To enable stabilisation work on the building, the effigies were removed to an adjoining shed, constructed for the purpose, in the summer of 1841 (ibid., 14).

[54] Richardson, *Effigies of the Temple Church*, 15.

surfaces. Certain statements in his general remarks on the restoration of the effigies give cause for concern. For example:

> . . . the various coatings above-named [paint, dirt and whitewash] which enveloped the Effigies, varying from one-eighth to half an inch in thickness, were first carefully removed with a fine tool prepared for the purpose. This done, the Effigy was generally found to be extensively decayed, the decay having proceeded in many cases from within as well as from without. The three stone figures were free from internal decay [i.e the freestone figures, RCHM nos. 8, 9 and 12], but covered with a crust which had to be removed.

One wonders how much original surface came away with the 'coatings' and 'crust' as they were removed. His work received severe criticism at the time, with one critic accusing him of being 'a charlatan who has planed down the effigies'.[55] Moreover, it is clear from Richardson's account that earlier restorations had been carried out,[56] and these need to be borne in mind too. Richardson also records remains of colour on the effigies but I shall not be discussing this, except in the one case where it may be relevant to the identification of the effigy.

The effigies will be discussed in their approximate chronological order (in the opinion of the present author); the important aspects of their restoration will be outlined and attention will be drawn to significant features. References to the drawings by Kerrich, Stothard, the Hollises and Richardson are given in the Table, pp. 96–7 above, and will not be repeated here. Richardson's published text for each effigy will be found near his relevant plate and will also not be referenced here, unless the information cited derives from his general discussion at the beginning.

---

[55] Augustus Hare, quoted in R. Gunnis, *Dictionary of British Sculptors 1660–1851*, rev. edn, London 1968, 320. Although Esdaile considered that 'seven [of the effigies] are so much recut that they can scarcely be described as medieval work at all' (Esdaile, *Temple Church Monuments*, 66–7), she took a more sympathetic view of Richardson's role, maintaining that he was merely following orders; nevertheless, she describes his restoration of the Temple effigies as 'a melancholy episode in his career' (ibid., 43–4). According to Esdaile (ibid., 67), Richardson was proposing further work on the effigies in 1853, but an examination of the text of his letter of 25 April, preserved in the Bench Table minutes (ITA, BEN/1/20, fol. 21ᵛ, 26 April 1853), suggests he was only proposing minor work 'at a moderate cost to obviate the injury inadvertently committed shortly after they were restored' (I owe this reference to Celia Charlton). No further details of the 'injury' or proposed work are given. Richardson also said he regretted that the Purbeck marble cross-slab discovered during the excavations (see n. 5 above) had been reburied, and proposed it now be 'recovered and restored'. Richardson also restored medieval effigies at Chichester Cathedral in 1843: see H. A. Tummers, 'The Medieval Effigial Tombs in Chichester Cathedral', *Church Monuments*, 3, 1988, 33; and at Elford (Staffs.) in 1848–9: see E. Richardson, *The Monumental Effigies, and Tombs, in Elford Church, Staffordshire: with a Memoir and Pedigree of the Lords of Elford*, London 1852. For Richardson's restoration of medieval effigies, see also I. Roscoe, E. Hardy and M. G. Sullivan, *A Biographical Dictionary of Sculptors in Britain 1660–1851*, New Haven and London 2009, 1034.

[56] Richardson, *Effigies of the Temple Church*, 14–15.

RCHM no. 5 (Plates 56, 58A)

Because of its low relief, lack of head and foot supports, and simple and rather stiff composition, this effigy is generally regarded as the earliest. However, a note of warning needs to be sounded about limited depth of carving necessarily indicating an early date, as this could simply be a consequence of the depth of slab available to the sculptor. This is especially relevant for effigies in Purbeck marble, where the bed thickness was limited and thinner pieces might be used for economy. Of this effigy, Richardson says:

> The state of decay and dilapidation of this figure far exceeded that of any of the others. The whole of the upper part of the face to the lower points of the eyes, nose, and mouth, the most prominent portions of the right arm, shield and surcoat, had perished; and the feet and legs nearly to the surcoat had been replaced in Caen stone.

Kerrich simply comments that 'This figure is very much defaced', but the overall impression is not encouraging. However, we can probably be reasonably confident about the overall attitude, with the straight legs, the right arm on the breast and the shield carried low down. Indeed Kerrich's fairly rough sketch shows all the main elements except the feet. The large spherical chape at the end of the scabbard is clearly Richardson's creation for which there appear to be no medieval precedents. The feet were restored by Richardson at an improbably upright angle given the low relief of the rest of the figure, and it is clear from his description and from Kerrich's drawing that there was no evidence for this. The feet are likely originally to have lain flatter and closer to the slab. The head apparently lacked any carved representation of mail, and this will be considered below (p. 121).

RCHM no. 10 (Colour Plate IV, Plates 45, 56, 57)

This effigy is also in low relief. Richardson records that it was 'broken transversely in four pieces'. He states that he restored part of the sword, and refers to various minor defects including parts of the foliage and the sword and scabbard (the damage to which can be seen in the Hollis view), and he also mentions traces of colour. Apart from the reported damage the impression is that the effigy was otherwise in fair condition. This effigy is unique among those in the Temple Church in having integrally carved stiff-leaf foliage flanking the pillow,[57] and this is further discussed below (p. 129). Kerrich omitted to show this foliage in either of his drawings, probably indicating that it was of little interest to him.

---

[57] For foliage on the slabs of other thirteenth-century English effigies, see Tummers, *Early Secular Effigies*, 34 ff. RCHM no. 10 (Tummers no. 1) is discussed at 36.

RCHM no. 6 (Plates 56, 59A)

The helmet and carvings on the shield will be discussed in due course (pp. 116–17, 120–21 below), but we should note here that Richardson says that 'the mutilation and decay of this figure were very considerable'. As well as noting various points of serious decay he also says that 'the figure, from the crown of the helmet through the body to the knee, was divided into two large pieces'; this was a horizontal break which can still be detected. The slab was considerably thicker than on the other effigies, so much so that Richardson reduced its thickness and reused the Purbeck marble gained to restore the original width of the plinth and parts of the effigy.[58] Stothard's drawing provides a good impression of the state of this figure before Richardson's work, and agrees well with the drawings by Kerrich.

RCHM no. 3 (Plates 56, 60A)

Richardson records that 'this Effigy was in a fine state of preservation. The defects were trifling.' The attitude of both arms crossed on the breast appears to be unique in Britain.[59] The eyes were also said to have been closed, and although in view of the war damage this is now impossible to determine with certainty, it seems probable from Stothard's drawing.[60] Showing effigies with closed eyes is rare in northern Europe, though common in Italy.[61] The unusual head covering of this effigy is discussed below (p. 121).

RCHM no. 4 (Plates 56, 61)

According to Richardson, the defects of this effigy were relatively minor, and Kerrich's drawings support this view. Part of the right leg and the scabbard were detached but remained present (the leg was lost in the war damage). The support of the feet on two small grotesque heads (not shown or noted by Kerrich) is commented on below (p. 127 f.). Sadly, one of these supports is now completely lost and of the other scarcely any original surface remains. The padded 'head band' is discussed below (p. 121).

[58] Richardson, *Effigies of the Temple Church*, 15.

[59] This attitude is found occasionally in France: for example on the effigy of a bishop at Rouen, attributed to Rotrocus de Warwick, d. 1183 (Bauch, *Mittelalterliche Grabbild*, 45, Abb. 54, 55). Mark Downing has drawn my attention to an effigy in St Mark's, Bristol, which comes close to this position, but the figure's right hand rests on the corner of the shield (see A. C. Fryer, 'Monumental Effigies by Bristol Craftsmen (1240–1550)', *Archaeologia*, 74, 1925, pl. II, fig. 3).

[60] Kerrich's drawings, which are from the side, do not assist in determining this.

[61] For discussion of this feature and a list of other thirteenth-century examples in England, see Tummers, *Early Secular Effigies*, 23–5.

RCHM no. 7 (Plates 56, 58B–C)

This was the first effigy Richardson restored, in order to demonstrate what could be achieved.[62] In its post-Richardson state, this effigy is in my view the most elegant. Unfortunately the legs were completely restored by Richardson, replacing earlier restorations in Caen stone, though Richardson says that their original outline could be traced from fragments on the plinth. Richardson reported that 'The hood, cushion, face, surcoat . . . the belts, buckles, scabbard, and ring mail throughout, were much decayed in places'. One would like to know more, but unfortunately we only have the evidence of a few pre-Richardson sketches by Kerrich (two showing the head and one the torso). However, the parts drawn by Kerrich appear to have been reasonably well preserved. Richardson specifically says that his restoration of the spurs on this effigy was 'taken from those of a former restoration, with some assistance from those in Plate 9 [RCHM no. 3]'.[63]

The remaining two effigies are in Reigate stone and, probably for this reason, suffered less in the war damage than the others.

RCHM no. 8 (Plates 56, 62)

In addition to a number of breakages, Richardson recorded that 'the left [hand], excepting the tip of the fingers, had long since been replaced by plaster of Paris, which covered the tips of the fingers that remained. This repair wrongly represented the mail as divided at the fingers. The sword hilt and scabbard from below the left hand were gone, and also the snout and tongue of the dragon.' Richardson's statement that the sword *hilt* was missing from below the left hand is confusing if we assume he means the *effigy's* left hand, since no part of what could be called the hilt is below that hand (he may have meant the right hand). However, it is clear from drawings by Kerrich and that published by Gough (Plate 87),[64] that the central part of the hilt had survived, but that Richardson replaced the quillons (again now missing since the war damage). Richardson tells us that his restoration of the sword-guard of this effigy was copied from that on RCHM no. 10 and that there were only traces of the original length of the scabbard (which, as it was largely undercut, probably means he found the remains of a support for it at or near its tip).

    One might reasonably doubt that the unusual lobed pommel was there before Richardson's restoration. If it had been one would have expected Kerrich's drawings to show it, whereas he only gives a sketchy outline. On the other hand, if Richardson had found no evidence for its original shape, it is curious that he chose to restore it to such a relatively unusual form. In describing the effigy he merely says 'The sword-hilt is in

---

[62] Richardson, *Effigies of the Temple Church*, 14.
[63] Ibid., 15.
[64] Gough, *Sepulchral Monuments*, 1/1, pl. XIX (fac. p. 50).

the form of a scallop shell', implying he was certain about it.[65] A possible explanation is that the original form of the pommel was hidden by the 'crust' which covered this and the other freestone effigies, described by Richardson in one of the sections quoted above (p. 105).

While we may doubt the crispness of the some of the carving on this effigy, there is no doubt that it was originally of the highest quality, and Kerrich's general view (Plate 62A) indicates that it was then reasonably well preserved.

RCHM no. 9 (Plates 46, 56, 60B)

Richardson says that 'The principal defects were the nose, the right hand and part of the left, the sword from the hilt downwards, one entire side of the plinth, a portion of the upper part of the shield, for which a piece of stone had long ago been substituted but never worked down.' He then adds that 'The decays, although numerous, were not deep'. It is this last sentence which gives possible cause for alarm and suggests that there *may* have been extensive recutting. Kerrich noted 'It is so defaced I cannot see whether the Armour of the Head or Neck be Maille or not'[66] and that was certainly not the case when Richardson had finished with it. However, we should also note the generally fuzzy appearance of the drawings by Stothard (Plate 60B), which is not typical of his style, and must be due to the 'crust' which coated the three freestone effigies (see p. 105 above), though this is not apparent in the drawings of several of the other effigies.[67] This same crust, rather than damage, could have been the cause of Kerrich's uncertainty over what he was seeing. Richardson also says that there were only traces of the original length of the scabbard and small portions of the upper parts of the sword.[68] Richardson says he found more colour on this effigy than on any of the others.

The small beast supporting the corner of the shield of this effigy, interpreted by Richardson as a squirrel, would appear to be the earliest example of this feature. From one of Kerrich's drawings (Plate 62) it is apparent that there was originally something similar on RCHM no. 8: it was already then missing but a stump remained. It was restored by Richardson as a knobbly lump, possibly intended to suggest the shape of a beast (and it is interesting that Richardson resisted the temptation to restore it as

[65] Richardson, *Effigies of the Temple Church*, 26. For a post-war photograph by the late A. F. Kersting, see A. Tomlinson, *The Mediaeval Face*, London 1974, 11. For other examples of lobed pommels on effigies, see J. B. Ward-Perkins, 'Persistence of Viking Types of Swords', *Antiquaries Journal*, 21, 1941, 158–61. If authentic, it is uncertain whether the Temple Church example should be classified as an example of the group Ward-Perkins identified or as a cockle shell, for which see R. E. Oakeshott, *The Sword in the Age of Chivalry*, London 1964, 102 (type G2) and pl. 44C; idem, *Records of the Medieval Sword*, Woodbridge 1991, 10 (type G2), 232.

[66] The lack of mail on the head in the Lethieullier collection drawing of the 1730s (see p. 101 and n. 30 above, and Plate 86) suggests it was already then difficult to discern its original state.

[67] Of the other two freestone effigies, Stothard did not draw RCHM no. 8 but his drawing of RCHM no. 12 (the fourteenth-century effigy) has the same fuzzy appearance: Stothard, *Monumental Effigies*, pl. 38.

[68] Richardson, *Effigies of the Temple Church*, 15 n.

a beast on the lines of that on RCHM no. 9). Beasts in this position are no doubt just a means of decorating the small piece of stone retained in this position to support the corner of the shield when there was considerable undercutting of the remainder.[69] The decoration of the top edge of the slab, under the cushion, with battlements will be commented on later.

Tomb chests, etc.

We have no firm idea of how the effigies were originally displayed. We cannot even say whether they were always freestanding or against a wall. However, if they were always in the Round, the former seems more likely because the curved walls would permit only two positions (north and south) where effigies could be placed against the wall and orientated on the east–west axis, as was normal for funerary monuments before the Re-formation. While it seems likely that the effigies would have been raised at least a little above the level of the pavement (and Richardson recorded that the plinth of RCHM no. 6 was quite thick), the evidence for this elsewhere in England in the thirteenth century is limited, as many effigies now rest on the floor or on later tomb-chests.

From thirteenth-century England, apart from the five effigial tombs in Westminster Abbey, Tummers identified only three other examples of contemporary tomb-chests supporting secular effigies.[70] To these can be added a number of ecclesiastical effigies, such as a late-twelfth-century example at Exeter Cathedral[71] and that of Archbishop Walter de Gray (d. 1255) at York Minster, which are both raised on low tomb-chests (the latter with the addition of a canopy).[72] Archbishop Godfrey de Ludham's tomb, also at York, has a cross-slab supported on low, open arcading.[73] However, the lid of de Gray's coffin, which had a painted image that was hidden when the main tomb was built, has a moulded edge and was clearly designed to stand above the level of the pavement.[74] There seems no reason why some sculpted effigies should not have been

[69] Other examples of this feature can be found down to the middle of the fourteenth century, after which shields on effigies are very rare. Two examples on effigies dating to the early and mid-fourteenth centuries may be seen at Warkworth (Northants.): A. Hartshorne, *The Recumbent Monumental Effigies in Northamptonshire*, London 1876, resp. 79 and pl. fac. 80; and 17–19, 25 and pls. fac. 18, 20 (nos. 3–7), 26 (nos. 1–5).

[70] Tummers, *Early Secular Effigies*, 28.

[71] Prior and Gardner, *Medieval Figure-Sculpture*, 574, fig. 648.

[72] H. G. Ramm et al., 'The Tombs of Archbishops Walter de Gray (1216–55) and Godfrey de Ludham (1258–65) in York Minster, and their Contents', *Archaeologia*, 103, 1971, 101–47, esp. 110–11 (figs. 2, 3), pl. xxxvi. See also S. Brown, *'Our Magnificent Fabrick': York Minster, an Architectural History c.1200–1500*, Swindon 2003, 37–42; M. J. Sillence, 'The Two Effigies of Archbishop Walter de Gray (d. 1255) at York Minster', *Church Monuments*, 20, 2005, 5–30 and col. pl. i.

[73] Ramm et al., 'Tombs of Archbishops', 131–4 (just visible in pl. xxxvi) where it is stated that Archbishop de Bovill's tomb was originally similar, though higher, but the arcaded superstructure was lost in the fire of 1839. Sillence ('Two Effigies', 21–2, 19, figs. 17, 18) has suggested that these lost parts may have been an addition to the original design. See also Brown, *York Minster*, 42–3.

[74] Ramm et al., 'The Tombs of Archbishops', 120, 111, fig. 3. For the painted image, see also Sillence, 'Two Effigies', esp. 6–12.

positioned in the same way. Richardson suggested that the well-finished outer faces of the Purbeck marble coffins discovered in 1842 indicated that they were originally visible above ground, possibly supporting effigies (p. 98 above). Two Purbeck marble effigies of bishops at Rochester Cathedral form the lids of such raised Purbeck marble coffins, and there are other raised coffins in the same material which similarly support plain slabs or cross-slabs at Rochester and also at Winchester Cathedral.[75] The available evidence indicates a wide variety of ways in which the Temple Church effigies could originally have been displayed.

WHOM DO THESE EFFIGIES COMMEMORATE?

It is highly improbable that any of the Temple Church effigies represent full serving members of the Order of the Temple, as all modern authors seem to agree. Indeed the idea that they commemorated Knights Templar was rejected by Addison and doubted by Richardson as long ago as 1843.[76] It is much more likely, as suggested by Addison, that they represent lay patrons who may have become Associates or *Confratres* — that is, those who were received into the Order in exchange for donations but who did not have to take the threefold monastic vow of poverty, chastity and obedience, with the possible exception of those Associates who were received as fully professed brothers on their deathbeds (who included William Marshal the elder, discussed below).[77] Even if some of the effigies do represent knight-brothers of the Order, none has any feature that distinguishes it from other thirteenth-century effigies in England. Esdaile said that the Temple effigies cannot represent knight-brothers because they do not wear the mantle of the Order,[78] but monuments to members of the other military orders show that it cannot be assumed that they would be shown wearing the mantle when depicted in armour.[79] If the Temple effigies represented members of the Order one might expect them to have been depicted with the beards which Templars appear to have worn.

[75] S. Badham, B. and M. Gittos and P. J. Lankester, 'List of Purbeck Marble Coffin-Shaped Slabs', Pt III (*recte* IV), *Church Monuments Society Newsletter*, 11/2, Winter 1995/6, 45–50, at 49–50 (Winchester); Pt IX, ibid., 14/1, Summer 1998, 22–4, at 23–4 (Rochester).
[76] Addison, *Temple Church*, 87–8. Richardson, *Effigies of the Temple Church*, 13. See also W. S. W[alford], 'On Cross-Legged Effigies Commonly Appropriated to Templars', *Archaeological Journal*, 1, 1845, 49–52.
[77] Nicholson, *Knights Templar*, 124. For the other terms used for Associates and the distinctions between them, see ibid., 132–3. For Associates received as fully professed brothers, see Park, pp. 69–70, 76–7, 81 above.
[78] Esdaile, *Temple Church Monuments*, 63.
[79] An example, admittedly dating from a hundred years after the suppression of the Templars, was the double effigial incised slab to the Hospitallers Sir Jehan de Parfondrieu, Master of the Chartraines and his brother Sir Arnolt, Commander of Flemalle (1413), now lost but formerly at the Flemalle Grande, Liège, Belgium, where the cross of the order was worn on the left breast on a sleeveless military gown reaching to just above the knees (F. A. Greenhill, *Incised Effigial Slabs*, 2 vols., London 1976, I, 147, II, pl. 58b; W. F. Creeny, *Illustrations of Incised Slabs on the Continent of*

While it is possible that the Master, commanders of houses and other high officers of the Order would have been commemorated by funerary images, it seems unlikely that other full serving members of the Order would have been accorded this distinction, or that they would have been buried within the church rather than in the cemetery. Nor can one assume that any members of the Order who were privileged to have a tomb image would have been depicted in armour. In his survey of European incised slabs, Greenhill concluded that it was more common for members of the military orders to be shown in their normal day dress.[80] Firm conclusions are not possible because medieval funerary images to members of the military orders are not very common and, among those that do survive, those of the Templars seem to be the least numerous: the paucity of examples is probably at least partly due to the Order's relatively early demise.[81]

Any attempt to identify the effigies naturally begins with the evidence for notable people who have been buried in the church. The famous William Marshal the elder, earl of Pembroke, who became Regent on the accession of Henry III and died in 1219, was buried in the Temple Church, almost certainly in the nave;[82] and his two sons William (who died in 1231) and Gilbert (who died in 1241), both in turn earls of Pembroke and hereditary Marshals, were buried nearby.[83] This was clearly known to the antiquaries from an early date, and the first to mention the burial of these three in the Temple seems to be John Stow, in the first edition of his *Survey of London*, published in 1598.[84] He says that five of the effigies were cross-legged and that the other three were straight-legged (which agrees with the surviving effigies), but he goes on to say that the first three cross-legged effigies represented, in this order, William the elder, William the younger and Gilbert. Unfortunately we cannot tell which effigies he was referring to

Europe, Norwich 1891, 52 and pl. fac.). Greenhill (ibid., I, 147, II, 116) also mentions an earlier slab, of c.1360, in the Musée des Beaux Arts at Troyes, depicting a Hospitaller in armour and commemorating Brother Jehan de Nanthieul, Prior of Aquitaine and Lieutenant of the Priory of France.

[80] Greenhill, *Incised Slabs*, I, 147 (Walford, 'On Cross-Legged Effigies', had reached a similar conclusion in 1845). For example, the incised slab commemorating Brother Gérard (d. 1273), Commander and founder of the House of the Templars at Villers-le-Temple, now in the church of Saint-Pierre at Liège in Belgium (illus. Greenhill, *Incised Slabs*, II, pl. 121a; see also H. Kockerols, *Monuments funéraires en pays mosan — Arondissement de Huy — Tombes et épitaphes 1000–1800*, Malonne 1999, 50, no. 2). Gérard's dress is quite similar to that worn by Templars in three other 13th-century images: a manuscript of Alfonso X of Castile's 'Book of Chess' (El Escorial, Biblioteca del Monasterio de El Esorial, MS T.I 6, fol. 25), and by the Master of the Temple, in a manuscript of Jacquemart Giélée's *Renart le Nouvel* (Paris, Bibl. Nat., MS Fr. 372, fol. 59) and a group of four Templars on the tomb-chest of Don Felipe in the church at the Templar Commandery of Villasirga (Villalcázar de Sirga), Spain (all reproduced in Nicholson, *Knights Templar*, 125–7, pls. 4.9, 4.12 and 4.11).

[81] I have been unable to find any complete survey of medieval monuments to members of the military orders and I have been largely reliant on Greenhill's *Incised Slabs* and occasional references in other publications.

[82] For a detailed discussion of his death and place of burial, see Park, pp. 76–9 above.

[83] G. E. C[okayne], *The Complete Peerage*, 13 vols., London 1910–59, X, 368, 373, Gilbert's entrails were buried at Hertford Priory, after he was killed in a tournament nearby. For a more detailed discussion, see Park, p. 82 above.

[84] Stow, *Survay of London*, 327; *Stow's Survey*, ed. Kingsford, II, 50–51.

because we do not know how all the effigies were then arranged. However, it is likely that RCHM no. 9 was among those assigned to the Marshals because of the lion on the shield (see p. 116 below).

Camden, in the third edition of his *Britannia*, published in 1594 (which, like the earlier editions, was written in Latin), also identifies three of the effigies as representing the same three earls of Pembroke but adds a marginal note: '*In altero horum tumulo lit[t] eris fugientibus legi, Comes Penbrochiae, & in latere, Miles eram Martis Mars multos vicerat armis*',[85] the most probable translation of which is, 'On another tomb of these [Pembrokes] was read in faded letters, "Earl of Pembroke", and on the side, "I was a knight of Mars, and Mars vanquished many in arms."' Taken at face value, this implies that the monument with the inscriptions (not necessarily an effigy) was not among the three effigies Stow identified as commemorating the three named earls, i.e. it commemorated another earl of Pembroke. However, in Edward Gibson's English edition of 1695 the same marginal note begins 'On one of these monuments . . .', making it possible that the inscriptions were on one of the effigies; and it is possible that this less complicated meaning was intended in the earlier editions.[86] If so, this is the strongest evidence we have that one of the effigies commemorated an earl of Pembroke, and the inscription would have been appropriate to William Marshal the elder, though one or both inscriptions could have been added at a later date.

In addition to the three Marshals, Stow mentions one member of the Ros or Roos family as being buried in the Temple Church — Robert Ros, also known as Fursan. By a charter of 1226 Robert had given to the Templars his manor of Ribston in Yorkshire, together with the advowson of the church and his body for burial.[87] Robert was dead by 16 July 1227, when Archbishop de Gray confirmed this gift. In December 1226 the king had taken the homage of William de Ros for the lands of Robert de Ros falling to him by inheritance.[88] This could indicate that Robert was then already dead or merely that he had retired from secular life.[89] It seems probable that, like William Marshal the elder, he became a full member of the Templars rather than just a lay associate (*confrater*)

[85] W. Camden, *Britannia . . .*, London 1594, 321. There has been some confusion among previous authors over which edition first mentions the effigies. I have been unable to locate the relevant passage in the first edition of 1586, or in the editions of 1587 and 1590.

[86] It is possible that the difference between the two texts may be resolved by reference to Edward Gibson's papers relating to his edition of *Britannia* which are preserved at The Queen's College, Oxford. I am grateful for advice on this to John Blair. Philémon Holland's translation in the 1637 edition (p. 427) has, 'Upon William the Elder, his Tombe, I have some yeares since read in the upper part *Comes Penbrochiae . . .*', but this does not correspond with Camden's text, and the location of the inscription specifically to William the elder's tomb appears to have been invented by Holland.

[87] *Early Yorkshire Charters, vol. X: The Trusbutt Fee with some Charters of the Ros Fee*, ed. C. T. Clay, Yorkshire Archaeological Society Record Series, extra ser. vol. 8, 1955, 40–41 (no. 14). See also David Park, p. 81 above, to whom I am grateful for drawing this volume to my attention. Stow, *Survay of London*, 327, incorrectly gives Robert's date of death as 1245.

[88] *Early Yorkshire Charters vol. X*, 41.

[89] Cokayne, *Complete Peerage*, XI, 92–3.

because a further confirmation of his gift of Ribston, by his aunt, Hilary Trussebut (d. 1241), refers to him as 'brother Robert de Ros, my nephew'.[90]

The wording of Robert's charter might be read as an intention that he should be buried at Ribston, where there was a Templar Preceptory,[91] but David Park, in his contribution to this volume, points out that Robert left his body to the Order, not to a particular preceptory, and concluded that it is more likely that Robert was buried at the London Temple, and that the tradition recorded by Stow was correct. This view is supported by another document, the 'successio dominorum de Rose' (succession of the Lords of Ros) which is preserved in a collection of papers associated with John Leland, where Robert's gift of the manor of Ribston is recorded, and a little later it is stated that 'Robert Fursan was made a Templar and was buried in London.'[92] For my present purpose, it is sufficient to note that Stow evidently *believed* that Robert Ros had been buried in the London Temple Church, and this belief, repeated by later antiquaries, prompted attempts to try and identify one of the effigies as his.

To avoid confusion, brief reference should be made to the arms of Ros (or Roos) which appear on the shield of the fourteenth-century effigy (RCHM no. 12); however,

---

[90] '. . . fratris Roberti de Ros nepotis mei' (in the genitive): *Early Yorkshire Charters vol. X*, 42 (no. 15). See also Park, p. 81 above.

[91] *The Victoria History of the Counties of England: Yorkshire*, III, London 1913, 258–9.

[92] 'Robertus fursan factus est Templarius et Londini sepultus'; BL, MS Cotton Julius C vi, fol. 226, cited by Esdaile, *Temple Church Monuments*, 64, who gives *frater* instead of *factus* (I am grateful to Nigel Ramsay for a transcript and discussion of this entry). The date of this 'successio', which continues down to George de Ros (d. 1513), is not known, but it is not apparently in Leland's hand, though other papers bound up in the same manuscript are. Dr Ramsay has drawn my attention to what is probably a copy of the same document, made by Robert Glover, in the Bodleian Library, Oxford (MS Ashmole 848, fols. 2ᵛ–3ᵛ; see W. H. Black, *A . . . Catalogue of the Manuscripts Bequeathed unto the University of Oxford by Elias Ashmole*, Oxford 1854, cols. 609–612) which Glover says was copied from Leland's 'Collections'. This copy has not yet been examined by the present author.

It should be noted that Weever, *Monuments*, 443, appears to be the source of a later confusion in giving an inscription (repeated by Esdaile, *Temple Church Monuments*, 64): 'Hic requiescit / . . . R . . . Ep . . . Quondam Visitator generalis ordinis Milicie Templi, in Anglia & in Francia & in Italia. . .' (once Visitor General of the Order of Knights Templar in England, France and Italy), which he says was 'insculpted upon one of these crosse-legged Monuments [i.e. the effigies]; as I found it amongst other Collections by one studious in Antiquities, in Sir *Robert Cottons* voluminous Librarie: which he proues by pedigree of the said Lord *Rosses* [presumably that discussed at the start of this note], to haue been to the memory of one *Robert Rosse* a Templer, who died about the yeare 1245 [this date, also given by Stow, is a mistake], and gave to the Templars his Mannor of Ribston'. Esdaile, *Temple Church Monuments*, 64, claimed that the source of this inscription was BL, MS Cotton Julius D.14 (*sic*, and no fol. number is given), but the Julius D series of Cotton manuscripts only goes up as far as no. XI, and the present author has been unable to locate the correct reference. In fact it seems certain that Weever or his source was wrong in locating this inscription on one of the effigies (as realised by Addison, *Temple Church*, 124) because, apart from the name near the beginning, '. . . R . . . Ep.', minor spelling differences and the omission of the final 'in Italia', it is identical to an inscription recorded by Burton on a 'blue Marble [slab]' . . . 'in the body of the church' that had formerly been inlaid with brass, which commemorated one Constantius de Hoverio (W. Burton, *The Description of Leicester Shire*, London 1622, 235). For discussion of the lost indent, see David Park's paper, pp. 86–7 above.

we know that this effigy, which is discussed in more detail in David Park's paper above, was only introduced into the church in the late seventeenth century. David Park also cites evidence to suggest that Robert de Vieuxpont, who witnessed Robert de Ros's charter of 1226, was also buried in the London Temple Church, although Vieuxpont's name is apparently not recorded by any of the antiquaries.[93]

William Burton, in his history of Leicestershire, first published in 1622[94] (possibly based on his memories of 1593[95]), adds further names to the list of those commemorated by the Temple Church effigies: '*Vere* Earle of *Oxford*, *Mandevile* Earle of *Essex*' and '*Bohun* Earle of *Hereford*'. I have found no evidence that any of the earls of Oxford or the Bohuns who were earls of Hereford were buried in the Temple Church, and all the holders of those titles who died before the suppression of the Templars are recorded as being buried elsewhere, according to the *Complete Peerage*.[96]

The *Complete Peerage* also records the burial places of all six members of the Mandeville family who were earls of Essex, of whom only one was buried in the Temple — Geoffrey de Mandeville, the famous first earl.[97] On his death in 1144 his body was taken to the Old Temple at Holborn, but, as he had died under excommunication, his body could not receive Christian burial until absolution was granted posthumously in 1163, when the body was buried in the New Temple (the present site). Although the sources disagree on exactly where within the enclosure he was buried, it seems it was not within the main body of the church.[98] 1144 is far too early for any of the effigies now in the church, and, while it possible that Geoffrey was commemorated by an effigy erected later, there is no evidence for this. As Nichols pointed out, Burton's identification of one of the effigies as a Mandeville is not repeated by later London historians.[99]

As already noted, Gerard Legh's *Accedens of Armorie*, which cannot be regarded as entirely reliable, records painted arms on the shields of the effigies.[100] None of the remains of colour recorded by Richardson was substantial enough to enable specific heraldic arms to be identified or even suggested. Only two of the thirteenth-century

[93] Park, p. 81 above.

[94] Burton, *Leicester Shire*, 234–5.

[95] Esdaile, *Temple Church Monuments*, 63, assumes this, but Burton (*Leicester Shire*, 235) merely tells us he was admitted to the Society of the Inner Temple in 1593, which does not preclude his having made a later visit. Burton began his book in 1597 (C. Phythian-Adams, 'Leicestershire and Rutland', in *A Guide to English County Histories*, ed. C. R. J. Currie and C. P. Lewis, Stroud 1994, 229).

[96] Cokayne, *Complete Peerage*, x, 207–18 (earls of Oxford); vi, 459–66 (Bohuns, earls of Hereford). The first de Bohun to hold the title earl of Hereford was Henry (d. 1200). The previous two earls were Miles and Roger of Gloucester. Miles, like Henry de Bohun and his son and heir Humphrey, was buried at Llanthony by Gloucester and it seems likely that Roger, who became a monk, was buried there also (ibid., vi, 453, 455).

[97] Cokayne, *Complete Peerage*, v, 116–132. The last de Mandeville to hold the title was William, on whose death in 1226/27 the title passed, through his sister, to the de Bohuns.

[98] For the burial of Geoffrey de Mandeville at the New Temple, see Wilson, pp. 21–2 above; Park, pp. 68–74 above.

[99] J. G. N[ichols], 'The Effigy attributed to Geoffrey de Magnaville, and other effigies in the Temple Church', *Herald and Genealogist*, 3, 1866, 100.

[100] Quoted on p. 99 above.

effigies in the Temple Church have carvings on their shields, and in only one case is it certain that they are heraldic. As already mentioned, heraldry is also found on the shield of the fourteenth-century effigy (RCHM no. 12) discussed in David Park's paper above.

RCHM no. 9 displays on its shield a *lion rampant*. A red lion rampant on a vertically divided field of gold and green (*per pale or and vert, a lion rampant gules*) was borne by the Marshals, earls of Pembroke (sometimes the lion's tail is forked).[101] Since three members of the Marshal family are recorded as having been buried in the church, the wish to identify this effigy with one of them is understandable. However, the dates of death of the three candidates — 1219, 1231, and 1241 — are all, in my view, too early for this effigy, which should be placed at least after 1250 and more probably after the late 1250s (see p. 128 f. below). It is possible that the effigy was made retrospectively — like that, for example, ordered by Henry III in 1253 for his sister, Queen Joan of Scotland, who had died in 1235[102] — but that is pure speculation. Richardson says he found more colour on this effigy than on any of the others, but the only colour noted on the shield was traces of red on the field, and no colour was found on the lion.[103] This conflicts with the arms borne by the Marshals — a red lion on a gold and green field — though the red found by Richardson might have been part of a ground for gilding. Sadly this evidence is insufficient to confirm or deny that the arms were those of the Marshals. There were, of course, various other families who bore a lion rampant as the main charge in their arms.[104]

The surface of the shield of RCHM no. 6 is covered in decorative diapering. Radiating from the centre are eight decorated ribs each terminating in fleurs-de-lis, which have been interpreted as forming the heraldic charge of the *carbuncle* or *escarbuncle*. This charge probably originated as a shield boss with radiating bars to provide additional strength to the shield, and it is far from certain that it has any heraldic significance here. On the basis of this feature, the effigy was identified by Richardson as that of Geoffrey de Mandeville, earl of Essex.

It would appear that the first person to identify RCHM no. 6 as commemorating Geoffrey de Mandeville in print was Gough in 1786.[105] As Geoffrey died in 1144, Gough observed that this was the earliest example of heraldic arms so far discovered,

---

[101] For a summary of the arms recorded for William the elder and his sons, see *Rolls of Arms: Henry III*, ed. T. D. Tremlett and H. S. London, London 1967, 8.

[102] Liberate Roll for 1252/3 (TNA:PRO C 62/29, membrane 13) — see *Calendar of the Liberate Rolls Preserved in the Public Record Office: Henry III*, 6 vols., London 1916–64, IV: *1251–1260*, 91 (7 Dec. 1252), 138 (14 June 1253); Pipe Roll for 1253/4 (TNA:PRO E 372/98, membrane 17). This evidence has been mentioned by several earlier authors, but I am grateful to John Blair and James Collingwood for locating and transcribing the entries, of which the latter appears never to have been published in full and has previously been inaccurately or incompletely referenced.

[103] Richardson, *Effigies of the Temple Church*, 25.

[104] Some with variations to the tail and some with major or minor marks of difference. For those recorded in the thirteenth century, see C. Humphery-Smith, *Anglo-Norman Armory Two: an Ordinary of Thirteenth-century Armorials*, Canterbury 1984, 59 ff; see also *Dictionary of British Arms: Medieval Ordinary*, I, ed. D. H. B. Chesshyre and T. Woodcock, London 1992, 107 ff.

[105] Gough, *Sepulchral Monuments*, I/1, second or main Arabic pagination, 23–4.

a view refuted by J. G. Nichols in 1866, who realised the effigy could not be that early and argued that the escarbuncle here was not heraldic.[106] Gough's basis for his identification was the escarbuncle on the shield, since a passage (which he cited) in the Chronicle of Walden Abbey relates that Geoffrey added the escarbuncle to his shield when he was girded with the sword of the earldom of Essex.[107] But this section of the Walden Abbey Chronicle was condemned as unreliable in 1892 by Round, who also pointed out that there is no evidence of this charge in the arms of any of Geoffrey's descendants,[108] who bore arms of red and gold quarters.[109]

In 1866 Nichols drew attention to three plain narrow zig-zag bands crossing the shield horizontally,[110] which would be blazoned heraldically as *three bars dancetty*, and on this basis he drew attention to several individuals or families who bore arms involving *bars dancetty* or *wavy*.[111] However, as no member of any of these families is recorded as having been buried in the Temple Church, this does not help further with identifying the effigy. The three *bars dancetty* (if that is what they are) are very narrow, and, while they were noted by Richardson and appear in his drawings and on the pre-1941 photographs of the effigy, they are absent from the earlier drawings by Stothard and Kerrich. It seems most unlikely that Richardson would have invented these features entirely (though the possibility remains that he reconstructed them from too little evidence); their significance, however, remains uncertain.

When the first complete edition of Stothard's *Monumental Effigies* was published in 1832, with text by Alfred Kempe, RCHM no. 9 (the effigy with the lion on the shield)

---

[106] Nichols, 'Geoffrey de Magnaville'.

[107] Gough, *Sepulchral Monuments*, 1/1, 23–4. He may well have just been repeating an idea already current among antiquaries. It may be significant that a shield with a field of *quarterly or and gules*, thought to have been used by Geoffrey and certainly used by his descendants (see A. R. Wagner, 'Heraldry', in *Medieval England . . .* , ed. A. L. Poole, Oxford 1958, 1, 350–52) and also a shield of the same arms charged with *an escarbuncle* are both included in Legh's *Accedens of Armory* of 1576, respectively fols. 25ᵛ, 101ʳ — a book which was dedicated to the Inns of Court and in the course of which the narrator visits the Inner Temple. Although no identification is given by Legh for either coat of arms, their inclusion may suggest that the passage in the Walden Abbey Chronicle concerning Geoffrey's arms was already known at that date. Whether the association had already been extended to the effigy is impossible to say.

[108] J. H. Round, *Geoffrey de Mandeville: a Study of the Anarchy*, London 1892, 395. The passage concerned occurs in what appears to be a summary of lost chapters from Book 1 of the original text of The Chronicle (which is now called 'The Book of Walden Abbey') which occurs in two other texts, now known as the 'Walden Annals' and the 'Roll of Founders': see *The Book of Walden Abbey*, ed. D. Greenaway and L. Watkins, Oxford 1999, pp. lviii–lix and appendix 1 (the escarbuncle passage is quoted on p. 168). Despite this, it still seems most unlikely that the escarbuncle passage occurred in the original version of 'The Book'.

[109] Wagner, 'Heraldry', 350–52. In the thirteenth century the quarters were arranged both as *or and gules* and *gules and or*, though it is unclear whether this indicates intentional differencing (see also *Rolls of Arms: Henry III*, ed. Tremlett and London, 7–8).

[110] These features had also been noted by Richardson but without further comment: *Effigies of the Temple Church*, 19.

[111] Nichols, *Geoffrey de Magnaville*, 104. The modern spelling of *dancetty* and the usual current term *wavy* have been used here in preference to Nichols's *dancettée* and *undée*.

was still identified as William Marshal the elder in Kempe's text, though Stothard's caption to the plates was more circumspect: 'Supposed to represent one of the Mareschals, Earl of Pembroke'.[112] By 1876, when the second edition was published, John Hewitt in his additional notes to the original text said that the effigy was 'formerly attributed to William Marshal . . . who died in 1219, [but] has more recently been attributed to his son who died in 1231', but he then cast doubt on that identification too on the grounds that the colour found on the shield (by Richardson) did not accord with the Pembroke arms,[113] though, as I have already said, I believe the evidence is inconclusive.

This reidentification of RCHM no. 9 had first appeared over 30 years earlier in two publications of 1843. In his *Effigies of the Temple Church*, Richardson had proposed new identifications for several of the effigies. In addition to identifying RCHM no. 9 as William the younger (d. 1231), RCHM no. 10 became William Marshal the elder, RCHM no. 8 became Gilbert Marshal (d. 1241), and RCHM no. 7 became Robert Ros (d. 1227) who, as already noted, was believed to have been buried in the Temple. All these identifications seem to be based on nothing more than Richardson's (or his source's) view that the effigies appeared to him to be of approximately the right date for the dates of death of the three men concerned. Richardson retained Gough's identification of RCHM no. 6 as Geoffrey de Mandeville.

Richardson's book was preceded in the same year by Addison's *The Temple Church*.[114] This anticipated Richardson's identifications of RCHM nos. 10, 9 and 8, but identified as Robert de Ros (d. 1227) RCHM no. 12 (the fourteenth-century effigy) in preference to Richardson's RCHM no. 7. It is not clear whether one author was copying the other or whether both were following new ideas that were already then in circulation. Both authors acknowledge each other generally, though apparently only Richardson's views on the effigy attributed to Geoffrey de Mandeville (RCHM no. 6) are specifically mentioned (by Addison).[115]

In conclusion, there is no certain evidence for assigning firm or even probable identities to any of the thirteenth-century military effigies, and several of the present 'traditional' identifications can be traced no earlier than Addison's and Richardson's books of 1843. On the evidence of the inscriptions recorded by Camden, probably on one of the effigies (see p. 113 above), it is possible that one of them commemorates an earl of Pembroke, most probably William Marshal the elder, but we cannot definitely say which effigy. Stylistically RCHM no. 10 is a possible candidate, but it is not cross-legged whereas Stow says the three Marshals were all commemorated by cross-legged effigies.[116]

---

[112] Stothard, *Monumental Effigies*, pls. 26–7 and adjacent text (1876 edn), 48. The drawings were made in February 1811 and etched by Stothard in April 1811. I am grateful to Richard Knowles for advice on this.

[113] Stothard, *Monumental Effigies* (1876 edn), 48–9, pls. 26–7.

[114] Addison, *Temple Church*, the dagger footnote on pp. 124–5; and a note in Richardson's *Effigies of the Temple Church*, 10, makes it clear that Addison's book was published first.

[115] Refs. as in preceding note and Addison, *Temple Church*, 94–5.

[116] Stow, *Survay of London*, 327. William Marshal the elder's effigy is also said to be cross-

ARMS AND ARMOUR

All the thirteenth-century effigies are shown in similar body armour of a kind typical of the thirteenth century, but difficult to date more closely. Since almost no European armour survives from this period, our understanding relies heavily on contemporary illustrations. The best general account of the development of European armour is still that by Claude Blair, published in 1958, on which the following account is based.[117] A key manuscript for illustrations of thirteenth-century armour is the Picture Bible in the Pierpont Morgan Library in New York.[118] It has been variously dated from the 1240s to the 1260s, but the general consensus now seems to be about 1240–50.[119]

A knight about to put on his armour would probably have been dressed in drawers, a shirt and thick hose. The first items to be put on were the long mail hose or chausses, which probably reached to about the mid-thigh or a little above and were presumably supported by straps attached to a waist belt.[120] Relieving straps would probably have been threaded though the mail below the knee to prevent sagging; these are not now visible on any of the Temple effigies, though they are on some others.[121] The next item to be put on was a thick, long shirt or padded shirt-like garment now generally called an aketon (though the term gambeson may sometimes have been used for it[122]). These undergarments are not normally visible on effigies since they were covered by the mail

legged in an unpublished manuscript of about 1632 (Inner Temple Records, MS 32, p. 2; see *Catalogue of Manuscripts of the Library of the . . . Inner Temple*, ed. J. Conway Davies, III, Oxford 1972, 1076). This agrees with RCHM no. 9, which was that identified as William the elder until about 1843 (see p. 118 above), and it is possible that this identification had remained unchanged since the late 16th century. In his contribution to this volume, David Park argues, on the basis of perspicacious observations, that the case for identifying RCHM no. 10 as William Marshal the elder is much stronger than I have concluded here (see Park, pp. 79–80 above).

[117] Blair, *European Armour*, esp. chap. 1, 'The Age of Mail'.

[118] MS M.638. Commonly known as the Maciejowski or Shah Abbas 'Bible' after its seventeenth-century owners. Published in facsimile by S. C. Cockerell, M. R. James and C. ffoulkes, *A Book of Old Testament Illustrations of the Thirteenth Century*, The Roxburghe Club, Cambridge 1927, and again (in colour), together with an abridged version of Cockerell's text, in S. C. Cockerell and J. Plummer, *Old Testament Miniatures*, New York 1969. Two separated leaves are in the Bibliothèque nationale de France, Paris (MS nouv. acq. lat. 2294), and a further leaf is in the J. Paul Getty Museum, Los Angeles (MS Ludwig I.6).

[119] For a summary of the dating and attributions (to Paris, northern France, Flanders, England and Italy), see H. Stahl, *Picturing Kingship: History and Painting in the Psalter of St Louis*, University Park, PA, 2008, 98, and for his own suggested dating of 1239/41×1244, see ibid., 209.

[120] For the chausse generally, see D. J. La Rocca, 'Notes on the Mail Chausse', *Journal of the Arms and Armour Society*, 15/2, September 1995, 69–84.

[121] For example, that commemorating William Longespée the elder in Salisbury Cathedral: Stothard, *Monumental Effigies*, pl. 17; repr. in Blair, *European Armour*, 22, fig. 4.

[122] Claude Blair pointed out to me that there is evidence to suggest that 'aketon' was used to refer to the quilted garment worn under the mail shirt, and 'gambeson' to the similar garment worn over it, or independently as a defence: see C. R. Beard, 'Order for a New Trial', *Fragmenta Armamentaria*, ed. F. R. Cripps-Day, v, Frome 1941, 118–19.

shirt or hauberk, but they are visible in the Morgan Picture Bible; this manuscript also gives a clear view of the hauberk, which on effigies is usually largely hidden by the sleeveless surcoat (which armour students now prefer to call a gown).[123]

By the thirteenth century the mail shirt normally had an attached hood (the coif) and attached gauntlets, normally of mitten form (called mufflers), again shown in the Morgan Picture Bible,[124] but sometimes — as in the case of one of the Temple Church effigies (RCHM no. 10) — with divided fingers. The mail coif was normally worn over a thick or padded textile coif, sometimes with the addition of a hard plate or leather defence, again shown in the Morgan Picture Bible.[125]

The attached mail coif had a flap on one side, called a ventail. This was held in place by laces, attached near the brow, normally on the wearer's left side, and this is clearly shown on three of the Temple effigies (RCHM nos. 7, 8 and 9).[126] When unfastened, this enabled the coif to be thrown back off the head, as seen on the fourteenth-century effigy (RCHM no. 12; Plates 52–3). In the case of RCHM no. 8, as left by Richardson, a lace is threaded through the mail right round the face opening of the coif to enable a good fit when tightened. This is plausible, but Kerrich was 'not certain whether the circle next the face be maille or not'. The mail mittens could also be removed from the hands, probably by means of slits in the palms (which were made of leather for obvious reasons), and allowed to hang down, as shown on the brass to Sir William de Setvans at Chartham (Kent), which is approximately contemporary with RCHM no. 12.[127]

The final item which is present on all the Temple effigies is the shield. On thirteenth-century effigies this can vary considerably in size but tends to be fairly large. It was mainly supported by the forearm passing through one or more straps attached to the inside of the shield (often called enarmes; the later English term is braces). These straps are only rarely visible on effigies, but a single strap is shown on one of the Temple effigies (RCHM no. 8; Plate 62B).[128] The inclusion of this detail further demonstrates the very high quality of this effigy. Additional support for the shield was often provided by a strap worn over the right shoulder (called a guige) and this is visible on all the Temple Church effigies.

That summarises the typical armour seen on all the thirteenth-century Temple Church effigies, but some of them show additional features. RCHM no. 6 wears a cy-

---

[123] The hauberk is visible in the Morgan Picture Bible, fol. 3ᵛ; Cockerell et al., *Illustrations*. In commenting on illustrations in the Maciejowski manuscript which appear to show the hauberk being put on over an ordinary shirt, Claude Blair (*European Armour*, 32–3) suggests that the necessary padding may have been incorporated into the lining of the hauberk.

[124] The coif and mufflers are again visible in the Morgan Picture Bible, fol. 3ᵛ; Cockerell et al., *Illustrations*.

[125] Fol. 11ᵛ; Cockerell et al., *Illustrations*.

[126] The ventail is still visible on RCHM nos. 8 and 9, but no longer on RCHM no. 7, the head of which suffered badly in the war damage.

[127] *The Earliest English Brasses: Patronage, Style and Workshops 1270–1350*, ed. J. Coales, London 1987, 87, fig. 74.

[128] I am indebted to Celia Charlton for checking that this feature is still visible. As it was drawn by Kerrich, it cannot have been invented by Richardson.

lindrical helmet, with central ridge or seam and a stout 'chin strap'. Various authors and antiquaries have debated whether there was an attached vertical bar to protect the nose (a nasal) but my reading of the evidence is that there was not. The closest comparative English illustration I have found is the helmet worn by the leading knight in the scene of the Martyrdom of St Thomas of Canterbury from a Psalter in the British Library which been dated to c.1220.[129]

One of the effigies (RCHM no. 3; Plate 60) wears an arming cap — that is, a padded version of the civilian close-fitting hood or coif, designed to provide additional protection below the armour — in this case with a padded ring around the temples. Where, as here, the cap with the padded ring is worn over the coif, the ring was presumably intended to support the great helm by engaging with the latter's lining. RCHM no. 4 (Plate 61) wears a similar padded ring, apparently attached to a skull cap, but with no visible means of holding it in place. Coifs with padded rings, worn both over the mail coif and directly on the head, are depicted on statues on the west front of Wells Cathedral.[130] None of the Temple Church effigies wears a great helm, but they appear on a few other effigies such as those at Walkerne (Herts) and Twyford (Bucks),[131] both also in Purbeck marble and stylistically related (see p. 131 ff. below).

One of the Wells west front statues also wears an extra protective collar,[132] not of mail but probably of leather, and it is possible that this is what we see on RCHM no. 5 (Plates 56, 58A), where the neck lacks any carving to represent mail. However, the smooth surface of the neck seems to extend over the whole head, rather like a Balaclava. This is somewhat puzzling, and Kerrich annotated his drawing: 'The Armour of the Head and neck does not appear to be maille yet I should suppose it is'. As Richardson tells us that he found this effigy in very poor condition no firm conclusions can be drawn about the original state of the head, though it is worth noting that the head and neck were shown as lacking any carved mail in the earliest surviving drawing made in the 1730s, in the collections of Smart Lethieullier (Plate 85).[133]

The two Reigate stone effigies (RCHM nos. 8 and 9) display additional protection for the knees, not seen on the other thirteenth-century Temple Church effigies. These are almost certainly the lower ends of padded tubes (called gamboised cuisses), which extend up under the skirt of the hauberk to protect the thighs. Once again the Morgan

---

[129] BL, MS Harley 5102, f. 32: N. Morgan, *Early Gothic Manuscripts [I] 1190–1250*, London 1982, 88–9, no. 40, ill. 138. A similarly shaped helmet, apparently with a nasal, is worn by an effigy originally at the Abbey of Étival and now in the Musée Archéologique, Le Mans, attributed to Raoul I de Beaumont, ? after 1210 (for references, see n. 191 below).

[130] Colchester nos. 124–6 (L. S. Colchester, *The West Front of Wells Cathedral*, Wells 1951 and later editions); illus. in *Courtauld Institute Illustration Archives, Archive 1, Cathedrals and Monastic Buildings in the British Isles, Pt 2, Wells b North West Tower*, ed. P. Kidson and P. Tudor-Craig, London 1977, nos. 1/2/62–67; see drawn details in Blair, *European Armour*, 34, figs. 11, 12; and descriptions in J. Sampson, *Wells Cathedral West Front: Construction, Sculpture and Conservation*, Stroud 1998, 210–11.

[131] For references see n. 189 below.

[132] Colchester no. 124. For references see n. 130 above.

[133] BL, Add. MS 27248, fol. 90; see n. 30 above.

Picture Bible (fol. 3ᵛ; see n. 118 above) is most helpful in showing a figure in the process of putting them on.

On one of the Reigate stone effigies (RCHM no. 8) we catch a glimpse of another piece of armour. Through the arm-hole of the gown under the figure's right arm a line of straps is visible (Plate 62c). The same feature appears on an approximately contemporary effigy at Pershore Abbey (Worcs.).[134] This is the side-fastening of some form of body protection worn over the mail shirt but under the gown. What form this protection took is uncertain from the limited parts visible, but it may have been composed of metal plates, hardened leather or possibly baleen.[135] Such protection for the torso, consisting of a series of separate metal plates riveted to the inside of a fabric covering (now called 'a coat of plates' but in the Middle Ages called 'a pair of plates' or simply 'plates'), is shown on the figure of St Maurice at Magdeburg Cathedral, dating to the 1240s, where it is worn over the mail hauberk and the rivet heads are visible.[136] No rivets are visible on the small parts of the relevant garments visible on the Temple Church or Pershore effigies, but they could have been painted on. The earliest 'complete' excavated coats of plates are from the mid-fourteenth century[137] but some smaller surviving fragments could be earlier.[138]

The swords, in so far as their present form is original, all have straight blades and simple cross-hilts, typical of the 'knightly' swords worn throughout the Middle Ages. While swords of this type with one-edged blades were not unknown in this period, the vast majority were sharpened on both edges, as in the case of RCHM no. 10, which is the only Temple effigy to show the sword exposed.[139] The sword belts are all of a very simple type used throughout the thirteenth-century, consisting of a single belt with the scabbard attached directly to it. RCHM no. 6 shows a single additional, narrower

[134] Blair, *European Armour*, 49, fig. 17; for a view of the whole effigy, see Tummers, *Early Secular Effigies*, pl. 52. I know of no visual evidence for the existence of this feature on the Temple effigy earlier than Richardson's post-restoration drawings (*Effigies of the Temple Church*, pl. 8) though in the accompanying text he describes this feature as already existing and he would have had no reason to invent it.

[135] Sometimes called whalebone, but in fact a softer material from the mouth of certain types of whale; see R. Moffat, J. A. Spriggs and S. O'Connor, 'The Use of Baleen for Arms, Armour and Heraldic Crests in Medieval Britain', *Antiquaries Journal*, 88, 2008, 207–15.

[136] See B. Thordeman, *Armour from the Battle of Wisby 1361*, Stockholm 1939, 285–7, figs. 288, 289; also P. Williamson, *Gothic Sculpture 1140–1300*, New Haven and London 1995, 176–7, pl. 262 (front view only). Another early example (where the coat of plates is also worn over the mail hauberk) is the figure of a sleeping guard on a reliquary in the Provinzial Museum, Hanover: Thordeman, *Battle of Wisby*, 289, fig. 290; Blair, *European Armour*, 49, fig. 18.

[137] See Thordeman, *Battle of Wisby*. The Temple and Pershore effigies are discussed on p. 302 (RCHM no. 8 is illus. at p. 305, fig. 311), where the strap-fastened protection is interpreted as a plastron of *cuir-boulli* (hardened leather). For coats of plates shown fastening at the sides see ibid., Armours nos. 22 (pp. 381–5) and 25 (pp. 392–404).

[138] I am grateful to the late Claude Blair for his views on this point.

[139] For medieval swords generally, see C. Blair, *European and American Arms c.1100–1850*, London 1962, 1–5 (useful short summary); also Oakeshott, *Sword in the Age of Chivalry* and *Records . . .* but, for errors in the latter, see review by A. V. B. Norman, *Antiquaries Journal*, 70, 1990, 490–91.

diagonal strap joining the sword-belt to a point a short way down the scabbard.[140] The evidence of the stylistically similar effigy at Walkerne (Herts.) points to there almost certainly being a matching diagonal strap on the other side of the scabbard.[141] Together, these straps would have prevented the scabbard from swinging back and forth.

When in their scabbards, swords were normally carried on the left side. It has sometimes been observed that RCHM nos. 3, 4 and 6 (Plates 59A, 60A, 61) wear their swords on the opposite side, and this is also true of the effigy at Merevale (Warwicks.) (Plate 59B). Showing the scabbarded sword on the figure's right side seems to be an artistic invention. The swords are not carried against the hips, as seen on the other effigies, but have been allowed to slip round with their belts so that they lie flat on the slab to the figure's right. By showing the sword lying on the slab, the sculptor avoided the problem that, in its conventional position, part of the scabbard would project beyond the lower edge of the gown and might require considerable or complete undercutting and support. It would have been impossible to carry swords in the manner shown on the three Temple effigies and that at Merevale when fighting, and it would have severely impeded progress when walking.

The Monumental and Effigial Context

The introduction of the monumental effigy in England has usually been dated to the second half of the twelfth century. However, Sally Badham has recently argued for an earlier date for the surviving parts of an effigy, apparently in civilian dress and inscribed to Aubrey de Vere (probably the first of that name, d. 1141); it was originally at Colne Priory (Essex) and is now at St Stephen's Chapel, Bures (Suffolk). Badham pointed out that a later date for the introduction of effigies to England would leave this country some way behind similar developments in France.[142] Despite the very early example at Bures, the earliest English effigies, dating to before 1200, otherwise commemorate the clergy, usually senior clergy. The earliest effigies in the Temple Church (RCHM nos. 5 and 10) are therefore among the earliest secular effigies in the country, very likely predating the effigy of King John (d. 1216) at Worcester Cathedral, which was probably

---

[140] For drawings of all the sword-belts on the Temple effigies, see Hartshorne, 'Sword Belts'. On several of the sword-belts and guiges decorative metal mounts and bar-mounts are shown. For surviving examples, mostly from excavations, see G. Egan and F. Pritchard, *Dress Accessories, c.1150–c.1450*, London 1991, 162–243 ('Mounts'), esp. 209–15 ('Bar Mounts'), where Temple Church effigies RCHM nos. 3, 8 and 9 are illus. at 210–11. The guige of RCHM no. 8 has shield shaped mounts which would probably have borne the owner's arms. For armorial mounts, see Egan and Pritchard *Dress Accessories*, 181–4, and *The Medieval Horse and its Equipment, c.1150–c.1450*, ed. J. Clark, London 1995, 69–71.

[141] For references to the Walkern effigy, see n. 189 below.

[142] S. Badham, 'Our Earliest English Effigies', *Church Monuments Society Newsletter*, 23/2, Winter 2007/8, 10–11. Badham also draws attention to another possibly early effigy, now built into the east wall of Bathampton Church (Somerset).

made about 1230–40, contemporary with the placing of the body in a new sarcophagus in 1232.[143]

In his study of thirteenth-century secular effigies in England, Tummers listed about 215 examples: about 140 in armour ('knights'), about 45 females in civil dress ('ladies') and about 30 males in civilian dress ('civilians').[144] Dating effigies to before or after 1300 is not always easy, and subsequent revisions of dating[145] and new discoveries will have changed Tummers's totals slightly, but they are sufficiently accurate for a general overview. An equivalent survey of thirteenth-century ecclesiastical effigies has not yet been published, and dating such effigies is often difficult because the mass vestments (in which they are almost always depicted at this period)[146] remained essentially unchanged. However, there appear to be fewer thirteenth-century ecclesiastical than secular effigies, with the vast majority representing the higher clergy (bishops and heads of monastic houses, as in the case of the example in the Temple Church, discussed in David Park's paper above), probably because the ordinary parish clergy had not, in general, yet aspired to this type of monument and some of the higher clergy preferred flat slabs (which were more suited to burial in the eastern parts of their churches, where taller monuments might obstruct the liturgy). By the end of the century, some members of the higher clergy were among the first to be commemorated by a slab enhanced by brass inlay (the 'monumental brass', which had by then become available in England), and were probably responsible for initiating the steady growth in the popularity of this type of monument throughout the fourteenth century.[147]

The Temple effigies display a variety of poses and features. RCHM nos. 4, 5 and 10 are relatively stiff with straight legs. The remainder have crossed legs, though are by no means uniform, and this attitude will be discussed below. All but three of the heads of the thirteenth-century effigies are supported on a roughly rectangular single cushion, set square.[148] The exceptions are RCHM no. 6, where the cushion is set diamond-wise, RCHM no. 10, which has an octagonal cushion, and RCHM no. 5, which has no head support. The line of battlements carved on the head end of the slab, below the pillow,

[143] *Annales Monastici*, ed. H. R Luard, 5 vols., London 1864–9 (Rolls Series, 36), I, 84 (Chronicle of Tewkesbury Abbey). See also J. Martindale, 'The Sword on the Stone: Some Resonances of a Medieval Symbol of Power: the Tomb of King John in Worcester Cathedral', *Anglo-Norman Studies*, 15, 1992, 199–241.

[144] Tummers, *Early Secular Effigies*, list at 135–47.

[145] For the proposed redating of one group, see n. 183 below.

[146] Bishops and mitred abbots are usually represented in full pontificals with at least the dalmatic and sometimes the tunicle as well showing below the chasuble.

[147] For early brasses in England, see: *Earliest English Brasses*, ed. Coales, esp. N. Rogers, 'English Episcopal Monuments', 8–68; S. Badham and M. Norris, *Early Incised Slabs and Brasses from the London Marblers*, London 1999, part I. Sally Badham (pers. comm.) points out that the picture of the influence of ecclesiastical monuments on commemorative fashions may have been skewed by the loss (as a result of the Dissolution) of early secular monuments in monasteries, which were in the twelfth century the preferred place of burial of lay magnates.

[148] RCHM no. 9 has an additional rectangular support below the cushion with shallow concave sections projecting on either side, but it is unclear what it represents.

of RCHM no. 9[149] may have some special significance since it appears to be unparalleled. However, Richardson's suggestion that it represents the governorship of the king's castles of Cardigan and Carmarthen seems unlikely, and its significance remains unknown.

RCHM nos. 5, 7 and 6 have their right hands placed flat on the breast,[150] RCHM no. 3 has both hands crossed on the breast,[151] RCHM no. 4 has his hands in prayer (like the fourteenth-century effigy, no. 12), RCHM no. 10 holds his drawn sword by his side and RCHM nos. 8 and 9 handle their scabbarded swords, an action echoed in the more lively attitude of their bodies. Shields are present on five of the Temple effigies, and vary in size; they are held high up on the effigies' left sides, except for RCHM no. 5, where it is held lower down. RCHM nos. 3, 5, 6 and 7 have no foot supports; the feet of RCHM no. 4 rested on two human heads; those of RCHM no. 8 rest on a dragon; and the remainder have their feet supported by a lion. All these aspects have been discussed at length by Tummers,[152] and so, with the exception of two features, they will not be further discussed here.

Attempts to devise a chronology of thirteenth-century military effigies generally, based on such features as the size of the shield and the length of the gown (worn by all the Temple effigies), have different results depending on which feature is chosen. For example, while it is likely that the general trend in the length of gowns was from long to short, the shortest gown is worn by RCHM no. 5, which also exhibits relatively low-relief carving, straight legs, and a lack of supports for the head and feet, all of which are features suggestive of an early date. Straight legs on thirteenth-century effigies are generally regarded as an early feature which preceded the fashion for crossed legs, a fashion which became virtually universal until about 1350. Yet one of the earliest surviving monumental brasses — that of Sir John d'Abernon II, at Stoke d'Abernon (Surrey), now dated to about 1327 — has straight legs.[153]

The dating of thirteenth-century effigies, including those in the Temple Church, must be to some extent subjective. The difficulties of dating were fully acknowledged by Tummers, who sought to establish a relative chronology which relied to a significant extent on the attitude of the figure.[154] Drapery style may give some clue to date, but its definition is often illusive. These and other approaches to dating will be discussed below, but two other features will first be addressed in more detail: the crossed legs, present on five of the eight thirteenth-century Temple Church effigies, and the different foot supports.

---

[149] Illus. by Richardson, *Effigies of the Temple Church*, pl. 7.
[150] For other examples, see n. 191 below.
[151] For other examples, see n. 59 above.
[152] Tummers, *Early Secular Effigies*, esp. 'Attitude' (chap. 4).
[153] P. Binski in *Earliest English Brasses*, ed. Coales, 93, fig. 87.
[154] Tummers, *Early Secular Effigies*, 'Attitude' (chap. 4) and 'Summary and Conclusion'.

Crossed legs

Early accounts of the effigies often mention that some of them were cross-legged. In fact five out of the eight are shown with legs crossed, and this was noted in the earliest reliable account of the effigies, by John Stow, published in 1598.[155] It is now generally accepted that the cross-legged attitude has nothing to do with actual or intended participation in the Crusades, though the contrary view — supported by Panofsky as late as 1964[156] — remains common in popular belief. The subject of crossed legs on effigies has been thoroughly discussed by Tummers[157] and so will be dealt with only briefly here.

The earliest instance of a connection between crossed legs and crusading found by Tummers was that by Stow, mentioned above, writing about the Temple Church effigies: 'images of armed knights, five lying crosse legged, as men vowed to the holy land, against the infidels and unbelieveing Jewes'.[158] Tummers has charted the historiography of the idea, showing that doubts expressed about a connection between crossed legs and Templars by Lethieullier as early as the 1772 had developed to the point where Walford, writing in 1857, doubted that the cross-legged attitude had any symbolic significance, adding that 'It may have been only a matter of artistic arrangement.'[159]

Although a precedent for crossed legs can be found in Romanesque figure-sculpture (and manuscript illumination) and to a lesser extent in classical sculpture, it is not known why this convention was originally adopted for effigies in England, but it is an almost exclusively English phenomenon and almost entirely confined to military effigies.[160] Indeed the vast majority of English military effigies up to about 1350 are

[155] J. Stow, *Survay of London*, 327. On each of the Purbeck marble effigies (RCHM nos. 3, 6 and 7) the figure's right leg is crossed over the left; on the Reigate stone effigies (RCHM nos. 8 and 9) the left leg is crossed over the right.

[156] E. Panofsky (ed. H. W. Janson), *Tomb Sculpture: Four Lectures on its Changing Aspects from Ancient Egypt to Bernini*, reissue with new foreword, London 1992 (orig. publ. London 1964), 56. In a more recent work, Rachel Dressler, *Of Armor and Men in Medieval England: the Chivalric Rhetoric of Three English Knights' Effigies*, Aldershot 2004, 80 ff., has sought to re-establish a link between such effigies and crusading, but her argument is unconvincing; see S. Badham and P J. Lankester, 'Of Twenty-Five Years of the CMS, "Knights" in Armour and Crossed Legs', *Church Monuments*, 19, 2004, 135.

[157] Tummers, *Early Secular Effigies*, 117–26.

[158] Ibid., 169, n. 458. Stow, *Survay of London* (1598), 327. Tummers thought Stow probably had in mind Knights Templar rather than crusaders in general, though the similar explanation offered by Camden (*Britannia*, 1594, 321) is also given without qualification. An interesting alternative (though equally fanciful) explanation is given by Schellinks, who visited in 1661 and described five of the effigies lying 'with their legs crossed, as is the custom in the Holy Land to distinguish them from Turks and Jews' (Schellinks, *Journal*, 58).

[159] Tummers, *Early Secular Effigies*, 118, 169, nn. 456, 457, citing S. Lethieullier, 'Observations of Sepulchral Monuments . . .', *Archaeologia*, 2, 1773, 294; and W. S. Walford, 'Effigy in Aldworth Church, Berks . . .', *Archaeological Journal*, 14, 1857, 148.

[160] For a few male and female civilian effigies with crossed legs, see Tummers, *Early Secular Effigies*, 103; to which can be added an example of the 1370s at Chichester Cathedral (see Tummers, 'Medieval Tombs in Chichester Cathedral', 32).

shown with crossed legs, though, as Tummers pointed out, not all crossed in the same manner.[161] Possible reasons for the origin of the convention are that it achieved a more satisfactory artistic composition (as suggested by Walford[162]) or that it was done for technical reasons when effigies began to be carved in higher relief. Both seem plausible explanations, though several other ideas have been advanced.

Foot supports

Four of the eight thirteenth-century effigies have beasts supporting their feet, a feature which is commonly found on effigies.[163] In the thirteenth century, the beasts at the feet of military effigies are normally lions, though one of the Temple effigies has a dragon (RCHM no. 8),[164] while the beast at the feet of another has been interpreted as a leopard (RCHM no. 10).[165] Conversely, ecclesiastical effigies usually have dragons, and on some effigies both a lion and a dragon is found. The significance of these beasts is often explained by verse 13 from Psalm 90 (in the Vulgate, now 91): 'Super aspidem et basiliscum ambulabis et conculcabis leonem et draconem' (You will walk on the asp and the basilisk, and the lion and the dragon you will trample under foot), and Canon David Meara has drawn attention to a sermon on Psalm 90/91 by St Augustine of Hippo, which shows how the lion was seen as representing diabolic threats of tyranny and persecution while the dragon was regarded as representing threats of heresy.[166] Meara also pointed to other verses, such as that from the First Letter of Peter, 'Be sober, be watchful. Your adversary the devil prowls around like a roaring lion seeking some one to devour.'[167]

The significance of the two grotesque human heads supporting the feet of RCHM no. 4 is uncertain. They may represent the triumph over earthly adversaries.[168] Their appearance as left by Richardson argues against their depicting angels, and sadly the war damage has since destroyed all useful evidence for their form. If they were intended as the heads of angels, it might have been a reference to the verses of Psalm 90/91 immediately preceding those just quoted: 'For he will give his angels charge of you . . .

---

[161] Tummers, *Early Secular Effigies*, 107 ff.

[162] Walford, 'Effigy in Aldworth Church', 148.

[163] Foot supports are discussed at length by Tummers, *Early Secular Effigies*, 40–44.

[164] Tummers, dealing with thirteenth-century English effigies, only identified one other example of a dragon at the feet of a military effigy — at Kirton-in-Lindsey (Lincs.; Tummers, *Early Secular Effigies*, 42, pl. 99).

[165] RCHM, *The City*, 141: 'smooth-haired beast (?leopard)'; Tummers, *Early Secular Effigies*, 42: 'definitely a leopard'.

[166] D. Meara, 'The Lion and the Dragon', *Monumental Brass Society Bulletin*, no. 54, June 1990, 442–4.

[167] 1 Peter 5.8. All biblical quotations are taken from the Revised Standard Version.

[168] See G. Henderson, 'The Damnation of Nero, and Related Themes', in *The Vanishing Past: Studies . . . presented to Christopher Hohler*, ed. A. Borg and A. Martindale, BAR International Series 111, 1981, 39–42. Something similar may be intended by a crawling man at the foot of the military effigy at Whitworth (Co. Durham), mentioned by Tummers (*Early Secular Effigies*, 44; see illus. in Stothard, *Monumental Effigies*, pls. 24, 25, (1876 edn) p. 46).

On their hands they will bear you up, lest you dash your foot against a stone.'[169] As these words were also used by the devil to tempt Christ,[170] the combat between good and evil would thus be recalled, as it is with the lion and the dragon.

Stylistic context and dating

Approaches to dating effigies include consideration of the attitude of the figures, the style (mainly of drapery), and considering individual effigies in the context of stylistic groups of such monuments. Such arguments are, however, often imprecise, and there is considerable room for reasonable differences of opinion.

Tummers has argued for the importance of the attitude of an effigy for its dating. Altogether there is a great variety of poses among the Temple Church effigies, which is characteristic of English thirteenth-century military effigies, and is to some extent also true for the first half of the fourteenth century. Although then a relatively quiet attitude with the hands joined in prayer or gently handling the sword and the legs crossed in a relaxed manner increasingly becomes the norm, there are some notable exceptions.[171]

Three of the cross-legged Temple effigies have their legs crossed in a quiet and relaxed manner, but the two in Reigate stone (RCHM nos. 8 and 9) do so more energetically and should probably therefore be dated later than the others. Tummers chooses a late thirteenth-century date for these two, with which I tend to agree. However, a problem is posed by the remarkable effigy at Dorchester Abbey (Oxon.), where a very energetic pose is combined with a drapery style that would suggest a date earlier in the century.[172] Could any of the effigies identified by Richardson as commemorating the three Marshals be as early as their dates of death (1219, 1231 and 1241)?

The pre-Richardson side view of RCHM no. 9 by Stothard shows one small feature which might point to a date just on the cusp of the change in drapery style that is observable in English sculpture around 1260. Discussing seals, Heslop has usefully summarised this change as follows:

The period around 1260 was a time of transition from late, developed trough-folds (*Muldenfaltenstil*), of a type familiar from the drawings of Matthew Paris, to the triangular broad-fold style of, for example, the Douce Apocalypse. On English episcopal seals this transition period was over very rapidly. It begun in 1257 with the seal of Hugh Bishop of Ely and was virtually complete within 10 years.[173]

---

[169] Psalm 91.11–12.

[170] Matthew 4.6; Luke 4.10–11.

[171] For example, several of the effigies at Aldworth (Berks.), especially that in the eastern recess on the north side, and the similar wooden effigy at Chew Magna (Somerset): Walford, 'Effigy in Aldworth Church', both illus.; for Aldworth, see also Stone, *Sculpture in Britain*, esp. 167, 175, and pl. 121. Although doubts have been expressed on the authenticity of the Chew Magna figure, it may well be fourteenth-century and was accepted by Stone (ibid., 167, 175).

[172] P. J. Lankester, 'A Military Effigy in Dorchester Abbey, Oxon.', *Oxoniensia*, 52, 1987, 145–72, esp. 172.

[173] T. A. Heslop, 'Cistercian Seals in England and Wales' in *Cistercian Art and Architecture in the British Isles*, ed. C. Norton and D. Park, Cambridge 1986, 270.

The hesitant beginnings of this change can be seen as early as the Purbeck marble effigy of Archbishop Walter de Gray (d. 1255) in York Minster, probably made fairly soon after his death.[174] It is seen again on the effigy of Bishop Giles de Bridport (d. 1262) at Salisbury Cathedral,[175] and on the angels flanking the canopy at the head of this effigy we see the beginnings of the development of the individual projecting folds into a heavier form; this can also be seen in the angels in the Purbeck marble tracery of the north side of the canopy, and on the demi-effigy commemorating the heart burial of Bishop Aymer de Valence (d. 1260) at Winchester Cathedral.[176] Stothard's side view of RCHM no. 9 shows these same broader, more bulky folds on the skirt of the gown, one of them breaking at a sharp angle (vertically above the tip of the shield; Plate 60B) which was a characteristic of the developed new style. As ever, we must be cautious in reading the evidence (especially as Richardson's comments and the generally fuzzy appearance of Stothard's drawing indicates it was then covered with a thick layer of paint or limewash)[177] but if the evidence is accepted, a date before the late 1250s for this effigy seems improbable. No similar 'angled' drapery appears on RCHM no. 8, which might suggest that it is slightly earlier, but I doubt it is as early as 1241 when Gilbert, the last of the three Marshals, died.

As already noted, the earliest of these three effigies (RCHM no. 10) has foliage by its pillow, and I am grateful to Dr Pamela Tudor-Craig for giving me her opinion on its date. On the basis of what is visible in the Hollises' pre-Richardson drawing (Plate 57A), Dr Tudor-Craig compares this foliage with one of the vault bosses of the choir ambulatory of Canterbury Cathedral, dating to the 1180s, and doubts that its occurrence on the Temple effigy can date to after c.1220. This would put the effigy a little earlier than it has been dated by some other authorities such as Tummers, but some caution must be expressed because certain details of the stiff-leaf as shown by the Hollises are not quite identical with those shown in the post-Richardson views (e.g. Plates 45, 56), raising the question of whether the foliage was altered by Richardson or whether the Hollises' interpretation was influenced by damage or surface coatings then present.

If this effigy does date to before 1220, it would fit very conveniently with the date of death of William Marshal the elder in 1219. However, it must be stressed that this identification (which frequently appears in captions to photographs of the effigy in the non-art-historical literature) can only be regarded as, at best, tentative, and it should be noted again that there appears to be no evidence that the effigy was so identified before the publication of Addison's and Richardson's books of 1843. It should also be remembered that Stow, in 1598, said that William the elder's effigy was cross-legged, in contrast to this effigy which is not.[178]

[174] Brown, *York Minster*, 41.

[175] See M. E. Roberts, 'The Tomb of Giles de Bridport in Salisbury Cathedral', *Art Bulletin*, 65, 1983, 572, fig. 26; the relevant folds of the chasuble are badly damaged.

[176] Ibid., 568–9, 573, figs. 28, 29; 574, figs. 32, 33.

[177] See p. 109 above. However, this angled fold is still visible today, and there is a similar fold at approximately the same point on the other side of the effigy.

[178] See, however, David Park's paper above (pp. 79–80), which argues that this effigy is most likely to be that of the first William Marshal.

It has already been noted that six of the eight effigies discussed here (as well as the coped grave marker) are in Purbeck marble, and it is some of these which offer the best prospect of being fitted into a larger stylistic grouping. Purbeck marble is not a true marble but the most commonly used of a number of polishable limestones that were exploited in the Middle Ages for a wide variety of products, such as architectural elements (as in the Temple Church), tapered grave-markers often decorated with an incised or relief cross ('cross-slabs'), and monumental brasses and fonts.[179] There are about 100 surviving medieval effigies in Purbeck marble, almost all in England[180] and virtually all dating to before 1350.[181] Of these a little under half are shown in armour.

A distribution map of all English effigies in this stone indicates two main geographic groupings: one towards the south-west, around the area of the quarries in Dorset; and another, more extensive distribution, mostly spreading north and north-west from London.[182] Many of the Purbeck military effigies can be assigned to one of two stylistic groups, which can be related to these two geographical distributions (even though the stylistic and geographic groupings do not exactly match), and this was recognised by Prior and Gardner as long ago as 1912.[183] Since then the groups have been extended and refined by other researchers including Tummers, Gittos and Gittos, and

[179] For general accounts of the medieval Purbeck marble industry, see n. 48 above. For a coped grave marker in the Temple Church and for another found there, see n. 5 above.

[180] Author's unpublished lists. This includes fragments and a few effigies in very low relief. For an important initial list of Purbeck marble effigies (now requiring some corrections and additions), see R. Leach, *Investigation into Purbeck Marble*, 25–33. For a few examples in Ireland, see B. Gittos and M. Gittos, 'Irish Purbeck: Recently Identified Purbeck Marble Monuments in Ireland', *Church Monuments*, 13, 1998, 5–14; for an example at Lisieux, Normandy, see A. Gardner, *A Handbook of English Medieval Sculpture*, Cambridge 1935, 174 n. 1, and rev. edn, *English Medieval Sculpture*, Cambridge 1951, 152 n. 1 (the material confirmed by the present author); illus. in Bauch, *Mittelalterliche Grabbild*, 82, Abb. 116. For other examples of Purbeck marble in Normandy and evidence for export, see Blair, 'Purbeck Marble', 44.

[181] For a rare late example of a Purbeck marble effigy in moderate relief at Minster-in-Sheppey (Kent), see J. Hewitt, 'Effigy of a Knight of the Fifteenth Century', *Archaeological Journal*, 6, 1849, 351–8 and pl. fac. 351; C. Blair, 'A Late Purbeck Marble Effigy at Minster, Isle of Sheppey, Kent', *Church Monuments Society Newsletter*, 8/2, Winter [1992/]1993, 33–6. Abbot Spofford of St Mary's Abbey (later bishop of Hereford, d. 1456) was commemorated by an effigy cut in very low relief on a Purbeck marble slab, now broken and incomplete and in the Yorkshire Museum (acc. no. YORYM: 2001.13018); see Royal Commission on Historical Monuments: England, *City of York*, IV, 1975, 23, fig. 26; and, for a slightly different reconstruction, C. Wilson and J. Burton, *St Mary's Abbey, York,* York 1988, p. 18 (illus.). However, according the latter reconstruction, the slab is tapered and it is possible it is an earlier slab that was re-used.

[182] See map in Leach, *Investigation into Purbeck Marble*, 28.

[183] Prior and Gardner, *Medieval Figure-Sculpture*, 552, 555, 588–96. Their view of the division between the two groups of military effigies produced in London and the south-west is clearly set out in the first parts of their Tables A and B (552, 555). It underpins their discussion of the 'The Purbeck-Marble "Knights" 1225–1270' (588–96) but is here sometimes somewhat obscured in the discussion of other matters, such as the change from the quiet cross-legged to a more lively cross-legged attitude. It is now apparent that their dating of the south-western group is too early and arguments have recently been advanced for placing most if not the whole of that group after 1300:

the present author.[184] The distribution pattern of the south-western group, especially when considered with stylistically related male and female civilian effigies,[185] points very strongly to production at or in the region of the quarries. Whether the distribution of the other group indicates London production, as proposed by Prior and Gardner and supported by later authors,[186] or marketing and distribution through London, as suggested by John Blair in the context of Purbeck marble products generally,[187] is debatable. As Blair pointed out, while the large numbers of marblers working at Westminster Abbey in 1253 is evidence for their employment in London in the mid-thirteenth century, it is not until after *c*.1280 that there is evidence for marblers becoming established citizens. None of the effigies in the 'London' group is located close to the quarries;[188] on the other hand no separate local and 'London' stylistic groups have so far been identified for any other Purbeck products such as architectural features, tapered grave-markers (including 'cross slabs') or fonts. The overall number of surviving effigies is really too small to draw a firm conclusion either way.

The distribution of what, for want of a better term, I shall call the 'London' stylistic group is illustrated in Fig. 6 (overleaf). While it is debatable how many effigies should be included in this group, I would include ten effigies in the core group (indicated by solid circles in Fig. 6). This includes three of the Temple effigies (RCHM nos. 6, 3 and 7; Plates 56, 59A, 60A, 58C),[189] which illustrate some of the main features of the group, the most obvious of which is the general attitude, described by Tummers as 'elegant'.[190] Legs are crossed in a broadly similar and fairly relaxed manner on all the members of the group and most have the right hand placed on the breast — an attitude

see C. Blair, J. A. Goodall and P. J. Lankester, 'The Winchelsea Tombs Reconsidered', *Church Monuments*, 15, 2000, 12–14.

[184] Tummers, *Early Secular Effigies*, 96–7; B. Gittos and M. Gittos, 'A Military Effigy at Welton, North Humberside' *Yorkshire Archaeological Journal*, 53, 1981, 126 (fig. 1), 129–31; Gittos and Gittos, 'Irish Purbeck', 12–13; Blair, Goodall and Lankester, 'Winchelsea Tombs', 12–14.

[185] Prior and Gardner, *Medieval Figure-sculpture*, 555, 598–599; Tummers and Blair et al., as cited in the preceding note.

[186] Andersson, *English Influence*, 55 ff., 'The London School of Purbeck Marble'.

[187] J. Blair, 'Purbeck Marble', 45–46.

[188] The nearest is Sullington (Sussex) but that could have been partly transported by sea.

[189] The other examples are in Sussex, at Lewes (Tummers, *Early Secular Effigies*, pl. 36) and Sullington (ibid., pl. 35); in Hertfordshire, at Eastwick (ibid., pl. 33), Walkern (ibid., pl. 20; also the drawing in Hollis and Hollis, *Monumental Effigies*, unpaginated) and Hitchin (Tummers, *Early Secular Effigies*, pl. 34); in Buckinghamshire, at Twyford (ibid., pl. 37); and in Warwickshire, at Merevale (ibid., pl. 31; Plate 59B in this volume). Other effigies related stylistically to the main group are at Great Haseley (Oxon.; Tummers, *Early Secular Effigies*, pl. 39) and Stowe Nine Churches (Northants.; ibid., pl. 32; Hartshorne, *Effigies in Northamptonshire*, pls. fac. 22 (left), 2 (nos. 7, 8)), and a further group at Farnborough (Warwicks. — a head only — Tummers, *Early Secular Effigies*, pl. 130); Cropredy (Oxon. — a torso) and Rushton (Northants.; ibid., pl. 21; Hartshorne, *Effigies in Northamptonshire*, pls. fac. 16 (left), 20 (no. 2)). For further references to all these effigies, see Tummers, *Early Secular Effigies*, esp. the 'List', 135–47.

[190] Tummers, *Early Secular Effigies*, 87.

FIGURE 6. Map of stylistically related Purbeck marble military effigies, centred on London

rarely found elsewhere on English effigies in other materials.[191] It is illustrated here by

[191] The hands on a few effigies in the south-west adopt this attitude or something close to it (including resting the hand on the near corner of the shield): see Tummers, *Early Secular Effigies*, 80–81. This attitude is found in France on two effigies formerly at the Abbey of Étival. One of them, now in the Musée Archéologique, Le Mans, with the hand partly covered by the shield, is attributed to Raoul I de Beaumont: J. Adhémar and G. Dordor, 'Les Tombeaux de la Collection Gaignières', Tome I, *Gazette de Beaux-Arts*, 6ᵉ Période, 84, 1974 (issue for Juillet–Septembre), 5–192, at 20, no. 60 ('d. after 1210'); Hurtig, *Armored Gisant*, 18 ff., pls. 10, 11 (after 1210 and before c.1225). The other, possibly now lost, is attributed to Raoul II de Beaumont, d. 1235: Adhémar and Dordor, 'Collection Gaignières', 37, no. 158; Hurtig, *Armored Gisant*, 24–5, pl. 20. However, it might be the same as another effigy, also in the Musée Archéologique, Le Mans (ibid., 23, 25, pl. 18). Another effigy, formerly at the Abbey of Boneval (a 'comte de Dunois?' of the 'twelfth century'), appears to have rested his hand on the corner of the shield (Adhémar and Dordor, 'Collection Gaignières', 20, no. 59; Hurtig, *Armored Gisant*, 20, pl. 12).

RCHM no. 6, shown alongside the very similar headless effigy at Merevale (Warwicks.) (Plate 59B). The lack of any foot supports is also characteristic of the group.

Departures from this attitude are seen on RCHM no. 3, with both hands crossed on his breast,[192] and at Walkerne (Herts.),[193] holding the hilt of the sword. At Sullington (Sussex)[194] the right hand is missing but appears to have rested on or near the sword pommel. Although the attitude of the figure is different, this latter effigy can be compared in certain details with RCHM no. 7, including the shape of the cushion and the form of the coif.

The dating of this group is problematic. None of the effigies can be certainly identified and the armour is of little help, though the related effigies at Rushton (Northants.) and Cropredy (Oxon.) display gamboised cuisses of the sort seen on RCHM nos. 8 and 9 and this probably places them at the end of the sequence, a view supported by the more lively attitude of the Rushton figure. Any reasonable dating of the group leaves unresolved problems. The difficulty is to find a date-span which accords with our understanding of the development of thirteenth-century sculpture in general, and of effigies in particular (however sketchy this may be), or at least which does not place such limitations on the dating of other pieces as would make the resulting general picture implausible. At the same time any such date-span cannot be infinitely elastic but must be of credible length, bearing in mind the extent of any stylistic developments between the earliest and the latest members of the group.

My own view is that the best fit is achieved by placing all the core members of this group between about 1240 and 1280, and this in agreement with the other main authors who have written on the subject since the early twentieth century, but I feel slightly uncomfortable about allowing such a long date-span — and therefore production — for such a relatively homogeneous group. There is a further possible problem.

Earlier the helmet of RCHM no. 6 was compared with one shown in a manuscript of c.1220. Attention should also be drawn to the rounded top of the shield shown in Stothard's drawing, but which was restored by Richardson as a slightly curved top with angled corners where it meets the sides. The rounded shape shown by Stothard could be due to damage, though looks rather too regular if that were the case, while the same regular rounded shape is shown in two drawings by Kerrich. If the shield of this effigy really was originally of the shape shown by Stothard and Kerrich this, combined with the evidence of the helmet, might suggest it should be dated somewhat before 1240 and that might have consequences for the dating of the group as a whole.[195]

---

[192] See p. 107 and n. 59 above.

[193] For references, see n. 189 above.

[194] For references, see n. 189 above.

[195] For the changes in the shapes of shields, see Blair, *European Armour*, 181. Fairly short shields with rounded tops and corners occur, for example, on the early thirteenth-century seal matrix of Robert FitzWalter; see *Age of Chivalry: Art in Plantagenet England 1200–1400*, ed. J. Alexander and P. Binski, London 1987, 397, no. 454. Longer curved-topped shields with rounded corners are more easily found on seals and in manuscripts in the twelfth century: for example on a leaf related to the Winchester Bible in the Pierpont Morgan Library, MS M.619; see *English Romanesque Art 1066–1200*,

CONCLUSION

Regrettably there is no reliable evidence to identify any of the eight thirteenth-century military effigies in the Temple Church, and there is room for wide differences of opinion of their dating within the century. It seems unlikely that any date to much before 1220, though arguments can be advanced for slightly earlier datings of RCHM nos. 5 and 10. My own view is that RCHM nos. 3, 4, 6 and 7 probably all date to between c.1240 and 1280 and RCHM nos. 8 and 9 to between c.1260 and 1280.

Given their importance, it is very sad that the effigies have not survived in better condition, but, even in their present state and despite the problems of dating them at all precisely, they are extremely important, both individually and as a group, and they include some of the earliest secular memorial effigies in this country. We must be grateful to those antiquaries and artists who recorded them with careful drawings and notes, especially Thomas Kerrich, Charles Stothard and the Hollises. We also owe some gratitude to Richardson. Although he intervened to an extent we would not now countenance, he nevertheless left us some record of the work he undertook, and, by consolidating weak areas and reattaching detached parts, he probably saved the figures from further loss, decay and neglect until they could be recorded by photography before the tragic damage which occurred in 1941 and with which this article began.[196]

London 1984, 57, 122, no. 65. It should be noted, however, that both curved- and straight-topped shields are shown in the Morgan Picture Bible, as on fol. 10ᵛ (for references, see n. 118 above).

[196] After this paper had been completed Celia Charlton kindly informed me that a report by Mr Harold W. Haysom on work undertaken to repair the damage the effigies sustained in 1941 had recently been located. It is a typed copy of the original manuscript report by Mr Haysom and is now Inner Temple Archives TEM/5/8. This discovery came too late to incorporate its contents into my main text but it is clearly a significant document. The report, dated November 1960, confirms that the 1941 damage to the effigies was considerable and that many had received deposits of molten lead during the fire which, in some cases, had penetrated through cracks in the stone and caused parts to lift off. The least damaged were the two effigies in Reigate stone (RCHM nos. 8 and 9), while the fourteenth-century effigy (RCHM no. 12) suffered no damage — apart from surface discoloration — owing to its location in the ambulatory. The work carried out to surfaces, to remove earlier coatings and the solidified molten lead, appears to have been somewhat more aggressive than modern standards would dictate, which is unsurprising given the advances in conservation thinking and knowledge during the last fifty years. With detailed study the report may provide further insights into Richardson's restoration work, but the only illustration is a sketch plan of the numbering (which is different from other numbering schemes so far encountered).

Robin Griffith-Jones

'An Enrichment of Cherubims':
Christopher Wren's Refurbishment
of the Temple Church

THIS PAPER WILL DISCUSS three projects for the refurbishment of the Temple Church: in 1682–3, 1695 and 1702. The first two were realised; the most prominent surviving records of the third — an exterior and an interior view by William Emmett — appear to represent as much an imagined past as a likely future for the church. The church was throughout these years under the control of the Common Law lawyers of Inner and Middle Temple. I will argue that the refurbishments were informed by the constitutional crises of the late seventeenth century in which these lawyers played leading roles. At the time of the first campaign, the Tories were pressing home their advantage after the dissolution of the 1681 Parliament; at the time of the second, James II had been dethroned, William and Mary were in power and the Whigs ascendant.

I will be asking what significance the lawyers — and Wren himself — might have seen in the church's architecture, layout and furnishings before and after these successive refurbishments. This will involve a discussion of the 'primitive churches' and of the Jerusalem Temple whose motifs were echoed in the Temple Church (as elsewhere in the last decades of the century).

In 1608 King James VI and I had granted the whole area of the Temple to Inner and Middle Temple in perpetuity,[1] on two conditions: that the Inns would accommodate

'An Enrichment of Cherubims': E. Hatton on the decoration of the organ-screen, *A New View of London*, 2 vols., London 1708, II, 564.

For help in the preparation of this paper I am most grateful to Emilia and Henrietta Amodio, Hannah Baker, Professor Sir John Baker, Celia Charlton, Dr John Clark, Professors Kerry Downes and Anthony Geraghty, Dr Nigel Llewellyn, the Revd Hugh Mead, Professor Wilfrid Prest, Dr Clare Rider, Dr Christine Stevenson, Professor Rosemary Sweet, and Mrs Lesley Whitelaw. The paper on the seventeenth century was due to be provided at the Conference and in this book by Thomas Cocke, and the present paper is dedicated to his memory.

[1] Two of the four Inns of Court, legal societies to one of which every barrister in England and Wales must still belong.

and educate those studying and working in the law; and that they would maintain the Temple Church at their own expense for the celebration of divine service.[2]

From then on the owners of the church — and the patrons of those who worked on it — were the two Inns, with their governing bodies (the Benchers) and in each Inn the Treasurer (presiding Bencher) for that year. The Inns were not answerable to the City or Lord Mayor for the management of the Temple in general, nor to the Bishop of London for their management of the church. It was already customary by 1620 for members of Inner Temple to sit on the south side, members of Middle on the north.[3]

Our chief concern will be with the last decades of the century. The church escaped the Great Fire by a few feet (Colour Plate VII). In 1675 John Playford, the clerk of the church (who had a shop in the church's porch and was the first publisher of Henry Purcell's music), reported to the Inns on the need for speedy repairs. He listed four concerns: 'the doors of the screen which parts the church are at this time . . . decayed and broken'; 'the pulpit is so rotten . . . as it is in great danger of falling'; the two bells in the steeple were both cracked and useless; and the two surplices were both worn out.[4]

The Benchers took seriously the need for repair, although chiefly, it seems, for the improvement of the seating.[5] Their plans were interrupted: on 26 Jan. 1678/9 a fire broke out to the west of the church, in Middle Temple. The fire reached the church's west end and damaged St Anne's Chapel (Colour Plate VII); the shops built against the Round were clearly a danger to the church itself as the fire approached and were pulled down.[6]

The cloisters, an arcade running south from the west porch, were destroyed. The Inns agreed — after prolonged debate — to accept a plan from Christopher Wren for their rebuilding; a drawing for the project survives (in Middle Temple's archives) in Wren's own hand (Plate 65).[7]

In May 1682 Wren reported on the state of the church. We will survey what con-

[2] For the Letters Patent, Williamson, *Temple*, 261–8. The Inns are obliged to maintain the Master of the Temple too, the church's principal minister: they provide a mansion next to the church and an annual stipend of £17 6s 8d, or half a mark per week. (There has been a welcome allowance for inflation.)

[3] MT.15/TAP.43.

[4] ITR III, pp. xl, 103.

[5] MTR III, 1296, 1304, 1314: May 1676 (the Bench seats); June 1677 and June 1678 (beautifying the Church and altering its seats; a model to be drawn and agreed on).

[6] With temperatures well below freezing, there was insufficient water with which to combat the fire. The flames were doused with beer instead. It was six years before Inner Temple settled the brewer's bill (ITR III, pp. xxx–xxxii).

[7] A. Oswald, 'Rebuilding the Temple', *Country Life*, 28 May 1948, 1072–5, at 1073. Cf. A. Geraghty, *The Architectural Drawings of Sir Christopher Wren at All Souls College, Oxford: a Complete Catalogue*, Aldershot 2007, 11: 'We can be sure that Wren gradually stopped making finished drawings in the 1680s. Instead, he began to produce a new kind of drawing: the freehand pen and ink sketch.' For further examples of such freehand drawings, see Geraghty nos. 79, 262, 155, 320, 410. Professor Geraghty points out to me that the Middle Temple drawing is one of Wren's latest known drawings; such a drawing by Wren himself shows the personal interest which he took in the project. Also in Middle Temple's archives is Wren's proposal for the cloisters, dated 24 September 1680.

fronted him then, and what changes he and his patrons made. Most care was lavished on the chancel. Twelve years later, the Inns turned their attention to the Round. And in 1702 a further campaign appears to have followed through the programme of the 1690s. In each case I will ask what significance, if any, the Inns and (in the early 1680s) Wren himself might have seen in the shape, history, effigies and current role of the church.

WHAT DID THE BENCHERS AND WREN SEE IN 1682?

We will move from the outside to the inside, and from west to east. Such evidence as survives suggests that the northern façade was plastered ragstone; such ragstone was revealed in the 1860s on the north wall of the Round, when the buildings against it were finally removed.[8] Some at least of the southern façade was already faced in ashlar. (An ashlar facing was still being installed or renewed in the years after Wren, in a long and sustained campaign.[9])

The buildings against and around the church involved more than just safety and rents; elegance and decorum were at issue too. The buildings over the west porch had been, in 1631, at least three storeys high (and still were at the end of the eighteenth century; see Plate 67); by 1634 there had been complaints that buildings against the church were obscuring its lights.[10] By October 1681 the Inns were in discussion concerning 'a shop under the arch of the porch and over against the west door of the Temple Rounds', and a stationer's engraved advertisement shows such a shop in the west porch (Plate 68).[11]

The shop will, in the following pages, prompt us to ask whether the west door could be used and, if so, how often it was. The print of 1676 (Colour Plate VII) seems to show three entrances: the west door; and others on the south and north side of the Round, used (we might surmise) by members of Inner and Middle Temple respectively.

---

[8]　The northern face of the Round in the 1860s is shown in a photograph (Plate 66). There were ample traces of medieval plaster on the undressed Kentish stone. The buttresses were disparate, revealing the church's piecemeal repair over time; see Gardam, 'Restorations', 106.

[9]　As Christopher Wilson points out (p. 27 n. 23 above), Essex and Smirke, *Illustrations*, 4, make clear that the south front of the Round had already been ashlared before St Anne's Chapel was built. Illustrations of the exterior by George Shepherd, 1811, published in C. Clarke, *Architectura Ecclesiastica Londini*, London 1819 (accessible on the Guildhall Library's Collage, http://collage.cityoflondon. gov.uk/collage, nos. 7167, 7177) show rubble facing on the lower portion of the chancel's south front 'from which some small buildings had lately been removed' and an ashlar facing on the north front (of which some was almost certainly hidden by buildings when Shepherd drew). For references to (re-)ashlaring in the 1820s and in 1842, Gardam, 'Restorations', 106.

[10]　Further details, MTR II, 778, 800 (1632), and Williamson, *Temple*, 540 (1634).

[11]　The advertisement's illustration was published (without the text) in the *Gentleman's Magazine*, 54 pt 2, Dec. 1784, opp. 911. The engraving was dated c.1678 by Lewer and Dark, *Temple Church*, 69, probably in deference to its reproduction in ITR III opp. 128, at the Inn's accounts for 1677/8. We return to the advertisement's text below.

Since any processional route down the west–east axis of the Round was apparently blocked by the medieval effigies, there may have been no call to have the west door in use.

The earliest surviving record of the Round's roof is in Wyngaerde's *Panorama* (1544) (Plate 63): a cone converging at about 45°.[12] An engraving of 1671, reissued in 1770, shows a conical roof with St Anne's Chapel hidden by buildings, and the southern roof of the Round squared off to cover them (Plate 64).

And so to the interior. The herald and antiquary William Dugdale wrote, 'Within a spacious grate of Iron, in the midst of the round walk, under the Steeple, do ly eight statues in Military Habits.'[13] His phrasing ('grate') suggests a single row.[14] Members of the Inns used the Round for lounging and conversation.[15] Heading eastwards towards the chancel, we have already heard from Playford of 'the doors of the screen which parts the church'.

A letter from William Davy (at the Golden Anchor, Fleet Street) to his friend Framlingham Gawdy, 16 November 1637, mentioned 'the pulpit removed to the side of the church'.[16] In 1641[17] the pulpit moved again.[18]

It seems likely there was no organ.[19] A window held the Royal Arms.[20] There were more monuments in the chancel than it is easy to envisage now. After the memorials

[12] Cf. ITR I, 229 (27 June 1563). Still conical, Stow, *Survey*, I, 271, pl. 44.
[13] Dugdale, *Origines*, 173. The Petyt MS 538 vol. 17, fols. 400 ff. mentions 'Barres of Iron' and 'Bars of strong Iron worke' (fols. 403, 412) round the effigies.
[14] On the eight effigies and the row of coffins discovered by Richardson in 1841, see Philip Lankester, pp. 95–9 above. J. Norden, *Speculum Britanniae, the First Parte: an Historicall, & Chorographicall Discription of Middlesex . . .* , London 1593, 33, seems almost defiant in his insistence that on the effigies the knights' 'names are not to be gathered, by any inscription, for that, time hath worn it out'. Weever, *Monuments*, 442, notes that the knights' identities 'cannot be gathered by any inscriptions'. In his manuscript (Society of Antiquaries MS 127, fol. 146ᵛ) he mentions that 'learned Camden told me' of the words Camden had read on the tomb of William Marshal.
[15] Cf. *Hudibras* III, 3 (published 1680), 759–72. (Records, ITR II, 443–63, speak of burials both in the 'round walk' and in the 'long walk', the side aisles of the chancel [ITR II, p. ci].) This use of the Round was of long standing; see the anonymous account of Middle Temple, *ante* 1540, Cotton MS Vitellius C IX, fol. 321a (quoted in Williamson, *Temple*, 127) and Norden, *Speculum*, 33. Dr Micklethwaite, Master of the Temple, was appalled by such 'profanation' in the 1630s and locked the Church; the Benchers objected, had new keys made and the Church reopened (ITR II, p. xcv; Misc. MSS xxii).
[16] Historical Manuscripts Commission, *Report on the Manuscripts of the Family of Gawdy* [10th Report, Pt 2], London 1885, 166 no. 998.
[17] Dr Micklethwaite had by then gone, and Dr John Littleton, scion of the notable Inner Temple family of which we shall hear more, was in post as Master; he was no doubt welcomed with relief after his predecessor's pretensions.
[18] ITR II, 263.
[19] The inventory of 1308 had mentioned two pairs of organs. In January 1518/19 an order was made for a levy in Inner Temple towards new organs (novis organis) (ITR I, 45). According to an Inner Temple memorandum of 1735: 'It does not appear there was any organ in the church before the year 1685' (ITR III, p. xlvii).
[20] 1665–6 (ITR III, 41), 1674–5 (104), 1679–80 (157).

above the altar, Dugdale recorded, 'On the south side of the Quire is a large monument of gray marble, raised above three feet from the ground' (to Sir Nicholas Hare, d. 1557, and to his wife).[21] By the 1670s the church was becoming cluttered; 'No monument shall henceforth be erected in the Temple Church on the Middle Temple side without the Treasurer's leave.'[22] The bishop's effigy was on a chest by the south-east corner (it was moved into its present niche in 1842); Plowden's monument (now in the link between Round and chancel, on the northern side) was nearly opposite, on the northern wall near its eastern angle.

Most significant for the character of the church's liturgy was the placing of the altar.[23] After the Restoration, the altar had, it seems, been once more placed lengthwise against the east wall when not in use. Middle Temple stipulated in the plans for 1677 that 'the model for the seats is approved of with these alterations: that the communion table do remain as it now is, to be removed into the body of the church upon administration of the sacrament'.[24] There was a crucifix, or perhaps (more modestly) a cross.[25] The decoration of the altar-area is unknown. Dugdale records two memorials 'upon two fair Tables of stone fixed to the East Wall, above the Altar'. In the early twentieth century the aumbries on the east wall were re-exposed: a row of four seems to have been interrupted by the creation of a large round-topped opening, 'perhaps for a mural decoration in the seventeenth century'.[26]

The church bore testimony to the century's political divisions. Dr Ralph Brownrigg, prevented in the Interregnum from taking up his diocese of Exeter, was Preacher at the Temple Church, 1658–9; the epitaph on his monument lamented the injustices done to him by his age's evil fate, 'bellis Schismatibus, Sacrilegiis et Regicidibus ferociente'; he was buried in 1660 'illucescente Car. II[di.] foelicissimo Reditu'.[27] (He was succeeded by John Gawden, so loyal to Charles I that he has been proposed as the author of *Eikon Basilike*.) One of the prominent monuments in the church was to Sir William Morton, his wife and son. Sir William had fought bravely for Charles I; he was captured

[21] Dugdale, *Origines*, 176.

[22] 28 January 1675 (MTR III, 1294).

[23] In 1637 Dr Micklethwaite successfully petitioned the King to command that the communion table, pulpit and reading place be ordered and placed as decently as in the King's own Royal Chapel. Instructions survive for 'The Usuall Forme of Administering the Holy Sacrament in the Temple Church', 1637–8; references to the vestments, altar and rail hint at the character of the service (in the 'Clerk's Book', ITR II, pp. lxxxix–xci; Misc. MSS xxii). In 1643 Parliament decreed that 'the rayles about the table and the crosses about the church be pulled down and the table removed from standing altarwise and the ground levelled' (Williamson, *Temple*, 413, MT.15/TAP.80a). Perhaps the steps were never removed. Careful phrasing, February 1644/5, records a burial 'above the steppes on the Middle Temple side at the upper end of the church close to the end where the altar lately stood' (ITR II, 360). Benchers' pews at the east end, ITR II, pp. xcvi–xcviii.

[24] MTR III, 1305 (July 1677). See further p. 164 below, on the 1683 decision.

[25] ITR III, 98 (1673–4): IT £3 10s 0d, 'For painting and mending the crucifix'.

[26] A suggestion by Sir Charles Peers in a report on the stonework to the Under Treasurer of Middle Temple, 19 May 1936.

[27] Dugdale, *Origines*, 179.

and imprisoned in the Tower, where he wrote *Jus regium, sive, Jus monarchiae Anglicanae* against the co-ordination of powers between King and Parliament.[28]

But these were not the only loyalties represented in the church. John Selden of Inner Temple, twice imprisoned for resisting the Stuarts' encroaching absolutism, was buried in 1654 at the narrow junction of the Round and Inner Temple's aisle.[29] Near him was buried his friend Sir John Vaughan, one of those who took on Selden's mantle at the Restoration.[30]

The church, then, belonged to no one faction. The Inns and their church were the nation in miniature, their members 'like so many atoms contributing jointly to the mass of confusion now before us'.[31] Families could, with their monuments, mark the church with the signs of their allegiance, and so — by the fact of the Inns' permission for such monuments — mark it with signs of the Inns' allegiance too. I will be suggesting that in the 1680s the Inns themselves, in their refurbishment of the church, made a programmatic statement of their own which the Inns themselves revised after the Revolution of 1688–9.

WHAT DID THE LAWYERS SEE IN WHAT THEY SAW?

Two features of the church call for scrutiny: its medieval effigies, and its Gothic architecture. Both relate to the church's documented and (by contrast) its imagined age. Until 1695 a Latin inscription over the door into the cloisters recorded the consecration of the church by Heraclius in 1185 (Plate 84).[32] But two traditions, apparently independent of each other, evoke a quite different — and *legal* — history. First, Weever (1631) wrote twice of the foundation of the Temple Church. First, in his preface: Dunwallo Malmutius, king of Britain,

> called the Temples which hee built, the Temples of peace and concord: one of which was in London, where now Blackwell Hall is, another in Fleete-Street, as yet

---

[28] Most of the Morton monument survives and is mounted on the south wall. He was 'perduellium Hostis ac praedonum malleus'.

[29] We shall be hearing more of Selden, and of his near-contemporaries Edward Coke and Edward Littleton (Baron Littleton of Mounslow). See Esdaile, *Temple Church Monuments*, 126: Coke's youngest son Clement predeceased his father and was buried in the Temple Church, 1629. Littleton's wife Anne predeceased her husband and was buried in the church, 1623; the monuments to Anne and to Sir Timothy Littleton, 1679, have both been lost: ibid., 57, 87. The heraldic brass (with a proud twenty-eight quarterings) to Edward, a grandson — who died young — of Baron Littleton and of Anne, survives; it now lies at the junction of the Round and chancel, in the central aisle.

[30] For his monument, Esdaile, *Temple Church Monuments*, 121.

[31] Edward Hyde, earl of Clarendon, *History of the Rebellion*, 1, Oxford 1702, para. 4.

[32] Esdaile, *Temple Church Monuments*, 9, records the history of this inscription as given in successive editions of T. Blount, *Glossographia*, London 1656, 1661, 1670, 1674, s.v. Templaries. On the consecration's date, as recorded on the inscription, see Appendix 1 to the present paper, p. 170 below.

called the Temple Church, wherein (or in some of them) himselfe, *Gorbomannus*, and other of the British kings, were interred, as by supposition it is delivered.[33]

And then in Weever's full account of the Church:

The first Founder hereof is not certainly recorded, some hold that it was built by Dunwallo Malmutius, about the year of the world's creation 4748 the precincts whereof he made a sanctuary . . .
Besides these priviledges unto Temples, hee constituted divers good lawes. Of which he writ two books, the one called Statuta municipalia, the other Leges iudiciariae. . . . He reigned forty years, died the year of the world's creation 4768, and was buried in this place, with other of the British Kings.[34]

These links between Dunwallo and the Temple Church could still be deployed in the eighteenth century. Edward Hatton acknowledged them in his *New View of London,* London 1708, and Boydell's print of the chancel, *c.*1750 (Plate 69) draws for its text on Hatton: 'There is a tradition that the church was founded by Dunwallo Malmutius, a British King Anno mundi 4748.'[35]

The second tradition surfaces on the advertisement we have already mentioned (Plate 68) for the stationer's shop in the church's west porch. At the top is the porch, with the motto 'Legibus Serviens, Deo Servit.' Under it are the Round's effigies and tomb-stone in two groups of five, between which is inscribed, 'Troes fuimus.' The allusion is to Panthus, lamenting the fall of Troy: 'Fuimus Troes, fuit Ilium et ingens / Gloria Teucrorum' (Vergil, *Aeneid* 2. 325–6). Thus the advertisement recalls the story of Brute, who escaped from the sack of Troy and made his way to England. And Brute was a figure as important as Dunwallo for those researching — with clear political and constitutional agenda — the history of England's laws. The effigies and the space in which they lay, already linked with Dunwallo and his laws, could be reimagined to evoke the origins, far more ancient still, of English nationhood and English law.[36]

[33] Weever, *Monuments*, 181; Weever is surely dependent here on Norden, *Speculum Britanniae*, 33. Geoffrey of Monmouth has Dunwallo buried 'near the Temple of Concord'; Gorbomannus was also for Geoffrey a 'great promoter of justice'. The writer of Inner Temple's Petyt MS 538, vol. xvii, fol. 400 (temp. Charles i) records, citing Norden, the suggestion that Malmutius had built a Temple of Concord on the land bought by the Templars, and had been buried there, 'for the teaching of his laws called Leges Molmutinae'; 'this story I will neither affirme nor disaffirme but leave it wholly to the Authors . . . Only this much I may say if it be true. It seems that by God's Providence this place was anciently designed to the profession and professors of the Laws of these Kingdoms' (fol. 401ᵛ). Inner Temple's Wilde MS, post-1764, distinguishes clearly — as Weever does not — between the Temple of Concord said to have been built on the site by Dunwallo and the 'present church', consecrated in 1185. For the site of Dunwallo's Temple, Strype's Stow, *Survey*, i, bk i, 4 proposes Blackwell Hall, suggesting as well (in a marginal note) St Paul's.

[34] Weever, *Monuments*, 441.

[35] The text accompanying G. Shepherd's view of the church from the north-west, 1811, in C. Clarke, *Architectura Ecclesiastica Londini*, London 1819, pl. 117, still refers to the story.

[36] A further hint that the Temple Church could be associated with Brute is offered by a version of William Emmett's engraving of its south elevation with an image of London Stone on

We are in the realm of 'the British History', popularised (and perhaps in good measure invented) by Geoffrey of Monmouth.[37] A summary of a few of its claims may be useful. The Trojan Brute escaped from Troy's destruction (when Eli was priest in Israel, *c.*1170 BC), made his way to England and founded the city that would become London; after a division of his kingdom between his three sons (into England, Scotland and Wales), his eldest son reunited the kingdom into one. Later kings included Lear. The dynasty changed with the usurping king Dunwallo Malmutius. Julius Caesar invaded after some fifty kings of the Molmutine dynasty had reigned.[38]

These motifs were not (any more than the Temple Church itself) the property of any one faction through the seventeenth century. James I's arrival in 1603 was greeted enthusiastically. Brute was evoked: he had been the first to reign over the undivided kingdom before dividing it between his three sons; James had now reunited the island. The Arch of Triumph over Fleet Street, constructed for the king's procession into his capital, bore the inscription, 'By Brute divided, but by you alone / All are again united and made one.' At least three authors in the king's first years traced James's own ancestry to Brute.[39]

But as the century's crises took shape, it became clear that the British History would be of greatest advantage to those who traced the origins of Common Law — and the source of its current authority — back beyond the Norman Conquest to an immemorial past. Edward Coke of Inner Temple, in the seventeenth century the most authoritative voice in English law, argued in the preface to his *Third Report* (1602) that the Common Law had been the law of England 'time out of mind of man';[40] the Common Law and its officers preceded the Norman Conquest, and such law 'was not altered or

the same sheet. (Accessible on Guildhall's Collage, http://collage.cityoflondon.gov.uk/collage, no. 6412.) London Stone was linked with Brute; see P. Ackroyd, *London: the Biography*, London 2000, 18–19. (London Stone was linked too with the confirmation of contracts, L. Gomme, *The Governance of London*, London 1907, 150–53, as was the font of the Temple Church, ITR II, pp. c–ci.)

[37] See T. D. Kendrick, *British Antiquity*, London 1950; R. J. Smith, *The Gothic Bequest*, Cambridge 1987. For the Inns' early medievalists, J. G. A. Pocock, *The Ancient Constitution and the Feudal Law*, Cambridge 1987 (rev. edn), 243. On the prominence among the early antiquaries of lawyers (with their professional interest in the history of the law), Kendrick, 114.

[38] Geoffrey of Monmouth, *The History of the Kings of Britain*, bk 1 *passim*.

[39] R. F. Brinkley, *Arthurian Legend in the Seventeenth Century*, Baltimore and London 1932, 1–25. For similar motifs, see Anthony Munday, *The Triumphes of Re-united Britaine*, 1605; William Harbert, *A Prophesie of Cadwallader, last King of the Britaines*, London 1604 (presenting James as 'our second Brute', trying to become the first king of all Britons since Cadwallader); Percie Enderbie, *Cambria Triumphans*, London 1661 (Kendrick, *Antiquity*, 101). Aubrey, writing the life of his own relative Henry Lyte (d. 1607), reports that 'Lyte began the genealogy of King James, derived from Brute; which his eldest son Thomas Lyte . . . finished and presented to King James': J. Aubrey, *Brief Lives*, ed. A. Clark, 2 vols., Oxford 1898, II, 41. In the late sixteenth century, the family bore the motto, 'Fuimus Troies', Kendrick, *Antiquity*, 100. For the myth's further political deployment, see T. Marshall, *Theatre and Empire: Great Britain on the London Stage under James VI and I*, Manchester 2000, esp. 114–22.

[40] *The Reports of Sir Edward Coke*, ed. J. T. Thomas and J. F. Fraser, 6 vols., London and Dublin, II (parts III–IV), 1826, p. x. For Coke and the 'Ancient Constitutionalists', see Pocock , *The Ancient*

changed by the conqueror'. Coke was suspicious of the ancient history being claimed by chroniclers, but not of the principle:

> If you will give any faith to them [annalium scriptoribus], let it be in those things they have published concerning the honour and antiquity of the common laws: first, they say that Brutus, the first King of this land, as soon as he had settled himself in his kingdom,[41] for the safe and peaceable government of his people, wrote a book in the Greek tongue, calling it the Laws of Britain, and he collected the same out of the laws of the Trojans. . . .
>
> The laws of England are of much greater antiquity than they are reported to be, and than any the constitutions or laws imperial of Roman Emperors. Now, to return to our chronologers, they farther say that 441 years before the incarnation of Christ, Mulumucius of some called Dunvallo M. of some Dovebant, did write two books of the laws of the Britons, the one called Stat. Municipalia, and the other Leges Judiciariae, for so the same do signify in the British tongue . . . the statute law and the common law.[42]

The laws of Brute and Dunwallo embodied the immemorial Common Law, which took historical and so legal precedence over any claims of royal prerogative which had been introduced by William the Conqueror or his heirs.[43] James vi's *The Trew Law* and *Basilikon Doron*, both of 1598, had made James's position clear on the supremacy of the king, before he assumed the English crown: the king's promises, made to his people in the coronation oath, are enforceable only by a third party, namely God, not by the people themselves. The kings are the authors and makers of the laws and not the laws of the kings. Kings are called Gods by the prophetical King David, because they sit upon God's throne in the earth, and have the account of their administration to give to

---

Constitution; G. Burgess, *The Politics of the Ancient Constitution*, Basingstoke 1990; idem, *Absolute Monarchy and the Stuart Constitution*, New Haven and London 1996.

[41] Coke has Brute die in 1103 BC, when Samuel was judge in Israel.

[42] Preface to the Third Report, Coke, *Reports*, II, pp. xiv, xviii–xix (cited by Weever, *Monuments*, 441, on Dunwallo's laws). Coke owned two copies of Geoffrey's History, one signed by Coke himself; A. D. Boyer, *Sir Edward Coke and the Elizabethan Age*, Stanford 2003, 144. He traced back to Dunwallo the rule that certain beasts of burden could not be distrained, 2 *Inst.* 32. He owned a manuscript transcript of Dunwallo's laws, dedicated to him by John Llewys of Inner Temple, who went on to write a history of Celtic Britain; Boyer, 141. For Coke's links with the early-seventeenth-century Society of Antiquaries, including Joseph Holland and Arthur Agarde, see Boyer, 146–7; Agarde and Holland both believed that the Britons were descended from the Trojans. James I, concerned by the political and constitutional implications of the research undertaken by those first antiquaries, closed their society down. Coke's claims did not go unquestioned: see 'On the Antiquity of the Laws of England', *A Collection of Curious Discourses*, ed. T. Hearne, Oxford 1720, 8, no. 2; and William Prynne, *Fourth Part of a Brief Register*, London 1664, 553 (Coke was 'a far better lawyer, than antiquary, historian, or record man').

[43] This was not to deny that the immemorial Common Law did admit some royal prerogatives. For Saxon law, see classically S. Kliger, *The Goths in England*, Harvard 1952.

him.[44] 'As to dispute what God may do is blasphemy, . . . so it is sedition in Subjects to dispute what a King may do.'[45]

Coke, by contrast, (so Coke himself claimed) insisted to the king that the king, being ignorant of the law, must submit to the superior learning of his Common Law judges.[46] Coke would not even discuss with the king any case in which James believed his prerogative was involved.[47] In *The Case of Commendams* Coke drafted the judges' reply to a letter from the king: the king's letter was 'contrary to law;' the judges' oath 'in express words is that in case any letter comes to us contrary to law that we do nothing by such letters, but certify your Majesty thereof and go forth to do the law.'[48] Of the judges, only Coke withstood the king's demand for a retraction. James famously maintained that 'the courts of common law were grown so vast and transcendent, as they did both meddle with the King's prerogative and had encroached upon all other courts of justice'.[49]

We will need to bear in mind, in all that follows, that the Temple Church was maintained by the Common Law lawyers of the Inns of Court. The Inns had secured their land from the king in 1608, and continued to court him.[50] Relationships could nonetheless be delicate. John Selden of Inner Temple was imprisoned in 1621 for helping to draw up the Commons' Protest as to their rights and privileges; Coke was imprisoned, 1621–2, for challenging the king's foreign affairs and asserting Parliament's right to discuss them. Coke proposed and Selden seconded the motion denouncing Buckingham. Selden helped draw up the Petition of Right. He was then imprisoned again, 1629–31.

The Temple Church as a shrine to Dunwallo was a shrine to England's ancient laws. The Inns could seek, in the 1680s and then the 1690s, to incorporate these laws and this church into their own narrative of the long-lasting constitutional crisis. And as

[44] James VI and I, *The Trew Law of Free Monarchies, or, The Reciprock and Mutuall Dutie betwixt a Free King, and his Natural Subiectes*, in C. H. McIlwain, *The Political Works of James I*, Cambridge, MA, 1918, 68, 62, 54–5. See further M. Lee, *Great Britain's Solomon: James VI and I in His Three Kingdoms*, Chicago 1990, 82–8.

[45] McIlwain, *James I*, 310 (21 March 1609/10).

[46] *Fuller's Case*, Twelfth Report, 63–5 (65), in Coke, *Reports*, VI (parts XI–XIII), 280–82. G. R. Elton, *The Tudor Constitution: Documents and Commentary*, Cambridge 1960, 234.

[47] R. G. Usher, 'James I and Sir Edward Coke', *English Historical Review*, 18, 1903, 664–75, questions Coke's account of his open defiance of the King. For further antagonism, McIlwain, *James I*, pp. lxxxvii, 310–13, 326–45.

[48] *Commendams* (1616): see L. Jardine and A. Stewart, *Hostage to Fortune: the Troubled Life of Francis Bacon, 1561–1626*, London 1998, 370–73, 380–83 (using J. Spedding, *The Letters and the Life of Francis Bacon*, 7 vols., London 1861–72, V, 349–54).

[49] Quoted in M. A. Judson, *The Crisis of the Constitution*, New Brunswick, NJ, 1949, 119. When Coke died, royal agents seized his papers; the last three parts of his *Institutes*, confiscated by the Crown, were published posthumously by order of the Long Parliament, 1644.

[50] W. R. Prest, *The Inns of Court 1590–1640*, London 1972, 220–37 (and in particular on the Inns' 'Court Connections', 223–31); idem, *The Rise of the Barristers*, Oxford 1986, 234–82 (with overviews of previous assessments, 234–5, 256–7). Williamson, *Temple*, 443–4, lists the Temple's regicides.

the political position and outlook changed, so did the narrative which the Inns sought to represent and reinforce by the layout and decoration of their church.

'The British history' of Brute and Dunwallo may seem a startling survival from the historiography of an earlier and less critical age. The myth was already under threat by the start of the seventeenth century, not least from the attack in Camden's *Britannia* (1586, already in its fifth edition by 1600).[51] When Michael Drayton retold the story at length in *Poly-Olbion*, his friend John Selden annotated his copy, 'I implore you not to credit the material derived from the British story.'[52] But the Presbyterian William Prynne in the 1650s was still invoking Brute in his plea for an organic parliament under sovereign law which could restrain the king: 'an Hereditary Kingdome and Monarchicall Government by Kings, was the original Fundamentall Government settled in this Island by Brute', but Brute's first act was to convene a Parliament.[53]

Weever himself was probably drawing on Norden's confident link between Dunwallo and the Church. But Weever, writing fifty years later, knew he might seem credulous to his readers: he cites *Poly-Olbion* but adds the parenthesis, 'take it upon the credit of the British Story'.[54] Now Weever was not blind: 'it appeareth by this inscription following over the church doore in the stoneworke, that this holy Structure was newly founded of farre later times, and dedicated to the honour of the blessed Virgine; yet I think it is farre more ancient' (71).[55]

How could Weever have been so ready to disbelieve the evidence of the church's own inscription? We do well to look at the church through a lens of legal and constitutional — not of architectural — history. The Inns had secured the land of the Temple less than three decades before Weever wrote. The Common Law lawyers of the 1630s had good reason to 'claim' the church, of which they now had the care, as a church of ancient legal associations, being in its origins the Temple of Concord — a name and role to relish — in which Dunwallo had been buried; and their successors in the 1680s and beyond will have been glad to see this romance kept alive. Better still, if the church

---

[51] For John Ross (Inner Temple) and his defence of the Molmutine Laws against Camden, see R. F. Hardin, 'Geoffrey among the Lawyers: *Britannica* (1607) by John Ross of the Inner Temple', *Sixteenth Century Journal*, 23:2, 1992, 235–49; extracts 103–4.

[52] Kendrick, *Antiquity*, 103, 109. Drayton asked Selden to provide 'Illustrations' (or commentary) to the first part of *Poly-Olbion*, 1612. Selden treated the story of Brute there with vast learning and only light irony, M. Drayton, *Poly-Olbion*, in *Works*, ed. J. W. Hebel, Oxford 1931–41, IV, 21–3. Drayton admitted he was retelling a story 'which now the envious world does slander for a dream' (I, 312) and defends it at length, x, 219–323. Spenser (*Faerie Queene*, II, x, 68–9; cf. Kendrick, *Antiquity*, 127–32) and Shakespeare (*Cymbeline* 3.1.55–62 (1610–11)) both deployed the story.

[53] W. Prynne, *The First and Second Part of a Seasonable Legal, and Historical Vindication and Chronological Collection of the Good, Old, Fundamental Liberties*, London 1654–5, 4, in Kliger, *The Goths*, 154.

[54] Weever, *Monuments*, 181. By 1708 R. Newcourt, *Repertorium Ecclesiasticum* . . . , 2 vols., London 1708–10, I.ii, 544, is dismissive of Weever's chronology, but not of Dunwallo.

[55] Norden too, *Speculum*, 33, had recorded, but without any reference to the inscription, that 'some say it was founded . . . about the yeere of Christ 1185. but it seemeth that this Temple is farre more ancient'. Weever himself in his MS (Society of Antiquaries MS 127, fol. 146ᵛ, marginal note) suggests that knights might have sought burial in the Round because of its 'religious fabricke', built (long after Dunwallo) in the form of the Sepulchre.

could find ways to appropriate, on behalf of the Common Law, the primordial Brute; a Cokean Common Law lawyer had good reason to enjoy, in the Temple Church, reso-nances of such heroes.

So much for the half-credited legends of Brute and Dunwallo. Viewed with Cokean eyes, the church bore yet further and valuable witness to the pre-Norman past; and this time the links could be woven from the most sophisticated architectural history of the time. A third part of Britain's history is coming into focus, once more in relation to the evolution and codification of law. Coke continues the story whose early parts we have already heard:

> 356 years before the birth of Christ, Mercia Proba, Queen and wife of King Gwintelin, wrote a book of the laws of England in the British tongue, calling it Merchenleg; King Alfred, or Alvred, King of the West Saxons, 872 years after Christ, wrote a book of the laws of England ... [King Edward] ex immensa legum congerie, quas Britanni, Romani, Angli, et Daci condiderunt, optima quaeque eligit, ac in unum coegit quam vocari voluit legem communem ... [56]

In April 1628 Digges, Coke, Selden and Edward Littleton appeared before the House of Lords to protest against imprisonment without due cause shown.[57] Digges opened with an appeal to Saxon antiquity:

> The Laws of England are grounded on reason, more ancient than books, consist-ing much in unwritten customs, yet so full of justice and true equity, that your most honourable predecessors and ancestors many times propugned them with a *nolumus mutari*; and so ancient, that from the Saxon days, notwithstanding the injuries and ruins of time, they have continued in most parts the same ... [58]

Here, then, was the next line of succession: through the laws of the Saxons and Danes. The Cokeans could find the pre-Norman basis for the English parliamentary constitution in the Saxon *witenagemot* or council. Such legal history was the intellectual cousin of that which deployed Dunwallo. Proponents were once more seeking in the pre-Norman polity the foundation and vindication of the constitution for which they worked in their own day.[59] Selden inferred from Tacitus' Germans (*Germania* 11) that 'whilst the Saxons governed, the Laws were made in the General Assembly of the State or Parliament'.[60]

---

[56] Coke, Preface to the Third Report, *Reports*, II, pp. xix–xx. Also Coke, Preface to the Eighth Report, *Reports*, IV, pp. iii–xi: William I promised to observe the ancient laws, especially those of Edward the Confessor.

[57] 7 April 1628, *A Complete Collection of State Trials*, ed. T. B. Howell, III, London 1816, cols. 83–126.

[58] Sir Dudley Digges in *State Trials* III, cols. 83–4.

[59] Coke, invoking as he did the Molmutine Laws, relied less on Gothicism. He did own a ma-nuscript copy of A. Horn's Saxonist *Mirror of Justice* (c.1290), and described the *witenagemot* briefly in I *Inst.* 110.a (II.10, § 164).

[60] J. Selden, *Jani Anglorum Facies Altera* (London 1610), quoted from Kliger, *The Goths*, 181–2,

From Coke and Selden in the 1620s to William Petyt of Inner Temple in the
1680s, there were 'ancient constitutionalists' who defiantly invoked the Saxon foundations of English law. William Petyt, 'having often read of the freedom of this Nation,
that no Englishman could lose his life or property but by Law, the Life and Soul of this
so famous and so excellently constituted Government, the best polity upon Earth', appealed as Selden had to Tacitus, the Saxons and the *witenagemot*.[61] Christopher Brooks
has shown that Gothic architecture was already, in the seventeenth century, an arena
for competing political and ecclesiological claims.[62] At the Temple Church the building
itself was available as a monument to a valued past: for in origin it looked *Saxon*. To see
how, we must loosen the hold which a now-familiar chronology has upon our minds.
Even the most observant antiquaries of the seventeenth century were wildly mistaken
in their dating of medieval buildings.

Roger North, treasurer of Middle Temple in 1684, an architect himself (who re-
designed Middle Temple's gateway) and a friend of Wren, analysed the development
of English architecture. The first of three periods was 'the antediluvian of the Danes
[that is, from the period prior to the Danish invasions] . . . This I suppose to be seen
in the church of Durham, and is the most antique of any.' Little remained of the other
churches built before the Danes by 'the Saxon kings', although North identified 'some
foot steps of this antiquity' at Gloucester and Norwich. After the inroads of the Danes
there came 'arches angular or as half a birds eye and the supports quadrat diagonall
and thredded, as Westminster Abbey'. This style 'lasted to the Edwards time, and then
a still finer sort of building came in', as exemplified at Salisbury. North describes and
illustrates a column from Salisbury; its 'conceipt is taken from the Temple Church in
London, which is more ancient'. Here North adds a further sketch, of a column in the
Temple's chancel. How, then, would North have described the Temple Church? Probably as a church of Saxon origin (whose 'foot steps' are still visible in the west door),
with the Round (re)built after the Danish invasions; the chancel, of indeterminate date,
inspired a late-thirteenth- or fourteenth-century Salisbury.[63]

Wren himself credited a church built on the site of the later St Paul's in 605, destroyed by the Danes and repaired by King Edgar (959–75). 'We have some examples
of this ancient *Saxon* Manner . . . such was *Winchester* Cathedral of old; and such at

in the English translation made by R. Westcott, *Tracts Written by John Selden*, London 1683, 32, 93–4.
It is telling that Selden merited translation in the 1680s.

   [61] W. Petyt, *The Antient Right of the Commons of England Asserted, or, A Discourse Proving by Records
and the Best Historians, that the Commons of England were ever an Essential Part of Parliament*, London 1680,
Dedication, 11–12 and 123, in Kliger, *The Goths*, 168–70.

   [62] C. Brooks, *The Gothic Revival*, London 1999, 23–48 ('The Rhetorics of Power: Gothic Lega-
cies 1600–1700'). A. Buchanan, 'Interpretations of Medieval Architecture, c.1550–c.1750', in *Gothic
Architecture and its Meanings, 1550–1830*, ed. M. Hall, Reading 2002, 25–30, 42, refers to Samuel Daniel's *Defence of Ryme*, 1602, in which architectural and constitutional Gothicism are already linked.
Kliger in *The Goths* finds most evidence for such associations in the eighteenth century.

   [63] R. North, *Of Building: Roger North's Writings on Architecture*, ed. H. Colvin and J. Newman,
Oxford 1981, 109–13.

this Day the Royal Chapel in the *White-tower* of *London*; the Chapel of St. *Crosses*; the Chapel of *Christ-church* in Oxford, formerly an old monastery.'[64]

Educated viewers in the seventeenth century could plausibly claim to see the Temple Church as a mausoleum for kings living hundreds of years before Christ, rebuilt by the Danes and Saxons in the aftermath of Rome's dominion. Common Law lawyers could see something more specific still: a shrine to the first founders of English law, given its present form by the Saxons who brought parliamentary government to England and by the Danes whose laws were honoured by both Alfred and the Confessor.

The end of the seventeenth century stirred memories of its start; among them, memories of the claims with which Coke and his circle had sought to protect the Common Law.[65] James I's speech of March 1610 — on the prerogative and duty of the king — was invoked by John Locke;[66] the speech was still relevant and remembered. Robert Filmer had written *Patriarcha* about 1630 in defence of royal power: the king was the author, interpreter and corrector of the Common Law; the constitution was the creation of the sovereign king. *Patriarcha* was finally published in 1680. William Petyt replied to Filmer's *Patriarcha* with *The Ancient Right of the Commons*, 1679–80.[67] Against Petyt, Robert Brady, Master of Caius, wrote A *Full and Clear answer to a Book written by William Petit, esq.*, 1681. Brady wrote under the auspices of Archbishop Sancroft, who had put him in touch with Dugdale; it seems to have been agreed that Brady's — and not Dugdale's — response to Petyt should be published.[68] Petyt replied in turn with *Jus Anglorum.*

Coke himself was well remembered in the 1680s. In an extended rebuttal of Coke (and in particular of the Preface to Coke's *Third Report*) Brady attacked the 'eminent Persons of the long Robe' for their Cokean appeal to immemorial law, even when these judges invoked such law to defend the king's prerogative.[69]

With the introduction of Sancroft we have moved close to Wren himself. Sancroft as Master of Emmanuel (Cambridge) commissioned the Chapel and Master's Gallery from Wren in the early 1660s. Sancroft became Dean of St Paul's in 1664, and building at Emmanuel began only in 1668; but Sancroft kept in touch about its progress and helped fund the work.[70] Sancroft invited Wren to comment on St Paul's in May 1666, on Wren's return from Paris. Within four months the Cathedral was destroyed by fire.

[64] *Report on Westminster Abbey to Francis Atterbury, Dean* (1713), Soo, *Wren*, 81–2. Aubrey, *Chronologia Architectonica* (Bodl. MS Top. Gen. c. 25), fol. 155^v (renumbered 6), recognised that the chancel's windows in the Temple Church matched those of Henry III's reign at Salisbury and elsewhere. At fol. 156 (renumbered 7) Aubrey compares capitals at Dore Abbey with capitals in the Temple's cloisters.

[65] Selden died in 1654; but the younger members of the circle — such as John Vaughan — outlived the Interregnum.

[66] *Second Treatise*, London 1690, chap. 18, para. 200 (also invoking the King's speech of 1603): to help establish the distinction between true kings and tyrants.

[67] Filmer was a target of Locke's *First Treatise*, London 1690, and of *Patriarcha non Monarcha*, London 1681, by Locke's close friend James Tyrrell.

[68] Pocock, *Constitution*, 194.

[69] R. Brady, *Complete History of England*, 2 parts, London 1685, I, 182–4.

[70] K. Downes, *The Architecture of Wren*, London 1982, 45.

WHAT DID WREN SEE IN WHAT HE SAW?

We can expect Wren to have been struck by two features of the Temple Church. First, it was surely a prime example of Wren's 'Saracenic' Gothic; and secondly, its Round Church recalled the Holy Sepulchre in Jerusalem.

First, its Gothic character. Wren wrote in 1713: 'This we now call the *Gothick* Manner of Architecture . . . I think it should with more Reason be called the *Saracenic* Style.' (The Saracens, expanding fast, built with small stones, and 'their Arches were pointed without Key-stones, which they thought too heavy.') And so, Wren concluded with reference to Westminster Abbey, 'the *Crusado* gave us an Idea of this Form; after which King *Henry* built this Church'. Henry III rebuilt the Abbey 'according to the Mode, which came into Fashion after the Holy War'.[71] Such a style was exactly what might have been expected in the Temple Church, built by the warriors of 'the Holy War' itself. Here was a church built in Saracenic style by the crusaders who brought that style to Europe.

Wren could, famously, design in Gothic style if it seemed appropriate. He wrote of his planned work for a central tower and spire at the Abbey (and could justly have claimed the same for his design for the west front):[72] 'I have made a Design . . . still in the *Gothick* Form, and of a Style with the rest of the Structure, which I would strictly adhere to, throughout the whole Intention: to deviate from the old Form, would be to run into a disagreeable Mixture, which no Person of a good Taste could relish.' Wren had prepared drawings for the Abbey, 'such as I conceive may agree with the original Scheme of the old Architect, without any modern Mixtures to shew my own Inventions'.[73] He could say — admittedly to his patrons at Salisbury, who needed to hear it — that the marble colonnettes at Salisbury (similar to those in the chancel of the Temple Church), though 'so long and slender', have 'a stately and rich plaineness'.[74]

So why did Wren and the Benchers not leave the Temple Church as a Gothic masterpiece? As Wren himself said, 'to deviate from the old Form, would be to run into a disagreeable Mixture'; and that is exactly the charge to which his classical work at the Temple Church has been subjected.[75] The Benchers might, of course, simply have insisted on such a style; but we need at least to ask what purposes — in Wren's or in the

[71] Soo, *Wren*, 82–3 nn. 25–30. C. Wren Jr adapted this passage in *Parentalia*, London, 1750, 306, in the context of his digest of Wren's 1668 report on Salisbury Cathedral, 'The Life of Sir Christopher Wren', pt 2 § 8. On Wren's use of 'Gothic', 'Saracen', 'modern' and 'freemason', see Soo, *Wren*, 293 n. 54. Cf. K. Clark, *The Gothic Revival*, New York 1962, 14–23.

[72] Soo, *Wren*, 210–18, 225. At Tom Tower, Wren 'resolved it ought to be gothic to agree with the Founders' worke, yet I have not continued soe busy as he began' (ibid., 218). Wren proposed for Westminster Abbey the recovery of a consistently Gothic north transept, ibid., fig. 29. He offered alternatives for the central tower, fig. 28. (The drawings, 1719–22, are by William Dickinson, Surveyor to the College, 1711–25.)

[73] Soo, *Wren*, 90, 92 n. 49. For such 'harmony of objects', ibid., 215 n. 57.

[74] Ibid., 215 n. 51 ('Report on Salisbury Cathedral', 63–4).

[75] See William Whyte's paper, pp. 199, 201 below.

Benchers' minds — were advanced by the juxtaposition of classical and gothic styles which his work introduced into the building.[76]

We must do justice, meanwhile, to the other dominant feature of the church, which Wren will certainly have recognised: its derivation, in shape, from the Holy Sepulchre. Wren wrote of the 'small Models of Wood, garnished with Mother of Pearl, of the holy Sepulchre at *Jerusalem* . . . usually made for Sale to Pilgrims and Foreigners'; he compared them to the models of the shrine of Diana at Ephesus.[77] And he was certainly alert to the significance which a building could have and to the passions and loyalty which a building could inspire: 'Modern *Rome* subsists still, by the Ruins and Imitation of the old; as does *Jerusalem*, by the Temple of the Sepulchre, and other Remains of Helena's zeal' (Tract 1, init.).

Wren had good reason to credit a close connection between the Templars and the Sepulchre. His family owned a copy of George Sandys, *A Relation of a Journey begun Anno Domini 1610 in Four Books*, London 1615.[78] Sandys described at length 'the Temple of Christ's Sepulcher'.[79] Rooms to the north of the rotunda had been part of the Templars' college; 'the Temples in *London* belonged unto them: where in the Church (built round in imitation of this) divers of their statues are to be seene, and the positure used in their burials' (168).

The Temple Church, then, as Wren found it, already had historical links with one of Constantine's great churches. We shall see Wren make good use of the connection.

[76] Christine Stevenson, with an eye on the illustrations to *Eniautas, or, A Course of Catechising: being the Marriage of all Orthodox and Practical Expositors upon the Church Catechism*, London 1674, points out to me that such a mixture of styles in interiors may not have been unpalatable. Brooks, *Revival*, 34, argues that in St John's Canterbury Quad and St Katharine Cree Laud had programmatically combined traditional church-gothic and a modish classicism redolent of the Stuart court.

[77] Soo, *Wren*, 153 (Tract 1), 172 (Tract IV). Soo (298 n. 100) draws attention to the minutes of the Royal Society on 29 March 1677: 'Mr. [Thomas] Povey produced a model of the Sepulchre of our Saviour at Jerusalem, said to have been made upon the place by the Maronites.' The model is described in one of the Society's eighteenth century inventories as 'A Model of the holy sepulchre in wood, inlayed with Mother of pearl.' For such models, see M. Piccirillo, *La nuova Gerusalemme: artigianato sacro al servizio dei Luoghi Santi*, Jerusalem 2007 (Studium Biblicum Franciscanum, Collectio Maior 51); cf. M. Biddle, *The Tomb of Christ*, Stroud 1999, 42–44. For the example in the collection of the Order of St John, Clerkenwell, see Plate 79.

[78] *A Catalogue of the Curious and Entire Libraries of that ingenious Architect Sir Christopher Wren, Knt, and Christopher Wren, Esq., his Son*, London 1748, facsimile in *Sale Catalogues of Libraries of Eminent Persons*, ed. A. N. L. Munby, 12 vols., London 1971–5, IV: 'Architects', ed. D. J. Watkin, 1972, 1–39 at 12, lot 109. Dugdale also knew that the Temple Church was built in the time of Henry II 'according to the form of the Temple near unto the holy Sepulchre at Jerusalem'.

[79] 'That famous Temple of the Resurrection of our Saviour, at Jerusalem . . . called a Martyrie, because is [*sic*] was a Testimoniall of our Blessed Saviour's Resurrection', R.T., *De Templis*, 1638, 22.

What did Wren and Those Who Followed Him Do?

In May 1682, the Inns received Wren's report.[80] Once more we survey the church, this time with our eye on the work undertaken by Wren and his successors.[81]

Benjamin Cole in 1737 (Plate 70) shows shops once more encasing St Anne's Chapel; just a hint of an arch appears, where the Round and chancel meet. Only at the Chapel's demolition in 1826 would its fuller remains be (briefly) seen again (Plate 43). Thomas Malton, 1792 (Colour Plate VIII) shows the shops round the chapel's west end.[82] Here the Round's lower windows (and perhaps the upper too) are bordered and etiolated by broad fillets of wood or stone. The upper windows have been shortened.[83] Cottingham would argue in 1840 that more light had once been admitted by the clearstorey windows; 'the modern wooden window frames should be removed and the glass carried back to the original stone window jambs. Great lightness would be effected by this restoration.'[84] Malton shows too a classical door and frame to the medieval entrance to the Round (also just visible in Plate 43), two bays to the south of the west door.[85]

Two aquatints show the Round's interior: one by Malton, the other by Rowlandson and Pugin.[86] Rowlandson's (Plate 72) shows the other — more modest — side of the square-topped doorway seen in Malton's exterior view; here too (one bay further to the left) is the blocked-up door to the lower floor of St Anne's Chapel. The chapel's walls will have taken all the sunlight from three of the Round's southern windows. The round window over the west door is occluded.[87]

Even before Wren started, then, the surrounding buildings were blocking out

---

[80] ITR III, 173. Middle Temple has a bill for plaster-work in the Church, 1682, with Wren's recalculations and the endorsement of Middle Temple's Treasurer, 'Let this bill be paid according to the allowance of Sir Christopher Wren' (MTA 2/TAP).

[81] We will make use of the engravings and aquatints of the eighteenth and early nineteenth centuries, though such later images must of course be treated with caution.

[82] T. Malton, *A Picturesque Tour through the Cities of London and Westminster*, 2 vols., London 1792–1801, II, pl. XLV; the interior view (our Plate 73), is Malton's pl. XLVI. So complete was the destruction of St Anne's Chapel in 1826 that the re-exposure of the undercroft in 1862 caused a stir: *Illustrated London News*, 22 March 1862, and *The Builder*, 29 March 1862; cf. Lewer and Dark, *Temple Church*, fig. 35.

[83] According to Billings, *Illustrations*, 38. His pl. V shows one window at what he believed to be its original length.

[84] Conveniently in Lewer and Dark, *Temple Church*, 182, col. 2.

[85] This 'Doric' door was closed off by Robert Smirke in 1819–25; T. Allen, *History of London*, 4 vols., IV, London 1827, 394–5.

[86] W. H. Pyne and W. Combe (for R. Ackermann), *The Microcosm of London* (with aquatints after T. Rowlandson and A. C. Pugin), 3 vols., London 1808–9, III, 173–6 (letterpress, and aquatint by J. Bluck).

[87] On the northern side the window next to the west door was wholly blocked (Rowlandson), and the next partly obscured by a monument (Malton). In 1682/3 payments were made both for whitening and colouring the body of the Temple Church and for 'whitening the rounds and cupola' (ITR III, 198). Masons were paid for polishing the columns.

much of the light that reaches the Round now. Wren may have introduced the fillets that reduced the Round's lower windows; he certainly added the solid, full-height screen between the Round and the chancel. Thereby he significantly reduced the light admitted to an already dark Round. It may be no surprise that a lanthorn was installed there in the 1690s.[88]

In 1706 the Round's pillars were wainscoted to a height of six feet;[89] they had, it seems, been left unclassicised by Wren. They are shown wainscoted by Malton, 1792 (Colour Plate VIII) and by Rowlandson, 1809 (Plate 72).[90]

So to the screen (Plates 73, 74).[91] As well as obstructing the light from the chancel to the Round, the screen divided the church starkly into two spaces. The Round, still Gothic and irremediably dark, was a (numinous but gloomy) space through which one walked to enter the chancel, bright and classically enhanced (Plates 69, 76). Here too there were refinements in the levels of light. Lamb Building is already shown on the print of 1671, set north–south across the present-day Church Court (Plate 71); only right at the church's east end, above and around the altar, will the sunlight have been uninterrupted.

The story of the organ itself has often been told.[92] For five years, 1682–7, the Inns argued over the installation of a new organ; it became, as Middle Temple's Parliament admitted, a 'tedious competicion'.[93] Two organ-makers were in contention: Father Smith and Renatus Harris. This 'Battle of the Organs' was finally resolved by Judge Jeffreys, of Inner Temple, who judiciously decided in favour of Smith, the candidate favoured by Middle.

Wren introduced black and white 'diamond' paving into (at least part of) the church, and raised the church's floor level;[94] the sanctuary was two steps — and the whole length of the side aisles one step — above the level of the nave's centre. Wren probably had his eye on the chancel's proportions, which the raised floor would flat-

[88] Its installation, ITR III, 337; its removal (May 1702), ITR III, 368. For the lighting of the church from the early seventeenth century, ITR II, pp. xxx, c, 53, 54.

[89] R. Hatton, *A New View of London*, 2 vols., London 1708, II, 563.

[90] J. Jekyll, *Facts and Observations relating to the Temple Church*, London 1811, 5, records that the 'wooden casings' around the columns 'have been lately removed.' J. Britton, *The Architectural Antiquities of Great Britain*, 4 vols., London 1807–14, I, 13, pl. 2 (engraved in 1805) shows them without wainscots (Plate 73); Rowlandson's image may have been a few years out of date by the time it was published in *The Microcosm*.

[91] The joinery for the whole church, 1682–3, cost £570 2s 6d, of which £45 was paid to 'William Emmett, Carver, for carving work about the altarpiece, pillar, pilasters, shields, festoons, etc.' For the Middle Temple accounts, see S. E. Harrison, 'The Wren Screen from the Temple Church, London', *The Collector*, 11, 1930, 107–13, and Lewer and Dark, *Temple Church*, 71. For further photographs of the pulpit, see Harrison, 111, and *Wren Society*, 10, Oxford 1933, 39, pl. xv.

[92] E. Macrory (ed. Muir Mackenzie), *Notes on the Temple Organ*, London 1911; Lewer and Dark, *Temple Church*, 73–75; D. S. Knight, 'The Battle of the Organs, the Smith Organ at the Temple and its Organist', *Journal of the British Institute of Organ Studies* 21, 1997, 76–98; the stories of sabotage may well have been embellished in the nineteenth century, 81.

[93] 2 June 1685.

[94] Importation of earth, ITR III, 198.

ten out into a more nearly classical balance; the chancel will no longer have given the impression of a soaring, vertically oriented space. (The stone seat along the Round's wall remained visible.) The pulpit, wrote Hatton,[95] 'is also finely carved and finnier'd, placed near the E. end of the middle Ile, the Sound-board is pendant from the Roof of the Church; It is enrich'd with several carved Arches, a Crown, Festoons, Cherubims, Vases, etc.'[96]

The Wrenian woodwork was sold in the refurbishments of the 1840s.[97] The altar-piece (Plate 77) and two columns were acquired by the Bowes Museum. After World War II the altarpiece was bought back for the church, still bearing the number, 'Lot 24', from the nineteenth-century sale. The pulpit (Plate 75) went to Christ Church, Newgate Street, and was destroyed in the war.

The Inns turned their attention to the church again in the 1690s. Middle Temple's Parliament decided, 14 June 1695, under the Treasurer Roger Gillingham: 'On Mr. Treasurer's report that he thought the Inner Temple would join in repairing the Church and beautifying the entrance . . . he may proceed alone according to Sir Christopher Wren's model and estimate.' Addison had found a notice that it was Treasurer Gilling-ham who 'marshalled the Knights Templars in uniform order';[98] and Middle Temple's accounts duly record the division of a single, railed set of effigies into two sets, with the old ironwork reused to make the new railings. The accounts read as follows:[99]

No. 131 [carpenter] / for cutting the way through the Knights Templers [scored out] / for 18. foote of oake at 14s p ftte for plate, 01:04:0 [sic][100] / for 7. dayes worke & ½, 01:00:0 / for moveing the Knights Templers 5. men all night, 00:15:0

. . .

No. 136 [painter] / for painting & blewing the railles round the Knights Tem-plers, 02:00:0 / for 9. C of leafe gold used in guilding the sd Iron raills and worke at 18s per C, 08:02:0 / for laying in oyle 9. stone monumts of the Knights Tem-plers at 3s a peise, 01:07:0 / for painting the top of a stone Coffin, 00:02:0 . . .

No. 137 [smith] for 4. spikes to fasten the Kirb for the raills in the Church, 00:01:6 / for cutting the Railes in two parts in the Church & peising & fitting them and altering & mending the standards & 6 new spikes for the balls & drill-ing the holes and peising out 5. of the barrs longer wth: 8 Li of new Iron & cut-ting & filing out 2. rivetts out of the flatt barrs and putting of them up, 01:10:0

[95] Hatton, *New London*, II, 563.

[96] The Inns' own joiners were used for the screen, organ loft, altarpiece, pillars, pilasters, rail and table. Emmett (n. 91 above) was paid £90 for the finer 'carving work'.

[97] The sales were advertised in *The Times* on 11 March 1841 (8), 26 February 1842 (8), 12 Octo-ber 1842 (8), 17 October 1842 (8), 24 October 1842 (8), 14 December 1842 (8) and 15 July 1844 (11). In the last the lots were offered without reserve.

[98] Addison, *Temple Church*, 93, quoting from *The Flying Post*, 2 January 1696. Cf. Philip Lank-ester's paper in the present volume, p. 99 n. 20 above.

[99] Lesley Whitelaw of Middle Temple has kindly transcribed the account, from pages badly burned by the ink.

[100] The account was for 18 ft of oak at 1s 4d per foot.

/ 20. for 2. new rayles & 13. barrs wth 100. C 3. qtrs & 15. Li at 6d the pound, 05:05:6[101] / For 4. workemen 3. days removing & plasing the Knight Templers, 01:16:0 / for a labourer 2. days to raise the ground, 00:04:00 / for a Carver 11. days to make good their Limbs and weapons at 4.s p day, 02:04:00[102]

There was now a west–east aisle through the Round. Work is also listed on 'the [paire of] Church doores next the Cloysters',[103] the 'reframed Church doors', 'the two outward new doores', 'the old doores of the Church' and 'the west dore'. Several of these records probably refer to the main west doors, perhaps being equipped either for regular or for ceremonial use. From these main doors straight through the Round to the central doorway in the screen and so to the chancel: here was a processional way, flanked by the effigies. The arch was repaired with a large quantity of new stone, and some of the capitals were reworked.

So we reach the final campaign. In February 1701/2 the Inns set up committees to confer over the repairs to the church's buttresses (Inner) or to its walls and roof (Middle).[104] By October an estimate had been received, for £1,000. The work may have been urgent: Inner Temple recompensed Lloyd in 1701/2 'for work done over his chamber occasioned by the falling of the steeple.' Our evidence for this work of 1701/2 includes two grand but enigmatic engravings.

We have encountered the William Emmett who worked for Wren on the church's woodwork. Also by one 'William Emmett' are two prints of the church (Plates 78, 82), one of which we have mentioned already in relation to the Round's effigies. Middle Temple's Parliament papers record that on 5 June 1702 'Mr. Emmett, a sculptor, presented four drafts of the prospect of the Church and the Hall, inside and outside, which he proposed to have engraved on copper plates and printed on royal paper before the

[101] Disregarding the 20., the account was for 1¾ cwt + 15 lb at 6d per lb. Philip Lankester points out that views of the new arrangement tend to show, on each of the two sets of railings, major uprights (standards) both at the corners and half-way along each rail; each set of railings, then, had eight standards. If the old, single set of railings had a total of ten standards (one at each corner, one half-way along each end-rail and two along each of the longer rails), six new standards were needed, each with spike and ball or fleurs-de-lis.

[102] The smith's account — for a relatively small sum — is given in surprising detail; perhaps the reworking of the old railings had been the smith's own proposal, for which he needed to justify the charge. The Inns paid again for painting the knights and for painting and gilding part of the ironwork around them in 1706/7 and 1724, and for painting the railing in blue without gilding and 'twice in oil the stone figures with the railings' in 1778 (MTA 15/TAM.125j; 138b,c; 208). For mending the knights and plaster of paris in 1707, 4s (ITR III, 407).

[103] Middle Temple paid its share, although the doors next to the cloisters were on Inner's land; even if the door on the north side of the Round still existed, the (more convenient) south doors were probably used by members of both houses. (The alleyway to the north door had the inauspicious name 'Pissing Alley'.)

[104] ITR III, 365, 370, 381–4 (specifying the south side, 383), 405 (the disbursements); MTR III, 1487, 1488, 1489, 1490, 1491. Accounts for 1702 record an estimate for 3,500 ft of ashlar stone for the side of the church and buttresses, for five windows with three lights each, built inside and out of solid block, and for Portland stone, total £960 (MTA 15/TAM.117).

end of Michaelmas Term; and offered to deliver two copies of each to Mr Treasurer for every Master of the Bench if they will pay him 4s. in hand, and 4s. on receipt of the prints.'[105] Four such engravings exist: the two of the church; one of 'The North Side of the Middle Temple Hall', closely comparable in style and layout to that of the church's 'South Side';[106] and one, the most sparely drawn of all, of the hall's interior, facing west.

If the 'steeple' had fallen onto the porch and so damaged Lloyd's stationery shop outside the west door, then Emmett had good reason to offer the Inns a new design for the roof of the Round and of the porch. The buttresses needed repair too; we shall return to the shape proposed for them by Emmett. The work may have proceeded slowly. In 1708 the Inns finalised their payments for the work; Inner paid too for 'coach hire and waterage to Sir Christopher Wren's', suggesting that he was asked for advice on or approval of the completed work.[107]

WHAT DID WREN AND THOSE WHO FOLLOWED HIM ACHIEVE WITH WHAT THEY DID?

Wren was refurbishing, not building the Temple Church; he had to strengthen the church's structure, but not devise it. (The 'steeple's' collapse in 1701/2 suggests that he should perhaps have paid rather more attention to the church's structure.) We could perhaps argue that in 1682 Wren was faced with an inflexible space, that the Benchers wanted a classical church, and that Wren simply did as much as he could to satisfy his clients: he abandoned the irremediably unclassical Round and made of the chancel, squared off by the screen, as classical a space as possible. As a task, it was all the simpler — and perhaps for Wren all the more congenial — for implementing, on a small scale, the plan he had adumbrated for St Paul's in the First Model (and had then realised, to his own great satisfaction, at St James's, Piccadilly): an auditory prefaced at the western end by a domed vestibule.[108]

There are clues, however, that Wren was making a more particular statement in the chancel's details and in the disjunction of the chancel from the Round; and that the character he impressed on the church was retained — and refined — by the Inns in 1695 and in 1702–6. The significance of the Round and its effigies had changed by 1695;

[105] MTR III, 1490.

[106] They bear similar subscriptions, each with the artist's name to the far right. The elaborate canopies to the smoke-hole and porch are already shown in the print of 1671.

[107] ITR III, 412.

[108] Anthony Geraghty points out to me the similarities: G. Higgott, 'The Fabric to 1670', in *St Paul's: The Cathedral Church of London, 604–2004*, ed. D. Keene, A. Burns and A. Saint, New Haven and London 2004, 187–9, figs. 108–10. The domed vestibule planned for St Paul's is known from Sir Roger Pratt's criticism, 1673 (*Wren Society*, 13, Oxford 1936, 25–6). For the limited area used for worship, J. Newman, 'Fittings and Liturgy in Post-Fire St Paul's', in *St Paul's*, 220–32. For Wren's own assessment of St James's, Piccadilly, see Soo, *Wren*, 115, with Clayton's plan, sections and elevation at figs. 31–2.

but the overall character of Wren's layout and decoration could be preserved. Let us then look back over the work's trajectory from the vantage point offered by Emmett's prints of 1702.

Which William Emmett made the engravings? The carver (b. 1641) was uncle to a second William Emmett; the nephew's designs for Whitehall (in the style of Inigo Jones) and another palace are in the British Museum, and in 1702 he made a series of engravings of St Paul's, apparently without authorisation from Wren.[109] All these, however, show a far greater mastery of perspective than the two Temple Church engravings. Were the church engravings, then, made by the uncle, who had actually worked with Wren on the church, 1682–3 and will have known the hopes that were borne then by the Benchers and by Wren for the church? Probably not; this elder William disappears from any records in the mid-1690s. We will take it that the nephew made or supervised the prints, seeing a natural market for them in the Inns.

The engravings are tantalising. Both are stylised; they are (for example in the shape of the Round's principal windows) incompatible with each other. In Emmett's view of the interior, all the Round's windows have been given gothic tops. Emmett has altered the proportions of the chancel's windows, to give more light and a more uniform height to the whole fenestration. He has narrowed the Round's columns and, as best he could, extended the rhythm and line of the chancel's columns westwards into the Round. The engraving *unifies* the space and its styles. The oddest feature is the open screen between the Round and the chancel, which probably recalls the screen that had been removed in 1682/3 for the installation of the organ-screen and (after a long delay) the organ; the effigies, on the other hand, are shown in the two sets of five into which, as we have seen, they were divided in 1695.

Emmett's south elevation raises questions of its own. The artist has moved the Round's south-west door one bay to the east, where it would be unusable for as long as St Anne's Chapel (which Emmett has omitted) still stood. The porch's dome could be built only if all buildings on the porch were foregone. Emmett was offering the Benchers a clear, uncluttered church. Was the dome on the Round's roof ever built? There is no sign of it in Cole's engraving (Plate 70). The buttresses on the Round are distinctive; we return to them below. Most telling is the overall impression that the windows, buttresses and roofing of the Round are here stridently distinct in character from those of the chancel. (Christine Stevenson points out that the eastern end of the gables may be topped with flaming urns, recalling the Great Fire, which was halted just yards from the church; see Colour Plate VII.)

These two engravings, then, seem to serve two different programmes: Emmett's

109 Biographical notes of the nephew in E. Croft-Murray and B. Hilton, *Catalogue of British Drawings [in the British Museum]*, London 1960, 1, 304–5 and pl. 119a, b; and in H. M. Colvin, *Biographical Dictionary of British Architects 1600–1840*, London 1978, 293–4. See also N. Davenport, 'Note on the Emmetts', *Wren Society*, 14, Oxford 1937, p. xxiii, and M. D. Whinney, 'John Webb's Drawings . . .', *Walpole Society*, 31, 1942–3, 48 n. 2. For the nephew's engravings of St Paul's, 1702–3, see R. Hyde, 'Images of St. Paul's', in *St Paul's*, 320; Emmett must have had a mole in Wren's office. The nephew had a younger brother in Inner Temple who became a Fellow of the Royal Society.

interior view unifies the space, belying its disparate styles; his south elevation stresses and even adds to the styles' variety. Why were these engravings made as they were? What function or functions did they serve?

The answer again lies in a self-consciously historical, almost archaeological interest: in an attempt to realise for the Inns the church's proper place in the history of Christendom, its architecture and liturgy. It may be helpful to outline in advance this next stage of our argument. Emmett's interior view portrays an integrated, purely Gothic space, light and airy. Wren, as we have seen, saw the origin of Gothic in Saracenic forms. This Saracenic connection is explored and extended in Emmett's south elevation; we shall see that the two domes, over the Round and the west porch, are its clearest marker. Such forms evoked their own forebears in turn: the early Christian churches which inspired them. The buttresses may well reinforce the allusion in Wren's altarpiece (in the Temple Church as so often elsewhere) to a building of greater antiquity and greater sanctity still: the Jewish Temple in Jerusalem. The conjunction of such motifs in Wren's work and then Emmett's engravings was not serendipitous or casual. What Wren began, Emmett brought to its conclusion: an epitome of the vast history in the Middle East out of which the London church of the Knights Templar had grown.

Our evidence will be drawn, for the next few paragraphs, from books and their illustrations. Guillaume-Joseph Grelot's *Relation nouvelle d'un voyage de Constantinople . . .*, Paris 1680, was translated as *A Late Voyage to Constantinople*, London 1683, with fourteen engraved plates, including illustrations of Hagia Sophia, and of three modern mosques.[110] The Wren family had both the French and English editions.[111] Also in Istanbul in the 1670s were George Wheler and a French companion, Dr Spon. Spon published an account of their journey in 1679; Wheler followed with *A Journey into Greece . . .*, 1682. The Wren family owned copies of both books.[112] Grelot and Wheler (Plate 80) both illustrated mosques, in closely comparable style.

We have encountered Wren's friend Roger North, treasurer of Middle Temple 1684. North wrote a memoir of his brother Sir Dudley North, who spent twenty years in Smyrna and Constantinople until his return home in 1680: 'no foreigner ever looked more strictly into the manner of the Turkish buildings than he had done'; and Wren, 'when he had the covering of the great dome of St. Paul's in deliberation', asked Sir Dudley about the Turks' covering their vaults with lead.[113]

Turkish domes would lead inevitably back to the great Christian domes of late antiquity.[114] 'When [the Turks] had occasion to build Mosques,' Grelot explained, 'they

[110] Hagia Sophia, figs. v–vii (90, 104, 116); the mosques, figs. xi–xiv (215, 219, 220, 225).
[111] Watkin, *Sale*, lots 207, 367.
[112] Ibid., lots 114, 318.
[113] R. North, *The Lives of the Right Hon. Francis North . . . .*, ed A. Jessop, 3 vols., London 1890, ii, para. 138. Reprinted in *Wren Society*, 19, Oxford 1942, 116.
[114] I gratefully deploy P. de la Ruffinière du Prey, *Hawksmoor's London Churches: Architecture and Theology*, Chicago and London 2000, esp. 17–46, in the following paragraphs. Peter Doll has written two valuable pieces on the importance of the Temple and of early churches in the theology, design and liturgy of seventeenth-century churches: P. M. Doll, *After the Primitive Christians*, Cambridge

took their Models from those of the Christians . . . And this is the reason that all the Mosques in Constantinople are but imperfect copies of Sancta Sophia.'[115] Wren himself speculated in Tract II on the ancestry of his own favoured vaulting (which he adopted for St Paul's), 'as appears at *St. Sophia*, and by that Example, in all the Mosques and Cloysters of the *Dervises*, and every where at present in the *East*'.[116] On 14 November 1677 Hooke recorded, 'To Sir Chr Wr at Mans with him and Mr Smith, a description of Sta Spohia.'[117] (Thomas Smith, FRS, lived in Constantinople, 1668–71 and described Hagia Sophia in *An Account of the Greek Church*.[118]) Du Prey draws attention to three drawings of S. Sophia by (or attributed to) Wren: one is a cross-section illustrating a dome and a half-dome.[119]

In 1689 George Wheler published another volume. *An Account of the Churches, or Places of Assembly, of the Primitive Christians* offered descriptions — based on the descriptions in Eusebius[120] — of the church at Tyre, the Holy Sepulchre in Jerusalem and the church of the Holy Apostles in Constantinople. Wheler then extrapolated from these sources the constituents of an ideal early Christian church (Plate 81); Wheler's church of 1689 is deeply indebted to his mosque of 1682.

So we come back to the engravings of William Emmett; their domes were clearly inspired by scholarship — and by engravings — such as Wheler's. Emmett, in his imagined elevation, was evoking two related traditions, both germane to the history of the Temple Church: the west end of Emmett's elevation evokes, by its two domes, the early Christian churches and the lessons learnt from them by the Saracens; the east end evokes the 'Gothic' lessons learnt in turn from the Saracens by the crusaders. Emmett makes of the church an object lesson in the styles of architecture which the Crusaders who built the Temple Church will have encountered in the Holy Land. Emmett could expect to find a ready market for his confection precisely and only among patrons with lively antiquarian interests; such were the patrons he had in the lawyers of the Temple. As we shall see, ecclesiological politics were also in play: Emmett's Church embodies

---

1997, and '"The Reverence of God's House": The Temple of Solomon an the Architectural Setting for the "Unbloody Sacrifice"', in *Anglicanism and Orthodoxy 300 Years after the 'Greek College' in Oxford*, ed. P. M. Doll, Oxford 2006. Dr Doll kindly drew my attention to the importance of these motifs. See too D. H. Smart, 'Primitive Christians: Baroque Architecture and Worship in Restoration London', Th.D. thesis, University of Toronto, 1997.

[115] Even the fountains in the forecourt had been known in some early churches, Eusebius, *Ecclesiastical History* x.4.39–40 (on the church at Tyre).

[116] Soo, *Wren*, 163, with useful diagrams, 164–5, and full notes, 294–5 nn. 61–6. Du Prey, *Churches*, 42: Tract II specifically cites Grelot on the domes of Santa Sophia.

[117] R. Hooke, *The Diary of Robert Hooke, 1672–1680*, ed. H. W. Robinson and W. Adams, London 1935, 328.

[118] Discussed by J. Loach, 'Anglicanism in London, Gallicanism in Paris, Primitivism in Both', in *Plus ça change: Architectural Interchange between France and Britain*, ed. N. Jackson, Society of Architectural Historians of Great Britain 1999 Annual Symposium, Nottingham 1999, 9–32 at 13–14.

[119] Du Prey, *Churches*, 44 and fig. 20.

[120] Tyre: *Ecclesiastical History* x 4.37–45; and in the *Life of Constantine*, Holy Sepulchre, III, 25–40; Golden Octagon at Antioch, III, 50; Church of the Apostles, IV, 58–60.

the rich heritage that had been handed down from the early Christian past to all the King's loyal subjects, free from any contamination by Rome.

The domes of Emmett's engravings, evocative on paper, were surely never realised (n. 12 above). But he was being loyal to a tone set by Wren twenty years before. Most distinctive in Wren's chancel was the pulpit placed in its centre (Colour Plate IX); the pulpit needs our attention in this context of early Christian churches.[121] The pulpit appears to have been centrally placed before Dr Micklethwaite had it moved in 1637; and we have seen the record of its second relocation in 1641. Wherever it was placed between the Restoration and Wren's work, Wren was probably reviving or continuing a local tradition. But in doing so he conformed the church's design to a floor plan he will have known from contemporary research into early Christian churches: in location and function alike, a two- or three-decker pulpit on the church's east–west axis was comparable to the ambo in an ancient church.[122] It will take a page or two to describe what would (we may suspect) have presented itself readily to Wren as a fitting way to meet a particular demand of the Inns: that the places in the church for Benchers (n. 23 above) and for other members be clearly distinguished within a single space.

William Beveridge in *Synodicon*, Oxford 1672, gave a plan and a full description of the interior of an early church (Plate 83); the ambo is centrally placed.[123] Wheler followed suit in his *Account of the Churches*, 1689. The principal use of the *ambo*, according to Wheler, was for reading the scriptures to the people, especially the epistles and

[121] G. Shepherd's image of the chancel, 1811, can suggest to modern eyes the deliberate (and drastic) occlusion of the altar: surely the pulpit and preaching are being emphasised, the sanctuary and sacrament belittled. As we shall see, this is probably a serious misreading. In Inner Temple's collection there is a view similar to Shepherd's: 'Interior View of the Temple Church from a Sketch taken in the Year 1803 (by G. J. Rhodes 1849)'.

[122] For the movable pulpit (and the organ-screen, dividing the choir from the nave) in Wren's St Paul's, see Newman, 'Post-Fire St. Paul's', figs. 154–6, 158. Wren's pulpit at the Temple was fixed; for its foundations, ITR III, 199. Cf. the design for St Clement's Danes with a central pulpit, from Wren's studio, Du Prey, *Churches*, 72, fig. 33. The chapel of Lincoln College, Oxford, built by John Williams, 1629–31 (and thereafter re-adorned only once, in the 1680s) still has a movable pulpit which in the 1990s was for Evensong occasionally placed on the chapel's axis and at the foot of the chancel steps. I can confirm (from my own sermons) that the preacher — and (from my congregations' reports) that the audience — experience the sermon quite differently when the preacher is in this way among but above the audience, and is clearly placed in conformity with the building's symmetries, orientation and scale.

[123] *Synodikon, sive Pandectae Canonum SS. Apostolorum, et Conciliorum ab Ecclesia Graeca receptorum*, Oxford 1672, II, appendix 71–7; the engraving 'Ichnographia Templorum Veterum' opp. 71. Du Prey, *Churches*, 35 fig. 14, reproduces a page from E. Scheltrate, *Sacrum Antiochenum Concilium*, Antwerp 1681 (pl. opp. 186), showing an ambo and four floor-plans with ambos. The famous ambo of Hagia Sophia was probably destroyed (or at least stripped) in 1204. Grelot, *Relation . . .* (p. 157 above), was not sure if this ambo 'or Preachers Pulpit' had been axially placed just in front of the doors of the Sanctus Sanctorum or to one side where the Mufti's *Mamber* stood in Grelot's own day (81, 120). Thomas Smith, describing Greek churches, said that in the nave 'a little higher [from the Quire's station] is the desk, where they read the Holy Scripture to the People. In the great Churches a Pulpit [Smith's footnote: *ambon*] is usually placed in the middle, but which they very seldome make use of', *An Account of the Greek Church*, London 1680, 65.

gospels; singers were also placed there; John Chrysostom was the first to preach from there (and not from the *bēma* within the chancel) by reason of the great numbers of people who gathered to hear him.

There was some discussion, exactly who had been placed where in a service of the primitive church. Beveridge had the catachumens and others in the narthex, the penitents (*hypopiptontes*) inside the nave but near its entrance. William Cave takes up the theme: the penitents were by the entrance of the nave; next to them was the 'Ambo the pulpit or rather Reading-desk, whence the Scriptures were read and preached to the people'; beyond the ambo towards the altar were the faithful.[124]

Wheler acknowledged that in his own day the distinction had faded between the Beautiful Gates leading from the narthex into the nave and the Holy Doors leading from the nave into the chancel; 'so I take the modern signification of *Narthex*, to be in general the *Nave* or *Body of the Church*' (85). But at the Temple Church Wren was able to resist this fusion. The Round formed a natural narthex (and had in it the font that belonged there);[125] Wren's own screen ensured that three doors led from that narthex into the nave; the central door was suitably larger than the side-doors.[126] In the centre of the nave stood the ambo-pulpit. Beyond the ambo-pulpit towards the altar were the Benchers.

Wren used the space and the traditions of the Temple Church to re-create the character of an early Christian church. The Temple Church may once have been thought of as a large collegiate chancel with a round nave; it was now, thanks to Wren, a large nave, and round narthex. The sanctuary was clearly defined at the east end, up two steps; and the pulpit served, by breaking the sight-line down the length of the church, as a form of chancel screen, marking the division between the Benchers to its east and others to its west. The 'faithful' of the primitive churches were now the Benchers of the two Inns; the 'catachumens' to the west of the ambo were now the Inn's junior members. In the 1680s Wren and his patrons created an early Christian church in honour of the Common Law.

We have so far glanced at Moslem architecture and at its early Christian precursors. Behind these, in turn, lies the memory of the most sacred building of all: the Jewish Temple in Jerusalem. So we move to the church's east end and to our last topic. Wren's characteristic altarpieces were designed to evoke the Holy of Holies; and in the Temple Church, once more through the pulpit, he reinforces the theme. Nothing here jars with Wren's primary concern: the collegiate hierarchy of the Inns and their liturgy. On the contrary, his work endorsed both; for the Inns' church and its worship now conformed naturally to the pattern set by the building whose dignity was sealed by God himself.

The Jerusalem Temple was the object of two famous scholarly reconstructions in

---

[124] W. Cave, *Primitive Christianity*, London 1673, pt I, chap. 6.
[125] The font is prominent in the narthex of Beveridge, *Synodicon*, our Plate 83.
[126] As at Tyre, Eusebius, *Historia* x 4.41.

the seventeenth century.[127] Wren had direct access to Jacob Judah Leon and his model of the Temple. Leon's models of both the Tabernacle and the Temple were brought to London in the mid-1670s. Constantijn Huygens provided Leon with an introduction to Wren; and in September 1675 (after Leon's death in July) Hooke recorded in his diary, 'With Sir Chr. Wren. Long Discourse with him about the module of the Temple at Jerusalem.'[128] Wren had from Leon and his model the refined and authoritative vocabulary with which to evoke the Jerusalem Temple.

Three areas in the Jerusalem Temple matter to us here.[129] Immediately inwards from the Court of the Israelite People was the first: the Court of the Priests, open to the sky, which held the great altar of sacrifice. Inwards to its west, behind a vast curtain, was the roofed building itself, divided into two areas: the outer was the Holy Place entered daily by priests (and only by priests) in which the seven-branched candlestick stood and the incense was burnt; the inner, westwards again and beyond another veil, was the Holy of Holies, a pure cube, into which only the High Priest ever entered and only on the Day of Atonement. Here (in Solomon's Temple) sat the ark of the covenant which held the tablets of the Law, was topped by the mercy-seat and was flanked by cherubim.

English Hebraists in the seventeenth century were at the forefront of scholarship on the Temple. Joseph Mead, a Cambridge polymath, had urged in relation to church services,

> And what if I should affirme, that Christ is as much present here, as the Lord was upon the Mercy-seat between the Cherubins? Why should not then the Place of this Memoriall under the Gospell have some semblable sanctitie to that, where the Name of God was recorded in the Law? In a word, all those sacred Memorialls of the Jewish Temple are both comprehended and excelled in this One of the Christians, the *Sacrifices, Shewbread,* and *Ark of the Covenant*; Christ's Bodie and Bloud in the Eucharist being all these unto us in the New Testament, agreeably to that of

---

[127] More famous of the two was (and is) Villalpando's, which Wren believed to be 'mere Fancy', Tract IV, Soo, *Wren*, 169; cf. Tract II, ibid., 159 (Villalpando's 'imaginary Scheme of the Temple of *Solomon*') and Tract V, 191.

[128] Hooke, *Diary*, 179. For the model, J. Bennett and S. Mandelbrote, *The Garden, the Ark, the Tower, the Temple: Biblical Metaphors of Knowledge in Early Modern Europe*, Oxford 1998, 150.

[129] The Temple existed in three forms and was mystically envisioned in a fourth. It had been built by Solomon (1 Kings 6.1–8.12 and 2 Chron. 3–5) and destroyed in 587–6 BC. Ezekiel was given visions of the Lord's chariot throne (Ez. 1), of its departure from the Temple marked for destruction (Ez. 10) and of a rebuilt Temple (Ez. 40–48); scholars still ask how closely this corresponded to any Temple that was ever built. Zerubbabel did rebuild the Temple (Ezra 2–6); Haggai prophesied (optimistically) that 'the glory of this latter house shall be greater than of the former' (Hag. 2.9). This Temple was in turn desecrated in the 2nd century BC and rebuilt by Herod the Great and his successors on the man-made Temple platform, which survived the destruction of AD 70 in which the Temple itself was razed to the ground; on this platform the Aqsa Mosque and the Dome of the Rock now stand. In the seventeenth century Christian scholars such as John Lightfoot were, unsurprisingly, chiefly concerned with the Temple that Jesus knew; Jewish scholars such as Leon Aryeh with the Temple of Solomon.

the Apostle, *Rom.* 3.25. '*God hath set forth Iesus Christ to be our hilastērion through faith in his bloud*', that is, our Propitiatory or Mercy seat.[130]

In the Temple Church, as elsewhere, Wren carried through just such a programme. The two tablets of the Law, given to Moses, had been placed in the Ark of the Covenant within the Holy of Holies; the two panels of Wren's reredos contained the Ten Commandments, which were protected by the overhanging pediment. The Ark had functioned as the 'mercy-seat', covering the Tablets and sprinkled with blood on the Day of Atonement; the altar in front of Wren's reredos was the mercy-seat of the new covenant and its bloodless sacrifice of thanksgiving. On each side of the mercy-seat had stood a cherub with outstretched wings; above the Decalogue Wren placed two cherubim. The hall and the Holy of Holies had been lined with wood and decorated with carvings in wood of cherubim, palm trees, knops and open flowers; swags of wheat, fruit and flowers adorned the Temple Church's wooden reredos.[131] Wren decorated the Temple Church's pulpit with four-winged cherubs; the number of their wings may well have been determined simply by decorative convenience, but any patron or observer alert to such motifs will have known that four-winged cherubs attended the throne-chariot of God seen by Ezekiel in his vision inspired by the Holy of Holies.[132]

Who belonged where in such a church, at what parts of the liturgy? Christ's whole people was a 'royal priesthood' (1 Peter 2.9). 'Having boldness to enter into the holiest by the blood of Jesus, by a new and living way, which he hath consecrated for us, through the veil, that is to say, his flesh; and having an high priest over the house of God; let us draw near with a true heart in full assurance of faith' (Hebrews 10.19–22). The faithful, then, take the place not just of the priests around the sacrificial altar in the Court of the Priests; they follow the great High Priest into the Holy of Holies. The first analogy could be realised by moving the communion table down into the aisle, a new Court of the Priests; the second by extending the chancel, as a new Holy of Holies, to accommodate communicants.

The role of the church's altar or table is fruitfully ambiguous. As the new mercy-seat, *hilastērion*, the altar or table belonged in the Holy of Holies, inseparable from the Decalogue which the old mercy-seat had housed. As the replacement of the altar, *thysiastērion*, on which the sacrificial animals had been slain, the altar or table belonged in the larger area, the Court of the Priests, outside the veils. Thomas Smith, speaking of the Greek churches, identified the sacrarium or chancel as indistinguishably *hilastērion* and *thysiastērion*.[133]

How, then, should a church's space be divided? Scholars have paid much attention to Beveridge and the chancel screen at St Peter's, Cornhill. 'It may be sufficient to observe at present,' preached Beveridge at the church's opening, 'that the Chancel in

[130] J. Mead, *Churches, that is, Appropriate Places for Christian Worship; both in, and ever since the Apostles Times*, London 1638, 55; Doll, 'Reverence', 213.

[131] Cf. Doll, 'Reverence', 213–15.

[132] Ezekiel 1.6, 11.

[133] Smith, *An Account of the Greek Church*, London 1680, 66.

our Christian churches was always looked upon as answerable to the Holy of Holies in the Temple.'[134] Beveridge acknowledged that the screen at St Peter's was the only such screen in the City's new churches;[135] and although he briefly adduced the example of the early Christians ('having purposely waved antiquity hitherto, I am loth to trouble you with it now') he defends the screen more emphatically for its present function: the creation of a space in which communicants can gather, for 'it is much better for the place to be separate than the people.'

In the Temple Church, Wren had a large and open nave with no scope for a second, east-end screen; he must demarcate two special areas, for the Benchers and for the reception of Communion. Once more the central pulpit/ambo gave him his solution. The division of space and function by the ambo of the early churches had a still grander precedent in the Levites' pulpit of the Jerusalem Temple, dividing the Court of the (Israelite) People from the Court of the Priests. Thanks to the unusual layout of the Temple Church, Wren could celebrate the full depth of this shared Jewish and Christian liturgical tradition.[136]

In his *Portrait du Temple* (1643) and *De Templo Hierosolymitano* (1665) Leon describes this pulpit of the Levites.[137] So did the great scholar John Lightfoot:[138] the Levites stood to sing, two and a half cubits above the Court of the People on a level with the Court of the Priests; in front of them was a *dukan*, wrote Lightfoot, 'which was the name of their desks, and which the learned render *Suggestus* or *Pulpitum*'. (Wren's generation will have been more familiar than we are with a cathedral's raised pulpitum.)[139] Leon and Lightfoot both placed this pulpit outwards from the altar in the Court of the Priests,

[134] 'The Excellence and Usefulness of the Common Prayer: Preached at the Opening of the Parish Church of St Peter's, Cornhill, the 27th of November 1681', *The Theological Works of William Beveridge*, Oxford 1842–6, VI, 367, 388; the sermon is discussed by du Prey, *Churches*, 32, and Doll, 'Reverence', 211. For the possibility that Wren or Hooke or both might have heard Beveridge's sermon, see du Prey, 32.

[135] It would be followed by the screen at All Hallows-the-Great on Thames Street, whose minister was William Cave.

[136] Long before Wren (and before the re-admission of Jews in the 1650s), the Temple's Round Church had looked to observers like a synagogue. Sir George Buck of Middle Temple referred without any apparent embarrassment to 'that fair round Synagogue-like Church, or Temple yet standing and flourishing' in the Temple, *The Third Universitie . . .*, London 1615 (in J. Stow, *Annales*, continued and augmented by E. Howes and G. Buck, London 1631). According to R.T., *De Templis*, 22, the Jerusalem Temple's three subdivisions corresponded to porch, nave and chancel; Christians, then, need not 'fear . . . to build a Christian church so like Solomon's Temple' out of worry that it would resemble a synagogue. Petyt MS 538 vol. 17, fols. 400 ff., describes the Old Temple in Holborn as 'in form circular resembling the church buildings & synagogall Chapple at Hierusalem' and the New as 'in a round and sinagoggical form' (fols. 401ᵛ, 403).

[137] J. J. Leon Aryeh, *Portrait du Temple de Salomon . . .*, Amsterdam 1643, 31; *De Templo Hierosolymitano . . . Libri IV, ex Hebraeo Latine recensiti*, Helmstadt 1665, 64.

[138] J. Lightfoot, *The Temple: Especially as it Stood in the Dayes of our Saviour*, London 1650, 186.

[139] In secular Latin, a platform or stage, in cathedrals a stone screen provided to shut off the choir from the nave.

overlooking the Court of the (Israelite) People.[140] Here was vindication enough for a two-decker pulpit to mark off the sacred area into which the congregation would move to receive communion. This was the new Temple's Court of the new 'royal priesthood, an holy nation'.

So the pulpit of the Temple Church neatly served a dual purpose: to demarcate the areas where the Benchers sat for Mattins and where the congregation as whole gathered for Communion. The dignity of the Benchers, at home within the larger sacred area, a new Court of the Priests, was elegantly represented and enhanced. Wren's plan was not accepted without prolonged debate; for it reignited the argument, over the placing and mobility of the Communion table. Middle Temple discussed this placing at three successive parliaments in 1683, finally minuting that 'on further debate, their Masterships declare themselves satisfied in the placing of the Communion table where now it is'.[141]

Leon's model of the Jerusalem Temple is lost; for its appearance, we must rely on Leon's various descriptions of the Tabernacle and Temple and on the illustrations in *De Templo*. His description of the Temple Mount as a whole emphasises the vast size of the retaining wall and its stones. We do well to notice the shape of Leon's vast buttresses on the retaining wall. Emmett's south elevation shows, on a far smaller scale, buttresses of a similar, scooped-out form.[142] Wren himself, with the pulpit, extended the sanctity of Jerusalem's sacrificial area half-way down the nave of the Temple Church; Emmett's design supported its façade with the buttresses that had supported the Temple Mount.

What Wren had created inside the church, Emmett imagined twenty years later in its elevation: a building in which the whole history of faith was encoded. The aim was perfectly aligned to the history of the Temple Church itself, built by the Knights Templar: an order based in the Jerusalem of the Temple, the guardians of Constantine's Holy Sepulchre and a leading force in the Holy War that brought Saracenic architecture to England.

[140] Lightfoot acknowledged that some scholars were surprised by the levites' *dukan*, since this had been the name too of the priests' desks at which the priests gave the blessing. The plan of the Temple proposed by Lightfoot was included only in the posthumous edition, *The Works of the Reverend and Learned John Lightfoot . . .*, ed. G. Bright, London 1684, I, opp. 1049; repr. du Prey, *Churches*, 28 fig. 11.

[141] MTR III, 1354–5; see p. 139 above, on the 1677 decision.

[142] J. J. Aryeh Leon, *De Cherubinis Tractatus*, Amsterdam 1647, 3–9; *Portrait du Temple de Salomon . . .*, Amsterdam 1643, 31; *De Templo Hierosolymitano . . . Libri IV, ex Hebraeo Latine recensiti*, Helmstadt 1665, 35–8, 64. G. Sandys, *A Relation of a Journey begun An. Dom. 1610 . . .*, London 1615, dissolved the link between the Templars and Jerusalem's Temple Mount, but his description (192) and illustration (193) of the Mount's Dome of the Rock, a regular octagon, could still catch the eye. 'In the midst of the shelving roofe, another upright aspireth, though lesse by farre, yet the same in forme and substance with the former, being covered over with a cupolo of lead' (192). Might such a description have inspired Emmett's roofing on the Round? W. Burton, *Description of Leicester Shire*, London 1622, 234–5, believed the church to have been built 'after the fashion of the Temple of *Salomon* in *Ierusalem*'.

What will the Refurbishments Have Signified to the Inns?

Several factors encouraged the turn to the Temple and to primitive Christianity in the late seventeenth century. The Temple's legacy countered any Romish claims to be the sole heirs of a holiness imparted to the Temple and its liturgy by God himself. The early Church, prior to Rome's decline into tyranny and superstition, was a model for pure Christian teaching and worship; the Constantinian Church embodied a relationship with the state and its divinely appointed ruler to which widely diverse factions of the seventeenth-century Church could appeal and could encourage the King to aspire.

Solomonic imagery had defined James VI and I. The first state entry of James VI of Scotland into Edinburgh was marked by a pageant of the Judgment of Solomon. 'I know not', he wrote in his 'Meditation on the Lord's Prayer, 'by what fortune, the diction of PACIFICUS was added to my title . . . but I am not ashamed of this addition: for King *Solomon* was a figure of CHRIST in that, that he was a King of peace.'[143] Bishop Montagu was charged with the edition of the king's works, and in his foreword 'To the Reader' praised the Solomonic James.[144]

It was important for the Anglican Church to trace its foundation back, past the arrival of Augustine from Rome, to King Lucius (the first king of England to become Christian) and to Constantine. As Constantine had caused the scriptures to be transcribed and distributed, so James had called the Hampton Court Conference and caused the Bible to be newly translated.[145] As Constantine built the Lateran, so 'our own religious Constantine' would rebuild St Paul's.[146]

And so through to the Restoration. London, centre of the Puritan revolution, had particular reason to flatter the King as his return drew near.[147] Carew Reynell looked

[143] 'His name shall be Solomon [*shalom* = peace], and I will give peace and quietness unto Israel in his days', 1 Chron. 22.9. Cf. also Bacon's dedication of *Novum Organum*, and 'Salomon's House' in *The New Atlantis*; and the sermons by William Laud on 19 June 1621, by John Donne on 26 April 1625 and by John Williams at the king's funeral (citing Villalpando's reconstruction of the Temple). Charles I picked up the theme: for James's depiction in the Banqueting Hall, see R. Strong, *Britannia Triumphans: Inigo Jones, Rubens and Whitehall Palace*, London 1980. The whole Whitehall project was indebted to Villalpando, as Philip II's Escorial had been.

[144] *The Workes of the Most High and Mighty Prince James . . .*, London 1616.

[145] Joseph Hall, sermon at St Paul's, 24 March 1613. Cf. John Gordon, *A Panegyricke of Congratulation . . .*, London 1603; idem, *Enōtikon*, London 1604.

[146] Bishop King of London, 'A Sermon at Paules Crosse, on behalfe of Paules Church', London 1620, 53–4. On the Constantinian Temple Bar, see J. Newman, 'Inigo Jones and the Politics of Architecture', in *Culture and Politics in Stuart England*, ed. K. Sharpe and P. Lake, Basingstoke 1994, 229–56; G. Parry, *The Golden Age Restor'd: the Culture of the Stuart Court, 1603–42*, Manchester 1981, 249.

[147] The Temple Church was not insulated from the crises around it. Among sermons which Evelyn heard in the Church were the following. 2 Dec. 1659: 'in the afternoone Dr. *Wild* at the *Temple* on 4: Phil: 5, recommending moderation in all our actions; how *summum jus* was *injuria*, etc.' 1 July 1660: 'Dr. *Gauden* at the *Temple* Church on 16: Act: 24 of *Paules* apologie & Confession before *Agrippa*, proving his submission to Authority, etc.' 29 May 1684: 'Being his Majesties Birth-day and

to Charles: 'You are a second Constantine to stay / Our Holy Church from falling to decay.'[148]

We will be wary of laying too much weight on old typologies. By the time of Wren's work at the Temple, the early Stuarts' rule was a fading memory; the Regicide itself was over thirty years in the past. Wren's own father and uncle, both fervently loyal to the early Stuart regime (a loyalty for which they had both suffered), were dead. But a church that called Solomon and Constantine to mind will also have called to mind the early Stuart kings who had basked in their glory. In 1682–3 the Inns had no reason to resile from such associations; indeed, they could ill afford to risk the king's displeasure. In the second half of the century, the Inns' prestige was falling: a barrister's route to prosperity and preferment generally lay outside their structures; senior members could afford not to be benched; a shortage of Benchers brought an end to the readings with which the Inns had educated their students; neither established barristers nor students saw reason to take chambers in the Inns or to eat in Hall or even to pay the minimum charge for commons. Financial crisis — even without the costs of repairing the damage from two major fires — was never far away.[149] The King who would challenge the City of London's observance of its charter (*Quo Warranto*) was not to be crossed by Inns who depended on a royal grant of their own. In their refurbished church of 1682–3, the Inns needed to make (without crippling expense) a statement of present loyalty and intended grandeur.

In that work of the early 1680s the Round was robbed of much of its light. The effigies were left alone, blocking the central walkway; movement through the Round to the chancel was inescapably circuitous, via the ambulatory. One reason for rebuilding the cloisters after the fire of 1678 was the recovery of their old role as a place for students' 'walking in evenings' and 'putting cases'; and we have heard from *Hudibras* that the Round, entered direct from the cloisters, was still used for such conferences.[150] The Round, then, will have been an extension to the cloisters with the added charm of being, in antiquarian eyes, a mausoleum or shrine to the knights of old. (For the introduction of the last effigy, *c.*1682 — an act of careful antiquarianism — see Appendix II below.) The 'real' entrance to the church will have been at the organ-screen, the Round's dark, medieval air giving way to the light, classical splendour of the chancel.

restauration, I went to the Temple Church where a stranger [perhaps Dr Sherlock, appointed in April] preached before all the Judges and that Society on 1.4. *Pet*: 15, a Theologo-political sermon, in order to obedience and Union'; J. Evelyn, *Diary*, ed. E. S. de Beer, Oxford 1955, III, 237, 249; IV, 380–81.

[148] C. Reynell, *The Fortunate Change*, London 1661, 6; cf. I. Basire, *The Ancient Liberty of the Britannick Church*, n.p. 1661, 6. For the King's Bedchamber at Greenwich and Villalpando's Temple, J. Bold, *John Webb: Architectural Theory and Practice in the Seventeenth Century*, Oxford 1989, 144 and pl. 98.

[149] D. Lemmings, *Gentlemen and Barristers: the Inns of Court and the English Bar 1680–1730*, Oxford 1990, chaps. 2–5. Roger North, some time after 1707, described the Inns as 'societies, which have the outward show, or pretence of collegiate institution; yet in reality, nothing of that sort is now to be found in them' (ibid., 33).

[150] R. North, *Lives*, I, 25–6, para. 20. For *Hudibras*, see n. 15 above.

Passage through the Round evoked the passage from King Brute to the British Constantine, from the ancient constitution to the laws of the Stuart monarchy. The kings of venerable, primordial law were acknowledged, absorbed into the development of English law and so left behind. The shadows of primordial law and its heroes were dispelled, as the viewer walked eastwards through the church, by the chancel's overall brightness and finally by the sunlight flooding into the eastern end of this Constantinian church, the Holy of Holies inspired by Solomon, king and judge.[151]

The Benchers were, it seems, proud of Wren's work. The Bishop of Rochester and Dean of Westminster, John Dolben — staunch royalist, brave soldier and famous preacher — was invited to reopen the church and to a dinner on 11 February 1682/3. John Standish, Chaplain in Ordinary to the King, preached at the church on the following Sunday, to celebrate the work's completion.

The church was as directly exposed to political crises in the 80s as it had been in the 30s. In 1684 William Sherlock was appointed as Master. Sherlock resolutely opposed James II's Romanising policy (and refused to read the Declaration of Indulgence in the Church) but was loyal to the King and his rights. In May 1685 he preached to the House of Commons: Roman Catholicism tended to disloyalty, but he asserted his own faith in the king. In 1686 he was appointed a chaplain to the king.

In 1685 the Inns appealed to Jeffreys (as Lord Chancellor) to settle their dispute over the new organ. Jeffreys was at the height of his public power; in each of the three years following the 'Bloody Assize' of 1685 Inner Temple offered him a play when he dined on Grand Day; in 1687 the Inn commissioned a portrait of Jeffreys from Kneller.[152] Judges were meanwhile under increasing threat of deposition: eleven were arbitrarily removed and replaced in 1676–85; early in 1686 six more were removed, four of them purged to prevent their sitting in *Godden v. Hales* on the king's power to dispense with a statute in a particular case.[153] Those who remained in office were conspicuously complaisant to the King. In summer 1686 the judges were being treated with disrespect on circuit.

In spring 1688 the king reissued the Declaration of Indulgence and ordered that it be read 'at the usual time of divine service' in the churches of London, 20 and 27 May. On 11 May the leading clergy of London met at Sherlock's house in the Temple and decided to ask the bishops to petition the king against the order; on Sunday 13 May the bishops of Ely and Peterborough and fifteen senior clergy met at the Temple to

[151] In the *Gentleman's Magazine*, 1842 pt 1, 655, EIC (Edward John Carlos; see Rosemary Sweet's paper, p. 188 below) was delighted by Willement's new stained glass: 'Whoever remembers the Temple Church in all its former glories of whitewashed ceilings and pillars and naked ground-glass windows, and was annoyed with the glare of light . . . will at once see how justly the ancient edifices were designed to receive its stained-glass windows.' It was clearly a familiar complaint that the church had been 'disagreeably light'.

[152] ITR III, pp. lv–lvi.

[153] A. F. Havighurst, 'The Judiciary and Politics in the Age of Charles II', *Law Quarterly Review* 66, 1950, 229–52 (and for the earlier part of the reign, 62–78); idem, 'James II and the Twelve Men in Scarlet', *Law Quarterly Review* 69, 1953, 522–46 (Havighurst points out that the Bloody Assizes only won their bad reputation after the Revolution).

organise defiance. Inner Temple, meanwhile, remained publicly loyal: on 16 December 1688 the Inn lit a bonfire to celebrate James II's return to London from Rochester.[154]

But the tide had turned. On 18 December 1688 James II left London and his kingdom. Over the coming months Inner Temple lit bonfires for the arrival of the prince of Orange, the arrival of the princess of Orange, the proclamation of the king and queen, and their coronation.[155] The first three crimes listed by the Commons as justification for excepting persons from the proposed Bill of Indemnity all involved the judges: asserting and promoting the king's dispensing power; committal and prosecution of the bishops in the *Seven Bishops' Case*;[156] and advising and promoting the Ecclesiastical Commission (responsible for expelling the president and twenty-five fellows of Magdalen College, Oxford). The final indemnity excluded Jeffreys (by then dead), Herbert,[157] Wythens,[158] Holloway,[159] Lutwyche, Heath[160] and Jenner.[161]

Dr Sherlock, non-juring, was suspended from his post, but nobody was appointed in his place, and he supplied other preachers to the Church at his own expense; in 1690, pleading the de facto rule of the new regime, he swore loyalty to the king in person, and the Inns repaid to him the expenses he had incurred in the provision of other preachers.[162] Roger North was non-juring too; he gave advice to Archbishop Sancroft and the other six non-juring bishops.

William Petyt, long derided by Sancroft's ally Brady, replaced Brady as acting keeper of the Tower records. Petyt advised the House of Lords (which was necessarily asking how James's abdication had affected the constitution) that the contract between king and people long preceded the Norman Conquest: and that the king had for centu-

---

[154] ITR III, 264.

[155] Ibid.

[156] The jury, despite sustained pressure, acquitted the bishops of seditious libel for declaring the illegality of the King's suspending power (that is, the power to abrogate a law generally) as exercised in the Declaration of Indulgence.

[157] Sir Edward Herbert, Middle Temple, the 'new very young Lord Chief Justice' (Evelyn), presided in *Godden v. Hales* and found in favour of Hales and the Crown. As a member of the Ecclesiastical Commission, he voted *against* the expulsion of the President and fellows of Magdalen. (This and the following notes are indebted to the *ODNB*.)

[158] Francis Wythens, Treasurer of Middle Temple in 1682, was expelled from the House of Commons in 1680 for his complaisance to the King, pronounced sentence on Titus Oates and accompanied Jeffreys to the West Country after the Monmouth Rebellion.

[159] Sir Richard Holloway, Inner Temple, concurred in the sentence on Oates, and was said to be particularly under Jeffreys' influence.

[160] Sir Richard Heath, Inner Temple, was in favour of the dispensing power, followed court instructions to find the seven bishops guilty and on circuit suggested to juries that those lighting bonfires to celebrate the bishops' acquittal be indicted for riot.

[161] Sir Thomas Jenner, Inner Temple, was appointed Recorder of London under Charles II's *Quo Warranto*, and endorsed the dispensing power. He fled London with James II and was captured with him; effigies of both were hanged and burnt by the London mob.

[162] Williamson, *Temple*, 651.

ries taken the oath to do justice before any man paid him homage. In February 1693/4 Inner Temple's portrait of Jeffreys was taken down.[163]

By 1695 the new regime was securely in place. It was time for the Round and its effigies to be better honoured. Divided into two rows, the effigies, as a guard of honour, would now flank the new central aisle through the Round and into the chancel. Even from the Round's southern door, the natural route through the church was now a left turn on entry from the cloisters and then a right turn up the aisle; when the new west door was open, progress through the church's space was truly unified.

A further programme of works was soon needed on the church, for safety as much as for decoration. In his engravings of 1702 Emmett followed the trajectory established by Wren in the 1680s and refined in 1695. His south elevation harmonised elements from the Jerusalem Temple, the early Christian churches and Saracenic Gothic; so the programme of the 1690s was, in the viewers' imagination, elegantly enhanced. Emmett's interior view expressed and idealised the whole church's unified Gothic splendour around just one fixture: the set of effigies laid out in two rows, flanking the new processional way from west to east along the whole length of the Church. The Inns' crests are on the screen, north and south; this is the Inns' medieval Church, under the Inns' own care, as Emmett imagined it had been, long before the organ-screen was built. William Petyt became treasurer of Inner Temple in 1702; he was among the most important of the buyers whom Emmett will have hoped to secure for his engravings.

The church's refurbishments, 1682–1706, were shaped by the particular — and shifting — links between the church's imagined past and its present patrons: the church had ancient effigies and traces of 'Saxon' style; famous lawyers in the Temple had throughout the century valued the story of Malmutius and his laws; others still, at the century's end, found among the Saxons the origins of the English constitution. In 1682–3 the church's Constantinian potential could confidently absorb the church's medieval past and supersede it. But when the political crisis had resolved itself into a new dynasty, the Benchers could in 1695 arrange for the ancient traditions and claims encoded in the Round to be finally given their due. By 1702, primitivism was riding high; two extravagant domes could at least be imagined. Here was an antiquity and dignity that owed no debt to Rome.

The Inns were obliged, by the Letters Patent of 1608, to educate lawyers and to maintain the church; everything they were doing to discharge the second duty emphasised their commitment to the first. Any Inner Templars entering their side of the church would, as they stepped from the Round into the Chancel, walk over the tomb of John Selden, twice imprisoned for defying the executive. Today's visitors will see, on the wall above, the memorial to William Petyt, who insisted on the basis of the ancient constitution that no Englishman could lose his life or property but by Law. *Troes fuerunt.*

[163] ITR III, 306.

Appendix 1: The Inscription Commemorating the Consecration of the Church

'On 10 February 1185 in the year from the Incarnation of our Lord 1185, this Church was consecrated in honour of the Blessed Virgin Mary by the Lord Heraclius, by the grace of God Patriarch of the Church of the Holy Resurrection.' The Latin inscription (Plate 84) was in the tympanum over a doorway (of which all trace has disappeared) from the Round to the cloisters, two bays to the south of the west door; a copy now surmounts the west door itself.

Esdaile, *Temple Church Monuments*, 6–9 records, from T. Blount, *Glossographia*, London 1656, s.v. 'Templaries' (4th edn, 1674, 636), the history of this inscription: defaced in 1656; restored in May 1671 and within a few days defaced again; destroyed by accident in the repairs of 1695. We might wonder if this final 'accident' was engineered to bring the mention of indulgences to an irremediable end. For the exact date:

(A) (i) Weever, *Monuments*, 441 (and Weever's manuscript in the Society of Antiquaries, MS 127, fol. 146^v) records the dedication-date on the inscription as 'II Idus' (MS: '2 Idus'), ie. 12 February. Similarly (ii) T. Dingley, *History from Marble* (now in the Bodleian Library, repr. in facsimile by the Camden Society, 94, 1866–7), with dates mentioned up to 1684, fol. cccxiv, reproduced by Esdaile, *Temple Church Monuments*, 7); (iii) Inner Temple's Wilde MS, drawing post-1764 on two MSS, one drawn up *c*.1633; and (iv) Inner Temple's Petyt MS 538 vol. 17, fols. 400 ff. at 403 ('2do Idus'). This last shows how hard it had become to read the inscription: 'But for that it is affirmed by some that this church was consecrated to I wot not what Saint called St Parnell . [misread from o·ERACLI?] I will for the Refutation thereof referre you to the Inscription over one of the Doors of the Church yet extant and legible in these words . . .'

(B) More familiar is the date IV. Idus or 10 February (which was a Sunday) given by (i) T. Blount, *Glossographia*, London 1656, s.v. 'Templaries' (4th edn, 1674, 636), (ii) Dugdale, *Origines*, 173 ('. . . PATRIARCHA, IV. IDUS'), (iii) J. Aubrey, *Chronologia Architectonica* (the fourth and unpublished part of *Monumenta Britannica*, Bodley MS. Top. Gen. c. 25), fol. 155^v (renumbered 6), (iv) a drawing on parchment (in Middle Temple's loose papers), inscribed on the reverse, 'The Inscription over the doors at the West end of the Temple Church taken of the Stone Aug: 2nd [or 3rd] 1695' (Plate 84), (v) R. Newcourt, *Repertorium Ecclesiasticum*, 2 vols, London 1708–10, I.ii, 544 ('. . . Patriarcha.+.IV.Idus'), (vi) Strype's Stow, *Survey*, I, Bk 3, 272 ('IIII·IDUS'); and (vii) Middle Temple's 'Downing MS', 1739 (A. R. Ingpen, *Master Worsley's Book*, London 1910, repr. 103).

In the medieval dating-system whereby the days leading up to the Ides, etc, are counted in straightforward and not reverse order, IV. Idus would be 9 February, the Octave of the Purification in the event that the Octave was observed.

Strype's Stow and the Downing MS record that when the stone was broken in 1695 (it was, according to Strype's Stow, 'in old Saxon letters' and 'hardly to be read before') it was happily preserved and exactly transcribed by Mr. George Holmes. We might wonder if the drawing by Holmes (who became Keeper of the Records of the Tower) is Middle Temple's drawing, (B, iv) above. A succession of (nearly) vertical strokes and stops could have made the date hard to read with precision.[1]

---

[1] Enough of the inscription survived the defacements, it seems, for the Antiquaries to commission a drawing from Signor Grisoni in 1718; see Rosemary Sweet's chapter, p. 180 below.

Appendix ii : The de Ros Effigy

The de Ros effigy (Plates 52–3) was, according to Hatton, 'brought from York, by Mr Serjeant Belwood Recorder of that City about the year 1682, and is said to be the Figure of one Rooce of an honourable Family'.[1] The effigy is likely to have come from Kirkham Priory.[2] It was already believed that there was an effigy in the church to 'the Lord Ros' or 'one Robert Rosse, a Templer, who died about the year 1245'.[3] Why then did Roger Belwood arrange for the extra effigy to be brought down then, and why did the Inns accept it?

Belwood was from a Yorkshire family; his grandfather is recorded as Rector of St Cross, York; his father Josias was also a 'clerk'.[4] Roger appeared for the Crown in four of the trials to which the Popish Plot gave rise.[5] His library was rightly described in 1827 as having been 'extremely choice'.[6]

Perhaps a clue lies in Burton's list of the effigies from 1622. Many Templars, he wrote, lie buried in the church, 'and men of the chiefest houses of Nobility, as *Vere*, Earle of *Oxford*, *Mandevile* Earle of *Essex*, *Marschall* Earle of *Pembroke*, *Bohun* Earle of *Hereford*, the Lord *Ros*'.[7] Vere and Bohun are unexpected inclusions. But they suggest a thread: all the names in Burton's list (read without reference, in each family, to the particular knights that we now link with the Church) appear among the surety barons of Magna Carta.[8] The charter was insistently invoked by Coke and his colleagues in the first decades of the seventeenth century.[9] We might wonder if Burton, called by Inner Temple in 1593, had heard stories of the charter's heroes being buried in the Inn's church.

Burton dedicated *Leicester Shire* to George Villiers, marquess of Buckingham, who had in 1620 married Katherine Manners, daughter of Francis Manners, earl of Rutland, and of Frances Knyvett. George and Katherine's son, the 2nd duke of Buckingham, was famously proud of his lineage and was descended from every one of the families listed by Burton. He was himself Baron Ros. Kirkham Priory is some twenty miles from the Villiers seat at Helmsley. In 1540/41 the Priory had been granted to the Knyvetts. We might make, then, a tentative suggestion: that the 2nd duke of Buckingham, a member of Middle Temple, had sufficient

---

[1] Hatton, *New London*, ii, 574.

[2] See David Park's chapter, p. 88 above.

[3] 'The Lord *Ros*', W. Burton, *Description of Leicester Shire*, London 1622, 234–5. 'One Robert Rosse . . .': Weever, *Monuments*, 443.

[4] W. Dugdale, *The Visitation of the County of York* [1665–6], Surtees Society 36, London 1859, 213 ('Bellwood of Leathley', north-west of York); P. Le Neve, 'Memoranda in Heraldry', in *The Topographer and Genealogist*, ed. J. G. Nichols, 3 vols., London 1846–58, iii, 26.

[5] *State Trials*, vii, 422 (Richard Langhorn), 833 (Lionel Anderson), 887 (John Tasborough and Anne Price) and 1166 (Mary Pressicks).

[6] H.W. Woolrych, *Memoirs of the Life of Judge Jeffreys*, London 1827, 34 and n. 2. The library was sold at auction after his death; the copy of the sale-catalogue, *Bibliotheca Belwoodiana*, is accessible on Early English Books Online.

[7] Burton, *Leicester Shire*, 234–5. Burton (the brother of Melancholy Burton) named his son Cassibelan after Cymbeline's great-uncle — testimony in itself of the father's interest in the British story.

[8] J. C. Holt, *Magna Carta*, Cambridge 1992, 483.

[9] F. Thompson, *Magna Carta: its Role in the Making of the English Constitution*, Minneapolis and London 1948, part iii passim.

interest in the Temple Church's links with his own ancestors and with Magna Carta, and sufficient influence at Kirkham, to endorse and make possible the effigy's transfer from Kirkham to the Temple.

Both of Katherine Manners's parents are relevant here, as follows.

The Lord *Ros.* Through her father, Katherine inherited the barony of Ros (of Helmsley) in her own right.

Mandevile Earle of Essex. On the death of Geoffrey (1215/16) and of his brother William (1226/7) Mandeville, earls of Essex, their sister Maud became countess of Essex. Maud was married to Henry de Bohun, earl of Hereford (d. 1220). From there we reach the Marshalls.

Marschall Earle of *Pembroke.* Henry de Bohun's grandson Humphrey (d. 1265) married Eleanor, granddaughter of William Marshal, 1st earl of Pembroke. Their great-great-granddaughter Elizabeth de Bohun married (in 1359) Richard FitzAlan, 10th earl of Arundel; and their daughter Elizabeth (d. 1425) married Thomas de Mowbray, duke of Norfolk (d. 1400). Muriel, great-great-granddaughter of Thomas and Elizabeth, married Sir Thomas Knyvett of Buckenham (1485–1512). Frances Knyvett (mother of the countess of Buckingham) was their great-granddaughter.[10]

Among the Knyvetts, Sir Henry (d. 1546), son of Thomas and Muriel and grandfather of Frances, calls for particular attention. He married Anne Pickering, who brought estates at Wiggington, Escrick and elsewhere into the family.[11] In 1540–41 some at least of Anne's estates were sold to Henry VIII,[12] and Henry VIII granted Kirkham Priory and its estates to Henry and Anne.[13] The manor of Kirkham remained in the family of Anne's children by her later marriage to John Vaughan.[14]

George Villiers, 2nd duke of Buckingham, more than once argued (according to Barillon, the French ambassador) that he had a legitimate claim to the English throne through his mother's connections with the house of Plantagenet.[15] Since his mother's death in 1649 he had himself been Lord Ros. In 1657 he married Mary, daughter of the Parliamentarian general Thomas Fairfax and of Anne, daughter of Lord Vere of Tilbury (the grandson of the 15th earl of Oxford). So we reach as well the last of the names linked by Burton with effigies in the Temple Church: *Vere,* Earle of *Oxford.*

The marriage of the 2nd duke resecured for his family the seat of the Barons Ros at Helmsley, only a few miles from Kirkham, which had been granted to Fairfax in the Interregnum.

In the constitutional crisis of the 1680s, Magna Carta was again being deployed, not least by William Petyt in *The Ancient Right of the Commons,* 1679–80.[16] We might wonder if

---

[10] I do not claim that this thread exhausts the links between these families.

[11] Among the Lascelles estates in Yorkshire inherited by Anne was the manor of Escrick. Anne's son Thomas Knyvett (uncle of Frances) was ennobled in 1607; he took the name Baron Knyvett of Escrick. For the Knyvetts' rise, see R. Virgoe, 'The Earlier Knyvetts: the Rise of a Norfolk Gentry Family', pt 2, *Norfolk Archaeology* 41, 1990–93, 249–78.

[12] For Wigginton, see the Victoria County History, *A History of the County of York, North Riding,* II, London 1923, 214–16.

[13] J. Burton, *Monasticon Eboracense,* York 1758, 377.

[14] See *North Riding,* II, 113–19 (s.v. Crambe). The priory itself was held by the Early of Rutland in 3 Ed. VI, who was granted a license to alienate it in 5 Eliz. (Burton, *Monasticon,* 377).

[15] D. C. Hanrahan, *Charles II and the Duke of Buckingham,* Stroud 2006, 198.

[16] See pp. 147–8 above. Thompson, *Magna Carta,* 372.

Belwood, disappointed in his hopes for advancement in London and knowing of the church's refurbishment by Wren, offered to the Inns, in this second Ros effigy, a felicitous reminder and reinforcement of an imagined connection between the Round and the barons of Magna Carta. The Duke of Buckingham had himself been called by Middle Temple in February 1664/5 (within months of Belwood). He served on a subcommittee investigating Titus Oates's claims; and he helped organise the festivities in November 1679, when Guy Fawkes's Day was translated to 17 November (the anniversary of Queen Elizabeth's accession) and a wax figure of the pope was burned.[17] The duke already had good reason to enjoy the Round for its (real or supposed) burials: of a Bohun, Mandeville, Marshal and Ros, on his own account; and of a Vere, on his wife's. The duke's politics were ambiguous, but Whiggish or even republican. He had no reason to resist the celebration of another family member in his Inn's shrine to Magna Carta.[18] On the basis of the present account, we will only need to refine the chronology we have suggested for the Inns' changing aspirations for their church: there was already a more prominent Whiggism in the Inns, when they accepted the effigy in the early 1680s, than Wren's programme — or indeed, in 1682, the layout of the Round — could readily accommodate.

[17] On Villiers's religious views (and their service of his political pragmatism), B. Yardley, 'George Villiers, Second Duke of Buckingham and Politics of Toleration', *The Huntington Library Quarterly*, 51, 1988, 317–31.
[18] On Villiers's later politics, see A. Hobson, 'To Overthrow all the Kingdom: The Later Political Career of George Villiers, 2nd Duke of Buckingham', *Royal Stuart Society Papers*, 56, 2000.

Rosemary Sweet

'A neat structure with pillars':
Changing Perceptions of the Temple Church in the Long Eighteenth Century

T HE EIGHTEENTH CENTURY CHURCH has suffered from a reputation for benign neglect of both the spiritual welfare of its flock and the upkeep and maintenance of its churches.[1] Whilst Methodist and Nonconformist chapels sprang
up across the country, outside London — where Wren's programme of church building
created a series of ecclesiastical set pieces in modern architecture[2] — the impact of the
eighteenth century on the physical structure of the Church was far less noticeable. This
fits in with the image of latitudinarian somnolence, typified by Parson Woodforde
— apparently more concerned for his dinner than divinity — which dominated the
broader perception of the eighteenth-century Church for many years.[3] It still holds
considerable sway in some quarters.[4]

As in so many other areas, this image owes much to the Victorians, who had an
interest in blackening the reputation of the eighteenth-century Church — whether for

I would like to thank Dr Clare Rider and Mrs Lesley Whitelaw for their time and help in guid-
ing me through the archives of Inner and Middle Temple, and Dr Phillip Lindley and John Sweet for
comments on earlier drafts of this article.

[1] Although arguing a revisionist case, the title of P. Virgin's study, *The Church in an Age of
Negligence: Ecclesiastical Structure and Problems of Church Reform*, Cambridge 1989, is indicative of the
traditional view of the eighteenth-century Church.

[2] J. Summerson, *Georgian London*, London 1986, 84–97. For a recent overview, see P. Jefferson,
The City Churches of Sir Christopher Wren, London 1996.

[3] 'The Church partook of the general sordidness of the age. It was an age of great material
prosperity, but of moral and spiritual poverty, such as hardly finds a parallel in our history', *The
English Church in the Eighteenth Century*, ed. C. J. Abbey and J. H. Overton, 2 vols., London 1878,
II, 4, quoted in J. Walsh and S. Taylor, 'Introduction: the Church and Anglicanism in the "Long"
Eighteenth Century', in *The Church of England, c.1689–c.1833: from Toleration to Tractarianism*, ed. C.
Haydon, S. Taylor and J. Walsh, Cambridge 1993, 1.

[4] See, for example, the militantly secular version of the eighteenth century offered by R. Porter in *English Society in the Eighteenth Century*, Harmondsworth 1982, and more recently idem, *Enlightenment: Britain and the Creation of the Modern World*, London 2000.

its erastianism, its moral laxity or its corruption — in order to legitimate the reforms which they imposed in the nineteenth century.[5] The Church, as Arthur Burns notes, was bundled together with 'Old Corruption'.[6] More recently, historians have shown up the limitations of that perspective, drawing attention both to the spiritual vitality within the Church of England and to the considerable amounts of money invested in 'improving' churches — new flooring, new galleries, new pews, new windows — even if the number of *new* churches built was limited.[7] The problem for the Victorians, however, was that eighteenth-century interventions were seen to have compromised the integrity of the medieval fabric. Nineteenth-century antiquaries and architects, who prided themselves on their ability to discern the original medieval form and the fact that they had 'rescued' so many buildings from the vandalism of intervening periods, could only see the eighteenth-century treatment of such buildings in terms of neglect or destruction.[8]

And indeed for architectural historians the eighteenth century is not a rewarding period to look at with regard to the Temple. The standard history of the Temple Church does not have a great deal to say about the Georgian period:[9] a few repairs here, some whitewash there; the occasional purchase of hassocks and prayer books; a bit of stucco on the walls and a flourish of gilding on the ironwork. Short of itemising the sums spent on mops, brooms and dusting cloths for Mr Richards the cleaner or on the fancy new tasselled cushions for the Benchers' seats, there is little more to add to the record of occasional flurries of activity interrupting much longer periods of benign neglect. Whilst other churches received new windows or were reglazed, for example, the sudden burst of enthusiasm for painting the glass of the east window in 1779 came to nothing.[10] A large part of Lewer and Dark's chapter on the Georgians is taken up with discussion of music and the preachers, until they reach the early nineteenth century when Robert Smirke's restorations are rightly given prominence.[11]

But if the emphasis is shifted away from the analysis of the physical fabric itself to a consideration of how the building was understood and interpreted, and how this

[5] A. Burns, 'English "Church Reform" Revisited', in *Rethinking the Age of Reform: Britain 1780–1850*, ed. A. Burns and J. Innes, Cambridge 2003, 136–62.
[6] A. Burns, *The Diocesan Revival in the Church of England, c.1800–1870*, Oxford 1999, 4.
[7] For recent revisionist views of the Church of England in the long eighteenth century, see J. Gregory, *Restoration, Reformation and Reform: the Archbishops of Canterbury and their Diocese*, Oxford 2000; *The National Church in Local Perspective: the Church of England and the Regions*, ed. J. Gregory and J. Chamberlain, Woodbridge 2003; *The Church of England*, ed. Haydon, Taylor and Walsh; F.C. Mather, 'Georgian Churchmanship Reconsidered: some Variations in Anglican Public Worship, 1714–1830', *Journal of Ecclesiastical History*, 36, 1985, 255–83. On church building see B. F. L. Clarke, *The Building of the Eighteenth-Century Church*, London 1963.
[8] See, for example, John Carter's essays in the *Gentleman's Magazine*; on Carter see J. Mordaunt Crook, *John Carter and the Mind of the Gothic Revival*, London 1995; on context see S. Bradley, 'The Gothic Revival and the Church of England 1790–1840', PhD thesis, University of London, Courtauld Institute of Art, 1996.
[9] See Mordaunt Crook, 'Restoration'; Gardam, 'Restorations'.
[10] ITR IV, 366, 1 Feb. 1779.
[11] Lewer and Dark, *Temple Church*, 80–93.

in turn influenced the nature of physical interventions in the fabric, the comparative absence of commentary and the low level of activity recorded in the archives become interesting in themselves.[12] The focus of this chapter, therefore, as the title suggests, is upon the perception and understanding of the Temple Church as a building — it will consider how the Temple Church was described, and will attempt to explain the improvements and repairs both in terms of how the structure was understood at the time, and in terms of the broader context of environmental or urban improvement. The Temple Church, it has to be remembered, was part of a much bigger complex of buildings, in the heart of London, in an area which provided a crucial link between the City of London and Westminster. It was frequented by lawyers and the general public. Changes to the church were carried out on the basis of an evolving understanding of its significance as a specimen of Gothic architecture, but also in the context of improvements to the physical environment of the Temple as a whole at a time when public space in eighteenth-century cities was undergoing improvement.

At a time when many Gothic buildings were criticised for their crude inelegance and the deplorable want of taste in their design, the Temple Church was, it seems, universally praised as one of the finest specimens of Gothic architecture remaining in London. This was, in part, a reflection of how many other potential competitors had perished in the flames in 1666. The fact that it had survived was in itself enough to single it out as a landmark and make it worthy of note. It served, like the official Monument, as a reminder of the full scale of the fire's destructive fury. But its unusual form also attracted attention in its own right. James Ralph, who wrote a pamphlet pleading for the modernisation and improvement of London, did not generally warm to the medieval buildings of the city, but even he allowed that 'the inside, indeed, may justly be esteemed one of the best remains of *Gothick* Architecture in this city; the form of it is very singular'.[13] Other accounts mention that it was 'finish'd with as much elegancy and proportion as the taste of those days would allow'.[14]

At this stage, however, the 'singular' form of the Temple Church conveyed little meaning. Some commentators noted that it was built after the model of the Holy Sepulchre at Jerusalem: but this was a perfunctory observation only, not least because so little was known, even in the eighteenth century, about the physical appearance of the Holy Sepulchre.[15] Francis Peck's reference to a 'neat structure with pillars' is, for the time,

---

[12] W. Whyte, 'How do Buildings Mean? Some Issues of Interpretation in the History of Architecture', *History and Theory*, 45, 2006, 174–5.

[13] J. Ralph, *A Critical Review of the Public Buildings, Statues and Ornaments in, and about London and Westminster*, London 1734, 25.

[14] F. Peck, *Academica Tertia Anglicana, or The Antiquarian Annals of Stamford in Lincoln, Rutland and Northamptonshire*, London 1727, 52.

[15] R. Pocock, *Description of the East*, 3 vols., London 1745, II, 16–17, noted that the wooden roof of the Holy Sepulchre was of cypress, and provided a ground plan of the building; but no further description of the appearance or architecture was given. The accompanying plate showed the ground plan and a view of the interior, illustrating the rounded arches and triforium of the circular part of the church. John Britton in his *Architectural Antiquities*, London 1807, was still relying on G. Sandys,

comparatively eloquent as a description.[16] But it was also because the early eighteenth-century eye did not read Gothic architecture either for mystic symbolism or to discern its structural or decorative qualities: even structures which were widely admired, such as those of ancient Rome, were represented in a somewhat terse manner, in terms of dimensions and the basic compositional elements. Gothic architecture, which could not be reduced to the classical orders, attracted still less notice. Thus the vaulting of the Round Church, the carving of the corbels in the arcade or around the west door, the elegance of the pillars in the nave — all these were scarcely noted, let alone described. The historic fabric, in fact, was of less interest than recent improvements carried out by benefactors whose names were still a living memory. Thus in Edward Hatton's account, published in *A New View of London* in 1708, the church was described as 'neat in its workmanship' and 'rich in its materials' and 'beautiful in its finishing'. But the longest part of the description was devoted to the recent improvements of whitewashing and gilding and painting, and the introduction of wainscoting and the fine new altarpiece, pulpit and organ screen by Sir Christopher Wren in 1678.[17] The altar piece, which was to excite so much hostile comment a century later, was said to be 'finely carved' and adorned with pilasters and columns, enriched with festoons of fruit and leaves and enclosed with a handsome rail and banister.[18]

Hatton's description, which would find its way into numerous subsequent accounts of London during the eighteenth century, made no distinctions between the modern and the medieval. The church was viewed as the composite of the different additions, ornaments and beautifications of succeeding generations: none of these had a higher value simply on the grounds of age, and no distinction was drawn between the different elements simply on the grounds of antiquity. Rather, the decoration of the church represented the piety of those who had paid for it; the tombs and inscriptions preserved the memory of those associated with the church who had been buried there.

A church, to oversimplify, existed as a monument to those who built it and improved it: not as an architectural feature in its own right. A church, as the seventeenth-century antiquary John Weever explained, was 'A Monument' and as such 'a thing erected, made, or written, for a memorial of some remarkable action, fit to be transferred to future posterities'.[19] By far the longest section of Hatton's and of many other

Sandys' Travels Containing an History of the Original and Present State of the Turkish Empire, London 1670, for a description of the appearance of the Holy Sepulchre.

[16] Peck, *Academica Tertia Anglicana*, 52.

[17] See Robin Griffith-Jones's chapter, pp. 135–69 above. The regilding and wainscoting was completed in 1706.

[18] E. Hatton, *A New View of London*, 2 vols., London 1708, II, 563. On Hatton's architectural descriptions, see B. Cherry, 'Edward Hatton's *New View of London*', *Architectural History*, 44, 2001, 96–105. Cherry observes (98) that 'No English guidebook of this period can compete with the thoroughness of Hatton's detailed and up-to-date descriptions of both pre- and post-Fire churches and their contents.'

[19] Weever, *Monuments*, p. i. Weever's categorisation of churches (and also books) as monuments was part of a general introduction to his theme. He subsequently proceeded to define monuments much more narrowly.

accounts detailed the various inscriptions recording the names and lives of all those who had been buried there.[20] The importance attached to inscriptions and funerary monuments was a characteristic feature of seventeenth- and eighteenth-century anti-quarianism. It represented the greater portion of 'church notes' of almost every anti-quary.[21] In *Ancient Funerall Monuments* John Weever had sought to explain why it was that so many people went daily 'to view the lively statues and stately monuments in Westminster abbey'. It was, he suggested, because the sight brought 'delight and admi-ration and strikes a religious apprehension into the minds of the beholders'.[22]

Whether visitors to the church in the early eighteenth century really felt 'delight and admiration' on viewing the monuments of Edmund Plowden and John Selden may be moot. But the crucial point is that the main interest of a church resided in the monu-ments and memorials which it contained. At this stage, in many accounts, the lawyers' monuments took precedence over the recumbent knights, many of whose effigies were frustratingly anonymous. As Weever noted, their 'names are not to be gathered, by any inscriptions, for that time hath worn them out'.[23] Hatton's description of the Knights Templar is one of laconic brevity in comparison with the interest they would command later in the century.

> In the middle of the Area lie the Marble Figures of 9 of the Knights Templers, some of them 7 foot and a half in length; they are represented in the Habit before described, cumbent in full Proportion, 5 in one Rank inclosed with Iron Rail, of which 3 are not cross legged; and 4 in another Rank all cross legged, and inclosed with Iron Rail.[24]

Hatton's account followed on from several pages of much more fulsome enumeration of more recent burials which extended over eight pages. We may contrast Benson's decision in 1840 to remove all the seventeenth- and eighteenth-century monuments from the Round and the nave, a change entirely in keeping with received opinion on the proper mode of church restoration at the time: the church should be restored as nearly as possible to its original form, removing plaques and monuments that obscured its shape or deformed its pillars.[25] This in itself is indicative of how radically the mean-ing of the church, its architecture and its monuments, changed in little over a century. The church's function was no longer primarily that of a monument, as described by Weever, but as a specimen of a particularly important stage in the evolution of Gothic architecture — the style which was by then regarded as definitively English and of

---

[20] Hatton, *London*, II, 564–75.
[21] P. Lindley, *Tomb Destruction and Scholarship: Medieval Monuments in Early Modern England,* Donington 2007, especially 90–137; R. Sweet, *Antiquaries: the Discovery of the Past in Eighteenth-Century Britain,* London 2004, 242–5.
[22] Weever, *Monuments*, p. xli.
[23] Weever, *Monuments*, 224.
[24] Hatton, *London*, II, 574.
[25] See William Whyte's chapter, pp. 195–200 below.

national importance.[26] By the nineteenth century it was, as the numerous publications attested, a building of considerable *antiquarian* importance. That is not to say that it was not of antiquarian interest in 1700; but rather, that the agenda of antiquarianism had undergone considerable change in the course of 100 years or so, and in the process, the meaning and interpretation of the Temple Church were also transformed.[27]

This raises the question of when and why this shift in sensibility occurred. The decision of the Society of Antiquaries to commission drawings of the tombs of the Knights Templar in 1718 from 'Signor Grisoni' should not be seen as indicative of a new antiquarian sensibility[28] — it followed rather in the spirit of seventeenth-century antiquaries such Weever and Sir William Dugdale, who had exhorted fellow antiquaries to make proper memorials of such tombs and monuments before they were destroyed. Of more interest, however, is the fact that Smart Lethieullier later informed the society that he had already had drawings made in 1736/7 for his private use (Plates 85–6).[29] Lethieullier's original interest in tomb sculpture, as far as one can recover it from his correspondence with fellow antiquary Charles Lyttelton, had originally been very much in the tradition of Weever: based upon the need to preserve the memory of the dead.[30] Over the years, however his interests developed as he and Lyttelton became increasingly aware of how the form and design of tomb sculpture and architecture were worthy of study in their own right.[31]

Lyttelton and Lethieullier were in the vanguard of an antiquarian movement which sought to re-evaluate the Gothic, and rescue it from the enormous condescension of eighteenth-century classicism. Their correspondence is full of observations on churches, in which they attempted to establish a chronological model of the development of Gothic architecture, and more precisely when the rounded Saxon arch, as the romanesque was then known, was replaced by the pointed arch.[32] Both Lethieullier and Lyttelton followed Christopher Wren's suggestion that the pointed arch had been introduced by returning crusaders, who had encountered the form in the East and brought it back to Europe. Accordingly, argued Wren, it ought to be called the 'saracenic' style.[33]

[26] See, for example, J. Britton, *Architectural Antiquities*, 5 vols., London 1807–35, I, 6.

[27] For an overview of the evolution of antiquarian studies in the eighteenth century, see Sweet, *Antiquaries*.

[28] 'February 25 1718 It was unanimously agreed at the Society of Antiquaries to take a drawing of the Knights Templars, and the tomb of the patriarch in the Temple-church, and the inscription over the door, and Mr Director [Talman] was ordered to employ Seignor Grisoni about that work, who was chosen by the Society when they shall have occasion for drawings', quoted in Gough, *Sepulchral Monuments*, I, 52.

[29] Gough, *Sepulchral Monuments*, I, 52.

[30] BL Stowe MS 752 fols. 3–12.

[31] Lethieullier's notes on the knights' tombs are now in the BL, Add. MS 27348, and the drawings made for him at fols. 90, 91; see Philip Lankester's chapter, p. 101 above. For the effigies' illustrations in *Sepulchral Monuments*, see Plates 87–8.

[32] BL, Stowe MS 752, fols. 1–105.

[33] C. Wren, *Parentalia*, London 1751, 306: 'He was of Opinion . . . that what we now vulgarly call the *Gothick* , ought properly and truly to be named the *Saracenick Architecture refined by the Chris-*

Wren does not appear ever to have referred specifically to the Temple Church as proof of this thesis — despite the obvious connection with the crusades and the simultaneous presence in the church of rounded and pointed styles. The experience of working at the church, however, could only have corroborated his views. The adjective 'saracenic' was widely used throughout the eighteenth century and often applied to the church: thus in 1783, for example, a print of the west door to the church was published in the *Gentleman's Magazine* as a 'View of the fine Saracenic Arch' of the Temple Church. The accompanying descriptive essay, written under the pseudonym Reuben d'Moundt, confidently affirmed that the Gothic was 'no more than the second manner of the Saracenic'.[34]

This was just one theory, amongst several, as to the origins of the pointed arch. As critics of the saracenic theory were not slow to point out, travellers to the East had brought back very few accounts of eastern buildings built in the pointed style.[35] Another theory argued that the style owed its inspiration to the intersection of arcades of rounded arches — as were found on the façade of St Cross at Winchester, or indeed, in the interior of the Round at the Temple Church.[36] The importance of the Temple Church, however, was that it illustrated the transition (combining as it did both rounded and pointed arches in the same structure) and that a reasonably certain date could (as it seemed) be fixed upon its building, thanks to the inscription recording the consecration by Heraclius in 1185.[37] 'The *semicircular, intersecting,* and *pointed arches* are all exhibited in this edifice', noted Britton, 'and we cannot hesitate in admitting that all these were constructed at one time.' The pointed arch system, he noted, was at the time 'in its infancy, and therefore too weak to effect complete conquest over its veteran rival'.[38] Furthermore, the Round exemplified the richness of carving associated with the Saxon or Norman style, as seen in the west door, for example, and the nave embodied

tians; . . . The Holy War gave the Christians, who had been there, an Idea of the *Saracen* Works, which were afterwards by them imitated in the West.' See also BL, Stowe MS 752, fols. 41, 45, 68ᵛ. It is interesting that, despite Lethieullier's interest in the monuments to the Knights Templar (see e.g. fol. 7), neither he nor Lyttelton ever refers to the Temple Church as an example of the transition from rounded to pointed arch, referring instead to St Cross or to Christ Church Cathedral, Oxford.

[34] *Gentleman's Magazine*, 53 pt. 2, 1783, 547–9. The print was also advertised in *St James Chronicle*, 19 Aug. 1783, and *Whitehall Evening Post*, 14 Aug. 1783.

[35] F. Grose, *Antiquities of England and Wales*, 8 vols., London 1773–6, I, 117.

[36] J. Bentham, *The History and Antiquities of the Conventual and Cathedral Church of Ely*, Cambridge 1771, 37.

[37] Ibid., 'The west end of the old Temple church, built in that reign [i.e. of Henry II], and dedicated by Heraclius patriarch of the church of the Holy Resurrection in Jerusalem (as appears by the inscription lately over the door), is now remaining; and has, I think, pointed and round arches originally inserted; they are intermixed; the great arches are pointed, the windows above are round; the west door is a round arch richly ornamented; and before it a portico or porch of three arches, supported by two pillars; that opposite to the church-door is round , the other two pointed, but these have been rebuilt.' Christopher Wilson's chapter, pp. 19–43 above, demonstrates that the Round was built significantly earlier than 1185.

[38] J. Britton, *Architectural Antiquities*, I, 13. See also EIC [Edward John Carlos] in *Gentleman's Magazine*, 94 pt 2, 1824, 408.

the lightness and elegance which characterised the eighteenth-century expectation of true Gothic architecture.

The Gothic Revival and interest in Gothic antiquities of the later eighteenth century helped shape a new appreciation of the beauty and significance of the Temple Church for the historical study of architecture. The publication of the print of the west doorway in 1783 which has already been noted was just one indication of the rising taste for Gothic antiquities. Descriptions became more detailed as the vocabulary for describing the different elements of 'Gothic' architecture became increasingly sophisticated and sympathetic to its unique qualities. Thomas Pennant published a widely referenced (and plagiarised) *Account of London* in 1790, which reflected the more analytical — if not yet archaeological — approach to descriptions of medieval buildings which had now become established. The entrance, he noted, was through a 'Norman' arch; within, the circular form was supported by six round arches, 'each resting on four round pillars, bound together by fascia'. Above each arch, he went on 'is a window with a rounded top, with a gallery, and rich *Saxon* arches intersecting each other'. On the lower part of the wall he noted were 'small pilasters meeting in pointed arches at top'; over each pillar was 'a grotesque head'. Interestingly, he had far less to say on the nave: observing only that it was square with narrow 'gothic' windows, and had evidently been built at a different time. Its more conventional form meant that, for Pennant at least, it was of less interest.[39] Pennant's choice of vocabulary is, it must be acknowledged, confusing (particularly his references to Saxon and Norman arches); but this betrays his own want of familiarity with the terminology, rather than any subtle distinction of style. As he would have been the first to admit, he was no architectural antiquary.

Thirteen years later, another popular topographical account of London was published, this time with a much more explicitly antiquarian content: J. P. Malcolm's *Londinium Redivivum* (1802), which illustrates the changing tenor of architectural descriptions of a medieval building by the early nineteenth century. Malcolm's account displayed much more attention to detail and employed more specialist vocabulary; the component parts of the building were isolated and individual elements described: 'The Antient Church, that is the Round,' he wrote, 'is a complete circle, the area of which contains six clustered pillars with fillets on the shafts, and Saxon capitals. Plain ribs and vaults from those to the exterior wall form a circular aile, with single pillars, answering to the clustered [pillars] . . . A range of pointed arcades extend round the basement; but the pillars between them are Saxon. A grotesque head projects over every pillar, and the mouldings are pierced into dentils.' The choir was four pillars in length; these were 'clustered, light and airy', and the walls were filled by 'lancet-shaped pyramidal windows' which gave 'an incredible lightness to the structure'.[40]

One could multiply the examples from John Carter, John Britton, J. T. Smith and

[39] T. Pennant, *Some Account of London*, 3rd edn, London 1791, 161.

[40] J. P. Malcolm, *Londinium Redivivum; or, An Antient History and Modern Description of London*, 4 vols., London 1802–7, II, 291.

other less distinguished authors, who, in time-honoured fashion, cut and paste their descriptions from other more authoritative sources.[41] Even the blandly anodyne comments of guidebooks, such as Samuel Ireland's *Picturesque Views* of 1800, effusively praised the architectural qualities of the Temple Church, referring to the 'beautiful Norman arch' and the 'beautifully intersecting arches' within 'the elegant choir', which acquired 'additional beauty' through being 'unencumbered with a gallery'.[42] With their forensic accuracy and careful perfection Nash's drawings, published by the Society of Antiquaries in *Vetusta Monumenta* 1828, provide unequivocal proof of the importance of the church to the antiquarian community (Plates 89–90).[43]

The story of the Gothic Revival which lay behind this more observant tone has been told elsewhere.[44] But it may be helpful here to summarize briefly some of the principal themes which contributed to this change in attitude. One of the most important was the gathering strength of a sense of English (as opposed to British), identity which attributed greater significance to the middle ages as the formative period in the emergence of the modern nation state, and to the Gothic style of architecture as the embodiment of the religious, political and legal history of that period and therefore preferable to the foreign (and pagan) import that was classicism.[45] The Gothic came to symbolise continuity of the established order of Church and State. Less parochially, the 'cosmopolitan' history of the eighteenth-century enlightenment similarly explored the decline of feudalism and the power of the church, allowing for the rise of the secular nation-state.[46] Associationist theory increasingly argued that the verticality and mystery of the Gothic interior — as opposed to the rational proportions of classic designs — encouraged meditation upon the deity.

More generally the middle ages began to acquire a romantic, picturesque gloss, best epitomised in Richard Hurd's *Letters on Chivalry and Romance* (1762) or the success of publications such as Thomas Percy's *Reliques of Ancient Poetry* (1765) The chivalric

[41] J. Britton, *Architectural Antiquities, Illustrations of the Public Buildings of London: with Historical and Descriptive Accounts of Each Edifice*, London 1825; C. Clarke, *Architectura Ecclesiastica Londinii*, London 1820, pll. 117–20; T. Allen, *The History and Antiquities of London, Westminster and Southwark an Parts Adjacent*, 4 vols., London 1827, IV, 393–6; J. T. Smith, *Antient Topography of London, Embracing Specimens of Sacred, Public and Domestic Architecture from the Earliest Period to the Time of the Great Fire of 1666*, London 1815, 4–7; W. Herbert, *Antiquities of the Inns of Court and Chancery*, London 1804, 259–60. For Smith's 'Part of the Vestibule', *Antient Topography*, 7, see Plate 91.

[42] S. Ireland, *Picturesque Views, with an Historical Account of the Inns of Court, in London and Westminster*, London 1800, 13–14.

[43] *Vetusta Monumenta*, 5, 1828, pll. 19–25.

[44] The standard account is still K. Clark, *The Gothic Revival: an Essay in the History of Taste*, London 1962. See also C. Brooks, *The Gothic Revival*, London 1999; M. McCarthy, *Origins of the Gothic Revival*, New Haven and London 1987; G. Worsley, 'The Origins of the Gothic Revival', *Transactions of the Royal Historical Society*, 6th series, 3, 1993, 105–50. For antiquarian attitudes to the Gothic, see Sweet, *Antiquaries*, 246–76.

[45] On the rise of English national identity in this period, see G. Newman, *The Rise of English Nationalism*, London 1987, rev. edn, 1997.

[46] K. O'Brien, *Narratives of Enlightenment: Cosmopolitan History from Voltaire to Gibbon*, Cambridge 1999.

Knights Templar who made their appearance in Scott's *Ivanhoe* (1817) had their roots in the eighteenth-century enthusiasm for knightly courtesy and a chivalric code of honour.[47] The pleasures of the antiquary, according to Stebbing Shaw, lay in the pleasing exercise offered to the imagination by churches, castles and the 'mouldering figures of the bold knights of chivalry'.[48] Gothic architecture meanwhile acquired new valency as the embodiment of both the sublime — with its soaring arches and 'dim religious light' of the interior — and the picturesque, as represented in, for example, the topographical tours of William Gilpin. Publications such as Francis Grose's *Antiquities of England and Wales* capitalised upon this growing taste for medieval antiquities, offering snippets from more forbidding tomes by James Bentham, Thomas Warton and Wren's *Parentalia* to a general readership.[49] Tellingly, the frontispiece to *Antiquities of England and Wales* depicted a ruined abbey and the tomb of a knight, followed by another plate showing a composite scene of a knight in armour below a castle, riding towards a monk outside a chapel. Grose knew his market: he also published a volume on military antiquities — that is a history of the English army, its armour and weaponry.[50] Joseph Strutt, an engraver who similarly identified a niche in the market for popular antiquities, published *Complete View of the Dress and Habits of the People of England* in the 1790s, using the evidence of knights' tombs for comments on Anglo-Norman armour.[51]

The Knights Templar as an institution had anyway become more familiar by the later eighteenth century. They were identified as key players in the narrative of the crusades, now recognised as a crucial era in the emergence of European nation states from the feudal system. Interest was further stimulated by Voltaire's determination to rescue the Knights from the imputations of heresy and corruption under which they had suffered since their dissolution.[52] Voltaire's anti-clerical arguments appealed to the rational sensibility of enlightened Protestants and found their way into many of the later eighteenth century accounts of the Temple Church.[53] In the 1790s the Abbé de Barruel attempted to revive the charges of heresy and treason against them, this time linking them to Masonic conspiracies.[54] Whilst Barruel's volumes were translated into English and reviewed in Britain, he failed to make the masonic mud stick, and his conspiracy

[47] M. Girouard, *The Return of Camelot: Chivalry and the English Gentleman*, New Haven and London 1987.

[48] S. Shaw, *History and Antiquities of Staffordshire*, 2 vols., London 1798–1801, I, p. v.

[49] Sweet, *Antiquaries*, 309–43.

[50] F. Grose, *Military Antiquities Respecting a Historical Account of the English Army*, 2 vols., London 1786–8.

[51] J. Strutt, *Complete View of the Dress and Habits of the People of England*, 2 vols., London 1796–9, I, 116–18.

[52] Voltaire, *An Essay on Universal History*, 4 vols., 2nd edition, London 1759, II, 62–8; P. Partner, *The Murdered Magicians: The Knights Templar and their Myth*, Oxford 1981, rev. edn 1990, 89–155.

[53] See, for example, Pennant, *Account of London*, 160.

[54] Abbé de Barruel, *Memoirs Illustrating the History of Jacobinism*, 4 vols., London 1797–8, IV, 119, 'Under the name of *Templar Masons*, it daily beheld new degrees invented, more and more threatening to the Kings and Pontiffs, who had suppressed the Templars.'

theories were largely ignored.[55] The imaginative link between masonry and the Knights Templar was briefly revived in the early nineteenth century by the German topographer, von Hammer, who claimed that not only were the Templars linked to the masons, but that they were also connected to the Assassins of the Syrian mountains, who were in turn the heirs to ancient Egyptian mysteries.[56] This innovative line of inquiry was taken up by Edward Clarke, in an essay published in Robert Billings's account of the Temple Church in 1838. Here he attempted to interpret the design and ornamentation of the church as a coded Masonic message.[57] The essay was not well received and was reviewed with withering scepticism in the *Gentleman's Magazine*.[58]

As a consequence of the growth of interest in the Knights Templar as an order, the tombs grew in importance as an attraction to the Temple Church. The monuments to the knights were believed to be among the most ancient in London, which in itself was sufficient to demand attention in a period when the evolution of the arts during the middle ages was coming under increasing scrutiny.[59] In 1809 the Rowlandson and Pugin image of the interior of the Church published in Ackermann's *Microcosm of London* (Plate 72) showed polite company in the Round, grouped in admiration around the effigies; they are not standing in the nave, which had been the focus of Boydell's earlier print (Plate 69). Correspondingly we find greater priority given to the tombs in the written descriptions from the late eighteenth and early nineteenth centuries. Richard Gough's account in *Sepulchral Monuments* (1786–91) made the most impact: this was the first detailed discussion of the monuments to be published, and was illustrated with the most accurate engravings to date (Plates 87–8). Gough's observations, although deficient in many respects, were far more extensive both in terms of the biographical information about the individual knights and in terms of describing the appearance of

[55] See, for example, *The Historical, Biographical, Literary and Scientific Magazine*, 3 vols., London 1800, II, 2–3.

[56] J. Von Hammer, *The History of the Assassins Translated by O. C. Wood*, London 1835, 216–17. In 1783 Reuben d'Moundt had argued that the Saracens 'had formed themselves into societies for the propagation of science: and the society called at this day *Free Masons* was of their institution' and that the Holy Sepulchre at Jerusalem was their 'first progeny'. He did not, however, make any connection with the Knights Templar and Freemasonry. He took the circular design of the Holy Sepulchre and of the churches built after its model to be a symbol of the deity, and one which had been anticipated in the stone circles of the druids. This was a thesis which had been put forward earlier, most notably by William Stukeley (himself a Mason). J. Britton, another Freemason and a devotee of Stukeley, also took up this thesis in 'An Essay towards an History of Temples and Round Churches', published in the first volume of *Architectural Antiquities*, 1–16, but the theory does not appear to have been widely discussed elsewhere.

[57] Billings, *Illustrations*, 1–26.

[58] *Gentleman's Magazine*, n. s. 10 pt 2, 1838, 288–92 at 291: 'The object of the architect was not to raise a mystic circle, but to support his building in the best way he could according to the fashion of the day.'

[59] Gough, *Sepulchral Monuments*, I, 7 n. 6: 'Maitland says, the duke of Exeter's monument at St Katherine's, near the Tower, is one of the antientest in London, except those in the Temple-church, forgetting that that of Rahere in St. Bartholomew's church by Smithfield is much older: unless he disputes the date of its erection.'

the effigies. Gough paid close attention to the details of the armour — the curve of the helmet, the ridge of the greaves, the pointed toes of the shoes — as well as making the conventional heraldic observations.[60] His description provided the basis for subsequent accounts until the 1840s and Richardson's restoration.[61] It was *Sepulchral Monuments* to which Pennant turned, for example, in the *Account of London*. Gough's comments appeared again in other popularizing topographical accounts of the early nineteenth century.[62] The first publication devoted in its entirety to the Temple Church, Joseph Jekyll's pamphlet of 1811, summarised the recent renovations, but was principally devoted to describing the monuments, which by now had acquired the reputation as the principal point of interest in the church, as well as providing a detailed account of the recent opening of the coffin under the tomb of the bishop, then assumed to be Heraclius.[63]

The corollary of this burgeoning interest in and appreciation of medieval architecture and antiquities was that more interest was shown in preserving and recording these monuments: antiquaries rapidly came to appreciate that much of the medieval fabric which they admired so much was falling victim not only to neglect but to improvement.[64] This is the hinterland to the ecclesiological movement of the nineteenth century which would have such a bearing on the restorations of the 1840s and subsequently.[65] In 1752 Smart Lethieullier had expressed doubts to Charles Lyttelton over Wren's 'improvements' to various cathedrals and churches: 'Inigo Jones's Portico to Old St Pauls, Introduced I fear the taste of adding a Horses Head to a Fishes tail, & Sir Christopher

---

[60] Gough, *Sepulchral Monuments*, I, 23, 37, 41–2, 50–52.

[61] Marion Roberts notes that, although Gough was attentive to the variations in medieval costume, he was unable to develop a satisfactory chronology of Gothic style through the study of tomb architecture. Thomas Gray, however, who was making his observations in the 1750s (around the same time as Smart Lethieullier), did develop a model of the stylistic development of funerary monuments: M. Roberts, 'Thomas Gray's Contribution to the Study of Medieval Architecture', *Architectural History*, 36, 1993, 62–3.

[62] Pennant, *Some Account of London*, 166–8; Smith, *Antient Topography of London*, 4–6; Malcolm, *Londinium Redivivum*, 292–4.

[63] J. Jekyll, *Facts and Observations Relating to the Temple Church, and the Monuments Contained in it*, London 1811; C. Scalia, 'The Grave Scholarship of Antiquaries', *Literature Compass*, 2/1, Jan. 2005, http://dx.doi.org/10.1111/j.1741-4113.2005.00166.x (accessed 10 May 2008); B. M. Marsden and B. Nurse, 'Opening the Tomb', in *Making History: Antiquaries in Britain, 1707–2007*, ed. B. Nurse, D. Gaimster and S. McCarthy, London 2007, 95–7: permission was given in 1774 to open the tomb of Edward I at Westminster; the tomb of Edward IV at St George's chapel Windsor was opened 1789; King John's tomb was discovered and opened at Worcester Cathedral in 1797; several tombs were opened by Richard Kaye and Richard Gough at Lincoln Cathedral in 1791 when the floor was being repaved; Bishop Grosseteste's tomb was opened at Lincoln Cathedral in 1782, and Sir Joseph Banks took a sample of liquid from the coffin for analysis. See also J. Ayloffe, 'An Account of the Body of King Edward I as it Appeared on Opening his Tomb in the Year 1774', *Archaeologia*, 3, 1775, 376–413; idem, 'An Account of some Ancient Monuments in Westminster Abbey', *Vetusta Monumenta*, 2, 1780; *Vetusta Monumenta*, 3, 1796, pl. 7.

[64] Sweet, *Antiquaries*, 285–307.

[65] S. Bradley, 'The Roots of Ecclesiology: Late Hanoverian Attitudes to Medieval Churches', in *'A Church as it Should be': The Cambridge Camden Society and its Influence*, ed. C. Webster and J. Elliott, Stamford 2000, 22– 44.

Wren &c. thought they might take the same Liberty when they came to be Employ'd in ornamenting & repairing the Ancient Cathedrals.'[66] Lethieullier anticipated here John Carter's fulminations against 'Wrenéan' improvements by some fifty years.[67] Similarly Reuben d'Moundt's essay on the Temple's west door published in 1783 complained of the 'absolute false concord in structure' between the new doorway introduced by Wren 'which has greatly disgusted the intelligent admirers of architecture'.[68] By the nineteenth century critiques of the incongruity of the altarpiece, the pulpit and the organ screen became a standard part of the commentary on the church.[69] By the same token the less deliberate accretions of whitewash and plaster (to which the Temple Church fell victim on several occasions during the eighteenth century) came under attack. Richard Gough expostulated against this practice — routinely recommended to church-wardens in various handbooks[70] — in a powerfully penned manifesto which prefaced his *Anecdotes of British Topography* (1768):

> That want of taste that suffers beautiful pilasters of English speckled marble to be daubed with plaister, or rich capitals and ornaments to be knocked off in every repair of our cathedrals, will justify throwing by a mutilated trunk, or selling imperfect brasses — Thus prebends sanctify the sacrilege of parish clerks.[71]

Gough was the leading figure of a group within the Society of Antiquaries who championed Gothic antiquities and their preservation. His protégé, John Carter, the Society's draughtsman, became one of the most forceful advocates of the Gothic in the late eighteenth and early nineteenth century. He set himself up against anyone who entertained a different vision of Gothic architecture and its historical importance from his own — whether on the geographical origin of the pointed arch (he was convinced that it was a purely English form) or on principles of restoration and improvement.[72] In the 1790s he had launched himself against Wyatt 'the Destroyer', whose 'improvements' at various cathedrals had necessitated considerable intervention in the physical fabric to introduce a cleaner, less cluttered interior, with clearer vistas and more open space.[73] Wyatt was implementing an eighteenth-century vision of what the Gothic *ought*

[66] BL, Stowe MS 752, fol. 68ᵛ, Lethieullier to Lyttelton, 15 July 1752.

[67] J. Carter, *Gentleman's Magazine*, 78 pt 2, 1808, 999.

[68] R. d'Moundt, *Gentleman's Magazine*, 53 pt 2, 1783, 548.

[69] *Gentleman's Magazine*, 94 pt 2, 1824, 406–8; J. Britton and A. Pugin, *Illustrations of the Public Buildings of London: with Historical and Descriptive Accounts of Each Edifice*, London 1825, 144.

[70] See, for example, J. Napleton, *Advice to a Minister of the Gospel*, London 1801; idem, *The Duty of Churchwardens Respecting the Church*, 2nd edn, London 1800.

[71] R. Gough, *Anecdotes of British Topography*, London 1768, p. xxvi. On Gough see R. Sweet, 'Antiquaries and Antiquities in Eighteenth-Century England', *Eighteenth-Century Studies*, 34, 2001, 181–206.

[72] Bradley, 'Gothic Revival', 130–35; J. Mordaunt Crook, *John Carter and the Mind of the Gothic Revival*, London 1995; Sweet, *Antiquaries*, 289–97.

[73] J. M. Frew, 'An Aspect of the Gothic Revival in England, c.1770–1815: the Antiquarian Influence with Special Reference to the Career of James Wyatt', 2 vols., D.Phil. thesis, University of

to look like.[74] Carter, Gough and a number of other antiquaries, however, entertained very different attitudes: churches and cathedrals represented the accretions of centuries. They were seldom, if ever, built in one stage. To tamper with the design and layout was unjustifiable. For restorers to introduce conflicting styles was unpardonable.[75] This archaeological approach, which was to become such a defining feature of antiquarianism and the ecclesiological movement during the restorations of the 1840s, was not, however, so widely accepted in the first three decades of the nineteenth century.

Robert Smirke, who was employed as surveyor in 1819 by the Inner Temple, and who was responsible for the restorations of the 1820s, operated in the tradition of Wyatt rather than Gough.[76] He was a classically trained architect without much genuine antiquarian interest in Gothic architecture. John Carter, indeed, would have had very little time for him, irrespective of his work at the Temple Church, not least because Smirke upheld the view that the pointed arch originated in mainland Europe rather than being the invention of native English genius.[77] His interventions have been well documented elsewhere.[78] Edward John Carlos, writing as EIC in the *Gentleman's Magazine,* took up Carter's cause and made pointed comments about architects who followed their own vision of Gothic ornament and design, rather than attempting to restore 'the pristine grandeur' of Gothic buildings.[79] Carlos was particularly damning of the decision to take down St Anne's Chapel, noting that 'a little caution might have saved the beautiful chapel'[80] — yet at the time Smirke had described it as being in such a ruinous state that demolition was the only practicable solution (Plate 43).[81]

But antiquarianism is not the complete story. There is another trajectory of change that should also be emphasised, because it was important in shaping the timing and nature of the changes to the Church in this period. Those who made the decisions

Oxford, 1976; idem, 'Gothic is English: John Carter and the Revival of Gothic as England's National Style', *Art Bulletin,* 66, 1982, 315–19.

[74] J. M. Frew, 'Richard Gough, James Wyatt, and Late 18th-Century Preservation', *Journal of the Society of Architectural Historians,* 38, 1979, 366–74.

[75] See Gough's comments on the restorations at Lichfield and Salisbury Cathedrals in *Gentleman's Magazine,* 59 pt 1, 1789, 401–3, pt 2, 873–4 and 1194–6. J. M. Frew, 'The "Destroyer" Vindicated? James Wyatt and the Restoration of Henry VII's Chapel, Westminster Abbey', *JBAA,* 134, 1981, 100–106.

[76] J. Mordaunt Crook, 'The Career of Sir Robert Smirke RA', D.Phil thesis, University of Oxford, 1962, 174–7, 332–4.

[77] R. Smirke, 'An Account of some Remains of Gothic Architecture in Italy and Sicily,' *Archaeologia,* 15, 1806, 363–79.

[78] Gardam, 'Restorations'; Mordaunt Crook, 'The Career of Sir Robert Smirke RA'; and Lewer and Dark, *Temple Church,* 85–9.

[79] EIC, *Gentleman's Magazine,* 94 pt 2, 1824, 208.

[80] Ibid., 'A little caution might have saved the beautiful Chapel, whose ruins now encumber the adjoining court. The curious crypt bears testimony to the strength of antient masonry. Its vaulting resisted the heap of fallen materials which covered it, when I witnessed, with the grief which every lover of antient art feels at the destruction of monuments of departed genius, the ruin which overwhelmed these remains.'

[81] ITR VI, 702, report of Subtreasurer 8 Nov. 1825.

concerning the fabric of the Church — certainly during the eighteenth and early nineteenth centuries — were not, by and large, antiquaries with a preference for the Gothic. They were lawyers, some of whom may have had antiquarian leanings, but who generally displayed these in works of legal antiquarianism rather than in architectural antiquities. Their priorities in ordering work to be done on the Temple, and in commissioning Smirke, were those of urban improvement: that is the more systematic ordering of urban space in accordance with classically derived principles of symmetry and proportion and accompanied by a diminished tolerance for disorder, dirt, projecting frontages and smoking chimneys.[82] The eighteenth-century urban aesthetic was one which valued order, straight lines offering perspective views, regularity and cleanliness. The removal of buildings — generally referred to as 'hovels' — built up against churches, and indeed any other public building, was a standard element in eighteenth-century projects of urban improvement.

The timing of the removal of the shops in 1810, which gave rise to Joseph Jekyll's pamphlet of 1811, may have had something to do with the rising volume of criticism directed against the buildings cluttering up the exterior of the church on the south side, which are to be found in a number of early nineteenth-century publications. 'It is much to be regretted,' wrote J. P. Malcolm, 'that the two Societies do not join to follow the example of the present enlightened Dean and Chapter of Westminster at the Abbey of St. Peter, by removing the houses from the front and sides of their interesting church, whose rich Saxon door is frequently obstructed by filth and offal.'[83] John Britton, writing in *Architectural Antiquities,* was likewise damning of the want of public spirit on the part of the lawyers: 'As the societies of the Middle and Inner Temple are equally interested in the stability of their public buildings, and as they have evinced a disposition to sacrifice a little private interest to general utility and beauty, we are surprised that they do not remove the several petty shops, &c which are built against the sides of this church, and which not only disfigure the building, but are highly injurious to its walls and foundations.'[84] And finally John Carter added his voice to the chorus of antiquarian disapproval in 1808 in the *Gentleman's Magazine*: 'It is surely a lamentable circumstance to find so much of the Nave of the Church shut out from view by hovels, for occupations the most mean and miserable.'[85]

For John Carter, and those who shared his views, the buildings on the exterior represented an unpardonable desecration upon the fabric of the church; for others they were unsightly simply because they did not conform with the eighteenth-century aesthetic of rationality, straight lines and clear vistas. One did not have to subscribe to the antiquarian agenda in order to see that the removal of these buildings from the exterior

[82] On urban improvement in general, see P. Borsay, *The English Urban Renaissance: Culture and Society in the Provincial Town, 1660–1770,* Oxford 1989; on London in particular, M. Obgorn, *Spaces of Modernity: London's Geographies 1680–1780,* New York and London 1998, 75–115; Summerson, *Georgian London,* 121–32.

[83] Malcolm, *Londinium Redivivum,* II, 291.

[84] Britton, *Architectural Antiquities,* I, 15. Compare Plates 70, 92.

[85] J. Carter, *Gentleman's Magazine,* 78 pt 2, 1808, 1000.

of the church would be desirable. Similarly, an appreciation of the need to repair the fabric's damage and decay, which was increasingly coming to light, was not necessarily predicated upon an antiquarian sensibility.[86] Samuel Ireland, author of *Picturesque View, with an Historical Account of the Inns of Court* (1800), had made similar complaints to those cited above,[87] but his agenda was not that of the outraged antiquary; rather he was pursuing an urban aesthetic of pleasing views and rational spaces. The Inns of Court, he observed, offered 'a situation, the most spacious and best selected for health and convenience, that London produces', but the pleasant potential was wasted as the approach was dark, 'mean and contracted' and the church 'encumbered with houses and shops of a mean cast of character, ill suited to the situation'. Opening up the approaches and clearing the area around the church would create a rational and genteel public space. This was a consideration that clearly influenced the thinking of the Benchers — as is apparent from the 'Plan of Improvement in Lambs' Buildings' drawn up when discussions were underway between the two societies for the removal of the buildings on the south side.[88] According to this document, the 'basis of the negociation [*sic*]' between the societies was the 'general Improvement of the view of the Church and particularly of the Round Tower which is now obstructed by the Buildings raised up to intercept it'.[89]

The first point to remember is that the Temple Church and the surrounding buildings were more open to the public than they are today: the area had always been a favoured place for strolling and contemplation: anecdotal evidence indicates that it was a space for promenading as early as the sixteenth century when John Stow had referred to the 'round Walk' in the Temple.[90] James Boswell used to stroll about the Temple ('a most agreeable place') with his friends; others would walk in the gardens.[91] Boydell's print of the Temple Church — with the theatrical curtains drawn back to show a stage occupied by polite company of both sexes — reinforces the sense of the church as social space, although the absence of the boxed pews and wainscoting around the pillars must render its overall accuracy questionable (Plate 69). Early-nineteenth-century accounts of London similarly recommended the Temple as a place for walking and recreation: 'The terrace before the Inner Temple hall is regularly and excellently paved,' Malcolm advised his readers, 'and facing the South, is always dry. This advantage attracts many visitors, who pass their leisure hours in conversation there with their friends, and in admiring the trees, walks, flowers, and moving scenes of the river.'[92] Not all visitors were

[86] Herbert, *Antiquities*, 260.
[87] Ireland, *Picturesque Views*, 9.
[88] The footprint of Lamb's Buildings is shown in the foreground of Cole's print, Plate 70.
[89] MTA 15/TAM 245, 'A Report on the Question of the Removal of the Buildings belonging to the Societies of the Middle and Inner Temple on the South Side of the Church', 13.
[90] J. Stow, *A Survey of the Cities of London and Westminster*, ed J. Styrpe, 2 vols., London 1720, I, pt. 2, 271.
[91] *Boswell's London Journal 1762–63*, ed. F. Pottle, New York and London 1950, 234.
[92] Malcolm, *Londinium Redivivum*, II, 289; see also Ireland, *Picturesque View*, 9. Malcolm's observations were reproduced in T. Allen, *The History and Antiquities of London, Westminster and Southwark*, 4 vols., 1827–8, IV, 395.

so 'polite', of course: barristers in the 1820s starting complaining regularly of the noise of children playing in the gardens, and steps were taken to tighten up the security and cut down on access.[93] Such measures again suggest a diminished tolerance for disorder of any kind within the space of the Inns of Court.

The pursuit of urban improvement transformed the appearance of many parts of London and other cities in the course of the eighteenth century and was clearly a factor in inducing the Benchers to clear the area around the church, but it should also be remembered that the removal of the shops around the church was not of itself a new idea at all, whether it was associated with urban planning, antiquarian sensibility or ecclesiological principles. Underlying these factors there was also a simple pragmatic concern for the long-term safety, convenience and durability of the fabric, which existed independently both of an aesthetic of clean lines and symmetry and of an antiquarian concern for the integrity of the building. The cluster of buildings around the church were always likely to be the targets of criticism, but they also represented profit: it was a matter of balancing the income to be derived from their rents against the 'nuisance' they caused to those in the vicinity and the future costs of repairing damage to the church fabric. In 1704 shops between the east end of St Anne's chapel and the east end of the Round had been removed; there had also been discussion between the Inner and Middle Temple as to the possibility of taking down those on the South side. In this instance it was a practical matter of securing the fabric of the church: for the 'better examining & securing the foundation wall and butterisses [sic] on the South side of the Temple Church'.[94] Similarly, the removal of some of the shops on the south side, or at the very least their chimneys, had also been mooted in 1769, on the grounds that they were unsightly and that the smoke created a nuisance.[95] In the same year measures were also taken to rail off the west end of the church in order to prevent persons from 'pissing' against the walls.[96] By this date at least, there seems to have been an effort to make the space outside the church more ordered and less offensive to the visual and olfactory senses.

It was precisely these issues again which seem to have instigated the first discussion of the removal of the shops against the south side of the church in the 1820s.

---

[93] ITR vi, 661, 6 July 1824: several barristers made a complaint that 'they are frequently disturbed from working in daytime by noise of boys and children allowed to play within the Temple, unchecked by porters who are supposed to keep order'. Another similar complaint was made 29 June 1827 (795).

[94] MTA 15/TAM 245, memoranda dated 20 June and 1 July 1704. ITR iii, 381–3, simply records repairs being ordered to the south side of the Church.

[95] The shops are shown in Cole's and Malton's views (Plates 67, 70). ITR v, 230, 3 May 1769: 'In the opinion of the Table no further interest should be granted in the buildings now Nathaniel Walthoe's and Firth's adjoining the Church, so that when they fall to the House they may be pulled down or made more commodious or ornamental as shall be thought fit.'

[96] ITR v, 230: 'On the proposal of the Masters of the Bench of the Middle Temple that the wooden rails now belonging to Lamb's Buildings should for the present be fixed before the whole western part of the Church, to prevent the nuisance by pissing against the same now complained of, a proportionable part of the expense thereof to be paid by this Society.'

Given that this part of Smirke's work involved protracted negotiations with the Middle Temple, who owned the leases for four of these shops, we have a clearer sense of what the Benchers' priorities were in making these changes. These four shops, which were occupied by hairdressers and tailors according to the memorandum, were

> offensive to the Neighourhood as well from their appearance as from the Smoke continually issuing from their Chimneys through the nature of the Businesses of the Occupiers both Summer and Winter It had therefore been very earnestly desired by the Master of the Temple and by Gentlemen occupying Chambers adjoining these nuisances that they should be entirely removed . . . but at the same time the Masters House and Garden the joint property of both Societies and more particularly the building called No 4 Lambs' Building, which belongs to the Middle Temple were benefited and greatly improved in value as Residences, and the Church was rendered more secure from Fire, and relieved from the effects of the Smoke which used to foul the Windows above the Shops and to penetrate into the inside through the Crevices and Openings in those Windows.[97]

The document goes on to observe that the benefits which had already been obtained by 'this sacrifice' on the part of the Inner Temple had encouraged a general hope which was shared even by 'Strangers who were in the habit of passing through the Lamb Building Court, as well as the Inhabitants' that the improvements to the 'appearance, air and security from Fire' of the area would be consolidated by the removal of the remaining buildings on the south side of the church.[98]

    Antiquarian and aesthetic considerations aside, the reasons for removing the shops from the church in the nineteenth century still had a pragmatic basis — as Britton had noted, they were 'highly injurious to its walls and foundations'[99] — but it is also important to set the improvements to the Temple Church in the context of other building and repair works being undertaken at the Inns of Court around this time. In 1818 the library of the Inner Temple had been extensively repaired and revamped — not least out of concern that it would reflect badly on the Inner Temple if its library did not match up to that of Lincoln's Inn, which had been rebuilt in the 1770s as part of a major programme of re-edification.[100] Nor was Robert Smirke employed simply to work on the church.[101] During his twenty-nine-year period of employment as Architect and Surveyor to the Inner Temple, he was also occupied on an extensive programme of repairs, renovations and building work across the Inner Temple. At the time that he was working on the Temple Church, for example, he had recently undertaken the gothicization of the hall,[102] and was carrying out work on the library and the Parliament

[97] MTA 15/TAM 245, 'Report on the Question of the Removal of the Buildings', 2 –3.
[98] Ibid., 3–4.
[99] Britton, *Architectural Antiquities*, I, 15.
[100] J. Allibone, 'These Hostells being Nurseries or Seminaries of the Court . . .', in *The Inns of Court: Essays by Jill Allibone and David Evans*, ed. H. Binet, London 1996, 8–17.
[101] Mordaunt Crook, 'The Career of Robert Smirke, RA', 174–7, 332–4; H. M. Colvin, *A Biographical Dictionary of British Architects, 1600–1840*, London 1978, 741.
[102] *Gentleman's Magazine*, 89 pt 2, 1819, 579.

Chambers: new buildings which were described in the *Gentleman's Magazine* as 'highly creditable to the public spirit and taste of the Society'.[103] We might note too that Smirke was also making increased provision for WCs throughout the Temple (including one adjoining the vestry).[104] The comfort of the barristers was doubtless the primary consideration here, but it seems to have been part of a programme to create a more sanitary environment, which was mirrored in the decision to erect additional railings outside the Church — presumably in a renewed attempt to stop persons pissing against the buttresses.[105] A similar interpretation might also be put on the decision of the Inner Temple to purchase in 1826 a run-down, disreputable and fire-damaged range of buildings adjoining Fleet Street. These had previously housed Joe's Coffee House, a brothel and the Maidenhead Public House 'which from its retired situation had become the resort of the very lowest and most desperate characters.' Smirke replaced them with Mitre Court in 1830–31.[106] His remit here evidently involved more than simply maintaining the fabric of the Inner Temple's buildings: his involvement was part of a plan to enhance the Society's reputation and public image. Their willingness to spend money on the improvement of the exterior of the Temple Church has to be seen in this context.

The importance of the eighteenth century for the Temple Church therefore, lies not so much in the changes to its physical fabric but in the transformation of its meaning as a building. In the early eighteenth century it was primarily a memorial to the lawyers of the Inns of Court and a reminder of the extent to which the Great Fire had ravaged London. The Knights' tombs were of interest chiefly for their connection with the nobility of thirteenth-century England. As a structure, it was a minor curiosity; its physical appearance was obscured by modern accretions; and, without the vocabulary to describe what was there, it was not possible for written descriptions to realise its form with any greater clarity. By the early nineteenth century it was renowned both for the knights' tombs and as an illustration of the historical evolution of Gothic architecture. Its importance as an exemplar of the transitional phase of Gothic architecture had been recognised, and its physical form was correspondingly more clearly defined and carefully delineated. The physical interventions of the early nineteenth century were in part inspired by the re-evaluation of Gothic architecture which had taken place in the eighteenth century but were also the product of a separate trajectory of improvement and order — the two impulses coincided comfortably in the need to remove the shops and hovels on the south wall of the Church but parted company over the fate of St Anne's Chapel.[107] Taken together, the result was that the Temple Church was now much more visible — both literally and figuratively.

[103] *Gentleman's Magazine,* 100 pt 2, 1830, 639.
[104] ITR vi, 787, 25 May 1827.
[105] ITR vi, 781, 11 May 1827, order for the 'centre of iron railing south of the Church to be 18 inches from the buttresses, and an iron railing to be placed round the new staircase on the north side of Middle Temple cloisters except against the doorway.'
[106] Mordaunt Crook, 'The Career of Robert Smirke RA', 177.
[107] T. H. Shepherd (1828) showed the Church's south side after Smirke's work had been finished and St Anne's Chapel demolished (Plate 92).

William Whyte

Restoration and Recrimination:
the Temple Church in the Nineteenth Century

A T ABOUT TEN PAST ELEVEN on the night of 10 May 1941, the inhabitants of the city of London were disturbed by the sound of air raid sirens. The noise heralded one of the worst nights of bombing London had ever seen, the longest and the last night of the Blitz. By the time the all clear was sounded, at some point between five and six o'clock in the morning, scores of fires had been started, and hundreds of homes had been destroyed. More than a thousand people had been killed.[1] All across London, from the Palace of Westminster to the terraces of Stepney and Bow, bombs fell indiscriminately. With the water mains burst and the Thames at low tide, there was simply no way of fighting the conflagration. Within the precincts of the Temple, the devastation was terrific, and at the heart of the destruction lay the Temple Church. It had burned through the night and was now a hollow shell. Everything within it had been destroyed (Plates 103, 104).

The damage to the Temple Church should have been a cause for regret — and even for mourning. Yet, for some at least, it was actually an occasion for rejoicing. Writing in 1945, Frank MacKinnon — a distinguished judge and member of the Inner Temple — spoke for this tendency. 'For my own part', he wrote,

> seeing how dreadfully the Church had been despoiled by its pretended friends a century before, I do not grieve so very acutely for the havoc wrought by its avowed enemies . . . If the Church is now once again truly restored, it can hardly fail to be far more beautiful than the Victorian vandals made it for us. To have got rid of their awful stained glass windows, their ghastly pulpit, their hideous

For their help with my research, I am extremely grateful to Dr Clare Rider, until December 2008 the archivist of Inner Temple, and to Mrs Lesley Whitelaw, archivist of Middle Temple. The Rev. Robin Griffith-Jones, the Rev. Elizabeth Macfarlane, and Dr Paul Williamson also provided me with important information. Thanks, too, to Zoë Waxman for advising on earlier versions of this essay and to members of the Oxford Modern Religious History Seminar, the Oxford Architectural History Seminar, and the Cambridge Modern British History Seminar for their comments.

[1] G. Mortimer, *The Longest Night: Voices from the London Blitz*, London 2003, 111, 324.

encaustic tiles, their abominable pews and seats . . . will be almost a blessing in disguise.[2]

Sure enough, the subsequent restoration by Walter H. Godfrey did everything it possibly could to efface the work of his nineteenth-century predecessors (Plate 108).[3]

In many respects, this response is understandable. In the 1940s, the reputation of nineteenth-century architecture stood at almost its very lowest ebb. Victorian buildings had come to be 'accepted as a national misfortune like the weather'.[4] Victorian restoration work was similarly condemned.[5] 'It is difficult to recall,' John Summerson wrote, 'the nausea we felt against the recent past.'[6] The Temple Church was, for those who knew it, a particular cause of distress, for it reflected an especially vigorous intervention by early-nineteenth-century architects. Between 1840 and 1843, and in the name of restoration, they had engaged in a wholesale reconstruction of the church (Colour Plate x).[7] They refitted, refurbished and effectively rebuilt the place.[8] The reredos, organ and pews were replaced; the windows, floors and marble columns were reconstructed (Plates 95–9). The seventeenth- and eighteenth-century memorials were removed (Plate 94), the medieval monuments were radically restored, a new bell tower was built and the whole structure made sound. Katharine Esdaile, the historian of the Temple Church monuments, counselled in 1933 that this 'reckless extravagance' should not be seen as 'intentional vandalism'. But it was, she implied, vandalism none the less.[9]

The bombing of the Temple Church did not, however, simply represent an opportunity to get rid of an unfortunate and ill-conceived exercise in restoration. It also meant the destruction of a particularly important example of early-Victorian taste. The features that made writers of the twentieth century shudder also made the Temple Church significant. Here were windows by Thomas Willement, the pre-eminent stained-glass artist of the 1840s (Plate 99).[10] Here were encaustic tiles by Herbert Minton, who in the first half of the nineteenth century was 'the most innovative and successful china merchant in the world'.[11] Here was a major restoration — to all intents and purposes, a re-creation — of the medieval effigies by Edward Richardson, one of the 'most notable

[2] F. MacKinnon, *The Ravages of the War in the Inner Temple*, London 1945, 33.
[3] Lewer and Dark, *Temple Church*, chap. 14.
[4] K. Clark, *Another Part of the Wood*, London 1974, 109.
[5] *From William Morris: Building Conservation and the Arts and Crafts Cult of Authenticity, 1877–1939*, ed. C. E. Miele, New Haven and London 2005.
[6] Quoted in M. Pawley, 'The Sense of the Modern', *Architects' Journal*, 16 and 23 December 1987, 28–30 at 28.
[7] It is striking that in 1903 T. G. Jackson referred to 'the "restoration" of the Church in 1842'. MTA 15/TAM/360, Jackson, Report, 18 February 1903, 2.
[8] Gardam, 'Restorations'
[9] Esdaile, *Temple Church Monuments*, 10.
[10] S. A. Shepherd, 'Willement, Thomas (1786–1871)', *ODNB* (accessed 21 Feb. 2008).
[11] E. Bonython and A. Burton, *The Great Exhibitor: The Life and Work of Henry Cole*, London 2003, 84.

sculptor[s] and archaeologist[s] of his day'.[12] Nor were the architects responsible any less impressive. Sydney Smirke, renowned for his round reading room at the British Museum;[13] Decimus Burton, well-known for his work as a domestic designer and town planner;[14] James Savage, whose St Luke's, Chelsea, was widely seen as the starting point of the Gothic Revival:[15] these were the big names of the day. The restoration of the Temple Church was one of the largest jobs going, ultimately costing somewhat more than £50,000.[16] It gave these men — and their clients, the representatives of the two Inns of Court — an unrivalled opportunity to impose their vision of church architecture on an iconic building. The result was a striking work of architecture; one that many Victorians believed to be both beautiful and appropriate. 'Considering that this work was begun thirty years ago,' wrote Charles Eastlake in 1872, 'the world of art may be thankful for the general success with which it was carried out.'[17] Even at the time, not everyone agreed, of course. But a project that could unite the stern unbending young Tory William Gladstone, the ambitious utilitarian designer Henry Cole, and the reforming bishop of London Charles Blomfield in their praise clearly had wide appeal.[18]

Nevertheless, the nineteenth-century restoration of the Temple Church has been the subject of surprisingly little research.[19] Although it was one of the most important projects of its period, attention has focussed elsewhere: on the earlier work of James — 'the destroyer' — Wyatt;[20] on the later campaigns of William Morris and the Society for the Protection of Ancient Buildings;[21] and on the contemporary controversy over work at another round church, St Sepulchre's, Cambridge.[22] The single sustained piece of research on this subject comes in J. Mordaunt Crook's important article of 1965, 'The

[12] Richardson, *Effigies of the Temple Church* (1843). See M. H. Grant, *A Dictionary of British Sculptors from the XIIIth century to the XXth Century*, London 1953, 203.

[13] J. Mordaunt Crook, 'Sydney Smirke: the Architecture of Compromise', in *Seven Victorian Architects*, ed. J. Fawcett, London 1976, 50–65.

[14] P. Miller, *Decimus Burton: 1800–1881*, London 1981.

[15] C. R. Eastlake, *A History of the Gothic Revival*, London 1871 (repr. New York 1970), 141–2. See also J. Britton, 'An Account of the Church of St Luke's, Chelsea', in J. Britton and A. Pugin, *Illustrations of Public Buildings of London*, 2 vols., London 1825–8, II, 205–18.

[16] MTA Court of Parliament P, 1840–46, 437. The *Gentleman's Magazine*, however, estimated the total cost at more than £70,000: *Gentleman's Magazine* 20, 1843, 301.

[17] Eastlake, *Gothic Revival*, 201.

[18] *The Gladstone Diaries*, ed. H. C. G. Matthew, 12 vols., Oxford 1968–94, III, 237; F. Summerly [Henry Cole], *A Glance at the Temple Church*, London 1844; *Ipswich Journal*, 29 October 1842, 1. See also J. Jebb, *The Choral Service of the United Church of England and Ireland*, London 1843, 153.

[19] Though of course the standard works on the Church itself do naturally address this theme. See esp. Lewer and Dark, *Temple Church*, 84–110, 121–7.

[20] J. Mordaunt Crook, *John Carter and the Mind of the Gothic Revival*, London 1995, 27, 33–41. For a defence of Wyatt's work, see A. Dale, *James Wyatt*, Oxford 1956, 7–9.

[21] C. E. Miele, 'The First Conservation Militants', in *Preserving the Past: the Rise of Heritage in Modern Britain*, ed. M. Hunter, Stroud 1996, 20–27; '"A small knot of cultivated people": William Morris and Ideologies of Protection', *Art Journal*, 54, 1995, 73–9.

[22] Wrongly identified as St Sophia in C. Dellheim, *The Face of the Past: the Preservation of the Medieval Inheritance in Victorian England*, Cambridge 1982, 82. For further details, see below.

Restoration of the Temple Church: Ecclesiology and Recrimination', itself a revision of a section in his doctoral thesis, submitted three years earlier.[23] Crook's account was an expert exploration of the work done to the building in the early nineteenth century. Robert Smirke's limited restoration of 1828, Crook showed, led to the refacing of the church, the demolition of St Anne's Chapel, the removal of the organ screen, and other, smaller changes. In the 1840s, he went on, Savage drew up plans which were intended to transform the church. But this was, as he showed, a far from unproblematic process. Most importantly, Crook revealed — and for the first time — that this had been the project which ended James Savage's career. He had wildly exceeded his estimates, had been tricked out of money by a mason, and had lost the confidence of his employers. The project was thus completed by Sydney Smirke and Burton. This was, undeniably, a personal tragedy for Savage. Nonetheless, his replacements essentially followed his lead — suggesting that something rather more than purely personal predilection was driving the restoration as a whole. The motive force for these changes, Crook concluded, was indeed a much broader alteration in attitudes towards church architecture. This was, in short, a moment at which 'ecclesiology engulfed antiquarianism'; or, in other words, the restoration was evidence of how new religious ideas were overcoming old archaeological assumptions.[24] Crook's account remains seminal: the starting point for any investigation of the Temple Church in the nineteenth century. Building on more recent research about both ecclesiology and antiquarianism, however, it is possible to suggest another conclusion.

This is not to say that either antiquarianism or ecclesiology is unimportant in the story of the Temple Church. Savage's, Smirke's, and Burton's work took place at a significant moment in the development both of English architecture and of the Church of England. The relationship between church reform and architectural debate in the nineteenth century is now increasingly well understood. The parallel action of the Oxford and Cambridge movements — the one set focussed on ecclesiology and known as the Tractarians, the other group known as the Ecclesiologists and absorbed by architecture — has been the subject of a number of important studies.[25] In particular, the significance of the Cambridge Camden Society and its journal, *The Ecclesiologist*, is now widely acknowledged. Deriving their theology from Pusey and Newman, and their aesthetics from Pugin and Cottingham, the Ecclesiologists sought to reform the Church by rebuilding it.[26] They looked back to the architecture and ethos of medieval

[23] See Mordaunt Crook, 'Restoration', and, in truncated form, 'The Victorian Restoration of the Church', in *The Inner Temple: a Community of Communities*, ed. C. Rider and V. Horsler, London 2007, 78–9. See also J. Mordaunt Crook, 'The Career of Sir Robert Smirke, R.A.', D.Phil. thesis, University of Oxford, 1962, 331–5.

[24] Mordaunt Crook, 'Restoration', 43.

[25] See especially P. B. Nockles, *The Oxford Movement in Context: Anglican High Churchmanship, 1760–1857*, Cambridge 1994, and J. F. White, *The Cambridge Movement: the Ecclesiologists and the Gothic Revival*, Cambridge 1962. S. A. Skinner, in *The Tractarians and the 'Condition of England': the Social and the Political Thought of the Oxford Movement*, Oxford 2004, makes the point that they were not solely interested in ecclesiology.

[26] N. Yates, *Anglican Ritualism in Victorian Britain, 1830–1910*, Oxford 1999, 48.

Christendom, and hoped to recreate it, believing that the symbolic power of Gothic buildings could not but influence worshippers within them.[27] Founded in 1839, their impact was soon felt all across the country, growing from a small band of Cambridge students into a large and influential pressure group. As Pugin put it himself in 1843, a notice appeared to have been affixed in every church porch: 'Beware of the [Camden] Society.'[28] As late as the 1890s, indeed, even architects who had formally rejected the Gothic Revival were still turning out churches that deviated in no single detail from the *Ecclesiologist*'s injunctions of fifty years before.[29]

The Temple Church restoration came just as this movement was beginning, and at first sight it does indeed look like yet another example of Ecclesiology in action. Just as the Cambridge Camden Society recommended, this was a church where non-Gothic details were to be effaced; where the 'hideous altar screen rich in pagan symbols, and . . . pulpit such as Gulliver might have sat under had he attended Divine Service in Brobdignag' were to be removed (Colour Plate IX).[30] The rich colours and rich symbolism of medieval art were to be restored. Moreover, this restoration was self-confessedly undertaken to eradicate what one contemporary described as 'the puritanic and revolutionary spirit' which had led to the church's 'desecration and disfigurement'.[31] The work at the Temple was believed by another to be 'the beginning of a peaceful crusade against the puritanic misdeeds which have been accumulating upon our buildings since the Reformation'.[32] Thomas Willement's work was likewise, as he put it, intended to counteract the 'puritanic spirit which prompted the destruction of stained glass . . . [and] obliterated or at least defaced the rich decoration of walls and ceilings'. This rhetoric — with its attack on the Puritans and its emphasis on what Willement called the practice of the 'primitive Christians' — all sounds strikingly Ecclesiological, if not Tractarian.[33] And the change did not stop there. The restoration was followed by a complete reorganisation of worship within the Temple Church.[34] A surpliced choir was introduced; daily service was instituted; there was even a proposal for those attending the church to be robed.[35] Given the interest taken by the Cambridge Camden Society in liturgical and musical reform,[36] this combination of architectural and choral revival can seem irresistibly Ecclesiological.

No doubt for this reason, the Master of the Temple, Christopher Benson, was

---

[27] See, 'Temples Worthy of His Presence': the Early Publications of the Cambridge Camden Society, ed. C. Webster, Reading 2003.

[28] A. W. N. Pugin, *The Present State of Ecclesiastical Architecture*, London 1843, 86.

[29] W. Whyte, *Oxford Jackson: Architecture, Education, Status, and Style, 1835–1924*, Oxford 2006, 15.

[30] Eastlake, *Gothic Revival*, 200.

[31] Addison, *Temple Church*, 44.

[32] Summerly, *Glance at the Temple Church*, 1.

[33] ITA TEM/2/6, Mr Willement's Report upon the Painted Ceiling, 2 November 1840.

[34] D. Lewer, *A Spiritual Song: the Story of the Temple Choir and a History of Divine Service in the Temple Church*, London 1961, 83–135.

[35] *Trewman's Exeter Flying Post or Plymouth and Cornish Advertiser*, 6 February 1845.

[36] D. Adelmann, *The Contribution of the Cambridge Camden Society to the Revival of Anglican Choral Music, 1839–1862*, Aldershot 1997.

deeply suspicious of the motives behind the restoration. As he had little control over the church and as he was frequently absent through ill health, however, he found himself powerless to thwart those changes which he believed to be objectionable, and was reduced to writing letters of complaint to those in charge. A broad Evangelical,[37] he was appalled at the 'Popish tendencies cloaking themselves with the name of Catholic' which he witnessed throughout the Church of England, and was convinced that the laity would not tolerate 'their Protestant Pastor reading their Communion Service in a Cope, like a Romish Priest, and his Curate in an Albe, with tunicles'.[38] There was no room in his world — much less in his church — for Ecclesiology.

Benson's attitude to the restoration was not wholly negative. After all, he had been the first person to suggest that the seventeenth- and eighteenth-century monuments should be removed.[39] He even preached at the opening service — returning from Italy specially to do so, and he praised those parts of the work which he found theologically acceptable.[40] Nonetheless, it is not surprising to find that the man who coined the term 'Tractarian' — and did not use it as a compliment — found some of the other changes made to the Church unsupportable.[41] In particular, Benson profoundly disapproved of the new altarpiece (Colour Plate xi), and expostulated that

> We cannot consider the lace embroidered article which is placed on the Top of what ought to have been a Communion Table, but is an Altar, to be consistent with the requisition, that 'a fair White Cloth' be put upon the Table . . . An Altar implies Sacrifice and is not consistent with any views of the Lords [sic] Supper, except those held respectively by papists, Laudians, Non-Jurors and Tractarians.[42]

The choral service of the restored church similarly appalled him. Admittedly, he had not approved of the old choir, consisting as it did, 'of a mixed quartet, who sat in front of the organ, and revealed themselves by withdrawing a curtain as the time for each psalm-tune came round'.[43] He had particularly deprecated the use of female singers 'in a collegiate Chapel appropriated principally for men'.[44] But he found the new choir and its music still less to his liking. Early in 1843, he sought to suppress its activities,[45] and he then fought a lengthy, but ultimately futile fight for control.[46] He resigned in

[37] See C. Benson, *A Theological Enquiry into the Sacrament of Baptism and the Nature of Baptismal Regeneration*, Cambridge 1817, which represents a subtle attack on the High Church doctrine of baptismal regeneration.

[38] C. Benson, *Rubrics and Canons of the Church of England*, London 1845, 29, 32.

[39] ITA TEM/2/4/1, Church Restoration Committee, 1840–41, 29 January 1841.

[40] *Illustrated London News* 1, 1842, 412, 5 November 1842.

[41] C. Benson, *Discourses upon Tradition and Episcopacy preached at the Temple Church*, 2nd edn, London 1839, p. iii.

[42] MTA Court of Parliament P, 1840–46, 406, 25 May 1843.

[43] J. S. Curwen, *Studies in Worship Music*, 2nd edn, London 1883, 347.

[44] MTA Court of Parliament P, 1840–46, 362, 25 November 1842.

[45] *Lloyd's Weekly London Newspaper*, 19 February 1843.

[46] Lewer, *Spiritual Song*, 110–13.

1845,[47] and was replaced by a Master who was happier with the High Church and willing to offer daily services both in term and out.[48]

In this battle, Benson's principal opponent was the barrister William Burge. He was the leading figure behind both the restoration and the choral revival. A convinced conservative, he was a pro-slavery, anti-Reform MP in the early 1830s. Nonetheless, he was far from a Philistine: a scholar and a writer, he was a Queen's Counsellor, a Fellow of the Society of Antiquaries and the Royal Society, treasurer of the Archaeological Institute, and a major authority on legal matters. Burge was determined to restore the Temple Church to its former glory — not least, one suspects, because it was where his first wife was buried in 1839.[49] In *The Temple Church: an Account of its Restoration and Repairs*, which was published in 1843, Burge made plain his belief that it was the duty of the two Inns to return the church to its original form; to root out the seventeenth- and eighteenth-century additions, which had 'destroyed its entire character', and replace 'those decorations, which excited the hostility of Puritanism'.[50] In his work *On the Choral Service of the Anglo-Catholic Church*, which came out a year later in 1844, Burge stated his principles still more clearly, arguing for a return to the practice of the pre-Reformation Church; for a daily choral service; and for music which, whilst it 'neither partook of, nor contributed to promote, the corruptions of the Church of Rome', was nonetheless truly 'Anglo-Catholic'.[51] Given these attitudes, it is no great shock to learn that Burge was a friend of the leading Ecclesiologist Alexander Beresford Hope,[52] nor that he was an admirer of the Tractarian poet F. W. Faber.[53] Nor indeed does Burge's public commendation of the Cambridge Camden Society's 'most beneficial influence in promoting Ecclesiastical Architecture' seem especially surprising.[54]

It would be wrong, however, to see the restoration of the Temple Church in the 1840s as a simple struggle between evangelicals and Ecclesiologists, a merely metropolitan equivalent of the battle over the Round Church — St Sepulchre's — in Cambridge. There, the Camden Society was called in to effect a restoration and found itself fighting with the Low-Church vicar over its decision to install a stone altar, something he believed to be blasphemous and which the Society increasingly believed to be an

[47] MTA MT.15/TEM/309, Resignation of Mr Benson, 1845.

[48] The new Master was Thomas Robinson, formerly chaplain to Bishop Heber, a defender of apostolic succession, and a critic both of Latitudinarianism and Evangelical enthusiasm. See Thomas Robinson, *The Last Days of Bishop Heber*, London 1830, 53 and *The Character of St Paul: the Model of the Christian Ministry*, Cambridge 1840, 14, 21, 25, 67, 73, 75.

[49] *Burge's Commentaries on Colonial and Foreign Laws*, ed. A. W. Renton and G. G. Phillimore, 5 vols., London 1907, 1, pp. ix–xiii. See also Royal Society Archive, EC/1840/18.

[50] W. Burge, *The Temple Church: an Account of its Restoration and Repairs*, London 1853, 24, 8.

[51] W. B. [William Burge], *On the Choral Service of the Anglo-Catholic Church*, London 1844, pp. xxx, iii.

[52] Beresford Hope was not alone in being one of Burge's creditors (ITA DIS/1/B1, W. Burge, Copy of Schedule and Balance Sheet, 3 August 1848, 14). But it is striking to note that he signed the accounts of the Archaeological Institute on Burge's behalf (*Archaeological Journal*, 3, 1846, 271).

[53] Burge, *Temple Church*, p. iii.

[54] Ibid., 11.

essential part of any church.[55] For all Benson's complaints, and his ultimate resignation as Master of the Temple, there was nothing like that here. The altarpiece he so disapproved of, for example, was not a radical departure from the old one, but was rather a Gothicised version of it. Canonically correct, it was framed by tables with the Creed and Ten Commandments on them. The restoration committee had firmly — and not a little self-consciously — insisted on providing 'a stout oak Communion Table' instead of a stone altar.[56] For all Benson's objections, this was certainly not intended to be an innovation — much less the introduction of papistical practices.

Nor were the liturgical changes made at the Temple strikingly ritualistic. The restored church — with its multiplicity of pews — prevented any sort of procession (Plate 97),[57] whilst the choir arose as a sort of afterthought.[58] It was initially highly unimpressive: repetitious in its repertoire, poorly rehearsed and badly organised.[59] The High-Church *Christian Remembrancer* condemned it and went on to complain about the lack of reverence shown towards the consecrated bread and wine.[60] This was scarcely the sort of objection that was usually made about Tractarian churches. Even after the inspirational choirmaster Edward Hopkins had reformed the choir and transformed the Temple's music, it was evident that the Temple Church was not a hotbed of ritualism. Hopkins rejected the emphasis on plainsong promulgated by the Tractarians in favour of what Walter Hillsman calls, 'a "warmer", more elaborate, Victorian repertoire'.[61]

It seems likely that, far from being an attempt to ritualise the Temple, the decision to revive a choir and to put its members into surplices reflected an effort to ape the common practices of Oxford and Cambridge college chapels.[62] It was certainly this that inspired the layout of the Church, with the Benchers seated in stalls 'as in Cathedral and collegiate churches'.[63] Likewise, the choir's dress was soon seen as strikingly antiquated. They 'remained', as one writer put it, 'uncassocked until the end of Hopkins' time; and the surpluses [*sic*] were of the old-fashioned "Cathedral" type', rather than reflecting the new styles introduced by ritualists.[64] Moreover, it is also worth noting that Thomas Robinson, the new Master, could scarcely be described as a ritualist himself. He was, in fact, an advocate of 'modern criticism' in biblical studies — something the

[55] E. Rose, 'The Stone Table and the Crisis of the Cambridge Camden Society', *Victorian Studies*, 10, 1966, 119–44.

[56] ITA TEM/2/4/2, Church Restoration, 19 August 1842.

[57] For the problems that this caused, see *The Times*, 27 October 1842, 3, and ITA TEM/3/10, Reseating in the Nave, 1906.

[58] ITA TEM/3/1 Committee upon Music in the Church, 1842–3.

[59] ITA TEM/3/5, Choir Committee, 1843.

[60] *Christian Remembrancer*, 5, 1843, 235–8. I owe this reverence to the Rev. Elizabeth Macfarlane.

[61] W. Hillsman, 'The Victorian Revival of Plainsong in English: its Usage under Tractarians and Ritualists', *Studies in Church History*, 28, 1992, 405–16 at 412. See also B. Zon, *The English Plainchant Revival*, Oxford 1999, 254.

[62] B. Rainbow, *The Choral Revival in the Anglican Church, 1839–1872*, 1970, repr. Woodbridge 2001, 38–9.

[63] MTA MT/15/TAM/272, Meeting of the Bench (13 July 1840).

[64] C. W. Pearce, *The Life and Works of Edward John Hopkins*, London n.d. [1910], 29.

Tractarians found anathema.[65] Together, he and Hopkins created a setting for worship which by the end of the century seemed remarkably Low Church. As one writer celebrated, there were

> No *superfluous* decorations here;
> No raised 'altar' forbidding to 'draw near',
> Sublime in its simplicity adorned,
> Christ's '*Table*' is for sweet communion formed.[66]

This was written in 1898, but even fifty years earlier it was clear that advanced Ecclesiologists would have been disappointed by the lack of evidence for ritualism.

Most strikingly, it is evident that the work at the Temple Church did not conform to the principles laid out in the *Ecclesiologist*. Indeed, it is remarkable that even anonymous antiquarians and moderate High Churchmen professed themselves somewhat disappointed by it. A correspondent in the *Gentleman's Magazine* regretted the fact that the altar had not been raised, and thus still stood 'at the same depressed level as it did before.'[67] The *Christian Remembrancer* welcomed the spirit in which the work had been done, but also deprecated its details. The reredos, it said, was ugly. The rediscovered piscina and bishop's tomb, it went on, should not have been hidden: 'This is vandalism, which we had no right to expect at the present moment from such a quarter.' Nor did the criticism stop there. The altar rails, it declared, were incomparable for their 'barbarism'. The lack of a screen; the absence of candlesticks; the failure to provide an alms bowl or a credence table or 'velvet embroidered copes': these all reflected a loss of nerve, it argued, an unwillingness to restore the church to its state under the Templars themselves.[68] As for the *Ecclesiologist*: whilst also expressing itself delighted at the 'spirit and generosity in which the works have been conducted', it too had a list — and a lengthy list — of complaints. All in all, it offered thirteen objections to the newly-restored Temple Church. Several were those also identified by the *Christian Remembrancer* and *Gentleman's Magazine*. Others — such as the height of the stalls, the absence of an aisle leading to the altar, the lack of a wicket gate at the west door, the presence of '*Altar-chairs*', and so on — were particular to the Cambridge Camden Society. What it meant, the *Ecclesiologist* concluded, was that however well intentioned it had been, the restoration was simply not '*complete*'.[69]

To some extent, it was only to be expected that the Temple Church should not live up to the more advanced ambitions of the Ecclesiologists. In form, function, and in governance it was profoundly different from the ideal parish church they were seeking to build. Even the Round Church in Cambridge proved somewhat problematic for them in these terms. The Ecclesiologists favoured the architecture of the late thirteenth and

---

[65] Robinson, *Character of St Paul*, 25.

[66] M. A. Clutton (1898), quoted in Pearce, *Hopkins*, 29.

[67] *Gentleman's Magazine*, 19, 1843, 31.

[68] *Christian Remembrancer*, 4, 1842, 611–23.

[69] *Ecclesiologist*, 2, 1842–3, 24, 98–9. See also J. M. Neale, *Hierologus, or, The Church Tourists*, London, 1843, 72. I owe the latter reference to Elizabeth Macfarlane.

early fourteenth centuries, yet St Sepulchre's was built in the 1120s. The Ecclesiologists preferred a screened-off Chancel and isolated eastern altar; but the Round Church's peculiar plan prevented this.[70] The problems presented by the Temple Church were still greater. The nave was Romanesque, still a style that was little known and — it must be said — little liked by the Ecclesiologists. It tended to be favoured by Low Churchmen.[71] The rectangular chancel was later, and a little more acceptable, but presented restorers with a still greater difficulty. In the 1840s, and for some time afterwards, the goal of any restoration was to return a building to its original form. A church, say, would be more authentic — even if entirely rebuilt — so long as the restorer had followed the presumed intentions of its first builders.[72] This was why, after all, the Ecclesiologists had removed all the Perpendicular additions to St Sepulchre's.[73] But what was the original form — the essence — of the Temple Church? It was not clear. Nor was the role of the church any plainer. This was, in every sense, a 'peculiar': effectively free from clerical control; free from state intervention; unencumbered by a parish or parishioners.[74] The Cambridge Camden Society offered little guidance for such a place.

More importantly still, the way the Temple Church was run prevented an outright Ecclesiological take-over. It was jointly owned by the two Inns of Court, with the Inner Temple responsible for the southern and the Middle Temple for the northern half. As a result, any change had to be approved by both sets of Benchers. This was what de-layed further restoration between Robert Smirke's works in 1828 and the start of Sav-age's project in 1840: they had just not been able to agree terms.[75] It also meant that no one person or group could wholly dominate proceedings. Even had anyone desired such a thing, it would simply not have been possible to force an unadulterated Ecclesio-logical programme through the joint committee set up by the two Inns of Court. The members of this committee were not young and impressionable men, nor likely to be easily seduced by the rhetoric of a group of Cambridge students. They included the sexagenarian David Pollock and septuagenarian John Newland from the Middle Tem-ple; the distinguished jurist Francis Holt and the renowned historian George Spence from the Inner Temple.[76] As it was, some members of the committee — including the independent-minded future Liberal Lord Chancellor, Richard Bethell — revealed them-

[70] J. Allibone, *Anthony Salvin: Pioneer of Gothic Revival Architecture*, Cambridge 1987, 116–18.

[71] T. Mowl, 'The Norman Revival in British Architecture, 1790–1870', D.Phil. thesis, Univer-sity of Oxford, 1982, I, 326. More generally, see K. Curran, *The Romanesque Revival: Religion, Politics, and Transnational Exchange*, University Park, PA, 2003.

[72] C. E. Miele, 'The Gothic Revival and Gothic Architecture: The Restoration of Medieval Churches in Victorian Britain', PhD thesis, New York University, 1992, 25, 84–5, 139, 184–8, 292–7, 532–5.

[73] C. E. Miele, 'Re-Presenting the Church Militant: the Camden Society, Church Restoration, and the Gothic Sign', in *'A Church as it should be': the Cambridge Camden Society and its Influence*, ed. C. Webster and J. Elliott, Stamford 2000, 257–94.

[74] Lord Silsoe, *The Peculiarities of the Temple*, London 1972, 51.

[75] Crook, 'Restoration', 40.

[76] MTA MT/15/TAM/277, Report of the Joint Committee, 3 November 1840; Court of Par-liament P, 424, 23 June 1843.

selves to be opposed to many of the Ecclesiologists' central ideals. Indeed, Bethell went so far as to complain about the expense of the restoration, shocked that money could be found for architecture whilst legal education languished for lack of funds.[77] It is true that William Burge was the dominant figure on the committee — the driving force behind the work — but he was, in the end, only one voice amongst several others. More than this, although he joined the Cambridge Camden Society, it is noteworthy that he did not do so until 1845, several years after the restoration was complete.[78]

For all these reasons, then, the work at the Temple Church cannot be fitted into any account of nineteenth-century church building that uniquely stresses the impact of the Ecclesiologists. The restoration came at a critical time in which the Cambridge Camden Society was getting going but was not yet the dominant — even domineering — force that it was to become. In recent years, historians like Simon Bradley, Peter Nockles and Nigel Yates have explored pre-Ecclesiological architecture, looking at the ways in which the impact of antiquarianism and a pre-Tractarian High Church tradition all contributed to liturgical and architectural reform in the years before the Camden Society was even founded.[79] They have shown that antiquarianism inspired the restoration of numerous cathedrals, churches, and college chapels in the early nineteenth century, with the desire to return these buildings to their supposedly proper form often leading to work which drew on pre-Reformation precedents. So strong was this impulse that even some evangelical institutions acquired suspiciously High Church ornaments.[80] This was true, for example, at Wadham College, Oxford; a place so fundamentally opposed to Tractarianism that the warden timed his compulsory lectures on the Thirty-Nine Articles to coincide with Newman's sermons at the University Church.[81] Yet, despite this, successive restorations in the 1830s and 1840s introduced new stained glass, a Gothic reredos and communion table. Strikingly, William Burge — whose arms are shown in a window in the ante-chapel — donated money to support this work.[82]

In other, more High Church contexts, the Cambridge Camden Society was even seen as a group of interlopers, with men like the impeccably orthodox Joshua Watson

---

[77] T. A. Nash. *The Life of Richard, Lord Westbury*, 2 vols., London 1888, I, 92.

[78] G. Brandwood, 'A Camdenian Roll Call', in *'A Church as it should be'*, ed. Webster and Elliott, 359–454.

[79] S. Bradley, 'The Gothic Revival and the Church of England, 1790–1840'; idem, 'The Gothic Revival and the Church of England 1790–1840', PhD thesis, University of London, Courtauld Institute of Art, 1996, esp. 227; Nockles, *Oxford Movement*, 214–19; N. Yates, *Buildings, Faith and Worship: the Liturgical Arrangements of Anglican Churches, 1600–1900*, Oxford 1991, 112–34, and *Anglican Ritualism in Victorian Britain*, 48–50. See also F. C. Mather, 'Georgian Churchmanship Reconsidered: Some Variations in Anglican Public Worship, 1714–1830', *Journal of Ecclesiastical History*, 36, 1985, 255–83.

[80] J. Fawcett, 'A Restoration Tragedy: Cathedrals in the Eighteenth and Nineteenth Centuries', in *The Future of the Past: Attitudes to Conservation, 1174–1974*, ed. J. Fawcett, London 1974, 75–111.

[81] C. S. L. Davies, 'Decline and Revival: 1660–1900', in *Wadham College*, ed. C. S. L. Davies and J. Garnett, Oxford 1994, 41–51.

[82] T. G. Jackson, *Wadham College, Oxford*, Oxford 1893; R. B. Gardiner, *The Registers of Wadham College, Oxford: 1719–1871*, London 1895, 229. Willement was also responsible for new windows in the hall.

declaring that 'the impertinence of these Camdenians is perfectly unendurable'.[83] It was pre-Ecclesiological High Churchmen, for example, who created iconic buildings like Leeds Parish Church, a place which also pioneered a distinctive — and distinctly pre-Camdenian — choral foundation, and which 'failed to conform to the *Ecclesiologist's* view of what a sound modern design should be'.[84] As Christopher Webster has put it, 'There is clear evidence that much of what the [Cambridge Camden] Society sought to achieve was already developing, and in some cases, was firmly established long before the Society's inception.'[85]

Given this background, it is easy to see why the restoration of the Temple Church was possible, why it was carried out in the way that it was, and why it proved to be such a disappointment to the Ecclesiologists. It was able to command the support of such a broad range of people precisely because it was not the work of a single church party. In this period, as Simon Bradley has shown, Churchmen of all sorts welcomed the restoration of old churches, seeing it as a way of affirming the historical continuity of the Church of England itself.[86] Specifically at the Temple, this meant seeking a connection with the Templars who had built the church. Indeed, they seem to have been far less controversial as exemplars than might have been expected. Certainly, they were less problematic than the generations that had followed them.[87] Despite the universally acknowledged importance of the Temple's most famous Master, Richard Hooker, for example, no one wanted to return the church to its state in the 1580s.[88] And everything introduced since then was written off as 'pagan', 'puritanic' or simply 'barbarous'.[89] This was a widely-held view; after all, it was precisely this assumption that led even Christopher Benson to welcome Willement's decorations, praising them for being 'in harmony with the grand beauty of a Gothic edifice'.[90] A belief in antiquarian restoration; a feeling that the Establishment should assert its antiquity; a sense that churches should be returned to — restored to — their original form: these factors were all present at the Temple in the 1840s, but they did not depend on the work of the Cambridge Camden Society.

The architects employed likewise owed little to teachings of the *Ecclesiologist.*

[83] Quoted in Nockles, *Oxford Movement,* 214.

[84] C. Webster, *The Rebuilding of Leeds Parish Church, 1837–1841, and its Place in the Gothic Revival,* London 1994, 24. See also D. Webster, '"A Mass sung to ancient music": the Society's Influence on Church Music', in *'A Church as it should be',* ed. Webster and Elliott, 331–47 at 342.

[85] C. Webster, '"Absolutely wretched": Camdenian Attitudes to the Late-Georgian Church', in *'A Church as it should be',* ed. Webster and Elliott, 1–21 at 17.

[86] Bradley, 'The Gothic Revival and the Church of England', 157.

[87] Though, for a rare, dissenting view, see E. Clarkson, 'Essay on the Symbolic Evidences of the Temple Church: Were the Templars Gnostic Idolaters, as Alleged?', in Billings, *Illustrations,* 1–26, which answers his own question in the affirmative.

[88] D. MacCulloch, 'Richard Hooker's Reputation', *English Historical Review,* 117, 2002, 773–812 at 808–12.

[89] For example, Addison, *Temple Church,* 43–4; J. Saunders, 'The Temple Church, II', in *London,* ed. C. Knight, 5 vols., London 1841–4, V, 17–32.

[90] *The Times,* 21 November 1842, 5.

James Savage, who drew up the plans, was a pioneering Gothic Revival architect, but — as Basil Clarke put it — 'There was a world of difference between Gothic set forth in the churches of James Savage and Gothic as explained by Pugin.'[91] Savage, in the final analysis, was just as happy in Greek as in Gothic; whilst for Pugin — and for the Ecclesiologists — there was a moral and religious difference between the two: Gothic was Christian and anything neo-classical simply Pagan.[92] Moreover, when Savage was replaced, his replacements not only followed his plan, but followed his example. Decimus Burton's other churches were, as Peter Bohan puts it,

> essentially of an earlier classical form but dressed up in simple Gothic detail. One senses that Burton adopted these non-classical styles after 1830 more to satisfy contemporary fashion than out of any genuine conviction as to their appropriateness.[93]

Burton's colleague in this project, Sydney Smirke, was no more a true Gothic man than him. Smirke had some antiquarian interests, but also an exclusively classical training, and his Gothic designs were, as J. Mordaunt Crook puts it, 'archaeological not ecclesiological'.[94]

The craftsmen and other experts brought in to assist with the work were, on the whole, more single-mindedly committed to the Gothic style. L. N. Cottingham, whose advice was crucial in persuading the two Inns of Court to undertake a wholesale restoration rather than just a repair, was popular with the Cambridge Camden Society.[95] Willement's windows, wall paintings and other decorations were also welcomed by the *Ecclesiologist* (Plates 96, 98, 99): he had, after all, also worked on the Round Church in Cambridge for the Society.[96] But Willement and Cottingham were not Ecclesiologists *pur sang*. Willement, for one, was 'an heraldic artist first and last': far more interested in coats of arms than in any more spiritual symbolism.[97] Nor were they in charge. In 1840, for example, Cottingham had absolutely insisted that a stone altar should be installed in the Temple Church.[98] The restoration committee did not even bother to report this,[99] and they certainly did not follow his suggestion.[100] Moreover, it was Savage, Smirke and Burton who were responsible for the direction of the work — and for

[91] B. Clarke, *Church Builders of the Nineteenth Century*, 2nd edn, London 1969, 72.

[92] M. H. Port, *Six Hundred New Churches: a Study of the Church Building Commission, 1818–1856, and its Church Building Activities*, London 1961, 81.

[93] P. Bohan, 'Burton, Decimus', *Macmillan Encyclopedia of Architects*, 4 vols., New York and London 1982, I, 356–8 at 356.

[94] Crook, 'Sydney Smirke', 53.

[95] J. Myles, *L. N. Cottingham, 1787–1847: Architect of the Gothic Revival*, London 1996, 23.

[96] *Ecclesiologist*, I, 1842, 126; 2, 1843, 99.

[97] H. T. Kirby, 'Thomas Willement: an Heraldic Artist's Notebook', *Apollo*, 43, 1946, 47–8 at 47.

[98] MTA MT/15/TAM/274, Report on the Temple Church by Cottingham, 26 October 1840, 3.

[99] MTA MT/15/TAM/277, Report of the Joint Committee, 3 November 1840, 13–19.

[100] ITA TEM/2/4/2, Church Restoration, 19 August 1842.

many of the fittings. The plan, which positively prohibited ritualism; the reredos and wooden communion table; the other details that the *Ecclesiologist* found so disturbing: these were all designed by the architects, men who did not share the Cambridge Camden Society's obsession with strict Gothic rectitude or theological correctness. Sydney Smirke's defence of the wall paintings, for example, was hardly couched in Camdenian language. Although the introduction of religious art might be considered controversial, he argued, the 'architects' duty was that of simple restoration'.[101] The evidence showed that the original structure had been ornamented; so ornaments there needed to be. This result was a restoration which could only disappoint those who believed that they had found the key to true, and truly Christian, church building.

Indeed, the wall paintings and stained glass introduced by the restorers owed very little to the teachings of the Camden Society. Whilst the Ecclesiologists were devoted to the idea of introducing sacred symbolism and religious art into church buildings, much of the work done in the Temple Church was suspiciously secular. Although there was room for Willement's image of Christ and the Evangelists in one window (Plate 98), many others simply showed individuals associated with the Church: the Grand Priors of the English Templars, the arms of Royal benefactors, and so forth.[102] On the arch between the round and the nave was painted 'in a style strictly according with the date of the architecture, six enthroned figures of those English monarchs who were connected with the history of the Knights Templars and with this Church' (Plate 99).[103] This was about evoking medieval aesthetics rather than recreating medieval religion; about the atmosphere rather than the theology of the late twelfth and early thirteenth centuries. This was far removed from the injunctions of the Cambridge Camden Society. Instead, the artists and architects took the period in which the Church was built as their inspiration — and sought to produce work that was in keeping with it. Thus, the new font was modelled on an example taken from Alphington, near Exeter, which was believed to be in keeping with the style of the Round.[104] Likewise, when it came to choosing encaustic tiles, the architect went to Westminster Abbey, where the floor of the Chapter House was believed to be of the same date as the Temple Church.[105] These developments, then, were driven by a search for historical accuracy instead of Tractarian doctrine — and they were all the more popular for that.

No architectural project is ever unanimously loved, and, to be sure, there were problems; there was inevitably recrimination. As J. Mordaunt Crook showed, the work cost far more money than was originally intended and ultimately destroyed James Sav-

[101] S. Smirke, 'An Account of the Temple Church', in *Quarterly Papers on Architecture*, ed. J. Weale, 4 vols., London 1855, III, 6.
[102] R. H. Essex, 'Descriptive Catalogue of the Plates Illustrating the Restoration of the Temple Church, London', in *Quarterly Papers on Architecture*, ed. Weale.
[103] Burge, *Temple Church*, 57.
[104] Smirke, 'Temple Church', 6. Smirke did admit, however, that the font was actually of an earlier date.
[105] Burge, *Temple Church*, 45–6.

age's career.[106] It drove the evangelical Christopher Benson from the Temple Church, and led to accusations of betrayal from serious High Church journals. The majority of those committee members who oversaw the project did not live long to enjoy it. Francis Holt died in 1844;[107] John Newland died in 1847;[108] David Pollock died in 1848;[109] George Spence went mad and killed himself in 1850.[110] And William Burge, who had been the single most influential force behind the restoration, went bankrupt in 1847 — owing the fantastic sum of £56,000. He was imprisoned in York Castle for two years, and died a few months after his release in 1849.[111] Nonetheless, the work at the Temple Church outlived them all. It was to be repaired again in 1860–64, when — in response to pleas by the Ecclesiologically-minded George Gilbert Scott[112] — J. P. St Aubyn and Sydney Smirke added a conical roof to the round (Plate 93), reroofed the clearstorey and reinstated the western porch.[113] In 1908 Reginald Blomfield raised the altar and modified the reredos, whilst in 1911 W. D. Caroë restored the porch and bell tower.[114] In 1929, the Gothic altarpiece was removed altogether and replaced with a simple curtain.[115] Yet even this did not affect the fundamental structure of the church, nor the way it functioned. The restoration of the early 1840s was left essentially intact. The idea of returning it to its state under the Templars — to what was believed to be its original, ideal form — remained unchallenged.

The services at the church were similarly unchanging in their form. There were occasional complaints that the sermons were too long.[116] There were repeated proposals to replace the stalls — not least because they had not been designed with a choral service in mind, and thus made the singing of the choir much harder.[117] Yet continuity remained the keynote — and much change was only in the minds of visitors. As the choirmaster Edward Hopkins observed in the 1880s, 'Years ago, people said I played too fast, now they say I play too slow; but I have kept the same time.'[118] Partly, this lack of change reflected the success of the choir and the popularity of the music; partly, it reflected the difficulty of getting both the Inns of Court to agree on any particular course

[106] See also *The Times* 9 July 1841, 7; 23 July 1841, 5.
[107] M. Lobban, 'Holt, Francis Ludlow (1779–1844)', *ODNB* (accessed 27 Feb. 2008).
[108] J. B. Williamson, *The Middle Temple Bench Book*, 2nd edn, London 1937, 214.
[109] J. M. Rigg, 'Pollock, Sir David (1780–1847)', rev. H. Mooney, *ODNB* (accessed 27 Feb. 2008).
[110] D. E. C. Yale, 'Spence, George (1787–1850)', *ODNB* (accessed 26 Feb. 2008); *The Times*, 17 December 1850, 6.
[111] ITA DIS/1/Bi, William Burge.
[112] ITA Bench Table Orders, 5 December 1862.
[113] J. P. St Aubyn, 'An Account of the Repairs at the Temple Church', *RIBA Transactions*, 1st series, 14, 1863–4, 153–6.
[114] Lewer and Dark, *Temple Church*, 136–7.
[115] Griffith-Jones, *Temple Church*, 71.
[116] *The Times*, 29 December 1860, 8.
[117] ITA TEM/3/10, Reseating in the nave, 1906.
[118] Quoted in Curwen, *Worship Music*, 350

of action. Yet, whatever the cause, the effect was clear. The church was frozen in about
1845 — and remained so until the bombs began to fall almost a hundred years later.

For *Country Life* — and, as we have seen, for others — the Blitz was scarcely a dis-
aster, and the 'destruction of the Victorian fittings was hardly a matter for regret'. It
was, the magazine went on to say, 'a grand opportunity . . . to undo almost all the pain-
ful effects achieved in the nineteenth-century restorations'. So the conical roof installed
by St Aubyn was removed and battlements reinstituted. The Wren reredos returned,
and plain natural oak benches were installed — with an aisle between them for proces-
sions. No attempt was made to paint the walls or the ceilings, and the glass, by Carl
Edwards, owed very little to early-Victorian taste. 'The interior', concluded *Country Life*,
'has come alive, is no longer a dull expressionless mask.'[119] This was, in many respects,
however, an unfair judgement. What was destroyed in the Blitz was not a run-of-the-
mill Victorian restoration. It was not just another example — like the thousands of other
examples — of the impact of the Ecclesiologists on the Church of England.[120] In that
sense, writers from Frank MacKinnon to *Country Life* were inaccurate as well as unjust.
It was something rather more interesting than that.

This was a monument to a moment in architectural and ecclesiastical history:
a period before the full impact of the Cambridge Camden Society had been felt. Here
was work by some of the leading architects of their generation — a generation that was
to be condemned by its immediate successors, and forgotten or merely disparaged by
succeeding generations. Here was a way of worshipping and style of music that was to
be hugely admired, but very rarely imitated (Colour Plate XII). Here was an attempt to
live out the antiquarian principles of its period; to remove all evidence of change and
to return the church to what was believed to be its original, ideal form. Here, until the
night of 10 May 1941 was a true period piece; and a period piece that will never — and
can never — be restored.

[119] A. Oswald, 'Temple Church Restored', *Country Life*, 124, 1958, 1104–5.
[120] J. Mordaunt Crook, *The Dilemma of Style: Architectural Ideas from the Picturesque to the Post-
Modern,* London 1987, 63, notes that by 1854 a quarter of all parish churches had been restored; by
1873 one-third.

Robin Griffith-Jones

'The latter Glory of this House':
Some Details of Damage and Repair, 1840–1941

THIS BOOK WOULD BE INCOMPLETE without addressing two aspects of the church's recent history: the age and degeneration of the carvings on the west doorway; and the night of the fire, 10–11 May 1941.[1]

THE WEST DOORWAY

The following is a tentative reconstruction of the work undertaken on the west doorway since the early 19th century.[2]

In the *Gentleman's Magazine*, 1783, (accompanied by a fold-out engraving of the doorway) Reuben d'Moundt identified among the capitals' figures Henry II on one side, Eleanor and the Patriarch Heraclius on the other; 'the figures are very perfect, and it would be almost a proof of deficiency in sight, to say that they have been impaired by time'.[3] His insistence suggests that the doorway's condition was giving rise to concern. The *Gentleman's Magazine* reported again in 1808 that the doorway was 'in excellent preservation'.[4] Substantial works were carried out on the church in 1811, and J. T. Smith's etching of the doorway, 1813, bore an inscription: 'Sacred Architecture: West Entrance to the Vestibule of the Temple Church. / External specimen of the decorated Norman Style (This beautiful specimen has now become more worthy of the attention of the antiquary, on account of the alterations it has undergone from the plasterers and painters in the late repairs of the church).'

The Society of Antiquaries still has Nash's drawings of the capitals (Plate 89); they

---

[1] The post-War repair of the church is well described by Lewer and Dark, *Temple Church*, 152–72.

[2] I summarise the accounts of the work in 1695 on p. 154 above. I will be drawing here on various papers in *Reports and Opinions of Architects and Surveyors regarding the Condition and Renovation of the Temple Church, 1842–1927* (Middle Temple Library).

[3] *Gentleman's Magazine*, 53 pt 2, 1783, 547–9.

[4] *Gentleman's Magazine*, 127 pt 2, 1808, 999.

were used for a plate engraved in 1818 and published in 1828 (Plate 90).[5] The carving of figures and foliage is all shown as crisp. R. W. Billings shows similar clarity in 1838, but with far less foliage under the faces in the innermost band of carving over the door.[6] We return below to two original voussoirs from this innermost archivolt, removed during the restorations of 1841–2 and now in the Victoria and Albert Museum. They match Nash's rendering (1818) more closely than Billings's (1838); we may surmise that Billings generalised the scant foliage that had survived under most of the heads, and that two of the few still showing the full decoration were preserved and ultimately reached the V&A.[7] According to Billings, 'there can be little doubt that the columns themselves are not original, as they are thicker at the bases than at the capitals. They were, most probably, restored at the time the church was wainscoted.'[8]

In 1841–2 Decimus Burton and Sydney Smirke reported: 'On removing the plaster and colouring that filled up the enriched archivolts, which are surprisingly perforated and sunk, we find that those carved stones are so perished as to be for the most part incapable of receiving reparations and that they ought to be entirely new. We find also that on close examination of the six shafts of the door jambs (originally of polished Purbeck marble) stone has since been substituted in some cases, whilst in others new Purbeck marble shafts have been supplied having a Roman entasis altogether unsuited to the style of the original work.'[9] None of the columns is, in 2010, of Purbeck marble.

The title page of T. S. Boys, *London as It Is*, 1842, is engaging for its portrayal of cobwebs, cracks and missing elements in the columns (Plate 100). Charles Ollier's accompanying notes reveal one reason for the doorway's prominence in the series: 'This is perhaps the most ancient doorway left in the metropolis. It is supposed to be, for the most part, nearly in its primitive state.'[10] The lithograph is based on a pencil drawing on tracing paper with the detail given: 'sketched 8.4.1840'.[11] By 1842, the artist was in a position to make a light-hearted comment on the famously lavish restoration finished, that June, after two years' work; he shows London as it was and soon, thanks to the graffiti of other — artistic — 'boys', will be again. The Temple Church must have been in the public eye in 1840, to merit inclusion; and certainly was, by the time of the series' publication in 1842.[12]

[5]   *Vetusta Monumenta*, v, London 1828, pl. xxiii.

[6]   Billings, *Illustrations*, Pl. xiii. Differences in the profile of the colonnettes and angle of the figures may be due to sketches made at different angles.

[7]   These two voussoirs are two of four stones from the west doorway now in the V&A; see p. 212 below.

[8]   Billings, *Illustrations*, 53.

[9]   *Reports and Opinions*, 2.

[10]   There were evidences, admitted Ollier, that the columns had been 'perverted by subsequent restorations' (*London as It Is*, 'Historical and Descriptive Notices'). The series was issued in a folder on whose cover was a vignette of the (even more totemic) London Stone; see p. 142 n. 36 above.

[11]   J. Roundell, *Thomas Shotter Boys, 1803–1874*, London 1974, 49 (as in an American private collection).

[12]   The series' extended review in *The Times*, 11 July 1842, 10, remarked that 'the ancient doorway to the Temple church' was 'a splendid piece of architectural, or rather, of antiquarian drawing'.

How much of the old stonework did Burton and Smirke renew? The *Gentleman's Magazine*, 18, 1842, 521 reported that 'the entrance porch is for the most part new, the extensively ornamented old door way having been partly renewed and the remainder reworked and restored'. Paul Williamson points out that the photographs in the Royal Commission volume of 1929 show the whole door in pristine condition, the voussoirs as crisp as the undoubtedly new jambs (Plate 101).[13] He concludes that Burton and Smirke extensively or completely renewed the voussoirs.

Williamson reinforces his point by reference to four stones from the west door now in the V&A.[14] Decimus Burton was listed as a donor of architectural fragments to the Royal Architectural Museum in 1855, and these four stones were part of the RAM collection in 1876 prior to their transfer to the V&A. It is at least likely that they were taken from the west doorway during Burton's restoration of 1841–2.

Two of these stones are voussoirs from the innermost archivolt.[15] The sketch by Neil MacFadyen, 1985 (Plate 102), clarifies their relation to the stones now in place. The V&A stones are 6 in. deep and 5 in. high. Immediately under the carved area is a horizontal return, 1¼ in. deep with a clear line of oil or wax ½ in. back from the front edge; behind this line, the stone's surface is rough-cut. The line marks the edge of the course once laid below the V&A's stones. The stones now in the archivolt show similar carved decoration, but a quite different shape of stone: the blocks are 15 in. deep and 7 in. high; beneath the principal carving is a hollow, 3¾ in. across, beneath which is a 10 in. horizontal return. The clear conclusion was drawn by Williamson and MacFadyen: this whole innermost order of the archivolt had been rebuilt in the 1840s.[16]

C. M. L. Gardam turned her attention to the V&A's foliate voussoir taken from the arch's outer order. Nash's engraving is compatible with the V&A stone, but the voussoirs presently in place are not: 'the four petalled leaves that curl back and meet point to point are spread much further apart on the doorway today, with a very large beaded

In the Guildhall Collection is an early-stage, less detailed proof of each plate. The proof of the doorway showed fewer cracks and cobwebs than the finished plate; in the plate's later stages Boys played up the doorway's mustiness.

[13] RCHM, *The City*, pl. 181.

[14] P. Williamson, *Catalogue of Romanesque Sculpture*, Victoria and Albert Museum, London 1983, nos. 45–8 (A.19, 20, 21, 22 — 1916), and 'The West Doorway of the Temple Church, London', *Burlington Magazine*, 127, 1985, 716.

[15] The following details are taken from N. MacFadyen, 'Temple Church, London: The Great West Doorway', Association for Studies in the Conservation of Historic Buildings, *Transactions* 9, 1984, 3–6 and P. Williamson, 'West Doorway'. The work of 1983–5, encouraged by George Zarnecki (MacFadyen, 6), undermined Zarnecki's own contention that much of the stonework on the doorway was original, 'The West Doorway of the Temple Church in London', in *Beiträge zur Kunst des Mittelalters: Festschrift für Hans Wentzel zum 60. Geburtstag)*, Berlin 1975 (repr. in G. Zarnecki, *Studies in Romanesque Sculpture*, London 1979), 245–53.

[16] Baylis, *Temple Church*, 9, noted that the porch visible in his day 'is slightly different' from the porch represented in J. Britton, The *Architectural Antiquities of Great Britain*, 4 vols., London 1807–14, I, 16, pl. 3, and in *Vetusta Monumenta*, 'but is probably more in accordance with the original.'

fruit in between'. In the second and third orders as well, Gardam observes differences between Nash's rendering and the present stones.[17]

There may well also have been a chemical intervention in the 1840s. Investigations in 1998 revealed that most (and perhaps all) of the ensemble, including the two voussoirs known to have been inserted in 1841–2, had been coated with a layer of white lead.[18] This suggested to the investigator that white lead was applied to the whole doorway after 1842 in order to unite the appearance of the old and the new stonework. Its effect will have been catastrophic. 'Because white lead is an excellent oil dryer, it was more often than not applied in that medium. If such were the case in this instance . . . we might well have established a reason for which the doorway began to decay at so rapid a rate through the course of the nineteenth century.' The subsequent work undertaken on the doorway 'lends weight to the hypothesis that an impermeable lead-based paint film applied to the stonework of the doorway had . . . in little over fifty years caused gross damage to it'.[19]

Deterioration was marked in the years after 1842; Smirke was consulted in 1856 and 1857.[20] In 1895 Blomfield reported that 'after a time [soon after 1842] the whole of the West porch seems to have been painted' to protect the new Caen stone from further decay. Blomfield recommended the removal of loose powdery stone and treatment with 'Fluate'. In 1907 T. G. Jackson reported that the stonework was 'in advanced decay, and urged rebuilding the arches in a durable stone, 'preserving the design of the ornamentation, which is no doubt a copy of the original'.[21]

By 1912 the Inns' surveyors feared 'that it will be requisite to re-instate the whole of the grouped, moulded and carved columns and arches'.[22] In 1912–14 W. D. Caröe cleaned away paint, putty and dirt, and so discovered that one or two outside pilasters on the north side had been renewed and painted black to harmonise with earlier work. After the paint's removal, Caröe treated the stone with Hemmingways Patent Siasic process.[23] Unsurprisingly, he turned his attention as well to the doorway's history, and reported that 'no evidence was found that the Doorway itself had ever been restored'.[24]

In 1926–7 Caröe reported again. He recommended treating the stone with mastic (to make up the decayed stones) and the application of Prof. Laurie's 'Siliconester'.

[17] Gardam, 'Restorations', 105.

[18] This coating had been identified in 1983 as 'limewash'.

[19] C. Weeks, *Conservation Report: Temple Church, Great West Doorway*, Cliveden Conservation Workshop, 1998, 4. Weeks found remains of medieval paint: numerous small traces of red ochre along the joints; one large island of red ochre; one large island of a grey colour seemingly comprised of a number of layers; and, on the abaci, numerous traces of a (red?) layer discoloured black.

[20] MTA, MTP.R (1855–60), 21 November 1856, 16 January 1857. The church's interior will have been causing concern too: *Pictorial World*, 19 October 1878, described the vault's paintings as fading 'very rapidly'.

[21] *Reports and Opinions*, 7.

[22] *Report on the Temple Church sent by the Surveyors of the Inner and Middle Temples*, 17 December 1912 (Middle Temple Library).

[23] Patented in 1910, patent no. 28284: based on the so-called water-glass technique (sodium or potassium silicates) with the further application of 'arsenic acid', Weeks, *Conservation*, 2.

[24] Report on the Temple Church, 17 December 1912, *Reports and Opinions*, 11.

Caröe now had further evidence to hand, with which to assess the dates of the door-way's parts. He wrote to the Under Treasurer of Middle Temple, 21 October 1927: 'It might interest you to know that we found the old Norman work cut away at the back of the new Eastern responds as well as at the back of the pillars of the doorway, from which there is no doubt whatever that no part of the existing pillars are part of the original Norman work. No documentary records can get away from the definite fact found upon the site.' He had, it seems, already reported to the Inns a change of mind from his view of 1912–14: 'I have pointed out before that this doorway is not ancient, but is a last-century construction, and probably an attempted imitation of a decayed doorway it now replaces.'[25]

So we come back, full circle, to the conclusions of Paul Williamson and Neil Mac-Fadyen, who investigated the doorway in 1983–5.[26] 'In 1983 the doorway presented a sorry appearance. Soot deposits on the stone, combined with traditional treatments of hot oil or wax and limewash, had resulted in an impervious skin of calcium sulphate with a build-up of moisture and chemical salts beneath. Where this skin had burst more rapid decay had set in, causing deep pitting and the loss of much fine carved work.'[27] In 1984 the doorway was cleaned by air abrasive methods, and some chemical consoli-dation (with Brethane) was undertaken.[28] In 1998, further cleaning was undertaken by laser.[29]

[25] Quoted in the report of Carden, Godfrey and MacFadyen, Architects, April 1970, 2.

[26] The report of Williamson and MacFadyen superseded the valuable paper by George Zar-necki, 'West Doorway'. Zarnecki, working with the architect W. E. Godfrey, argued that — with the exception of the columns, the carved jambs and probably some sections of the archivolts inserted in 1842 — the work is largely original. Zarnecki believed that 'the capitals and busts on either side of the doorway are made of only two blocks of stone and that, consequently, nothing has been inserted in this part of the doorway.' (The 1984 cleaning would reveal that the demi-figures 'are in fact carved from quite small stones including the innermost pair which were previously thought to be part of the main door jamb', MacFadyen, 'Temple Church', 5.) Zarnecki, 'West Doorway', 248, 252, suspected that the two least-weathered busts — the middle two on the northern side — had been 'somewhat recarved'.

[27] MacFadyen, 'Temple Church', 3. A fuller account of the stone's condition was given by J. Ashurst of the Department of Environment, August 1983 (report in the Estates Office, Middle Temple): 'The stones have not been washed directly by rain and have suffered from being in a semi-sheltered environment in which polluted moisture forms on the surface of walls, reacting slowly with the limestone to form a thin, crystalline skin of calcium sulphate. In time, parts of this sulphate skin split and disrupt the surface, shedding small flakes of sulphated stone. Traditional remedial measures of brushing in hot oil or wax have unfortunately exacerbated the situation by blocking the pores of the stones and encouraging the deterioration of the decaying areas; once a spall forms adjacent to an impermeable oily surface the exposed area becomes a sacrificial zone to which salts migrate, deepening and extending the crystallisation damage. Another problem associated with oil and wax is that dirt is easily attached to the surface and rapid soiling ensues. A common cosmetic solution to this is the application of limewash, or lime and size or casein; such a lime coat has been applied over the dirt and the oil at some time.' Ashurst seems not to have known of the further chemical interventions of the previous century.

[28] MacFadyen, 'Temple Church', records this work. The Brethane was applied to the whole of the innermost order of the arch and to the abaci, capitals and demi-figure of both jambs.

[29] Weeks, Conservation, records this work.

It is a sad irony, that successive well-intentioned chemical interventions since the 1840s are likely to have hastened just the decay they were intended to forestall.

10 MAY 1941

In London the night of 10 May 1941 was clear; the moon was almost full. The River Thames was at low ebb; water pressure was weak. The sirens sounded at 11.00 pm; the raid lasted all night. German crews flew two, even three sorties each; 571 German sorties were flown in all, dropping nearly 100,000 incendiaries.[30]

Three witnesses, all of them on fire-watch duty, later described the night in the Temple. Mrs Robinson, wife of the Subtreasurer of Inner Temple and resident in the Inn, was for part of the evening on the south side of the church, in the group trying to save Lamb Building (standing north–south across what is now the centre of Church Court) and Inner Temple Library (the next building to the south); she was also extinguishing canisters on the roof of King's Bench Walk (two hundred yards to the east). Stephen Benson was working with Mrs Robinson for much of the night. J. W. Morris, K.C., had been two courtyards to the west (in Brick Court) when he was told of the fire on the church's roof.[31] Mrs Robinson recorded later:

> Until the night of 10th–11th May I had never realised what an air raid could be like. That night was one of terror. Trouble started at 11:00 pm and right from the commencement everything was hectic. H.E.s fell in all directions — one explosion followed by another. . . . Incendiaries and H.E.s dropped incessantly. Planes were overhead all the time. The Temple Church caught fire and it was then we discovered that we could not get any water to it. We had to watch the fire spreading and were not able to do a thing to help.

The incendiary landed next to the parapet at the church's north-east corner; the fire spread south across the roof, then westwards along it. An attempt to place a ladder up the church's wall was abandoned; there would be no water to reach the roof.

Mr Morris went from Lamb Building, seemingly saved from danger from the church's fire, round to the north-west of the church, to Farrar's Building; sparks were flying from the church onto its temporary roof. So the Temple group missed the offer of help from the fire-party of Hoare's Bank, behind the Master's House and to the north-east of the church. The Bank's fire-party saw the incendiary land on the church (on the side nearest to the Bank) and ran a hose from the Bank's own well to the Master's House, the nozzle end being dropped into the Temple.

[30] Details from *The Blitz Then and Now*, ed. W. G. Ramsey, 3 vols., London n.d. [1987–9], ii, 608–18, with photographs of Ludgate Hill, 612–5.

[31] The recollections of Stephen Benson, J. W. Morris and Mrs Robinson were collected in Sir Frank MacKinnon, *The Ravages of the War in the Inner Temple*, London 1945, 22, 27–30. The present quotations from Mrs Robinson are taken from the transcript of an interview she gave about 2000 for Inner Temple's yearbook. She lived in Inner Temple until her death in 2007.

The Bank's fire-party shouted for the Temple firewatchers. No one responded; the Temple's firewatchers were variously on the church's south or on its north-west side. A porter from the Bank went round to the church, but was told that the Temple had the matter in hand and that the Fire Brigade was coming.[32]

But the Fire Brigade had no water. Mrs Robinson recalled:

> The fire brigade stood by helplessly. I asked the man in charge if he couldn't get the apparatus needed for relaying water from the Thames. He assured me that he had tried but the tide was too low. The fire was spreading and rapidly approaching the round. My husband . . . went into the Church and returned with his jacket covered with tiny globules of silvery lead which must have dripped from the piping.

Mr Benson also went into the Church, when the organ was already in flames and part of the roof had fallen in; he rescued a prayer book and an altar chair, to serve as memorials of the old furnishings.

The Senior Warden recorded:

> At two o'clock in the morning it was as light as day. Charred papers and embers were flying through the air, bombs and shrapnel all around. It was an awe-inspiring sight. . . . I saw an N.F.S. truck at the top of King's Bench Walk and noticed that the firemen were loading this with mattresses, blankets and equipment. I asked what they were doing and was told that their house was on fire and they were moving out. I felt rather helpless when I saw that even the professionals were leaving, but there was no water, and such fires could not be fought with axes alone.[33]

Inner Temple Hall caught fire and was ruined; the flames spread to Lamb Building, which was — after all the work to save it earlier in the night — destroyed. Mrs Robinson:

> It was not until 6:00am that the 'All Clear' sounded. We did not notice daybreak — the flames were so bright that there was no transition of night to day . . . All Sunday the fires raged . . . The fires burnt for several days — even a fortnight afterwards we had to call in the fire brigade to a fire which had started again in the cellar.

On 10 May 1,436 people in London were killed, over 2,000 injured, 14 hospitals damaged. Westminster Hall and the Abbey, the House of Commons, Law Courts, Mint, Mansion House, Tower and British Museum were all hit; the Temple Church, St Clement Danes, St Mary-le-Bow, Holy Trinity, Sloane Street, and St Columba's, Pont Street,

---

[32] Report [for Hoare's Bank by the Bank's fire-warden] on the Fire in Temple Church, West Fleet Street Area during Raid on Saturday 10th May 1941, in the archives of Hoare's Bank (Ref. no.: HB/7/B/9). I am grateful to the partners of Hoare's Bank for permission to publish this extract.

[33] *Middle Temple Ordeal* (by 'a lady member of and resident in the Middle Temple who took her part in the fight', according to the Foreword by Mr Justice Cassels), London 1948, 37.

were damaged or destroyed.[34] It was the worst night in London's Blitz; it was also the last. Hitler had already on 30 March informed his High Command that Germany would launch its attack on the Soviet Union on 22 June 1941, exactly one year after the fall of France; German attention and bombers were being diverted to the East.[35]

David Lewer records that on 11 May at about noon two members of the church's choir came into the church.

> The fire was still burning in the Round where huge baulks of timber had been placed over the effigies to protect them from blast, thus providing additional fuel for the flames. . . . The pews and choirstalls were reduced to lines of ashes, the words and music still readable on the fragile leaves of what had been rows of psalters and hymn-books.[36]

The damaged church and its environs were used at least twice to boost morale. A montage (now in the Guildhall Collection) of warriors in the roofless Round, from the Templars of old through to the service-men and -women of the 1940s, made of the War a new crusade and encouraged those who had inherited the church to match the resilience and Christian values of those who built it (Plate 106). In this drawing the effigies — and their spirit — have come alive.

[34] The German airman Robert Götz recorded his feelings as he returned home that night. 'Return flight from London. The moonlight reflections in the Channel are wonderful, fabulous. The attack and its dangers are behind us. These relaxed homeward flights, with the engines rumbling quietly and evenly, lull us into the feeling that nothing more can happen. Any attempt to speak is silenced by the sight of the wide, silvery, dreamlike landscape. Who could restrain himself from feeling deeply thankful?' See *The Blitz Then and Now*, II, 616, one of several passages translated from Götz's previously unpublished manuscript, *Bestrafte Träume*; for Götz's biography, ibid., 12. As Götz flew southwards across the Channel, British pilots were flying northwards, home from their own sorties on Bremen, Hamburg, Emden, Rotterdam and Berlin; on Monday 12 May *The Times* duly boosted morale with a report on their effect.

[35] How near had 10 May brought London to a collapse of morale and daily life? Reports differed. Quentin Reynolds (reporter of England's unflinching courage; see A. Calder, *The Myth of the Blitz*, London 1991, 223–7) later wrote that on this night 'Britain won the war', *Only the Stars are Neutral*, London 1942, 27–41. A second American journalist, Larry Rue, 'began to realise to what deep depths of their being the 10 May raid had shocked and shaken the people of London. It was just one raid too much' (in P. Ackroyd, *London: The Biography*, London 2000, 747).

[36] D. Lewer, *A Spiritual Song*, London 1961, 431. The Inns' surveyors had sought to have the effigies protected with sand, not timber, Lewer and Dark, *Temple Church*, 149. James Pope-Hennessey wrote an elegy on the effigies between 15 October 1940 (when Middle Temple Hall was damaged) and 10 May 1941. 'These two groups of Templar Knights, with their contorted legs and swirling jupons beneath their chain-mail tunics . . . have all the frozen beauty of eternally suspended motion, and the smooth sure elegance of birds: they seem to float upon the pavement of the Temple, beneath the early Gothic arches, like a flock of black swans' (C. Beaton, *History under Fire: 52 Photographs of Air Raid Damage to London Buildings, 1940–41*, with commentary by J. Pope-Hennessy, London 1941, 30). Cecil Beaton would return to the Temple for a more famous shoot, discussed below.

Subtler and more famous is the set of photographs of the church and its environs taken by Cecil Beaton, one of them published in *Vogue*, September 1941 (Plate 107). The magazine had been founded in 1916; here was its Silver Jubilee issue. 'It seems to us fitting,' wrote the leader, 'that in this war *Vogue* should come to full maturity: war-baby becomes war-woman.' The model, her back turned to the readers as she invites them to follow her gaze, looks at the memorial to the cloisters' reconstruction in the 1680s. The picture was titled, 'Fashion is indestructible.' Its caption read: 'Her pose unshaken, she reads about the other fire of London in which the earlier Temple was destroyed.' The article on the facing page was, 'Why Women read *Vogue*' by Cecil Willett Cunnington (the author, as *Vogue* reminded its readers, of *Why Women Wear Clothes*, London 1941): 'Fashions, formerly static, have become dynamic; that is to say, they are not satisfied merely to present a picture but their aim is now to imply action, mental as well as physical.' The new forms of fashion express women's 'complete competence in work or play'. Beaton's image was a more powerful statement of the theme: fashion itself and the calm assurance that valued it were both to be indestructible — not least in the man's world, now empty, of the Temple.[37]

Sir Frank MacKinnon (Treasurer of Inner Temple in 1945) compiled the report in 1944 from which some of the details above have been taken. MacKinnon reveals how far and fast taste had changed since the nineteenth-century refurbishments.

For my own part, seeing how dreadfully the Church had been despoiled by its pretended friends a century before, I do not grieve so very acutely for the havoc now wrought by its avowed enemies . . . If the Church is now once again truly restored, it can hardly fail to be far more beautiful than the Victorian vandals made it for us. To have got rid of their awful stained glass windows, their ghastly pulpit, their hideous encaustic tiles, their abominable pews and seats (on which alone they spent over £10,000), will be almost a blessing in disguise. An ancient text about the first Temple may even, I hope, be apposite. 'The latter glory of this house shall be greater than the former, saith the Lord of Hosts; and in this place will I give peace, saith the Lord of Hosts.'[38]

[37] *Vogue*, September 1941, 31–3.
[38] MacKinnon, *Ravages*, 33 (quoting Haggai 2.9 RV). Further lines from MacKinnon are quoted by William Whyte, pp. 195–6 above.

Black-and-White Plates

Plate 1

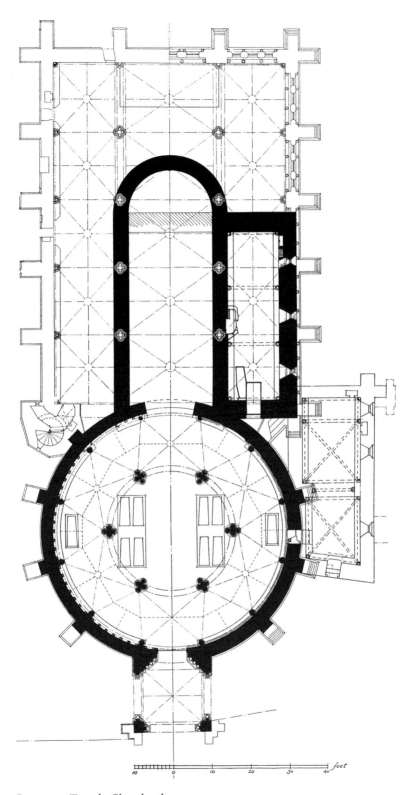

PLATE 1. Temple Church, plan

PLATE 2. Temple Church, west porch from north-west (west buttresses added in the 1860s and 1870s, upwards extension of aisle wall added in the 1950s)

PLATE 3. Saint-Denis, Benedictine abbey, chevet interior looking north-east

PLATE 4. Temple Church, upper part of nave pier

PLATE 6. Noyon Cathedral, north choir gallery, intermediate support

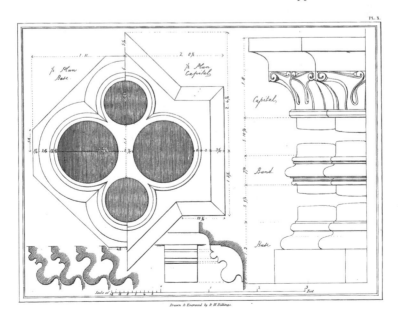

PLATE 5. Temple Church, plan and details of nave pier, from R. W. Billings, *Illustrations of the Temple Church*, 1838

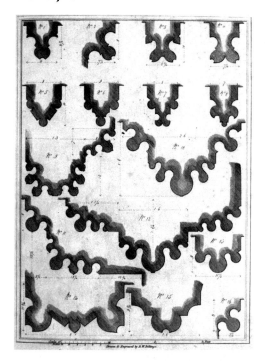

PLATE 7. Temple Church, profiles of nave aisle vault ribs (above) and nave main arcade arches (below), from R. W. Billings, *Illustrations of the Temple Church*, 1838

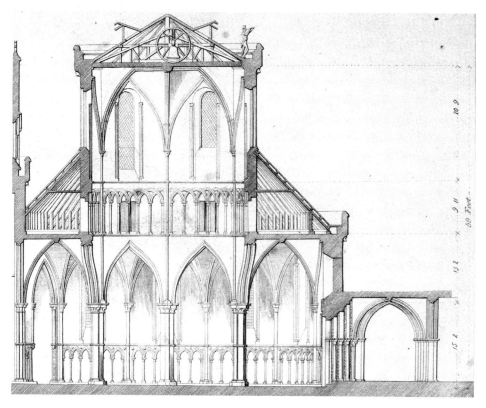

PLATE 8. Temple Church, east–west section through nave, from R. W. Billings, *Illustrations of the Temple Church*, 1838 (the left-hand clerestory window is shown opened out to its full original height)

PLATE 9. Temple Church, triangular vault compartment in north part of nave aisle

PLATE 10. Paris, St-Martin-des-Champs, Benedictine priory, detail of respond and vault on north side of axial chapel

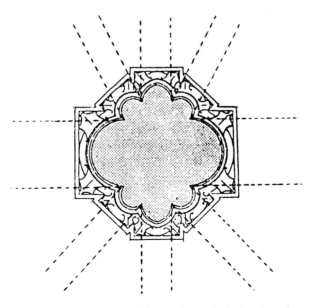

PLATE 11. Dommartin, Premonstratensian abbey, plan of choir pier, from C. Enlart, *Manuel d'Archéologie Française*, 1927 (broken lines showing projection of vault ribs added by C. Wilson)

Plate 12

PLATE 12. Temple Church, south part of nave aisle looking south-west

PLATE 13. Temple Church, quadripartite vault compartment in south part of nave aisle

PLATE 14. Namps-au-Val, parish church, vault of chancel looking east, from C. Enlart, *Monuments religieux de l'architecture romane et de transition dans la région picarde*, 1895

PLATE 15. Temple Church, capital of nave pier, detail

PLATE 16. Tournai Cathedral, capital of main arcade of north transept apse

PLATE 17. Temple Church, capital of nave pier, detail

PLATE 18. Temple Church, capital on north side of westernmost transverse rib of vault of 12th-century chancel

PLATE 19. Tournai Cathedral, north nave arcade, fifth free-standing pier from the east, capital on north-west face

PLATE 20. Tournai Cathedral, spur on base of main arcade of north transept apse

Plate 21

PLATE 21. Temple Church, west door, voussoirs

PLATE 22. Dommartin, hemicycle
capital, detail

PLATE 23. Dommartin, hemicycle
capital, detail

PLATE 24. Saint-Denis, chevet,
capital of columnar pier between two northernmost radiating chapels

PLATE 25. Berteaucourt-les-Dames, Benedictine nunnery, detail of west door

PLATE 26. Canterbury Cathedral, Benedictine priory, north-east corner pier of infirmary cloister (formerly with four shafts)

PLATE 27. Paris, Temple Church, interior of nave looking west, detail of engraving by Jean Marot (1619?–1679)

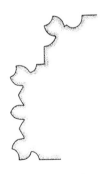

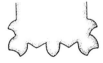

PLATE 28. York Minster, profile of choir main arcades and transverse ribs

PLATE 29. York Minster, choir crypt, base of pier at centre of north-east transept

PLATE 30. Ripon Minster, north choir aisle, vault respond

PLATE 31. Fontenay, Cistercian abbey, chapter house, pier

PLATE 32. Bridlington, Augustinian priory, capital from cloister arcade

PLATE 33. Temple Church, west porch, capital of east respond of north arch

PLATE 34. Bridlington Priory, capital (original setting unknown)

PLATE 35. Winchester, Hospital of St Cross, interior of choir looking south-east

PLATE 36. Temple Church choir, exterior, south side

PLATE 37. Salisbury Cathedral Trinity Chapel, view to north-east

PLATE 38. Winchester Castle hall, interior view to north-west

PLATE 39. Temple Church choir, piscina in south aisle

PLATE 40. Winchester Cathedral retrochoir, view to north-east

PLATE 41. Temple Church choir, head on north jamb of north lateral arch between nave and choir

Plate 42

PLATE 42. Temple Church, floor tiles found during the Victorian restoration of 1839–42

Plate 43

PLATE 43. Temple Church, St Anne's Chapel, 1823

Plate 44

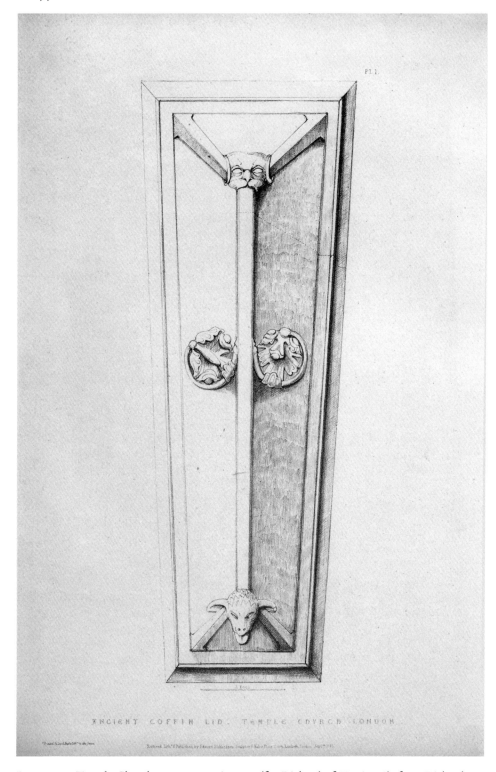

PLATE 44. Temple Church, grave cover in nave (for Richard of Hastings?), from Richardson, *Effigies of the Temple Church*, 1843

Plate 45

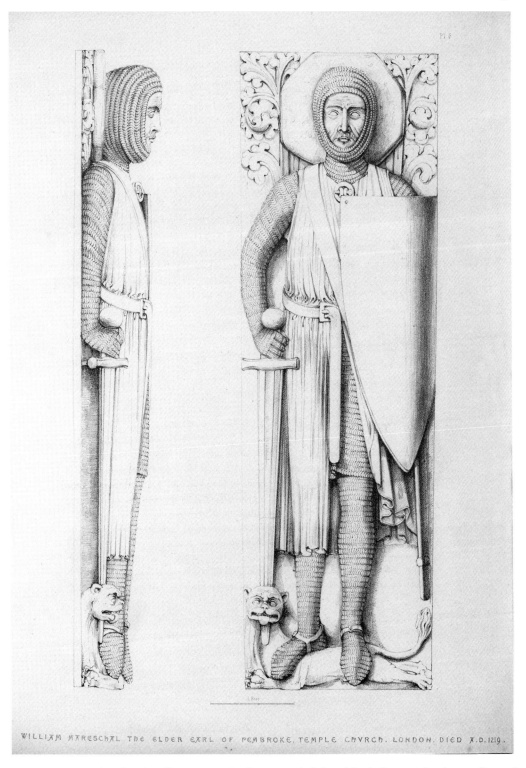

WILLIAM MARESCHAL THE ELDER EARL OF PEMBROKE. TEMPLE CHVRCH. LONDON. DIED A.D.1219.

PLATE 45. Temple Church, effigy in nave (William Marshal the Elder?), from Richardson, *Effigies of the Temple Church*, 1843

Plate 46

PLATE 46. Temple Church, effigy in nave (Gilbert Marshal?), from Richardson, *Effigies of the Temple Church*, 1843

PLATE 48. Temple Church, head of bishop's effigy

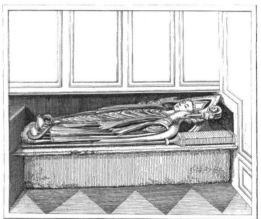

PLATE 47. Temple church, effigy in south choir aisle (Silvester de Everdon, Bishop of Carlisle?), from Richardson, *Effigies of the Temple Church*, 1843

PLATE 49. Temple Church, engraving showing original location of bishop's effigy in south choir aisle, from Smith, *Antiquities of London*, 1791–1800

PLATE 50. Temple Church, view of nave showing indent for brass in the foreground, from Clarke, *Architectura Ecclesiastica Londini*, 1819

PLATE 51. Temple Church, detail of indent for brass, from Clarke, *Architectura Ecclesiastica Londini*, 1819

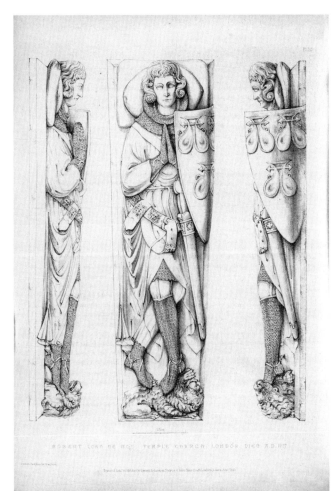

PLATE 52. Temple Church, effigy in nave south ambulatory of William de Ros?, from Richardson, *Effigies of the Temple Church*, 1843

PLATE 53. Temple Church, effigy of William de Ros? (detail)

Plates 54–55

PLATE 54. Bedale (north Yorkshire), effigy of Brian Fitzalan, from T. and G. Hollis, *The Monumental Effigies of Great Britain,* 1840–42

PLATE 55. Bedale, tomb of Brian Fitzalan, from E. Blore, *Monumental Remains of Noble and Eminent Persons . . .* , 1826

Plate 56

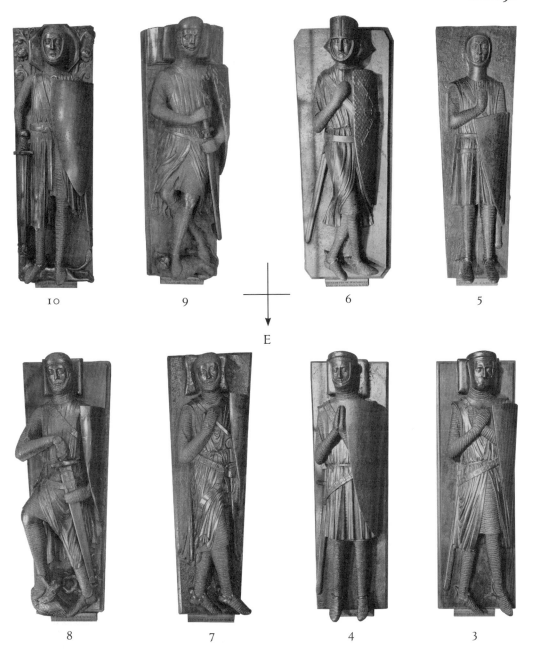

10   9   E   6   5

8   7   4   3

PLATE 56. Temple Church, layout of the thirteenth-century military effigies since 1842, from photographs by Bedford Lemere, c.1885

Plate 57

A

B

PLATE 57. Temple Church, Purbeck marble effigy, RCHM no. 10. A. Etching of a drawing, published by Thomas and George Hollis, 1840; B. After bomb damage in 1941

Plate 58

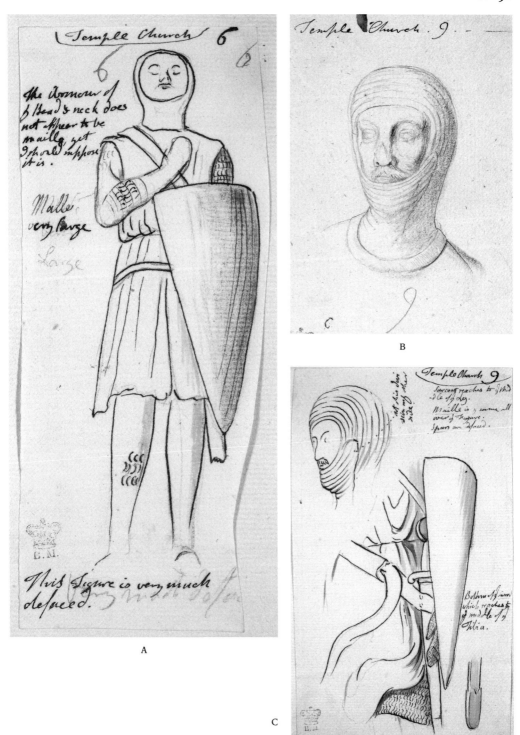

PLATE 58. Temple Church, Purbeck marble effigies. Drawings and notes by Thomas Kerrich (d. 1828). A. RCHM no. 5. B–C. RCHM no. 7

Plate 59

A

B

PLATE 59. A. Temple Church, Purbeck marble effigy, RCHM no. 6. Etching of a drawing by Charles Stothard, January 1812. B. Merevale (Warwicks), Purbeck marble effigy

Plate 60

A   B

PLATE 60.   A. Temple Church, Purbeck marble effigy, RCHM no. 3. Drawing by Thomas Kerrich (d. 1828). B. Temple Church, Reigate stone (?) effigy, RCHM no. 9. Etching of drawing by Charles Stothard, 1811

Plate 61

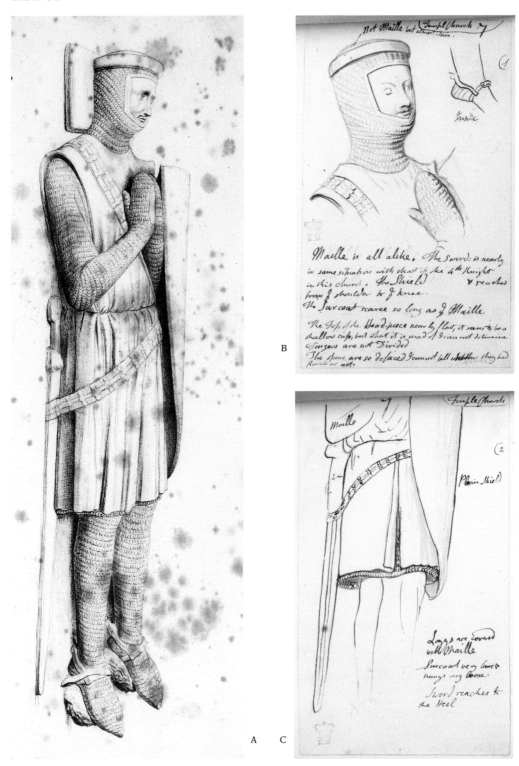

PLATE 61. Temple Church, Purbeck marble effigy, RCHM no. 4. Drawings and notes by Thomas
Kerrich (d. 1828)

Plate 62

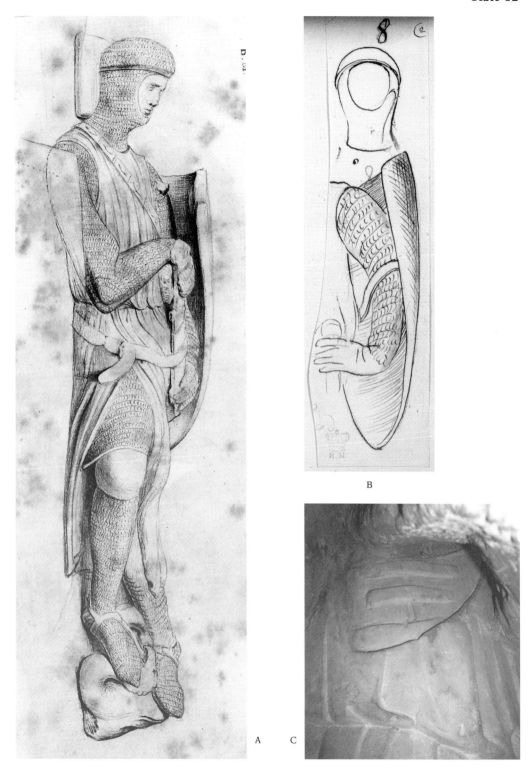

A   C

B

PLATE 62. Temple Church, RCHM no. 8. A–B. Drawings by Thomas Kerrich (d. 1828). C. Detail
showing the straps visible through the armhole of the gown

Plates 63–65

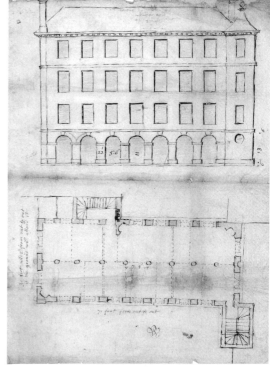

PLATE 63. Anthonis van den Wyngaerde, *Panorama of London* (detail), drawing, 1544

PLATE 65. Temple, design for cloisters by Sir Christopher Wren, 1680

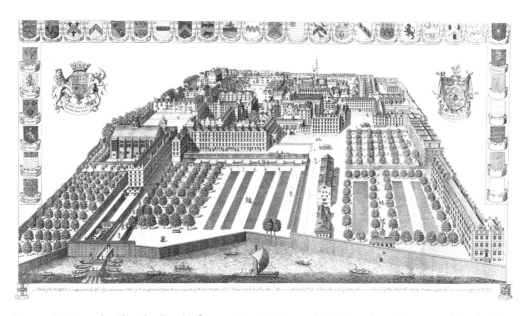

PLATE 64. Temple Church, detail of engraving, 'A View of the Temple as it appeared in the Year 1671'

PLATE 66. Temple Church, north face of nave, photograph 1861 following removal of neighbouring buildings

PLATE 67. Temple Church, exterior of nave looking north, aquatint by Thomas Malton, 1796

PLATE 68. Temple Church, west porch, advertisement for stationers J. Penn and O. Lloyd, n.d (perhaps late 17th century)

PLATE 69. Temple Church, chancel, engraving by L. Boydell after Thomas Boydell, 1750

PLATE 70. 'The South East Prospect of the Temple Church', engraving by Benjamin Cole, version of engraving by W. H. Toms, 1739

PLATE 71. Temple Church and Lamb Building (destroyed 10 May 1941), view from south-west, photograph c.1915–27

PLATE 72. Temple Church, interior of nave look-
ing south-west, aquatint by J. Bluck after
Thomas Rowlandson and Augustus Charles
Pugin, 1808–9

PLATE 73. Temple Church, interior of nave
looking east, engraving by W. Woolnoth,
1805, after Frederick Nash

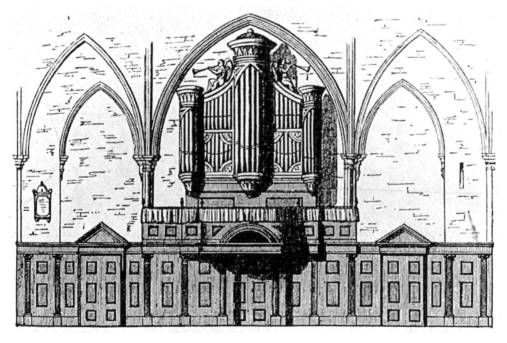

PLATE 74. Temple Church, Wrenian organ-case and screen looking west

PLATE 75. Temple Church, Wrenian pulpit after its move to Christ Church, Newgate Street

PLATE 76. Temple Church, 'View of the Interior from the Vestry Door', engraving by J. Le Keux after R. W. Billings, 1837

PLATE 77. Temple Church, Wrenian reredos

THE SOUTH SIDE OF THE TEMPLE CHURCH

PLATE 78. 'The South Side of the Temple Church', engraving by William Emmett, 1702

PLATE 79. Church of Holy Sepulchre, Jerusalem, 17th-century model

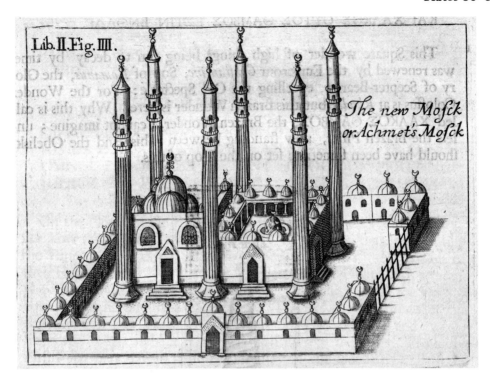

PLATE 80. Constantinople, 'The new Mosck or Achmet's Mosck', engraving from G. Wheler, 1682

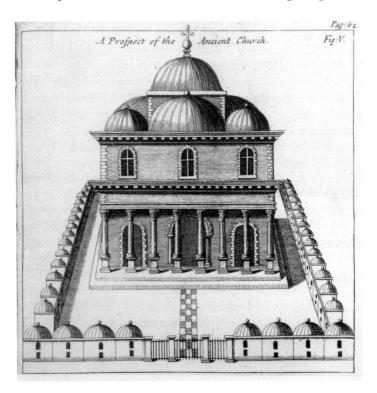

PLATE 81. 'A Prospect of the Ancient Church', engraving from G. Wheler, 1689

Plate 82

PLATE 82. Temple Church, section of nave looking east, engraving by William Emmett, 1702

PLATE 83. 'ICHNOGRAPHIA Templorum Veterum', engraving from W. Beveridge, 1672

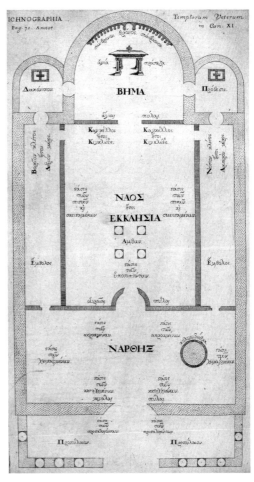

PLATE 84. Temple Church, copy (1695) of inscription over south-west door of nave

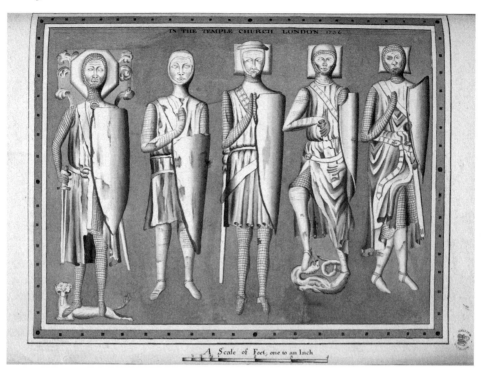

PLATE 85. Temple Church, drawing of southern set of effigies (as laid out 1695–1841), made 1736/7

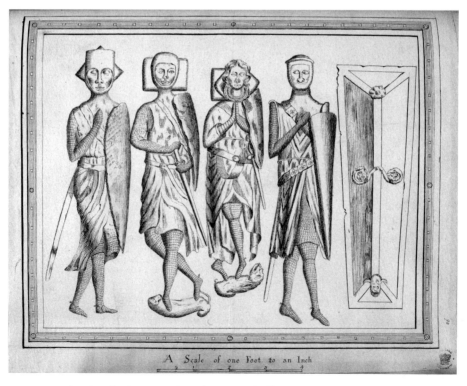

PLATE 86. Temple Church, drawing of northern set of effigies (as laid out 1695–1841), made 1736/7

PLATE 87. Temple Church, engraving of southern set of effigies (as laid out 1695–1841), 1786

PLATE 88. Temple Church, engraving of northern set of effigies (as laid out 1695–1841), 1786

Plate 89

PLATE 89. Temple Church, busts on west doorway, drawings by Frederick Nash, c.1818

Plate 90

PLATE 90. Temple Church, west doorway, engraving after Frederick Nash, 1818

PLATE 91. Temple Church, arcading in nave, drawn (1809) and engraved (1813) by John Thomas Smith

PLATE 92. 'The Temple Church, as Restored', engraved by J. Carter, 1828, after Thomas Hosmer Shepherd

PLATE 93. Temple Church, exterior from south after 1860–2

PLATE 94. Temple Church, monuments in triforium, photograph c.1915–27

PLATE 95. Temple Church, chancel from south-west, 1885

PLATE 96. Temple Church, chancel from north-east, 1885

Plate 97

PLATE 97. Temple Church, chancel from nave, 1885

PLATE 99. Temple Church, design for painted decoration over chancel-arch looking west by Thomas Willement, 1845

PLATE 98. Temple Church, design for east window of clerestory made and presented by Thomas Willement, 1845

PLATE 100. Temple Church, west porch and Round, lithograph by Thomas Shotter Boys, 1842

PLATE 101. Temple Church, west doorway, c.1915–27

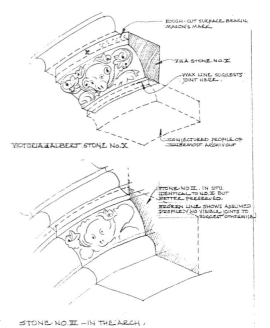

PLATE 102. Temple Church, two voussoirs of west doorway, one still *in situ*, the other in V&A, from drawing by Neil McFadyen, 1984

PLATE 103. Temple Church, 10 May 1941

PLATE 104. Temple Church, nave looking east as damaged on 10 May 1941

PLATE 105. The Temple, c.1945: View from Middle Temple Lane towards Temple Church

PLATE 106. Temple Church, warriors
of eight centuries gathered in nave,
gouache, after 10 May 1941

PLATE 107. Temple, cloisters, photograph by Cecil Beaton, 1941

PLATE 108. Temple Church, chancel from south-west, c.1954

PLATE 109. Temple Church, effigies in nave with V&A's plaster casts, photograph 2008

Index

ABBREVIATIONS

c   commander
gc   grand commander
gm   grand master
m   master
T   the Order of the Temple
Tr   Templar

Plate numbers are in **boldface** type, figures in *italics*.

Abingdon Abbey 72
Adam of Eynsham 68, 69
Adam the Mazun, Tr 12
Ailbe (Albinus), bishop of Ferns 83
Aimery of St Maur, m of T in England 76–9
Aldworth church 128 n. 171
Alexander II, pope 21
Alexander III, pope 71
Alphington 208
ambo 159–60, **83**
Amesbury Nunnery 83
Amesbury Psalter 78 n. 66
Amiens Cathedral 29
'ancient constitution' 147, 167
Anglo-Saxon Chronicle 70
Anselm, St 77
Ansfrid, concubine 72
Arles, Tr preceptory 14 n. 65
d'Aubigné, William 72 n. 34, 78 n. 63
Aubrey, John 142 n. 39, 148 n. 64, 170
Augustinian canons 51, 59
Avesnes-le-Comte church 32
d'Avranches, Hugh, earl of Chester 72

Balsall, Tr preceptory 5
Bathampton church 123 n. 142
Baudri of Bourgeil, archbishop of Dol 72
Beaton, Cecil 218 n. 36, 219

Beaulieu Abbey *50 Fig. 3*, 52
Beaumont family, monuments to 79 n. 71, 80
    n. 76
Beaumont, Robert de, earl of Leicester 23
Bedale church 90–91, **54, 55**
Becket, Thomas; *see* Thomas of Canterbury, St
Belvoir Priory 72 n. 34, 78 n. 63
Belwood, Roger 88, 171, 173
Benson, Christopher 179, 199–200, 206, 209
Benson, Stephen 216–17
Berteaucourt-les-Dammes Nunnery 34, **25**
Bethell, Richard 204
Beveridge, William 159–60, 162–3, **83**
Beverley Minster 91
Billings, Robert 185, 212
Blom, Roger 16
Blomfield, Sir Reginald 209, 214
Blount, Thomas 170
Boswell, James 190
Boydell, L. 141, 190, **69**
Boydell, Thomas **69**
Boys, Thomas Shotter 212, **100**
Bozon, Nicholas, Franciscan friar 6 n. 20
Brady, Robert 148, 168
Bridlington Priory 40, **32, 34**
Bridport, Giles de, bishop of Salisbury 80
Bristol, St Mark 107 n. 59
Britton, John 177 n. 15, 181, 185 n. 56, 189

Brownrigg, Dr Ralph 139
'British history' 141–3, 145
Brute 141–3, 145, 167
Buck, Sir William 163 n. 136
Buckler, John Chessell 62 n. 53
Burge, William 201, 205, 209
Burgh, Hubert de 7 n. 31, 9
Burton, Decimus 197, 207, 212, 213
Burton, William 115, 164 n. 142, 171
Burwell Castle 69

Caen, Saint-Étienne Abbey 26 n. 20
Cambridge Camden Society 198–9, 201,
    205–6, 208, 210
Cambridge:
    Emmanuel College 148
    St Sepulchre 197, 201, 203–4
Camden, William 100, 113, 118, 138 n. 14, 145
Camoys, Margaret de 87
Canterbury:
    archbishop's palace 49, 50
    Cathedral 24, 25 n. 19, 31 n. 37, 42, 62
      n. 53, 77, 78
    Cathedral Priory 34–5, 37, 49, 50 Fig. 3, **26**
Carlos, Edward John 188
Caröe, William Douglas 209, 214
Carter, John 176 n. 8, 187–9
Cartmel Priory 90
Cattermole, George **XII**
Caversham 76
Cecily, wife of William d'Aubigné 72 n. 34
Charles I 139, 165 n. 143
Charles II 166
Chartham church 89, 120
Chepstow 82
Chester Abbey 72
Chew Magna church 128 n. 171
Chichester Cathedral 50 Fig. 3, 52, 105 n. 55,
    126 n. 160
Cistercians 51, 73
Cîteaux Abbey 74
Clarendon Palace 50 Fig. 3, 52
Clarke, Edward 185
Cluny Abbey: Cluny III 29
Coke, Sir Edward 142–4, 146, 147, 148, 171
    family of 140 n. 29
Cole, Benjamin 151
common law and lawyers 142–5, 146, 148
Constantine 165–6
Constantinople:
    'Achmet's Mosck' **80**

Hagia Sophia 157, 158
Cottingham, Lewis 102, 151, 207
Cotton, Sir Robert 86 n. 120
Courtenay, William, archbishop of Canterbury
    77
Cressing, Tr preceptory 11, 70
Cropredy church 131 n. 189, 132 Fig. 6, 133
Crystal Palace 102
Cunnington, Cecil Willett 219

Danes 147
Davy, William 138
Despenser, Hugh le 15
Digges, Sir Dudley 146
Dijon, St-Bénigne 33 n. 41
Dingley, Thomas 170
Dinsley, Tr preceptory 5, 13
Dolben, John 167
Dommartin Abbey 30–34, 39, **11**, **22**, **23**
Dorchester Abbey 128
Douce Apocalypse 128
Drayton, Michael 145
Dugdale, Sir William 99, 100, 138, 139, 148,
    150 n. 78, 170, 180
Dunfermline Abbey 78
Dunstable Priory 40
Dunwallo Malmutius 140–45, 169
Durham Cathedral 38, 56 n. 26

early churches 157–60, **81**, **83**
East Harlsey church 89
Eastlake, Sir Charles 197
Eastwick church 131 n. 189, 132 Fig. 6
ecclesiological movement 188, 198–9, 201,
    203, 207
Edward I 7, 8
Edward II 15, 90
Edward III 14, 15
Edward the Confessor, St 65, 84
Edwards, Carl 210
Eleanor of Provence, Queen 7 n. 27, 9, 10, 64,
    83
Emmett, William (nephew) 154, 156–7
    engravings by 25, 98–9, 135, 141 n. 36,
      156–9, 164, 169, **78**, **82**
Emmett, William (uncle) 152–3, 156
Eu Abbey 78 n. 63
Eu, counts of 78 n. 63
Eugenius III, pope 21, 70 n. 12
Eusebius 158
Evelyn, John 165 n. 147

Everdon, Silvester de, bishop of Carlisle **V**, 85–6, **47–9**
Ewell, Tr preceptory 13
Exeter Cathedral 77, 110

Farnborough church 131 n. 189, *132 Fig. 6*
Farndon, Thomas 17
Faversham Abbey 35, 36
Faxfleet, Tr preceptory 14
Fécamp Abbey 72–3
Felipe, Don 112 n. 80
Ferns, bishop of 83
Fitzalan, Brian 90–91, **54, 55**
FitzWalter, Robert 133
Fontenay Abbey 39, **31**
Fontevraud Abbey 84
Foucarmont Abbey 78 n. 63
Fountains Abbey 56 n. 26
Foxe's Book of Martyrs 87
Furness Abbey 56 n. 26

Garway, Tr church *55 Fig. 4*
Gaveston, Piers 10
Gawden, John 139, 165 n. 147
Gawdy, Famlingham 138
Gentleman's Magazine 181, 185, 189, 203, 211, 213
Geoffrey, Tr almoner 64 n. 63, 77
Geoffrey of Anjou, Count 78
Geoffrey of Monmouth 141–3, 145
Gibson, Edward 113
Giffard, Walter, earl of Buckingham 72 n. 34
Gillingham, Roger 99 n. 20, 153
Glastonbury Abbey 35 n. 51
Godfrey, Walter 196, 215 n. 26
Goodrich 82
Gorbomannus 141
Gothic revival 182–4, 187, 199
Gough, Richard 98, 101, 116–17, 185–7, **87, 88**
Gray, Thomas 186 n. 61
Gray, Walter de, archbishop of York 85, 110, 113
Great Haseley church 131 n. 189, *132 Fig. 6*
Grelot, Guillaume-Joseph 157
Grendon, Walter de, Hospitaller Grand Prior in England 15
Grisoni, Signor 101, 170 n. 1, 180

Hadrian I, pope 58
Halberstadt Cathedral 78
Hare, Augustus 105 n. 55
Hare, Sir Nicholas 139
Harrington, Sir John 90

Hattin, battle of (1187) 20
Hatton, Edward 141, 153, 171, 178–9
Haysom, Harold W. 93, 134 n. 196
Hemel Hempstead church 40
Henry I 2, 70
Henry II 2, 6, 10, 20, 23, 41, 73
Henry III 7, 8, 9, 45, 48, 52, 63, 64–5, 80, 83–4, 116
Henry VIII 18, 36, 172
Henry of Blois 35, 41, 74
Heraclius, patriarch of Jerusalem 2, 20–21, 61 n. 50, 140, 170, 181
Hertford Priory 82
Hitchin church 131 n. 189, *132 Fig. 6*
Hollis, George 102, 105, 106
Hollis, Thomas 102, 105, 106
Holmes, George 170
Holt, Francis 204, 209
Hooker, Richard 206
Hopkins, Edward 202, 209
Hoverio, Constant de 86–7
Howden church 89
Hugh of Lincoln, St 67–8, 69, 82
Hynton, Nicholas de, Tr 12
Hythe church 50

Idonea, wife of Robert de Vieuxpont 81
Innocent II, pope 12
Ireland, Samuel 183, 190

Jackson, Thomas Graham 214
James VI and I 135, 142–3, 148, 165
James II 167–8
Jekyll, Joseph 186, 189
Jeffreys, George, Baron 152, 167–9
Jerusalem:
  Holy Sepulchre church 2, 24, 42–3, 54, 59, *60 Fig. 5*, 64 n. 64, 65, 150, 177, 185 n. 56
  Aedicule 43, 74
  models of 150, **79**
  Temple Mount 59–60, *60 Fig. 5*
  Aqsa Mosque 1, 59, 60 n. 44, *60 Fig. 5*
  Dome of the Rock (or 'Temple of the Lord') 59, *60 Fig. 5*
  Temple *60 Fig. 5*, 157, 160–63, 169
Joan, queen of Scotland 116
John, King 7, 10, 76 n. 52, 79, 80
John of Gaunt, duke of Lancaster 17
John of Stoke, Tr 12, 13

Kerrich, Rev. Thomas 101, 102, 105, **58**

Kilkenny 82
Kirkham Priory 88, 171–2
Kirton-in-Lindsey church 127 n. 164
Knaresborough Castle 90
Knyvett, Sir Henry 172

Lambert, marbler 34
Lambeth Palace, chapel 49–51, 50 Fig. 3
Lanfranc, archbishop of Canterbury 77
Langford, William de, custodian of the New
    Temple 15, 16
Langton, Stephen, archbishop of Canterbury 77
Langton, Walter, bishop of Coventry and Lich-
    field 9–10
Laon:
    abbey of Saint-Vincent 43
    Tr chapel 43, 55 Fig. 4
Larcher, Thomas, prior of the Hospital in
    England 15
Legh, Gerard 99–100, 115, 117 n. 107
Leland, John 114
Le Mans Cathedral 78
Lemere, Bedford 103, 56
Leon, Jacob Judah 161, 163–4
    model of Temple, Jerusalem 161, 164
Lethieullier, Smart, 101, 120, 180, 186, 86, 87
Lewes 131 n. 189, 132 Fig. 6
L'Histoire de Guillaume le Maréchal 76–7
Lightfoot, John 163
Lillers church 33, 35 n. 48
Lincoln, bishop of 21, 23 n. 14
Lincoln Cathedral 31 n. 37, 67
Littleton, Edward, Baron 146
    family of 138 n. 17, 140 n. 29
London:
    Blitz in 195, 216–19, 103–7
    Carlisle Inn 85
    Fleet Street 17, 142, 193
    Great Fire VII, 136, 156
    Hoare's Bank 216
    Holy Trinity, Aldgate 70, 81
    Hospital of St John at Clerkenwell 9, 10,
        16, 17
        church 2, 20–21, 48–9, 55 Fig. 4, 57, 61–2,
        65
    St Clement Danes 2
    St James, Piccadilly 155
    St Luke, Chelsea 197
    St Paul's Cathedral 148, 155, 157, 159 n. 122,
        165
    St Peter, Cornhill 162

Savoy Palace 17
Temple VII, 64
    cloisters 107, 136, 166, 65, 107
    excavation of (1999–2000) 46 n. 6
    Farrar's Building 216
    Inner Temple 17–18, 135–6, 166, 189,
        192–3, 204, 216–17
    Lamb Building 152, 192, 216, 217
    Master's House 216
    Middle Temple 17–18, 135–6, 166, 189,
        204
    Mitre Court 193
    New Temple 2, 4–18, 4 Fig. 1, 21–3
        churchyard 2, 21–2
        domestic quarters 12–15, 20
        financial and administrative centre 6–10
        garden 23
        Hospitaller possession of 14–16
        indulgences to visitors 58
        inventory (1308) 11, 13–14, 57–8
        lay access to 11–12, 14–15, 18, 58
        'Temple Bridge' 15
        treasury 6–10
    Old Temple 1–2, 21, 23, 67–71, 74, 115
    Temple Church; see Temple Church
    urban improvements 189–93
Temple of Concord 140, 141 n. 33, 145
Tower of 7, 9, 71
Victoria and Albert Museum 102, 212–13,
    109
Longespée, William the elder 119 n. 121
Longueville Priory 72 n. 34
Louis VII, king of France 24
Lucy, Geoffrey de, bishop of Winchester 63
Ludham, Godfrey de, archbishop of York 110
Lythegranes, Sir John de 90
Lyttelton, Charles 180

MacKinnon, Sir Frank 195–6, 210, 219
Magdeburg Cathedral 122
Magna Carta 80, 172–3
Mainz, Council of (813) 72
Malcolm, James Peller 182, 189–90
Malton, Thomas VIII, 86 n. 118, 151–2, 67
Mandeville, Geoffrey de, 1st earl of Essex 21–2,
    68–74, 81, 82, 115, 116–17, 118
Mandeville, Geoffrey de, 2nd earl of Essex 71,
    72
Margaret, queen of Scotland 77–8
Marshal, Gilbert 82, 112, 118, 46
Marshal, Richard 82, 84

Marshal, William the elder 11, **IV**, 64, 69–70, 76–80, 81, 82–3, 84, 112, 113, 118–19, 138 n. 14, **45**

Marshal, William the younger 11, 48, 64, 65 n. 66, 82–3, 84, 112, 118

Matilda, Queen 2, 35, 36 n. 53

Mead, Joseph 161

Melville, Harden **XII**

mercy-seat 161–2

Merevale 131 n. 189, *132 Fig. 6*, **59**

Michael of Baskerville, c of the New Temple 11–12, 13

Micklethwaite, Dr Paul 138 nn. 15, 17, 139 n. 23, 159

Mildenhall 69

Milites Dei (1145) 73 n. 37

Minton, Herbert 196

Montdidier, Payen de 70, 74

More, William de la, Tr gc of England 12–13

Morgan Picture Bible (Maciejowski Bible) 119–20

Morris, John, Baron 216

Morton, Sir William, monument to 139

Mosques 157

d'Mount, Reuben 185 n. 56, 187, 211

Nablus, Council of (1120) 1

Namps-au-Val church 32, **14**

narthex 160

Nash, Frederick 183, 211, **73**, **89**, **90**

Nesle-en-Vermandois church 30 n. 31, 33 n. 41

Newcourt, Richard 170

Newland, John 204, 209

Norden, John 145

Norreys, Roger, Tr 11

North, Sir Dudley 157

North, Roger 147, 157, 166 n. 149, 168

Norton church 90

Noyon Cathedral 25, **6**

Ollier, Charles 212

Omne datum optimum (1139) 70, 73 n. 37

Osmund, St 65 n. 66

Oxford:
  St Frideswide's Abbey 31 n. 37
  Wadham College 205

Paris, Matthew 8, 64 n. 64, 79, 82, 83, 128

Paris:
  Notre-Dame Cathedral 27
  Saint-Martin-des-Champs 27, 30, 36, **10**

Temple Church 26, 35–6, 43, 54, *55 Fig. 4*, 59, 63, **27**

Passelewe, Robert 8

Payns, Hugh de, gm of T 1, 70

'Peasants' Revolt' 17

Peck, Francis 177

Pennant, Thomas 182, 186

Percy, Eleanor 91

Pershore Abbey 122

Peter of Ottringham, T 12, 13

Peterborough Cathedral 31 n. 37

Petyt, William 147–8, 168–9, 172

Playford, John 136, 138

Plowden, Sir Edmund 139

Poblet Abbey 31 n. 36

Pollock, David 204, 209

Pont-l'Evêque, Roger of, archbishop of York 38–9

Pontigny Abbey 32

Portsmouth, Garrison church *50 Fig. 3*

Préaux Abbey 79 n. 71, 80 n. 76

Prynne, William 145

Pugin, Augustus Charles 151–2, 185, **72**

Purbeck marble 25, 28, 32–3, 34, 35, 37, 41, 42, 103–4, 130–32

Ralph, James 177

Ralph of Barton, Tr 12

Ramsey Abbey 22, 69, 71 n. 24
  Chronicle 69

Raven, William, Tr 5

Reading Abbey 77

Reigate stone 104, 134 n. 196

Ribston, Tr preceptory 81, 113–14

Richard II 15

Richard I, duke of Normandy 71, 73 n. 36

Richard II, duke of Normandy 72–3

Richard, abbot of Saint-Évroul 77 n. 60

Richard of Hastings, m of T in England 23–4, 74–5, 87, **44**

Richard of Herdwick, Tr 12, 13

Richardson, Edward 93–8, 100, 103–5, 106, 196

Ripon Minster 39, **30**

Robinson, Cecile 216–17

Robinson, Thomas 201–2

Roches, Peter des, bishop of Winchester 8, 60 n. 46, 63

Rochester:
  Castle 84 n. 103
  Cathedral 111

Roger of Wendover 9
Rome, Santa Maria in Cosmedin 58
Ros, Robert de 80–81, 88, 113–14, 118
Ros, William de 88, 91, **52, 53**
Rouen Cathedral 107 n. 59
Rowlandson, Thomas 151–2, 185, **72**
Rule of St Benedict 2
Rushton church 131 n. 189, *132 Fig. 6*, 133

Saint Albans Abbey 34–5, 40 n. 62
Saint Andrews Cathedral 38
Saint-Bertin Abbey 33 n. 43
Saint-Denis, abbey church 24–6, 31, 34, 37, 38,
    39 n. 60, **3, 24**
Saint-Germer-de-Fly 30, 37
Saint-Leu-d'Esserent 26
Saint-Omer 24
Saint-Omer, Osto de, m of T in England 24, 87
Salisbury:
    Cathedral 49–50, *50 Fig. 3*, 52, 64, 65 n. 66,
        80, 84, 119 n. 121, 147, **37**
    St George 51
    St Martin 51
    St Nicholas Hospital 51
Sampson, bishop of Worcester 77 n. 60
Sancroft, Archbishop William 148, 168
Sandys, George 150, 164 n. 142, 177 n. 15
Savage, James 197–8, 204, 207
Saxon architecture 147, 169, 181
Saxon law 146–7
Schellinks, William 99 n. 21, 126 n. 158
Scott, Sir George Gilbert 209
Selden, John 94, 140, 144, 145, 146, 147, 169
Seal of m of T in England 75
Senlis Cathedral 25
Setvans, William de 89, 120
Shepherd, George **IX**, 137 n. 9, 141 n. 35, 159
    n. 121
Sherlock, William 167–8
Shipley, Tr preceptory 71 n. 21
Skinner, Rev. John 101
Smirke, Robert 32 n. 39, 176, 188, 192, 198,
    204
Smirke, Sydney 197, 198, 207–9, 212, 213
Smith, John Thomas 211
Smith, Joseph Clarendon **II**
Smith, Thomas 162
Society of Antiquaries 101, 180, 187, 211
Solomon 165–6
South Cerney church 78 n. 65

South Witham, Tr church 53 n. 20, *55 Fig. 4*
Southwark Priory 61, 62
Spence, George 204, 209
Standish, John 167
St Aubyn, James Piers 209, 210
Staines 77
Starston church 76 n. 53
Stephen, King 2, 22, 24, 35, 70
Stothard, Charles Alfred 101–2, 105
Stow, John 80, 81, 100, 112, 113, 114, 126, 190
Stowe Nine Churches church 131 n. 189, *132*
    Fig. 6
Stukeley, William 185 n. 56
Suger, abbot of Saint-Denis 37, 39 n. 60
Sullington church 131 n. 189, *132 Fig. 6*, 133
Sussex marble 103

Tacitus 146–7
Templars
    admission to 5
    antiquarian attitudes to 150, 184–5, 206
    associates of 111
    burial 73
    chapels 54
    chapter meetings 3–5, 56–7
    daily timetable 2–3
    financial activities 6–10
    foundation of Order 1
    habit 1, 69–70
    provincial chapters 4–5
    Rule 2–3, 56–7, 73
    trial 5, 11
    visitors 86
Temple; *see* London: Temple
Temple Bruer, Tr preceptory 5
    church *55 Fig. 4*
Temple Church:
    brass 86–7, **50, 51**
    burials and monuments (post-medieval), 196,
        94; *see also* Brownrigg; Coke; Hare; Lit-
        tleton; Morton; Petyt; Plowden; Selden
    buttresses 164
    choir (chancel) **III, IX, X, XII**, 45–66, *50*
        Fig. 3, **36, 41, 69, 76, 95–9**
    altars (medieval) 13, 48, 57, 78
    altar (19th-century communion table) **XI**,
        139, 162, 164, 202
    aumbries 48, 139
    bishop's monument **V**, 85–6, 139, 186
        n. 63, **47–9**

consecration (1240) 10, 45, 83
floor-level 48, 152
mouldings 49, 52, *47 Fig. 2*
organ (from 1840s) **95**
painting (medieval) 52
painting (19th century) **X**, 208, **96, 99**
piscina 49, **39**
pulpit **XII**, 136, 159–60, 162–3, **75**
Purbeck marble, use of **III**, 46, 49
reredos **XI**, 153, 162, 210, **77**
sculpture 52, **41**
tiles (medieval) 52, **42**
tiles (19th century) 195–6, 208
window glass (medieval) 52–3, 84
window glass (post-medieval) 167 n. 151,
    195, 196, 208, **98**
consecration (1185) 2, 6, 20–21, 61 n. 50,
    140, 170, 181, **84**
damage to, 1941 46, 93, 195–6, 210, 216–19,
    103–6
doors 154
effigies in nave (13th century) **IV**, **VI**, 138,
    153–4, 171–3, 179, 180, 186, **45, 46, 56–62**
arms and armour 119–23
arrangement **VI**, 94–99, 138, 153
damage to, 1941 93, 134, **57**
drawings of:
    by Signor Grisoni 101, 180
    by Thomas and George Hollis, 101, 105
    by Thomas Kerrich 96, 101, 102, 105,
        106, 107–9, **58, 60–62**
    for Smart Lethieullier 101, 180, **85, 86**
    by Edward Richardson 102
    by John Skinner 101
    by Charles Alfred Stothard 101–2, 105
engravings of, for Richard Gough 98,
    101, 108, 116–17, 185–7, **87, 88**
heraldry 82, 115–17
plaster casts of 97, 102–3, **109**
polychromy 82, 100, 105, 115–16
restoration of 93, 104–5, 106–7
style 79, 82, 128–9
effigy in nave (14th century) 88–91, 171–3,
    52, 53
font 160, 208
from the south 70, 71, 78, **92, 93**
iconography of 24, 42–3, 59–61
liturgy **XII**, 139, 160, 162–3, 199–202, 209
nave (Round Church) 19–43, **I, VI, VIII,**
    138, 151–4, 156, 160, 166, 169, **2, 4, 5,**

7–9, 12, 13, 15, 17, 18, 50, 66, 67, 72,
    73, 91
arcading 31, 32, 35, 41, **I, 8, 12**
arches 25, **I, 3**
capitals 32–4, **15, 17, 18**
grave cover 74–5, 94, **44**
mouldings 26–7, 38, **7**
piers 25, 28, 30, 38, **I, 4, 5**
Purbeck marble, use of 28, 30, 32, 35, **I, 12**
triforium **94**
tympanum over south-west doorway 20,
    140, 170, 181, **84**
vaulting 27, 31, 32, 41, **9, 12, 13**
west doorway 34, 40, **II**, 75, 137, 187,
    211–16, **21, 89, 90, 100–102**
wheel window 25
organ 138, 152, **74, 95**
organ screen 152, **73, 74**
plan 24, **I**, 45–6, 54, *55 Fig. 4*
relics 11, 58
rood 57, 76–9
roof 156, 159, 209, **63, 70, 78, 92, 93, 103**
    steeple 154
shops and chambers adjoining 137, 151, 189,
    191–2, **67**
St Anne's Chapel 27 n. 23, 62, 136–7, 151,
    156, 188, 191, 193, 198, **43**
    undercroft 62, 151 n. 82, **43**
synagogues and 163 n. 136
vestry 13
west porch 22, 24, 40, 42–3, 71, 74, 137, 209,
    2, 33, 68, 100
    sculpture 40, **33**
Thame, Philip de 15–16
Thérouanne Cathedral 29
Theulf, bishop of Worcester 77 n. 60
Thomas, earl of Lancaster 15
Thomas of Burton, Tr priest 13
Thomas of Canterbury, St (Becket) 58, 71 n. 25,
    80, 87
Thomas of Standon, Tr 12, 13
Thorney Abbey 77 n. 60
Tintern Abbey 82
Tournai Cathedral 28–9, 33, **15, 16, 19, 20**
Tournai marble 28–9, 30 n. 31, 33–4, 35, 41
Trondheim Cathedral 39 n. 61
Trotton church 87
Troyes, Council of (1129) 1, 70
Trussebut, Hilary 114
Twyford church 131 n. 189, *132 Fig. 6*

Index

Urban II, pope 21

Valence, Aymer de 15, 89
Valence, Margaret de 87
Valence, William de 87
Vaughan, Sir John 140
Vieuxpont, Robert de 80–81, 115
Villalpando, Juan Bautista 161, 165
Villasirga (Villalcázar de Sirga), Tr preceptory
   112 n. 80
Villiers, George, 1st duke of Buckingham 171
Villiers, George, 2nd duke of Buckingham 171–3
Vipont, Robert, bishop of Carlisle 85
Virgil 141
Vogue 219

Walden Priory 22, 69, 70, 71, 72
   chronicle 22, 69, 71, 117
Walkern church 131 n. 189, *132 Fig. 6*, 133
Walpole, Horace 101 n. 30
Walter, Hubert, archbishop of Canterbury 62
   n. 53, 76, n. 52
Warwick, Rotrocus de, bishop of Rouen 107
   n. 59
Warkworth (Northants) church 90, 110 n. 69
Wastell, John 31 n. 37
Watson, Joshua 205
Weever, John 86 n. 120, 100, 140–41, 145,
   178–9, 180
Wells:
   bishop's palace 50, *50 Fig. 3*
   Cathedral 52, 79, 80
Werden, St Lucius 33 n. 41
Westminster Abbey 10–11, *50 Fig. 3*, 52, 65, 77,
   83–4, 87, 89, 110, 208

Wheler, Sir George 157–8, **80**, **81**
Whitworth 127
Wibert, prior of Canterbury Cathedral Priory
   37
Willement, Thomas **X**, **XI**, 167 n. 151, 196,
   199, 206–7, 208, **98**, **99**
William, St, archbishop of York 90
William of Hereford or Hertford, Tr 12, 13
William of Orange 168
William of Sens 34
William of Tyre 70 n. 12
William, son of Henry III 85–6
William the Lion, king of Scotland 80
Winchester Bible 133 n. 195
Winchester:
   Castle 50, *50 Fig. 3*, 52, **38**
   Cathedral 35 n. 51, *50 Fig. 3*, 51, 62–3, 64,
     74–5, 111, **40**
   Saint Cross Hospital 40–41, 181, **35**
Windsor Castle *50 Fig. 3*, 52
Worcester Cathedral 65, 77 n. 60, 79, 80
Wren, Sir Christopher 135–7, 147–8, 151–64,
   166, 169, 175, 178, 186–7, **65**
   and Gothic architecture 149
   and Saracenic architecture 149, 157–8,
     180–81
   drawings 136 n. 7
Wyatt, James 187–8, 197
Wycombe 81
Wyngaerde, Anthonis van den 138, **63**

York:
   Franciscan Priory 88
   Minster 38–40, 90, **28**, **29**